Rocky Marciano

Sport and Society

Series Editors
Benjamin G. Rader
Randy Roberts

*A list of books in the series
appears at the end of this book.*

Rocky Marciano
The Rock of His Times

Russell Sullivan

University of Illinois Press
Urbana and Chicago

Title page: Rocky Marciano and Harry Matthews,
July 28, 1952. (Stanley A. Bauman)

Library of Congress Cataloging-in-Publication Data
Sullivan, Russell.
Rocky Marciano : the rock of his times / Russell Sullivan.
p.   cm. — (Sport and society)
Includes bibliographical references and index.
ISBN 0-252-02763-9 (cloth : alk. paper)
1. Marciano, Rocky, 1923–1969.
2. Boxers (Sports)—United States—Biography.
I. Title. II. Series.
GV1132.M3S85   2002
796.83'092—dc21   2001008553

For my mother
Judith Ann Sullivan (1937–2000)
A champion

Contents

Preface

I am sometimes asked why I decided to write a book about Rocky Marciano. I wish that I could cite some sort of divine inspiration or perhaps a classical muse. But I cannot, for the truth of the matter is that this book started with a poster.

At least it was a large poster, one that covered much of a brick wall in my health club in the North End, the traditional Italian neighborhood of Boston. As I desperately (and vainly) tried to sweat out some unwanted pounds on the stationary bicycle, I would find myself frequently looking at the poster of Marciano belting his punching bag—and asking myself why I knew so little about him. After all, as a lifelong Boston sports fan, I knew all about the Hub's athletic deities, from the Kid and Yaz to Orr and Espo to Cousy, Russell, Havlicek, and Bird—but not Marciano. And, as a boxing fan, I was well familiar with the tales of great heavyweights such as Ali,

Louis, Dempsey, even Jack Johnson—but, again, not Marciano. The photographs that I frequently saw of Marciano in North End restaurants and taverns (Marciano bludgeoning another opponent, Marciano celebrating another victory, Marciano posing with another North End restaurant owner) only spurred my curiosity further.

So, when I decided to explore writing a book on sports—an old dream that had never completely faded—my thoughts naturally turned to Marciano. After receiving confirmation from my father that this was, indeed, a topic worth exploring, I decided to plunge ahead. I quickly discovered that there was a story, and one that had not been told enough—at least in the way I wanted to tell it.

That story does not equate a traditional biography. For sure, the pages that follow track Marciano's life, from his birth in 1923 to his untimely death in 1969, with plenty of biographical detail along the way. But the mere details of his life, career, and character (as interesting as they may have been) hardly represent the complete story of Rocky Marciano. His story also involves the glamorous and romantic boxing scene of the early 1950s, filled with rich personalities and more than its share of scandal and corruption. It also involves the way that Marciano's career reflected and intersected with larger societal trends such as race and ethnicity. And, most significantly, the story also involves the way that Marciano came to symbolize his times, the early 1950s. This story, then, is not simply about a heavyweight champion of the world but also about the era in which he reigned. Such a story seemed well worth telling.

I couldn't have told that story without getting plenty of help along the way. First and foremost, I would like to thank Richard L. Wentworth, a wise and patient editor who was devoted to this project from the day that it came across his desk. My thanks also go out to the other folks at the University of Illinois Press who helped with this book, including Terry Sears, Mary Giles, Jane Hoffman, Jane Carlson, and Dennis Roberts in addition to authors Richard Crepeau, and Randy Roberts. It was Randy, in fact, who returned my unsolicited telephone call and guided me to the Press and then later helped hone my manuscript with his incisive edits. For all of that, I am immensely grateful.

I would also like to thank the men I interviewed for this book—Furman Bisher, Jimmy Breslin, Bud Collins, Angelo Dundee, Lou Duva, Truman Gibson, W. C. Heinz, Roland LaStarza, Robert Lipsyte, Louis (Sonny) Marciano, and Peter Marciano. Each was exceedingly generous with his time and his insights. Thanks also to the individuals who went above and beyond the call of duty to help arrange these interviews, including Anita Collins, Julie Janofsky, Betty Mitchell, Alex Ramos, and Bob Reardon.

I would also like to acknowledge the hundreds of sportswriters of the early 1950s whose work I drew upon greatly in my research. I may not have interviewed them directly, but their voices are definitely heard in the pages that follow. And I would have never had a chance to incorporate those voices if not for all the librarians at Boston College, the Boston Public Library, Harvard University, the Providence Public Library, and Suffolk University who patiently and cheerfully retrieved dozens and dozens of dusty microfilm reels from the stacks.

Thanks to Stanley Bauman of Brockton, Massachusetts, a remarkable gentleman whose photography graces this book. Thanks also to Richard Johnson of the Sports Museum of New England, who gave me the idea of contacting Mr. Bauman in the first place. My thanks go as well to Ken Martin for the author's photograph; Lucy Bichsel for speed, expertise, and spirit on the technical front; and Renee Bella, Liz Cronin, Lindsay Elliott, and Gina Willard for invaluable production assistance.

Numerous individuals provided advice about writing and publishing, including Miriam Altshuler, Andrew Carroll, Monty Carter, Roy Craig, John Doerr, Eamon Dolan, Arnold Goodman, Cathy Greene, Matt Holt, Tom Horton, Jill Kneerim, Chris Mead, Bill Patrick, Cheryl Richardson, Danny Stern, Steve Sugar, Rachel Vail, Hack Wiegmann, Ron Zemke, and Susan Zemke. I thank them all.

Special thanks go to Phyllis Barajas for believing in the book when I really needed someone to believe; Warren Bennis for giving me his usual sage advice plus a lucky picture; Frank Catapano for contributing critical input and perspective; Larry Carr and Phil Harkins for displaying the understanding and flexibility that allowed me to pursue this project; Dan Gilligan for reading the manuscript even though he didn't have the time to do so; Keith Hollihan and Tim Schroer for serving as kindred spirits in word and deed; Honey Krotky, Paul Pilkons, and Phil Chisholm for keeping a secret; Caroline O'Connell for patiently and properly answering dozens of questions of every variety; Sal Ricciardone for editing the manuscript with skill and care; Brad Wiegmann for supplying the thorough review and personal encouragement that I so desperately needed at the time; Ellen Wingard for saying the right words at the right time, as usual; and Jon Zaroff, Vicky Zaroff, Kelly Crozier, and Matt Crozier for providing critical early support for this project. That I can call each of the above a friend makes me a lucky man indeed.

I am also lucky to have many other friends hailing from St. John's Prep, Yale, Harvard Law, and other ports of call. Space precludes me from naming them all here. Suffice to say, their friendship over the years has meant, and continues to mean, the world to me.

I have also been blessed with a supportive family, including the Sullivans of Hamilton, the Grants of Scituate, the Garveys of Woburn, and the Krotkys, Crishes, and the rest of "the family" in Youngstown. My brother Scott has always been in my corner, not just as a brother but as a confidant and as a friend. My father made enormous contributions to this book, providing guidance on the topic, a review of the manuscript, and perspective on the project. He also happens to be the greatest man that I have ever known.

My greatest thanks of all, however, is reserved for my wife Laura, who was with me every step of the way on this journey and gave of herself so selflessly and so enthusiastically throughout. Without her, this book would not have been possible. I should also add that, without her, *my* story (or life) would be not complete.

Last but not least, thanks to my sons Ramsey and Owen, each of whom is my pride and my joy.

Rocky Marciano

Introduction:
A Man for His Time

It was a simple time.

It was the early 1950s in America, and everything was finally and blissfully settled. The Great Depression was more than a decade removed. World War II was also finally behind us, as were the troublesome times that immediately followed the war, with all the uncertainty surrounding the reentry of servicemen into the mainstream of American life and the return of the women they had left behind to more traditional roles. Everything had returned to normal.

In many ways, the Age of Simplicity was a great time to be alive. Everyone seemed to know his or her place in the home, in the economy, and in society at large. And everyone bought into the American dream, as so powerfully conveyed by a dying medium (radio) and a rising one (television). With some hard work, you, too, could be like Ozzie and Harriet—have a nice home in the suburbs with a couple of kids, a couple of cars, and a white picket fence.

America was flush with postwar prosperity. The economy was booming, the optimism was infectious, and the possibilities seemed limitless. And everything seemed so remarkably simple. Simple men occupied the Oval Office—Harry Truman, an ordinary haberdasher from Missouri, followed by Dwight Eisenhower, an authentic, red-blooded American hero from the plains of Kansas. There were problems, of course—labor problems, foreign policy problems, even a nasty military problem in Korea—but they were nothing that we couldn't handle. Even the dominant issue of the day, the Red Scare of communism, was painted in black and white. Either you were a commie or you weren't. It was that simple.

The world of sports was simple as well. Baseball was king, and the best teams (the Giants, the Yankees, and the Dodgers) and the best centerfielders (Willie, Mickey, and the Duke) all played in New York. The Cooz and a hulking giant named George controlled the hardwoods, while a blur named Rocket dominated the winter ice. In football, the best quarterbacks were a milk chuggin' straight-arrow named Otto and a good ol' boy from Texas named Bobby. The best golfers were named Sam and Ben. And the heavyweight champion of the world was named Rocky.

It was a simple time. Or was it?

●   ●   ●

As a cultural icon of his age, and with the hindsight of half a century, Rocky Marciano reflects the era in which he fought: simple on the surface but considerably more complex in reality.

On one level, Marciano's story is indeed a simple one. He came, he saw, he conquered. In fact, he never lost. With his unblemished 49-0 record, he remains, even today, the only undefeated heavyweight champion in history. During his rise in 1950, 1951, and 1952, he beat all the other young up-and-comers (Roland LaStarza, Rex Layne, and Harry Matthews) vying for the title, as well as an old champion (Joe Louis) seeking to recapture past glory. Then, in September 1952, in a classic fight that ended with a classic knockout, Marciano defeated Jersey Joe Walcott to become champion. He would successfully defend his title a half-dozen times against men such as the wily Walcott, the enigmatic Ezzard Charles, and the colorful Archie Moore. In April 1956 Marciano suddenly retired, his perfect record and his legacy intact. The story line of his career had been straight, rising, and unbroken.

Along the way, Marciano enjoyed a huge amount of fame. He reigned atop the boxing world at a time when the sport was second only to baseball in terms of popular appeal. This meant that he fought a succession of big fights in big arenas and outdoor ballparks, mainly in New York, in front of crowds usually in excess of forty thousand. Marciano's title fights were events of glamour and romance that captured the attention of the nation and provided some classic boxing moments that rank, to this day, among the greatest in the sport's history. They also secured Marciano's status as "the heavyweight champion of the world." And in that era, unlike today, that title bestowed unparalleled fame, glory, and prestige upon its holder. Even those who harped upon Marciano's undeniable flaws as a boxer deemed him deserving to wear the most hallowed crown in sport. With the possible exception of a few baseball players such as Stan Musial and Ted Williams, Rocky Marciano was the most celebrated athlete of his age.

But Marciano was more than just a big man in a big sport still in its heyday. He was also a man of his age. And that age, despite its surface simplicity, was not without tension or complexity. While there was widespread prosperity and conformity, there was also significant change taking place beneath the surface of American life—change that would accelerate in the late 1950s and then emerge full-blown during the tumultuous 1960s. Two key components of this fermenting change involved race and ethnicity. The career of Rocky Marciano—which, like the era in which he fought, involved considerable complexity beneath the surface of simplicity—reflected the change in both areas.

As a white man in a sport increasingly becoming dominated by black men, Marciano reflected the curious, uneasy racial attitudes of his era. In the early 1950s, most whites still viewed blacks as second-class citizens, especially in the South, where Jim Crow still reigned. Even white Americans who favored integration were unwilling to push for fear of upsetting the cherished societal normalcy that had finally taken hold after so many years of tumult. Blacks were, by and large, willing to play along with the mandate of normalcy. They were willing to pursue progress through accepted channels and with considerable patience. Although the civil rights movement was on the horizon, it was not yet a movement—and would not be until Rosa Parks refused to go to the back of the bus in December 1955.

But, significantly, Rosa took her stand three months after Marciano's last fight. During his reign, the sharp edge was off the issue of race—particularly in the world of sports, given the heroic triumphs of Joe Louis and Jackie Robinson in the 1940s. As in society, the racial tension surrounding Marciano and his fights against black men remained very much beneath the surface. But it was there. It was there in the press coverage of Marciano, which was infused with special treatment for Marciano and racially inspired references to his black opponents. It was also there in the crowd reaction to Marciano. For some, if not many, Marciano was the Great White Hope. But no one trumpeted it—only because race relations were in a delicate "calm before the storm" phase.

The reaction to Marciano also reveals the ethnic tensions in society in the early 1950s. Only a few years before, ethnicity had played an enormous role in American society. First- or second-generation immigrants from Europe were not only defined by their ethnicity but also limited occupationally, educationally, economically, and otherwise. In the years after World War II, however, the concept of the melting pot emerged. Suddenly, the Italians, Irish, and other newer Americans of European descent were invited to join "old stock" Americans at the table.

Rocky Marciano was an Italian American. His ethnicity neither limited his opportunity nor hindered his success. It did, however, affect the way that people viewed him. Sportswriters invariably referred to Marciano as an Italian, although increasingly less so as his career progressed. They occasionally perpetuated ethnic stereotypes through him as well. On another front, Marciano became a towering hero among Italian Americans. In the Age of Simplicity, people rooted for their own. Ethnicity still mattered—not as much as it had before World War II but far more than it would at the dawn of the twenty-first century. Marciano came to symbolize ethnicity at its midcentury crossroads.

In fact, in terms of symbolism, Rocky Marciano came to personify his entire age. There was a set of qualities that were valued above all in early 1950s America: family devotion, loyalty, respect for authority, patriotism, religiousness, innocence, purity, hard work, decency, modesty, friendliness, gentleness, likeability, and, perhaps most of all, simplicity. These were the qualities that separated America from the evil communists. These were the qualities that composed that most precious of all things, the American Way of Life. These were the qualities that gave you a chance for the American Dream: that attractive wife, that well-paying job, and that little house with a white picket fence in the suburbs.

Rocky Marciano personally had many of these qualities. More important, the larger-then-life image that he acquired included them all. This was an era where sportswriters sought to lionize the athletes they covered, albeit only in a certain—and simple—fashion. What athletes stood for and what they did mattered; why they did it and what drove them to succeed did not. The fact that television was just catching on allowed sportswriters to engage in such two-dimensional hero-making. But television was beginning to change the way we view our sports heroes. Today, with lessening distance and more immediacy, it is no longer as important to recount an athlete's deeds. The focus is on the components of the psyche that allows the hero to scale such heights. Sportswriters (and the fans for whom they wrote) were largely unconcerned with such matters when it came to Rocky Marciano.

Nor were sportswriters of the early 1950s concerned with exposing Marciano's various character flaws. He had them, of course, as well as his share of peccadilloes, but sportswriters tended to gloss over them, adhering to their general credo of accentuating the positive and eliminating the negative. Today, we expect sports heroes to have flaws, and we accept them, warts and all. That was not an option in Marciano's time. You either wore the white hat or the black hat. Marciano wore the white hat. That Marciano genuinely had many of the qualities at the heart of his all-American-boy image—he was, for example, loyal and patriotic—was almost incidental. What was important was that he had enough of the desired qualities to wear the white hat. What he did not have enough of, the image-makers embellished; what he did not have at all, they made up; and what he had that did not fit the ideal, they omitted.

Ultimately, the sporting public saw in Rocky Marciano everything that was good and admirable in early 1950s America. He was a family man. He was modest. He was pure and innocent. He was friendly and likable. He was devoted to his parents. He was religious. He was patriotic and had served his country. He respected authority and obediently carried out the orders of his elders. He was loyal to his old friends and his old hometown. He worked hard for his success. And he was simple. As a result of all of these qualities, Rocky Marciano got it all: the pretty wife, the darling little daughter, the money, and even the brick house in the suburbs.

To his contemporaries in the Age of Simplicity, Rocky Marciano was the heavyweight champion of the world who also happened to represent the best the country had to offer. He personified the American Way of Life and was living the American Dream. He was, in short, a man for his time.

Now, decades after his retirement and premature death from a airplane crash, Marciano stands as a powerful symbol of his era. Unfortunately, all that is usually remembered about him is the fact that he was 49-0. Neither his story nor all the symbolism surrounding it is quite that simple.

Part 1: Rising

1 Holyoke

It was St. Patrick's Day in the year 1947, and the good, hard-working people of Holyoke, Massachusetts, had several options for their evening's entertainment.

They could, of course, visit their favorite neighborhood tavern and raise a pint or two to celebrate the traditional Irish holiday. If they were in the mood for a special celebration, they could go to O'Brien's Ballroom at the local chapter of the Knights of Columbus, which was staging a big holiday dance featuring Gordon Corlies and his orchestra, or to the Ancient Order of Hibernians Hall, which was offering Joe O'Leary and his Irish Minstrels plus Irish tenor Tom Quinn. They could always take in a movie—*Humoresque* starring Joan Crawford and John Garfield was playing at the Victory, while *The Man I Love* with Ida Lupino and Robert Alda was on the screen at the Strand. Or, if they preferred a quieter evening, they could stay home with the family and listen to the radio, perhaps the *Lux Theatre* on WMAS or the special half-hour of Irish tunes on WHYN (sponsored by Griffin's Package Store). More cutting-edge home entertainment beckoned if they were lucky enough to be one of the few to own that new invention called television.

Or they could go to the fights. In those days, with television in its infancy, a night of live boxing was a viable option for those who wanted action and thrills. For a few bucks, you could see fighters of all different weight classes—maybe not world champions, but young men willing to give an honest day's effort for an honest day's pay. That very night in Holyoke, promoter Oreal D. Rainault had lined up an attractive fight card for a show at the Valley Arena. The main event promised to be a donnybrook, with a middleweight named Saint Paul set to battle Tee Hubert.

On that St. Patrick's night in Holyoke, 1,200 fans paid their way into the Valley Arena to see Rainault's show. They saw Tee Hubert rely on his left hand to beat Saint Paul. They also saw several good fights on the undercard. The opening bout in particular was a wild one. It was a heavyweight fight featuring one of Holyoke's own, Les Epperson. Those in the know among the Holyoke fight crowd recognized Epperson's potential. He had fought well in the amateurs, and Baron Cohen, the Valley Arena matchmaker, was convinced that he was a good prospect. On this St. Patrick's night in Holyoke, he was fighting for the very first time as a professional.

Not much was known about Epperson's opponent. One thing was sure: He had never appeared in a Holyoke ring. In fact, he, like Epperson, had never fought professionally before. An ex-GI who lived in Brockton, Massachusetts, he had just gotten a job with the Brockton Gas Company and was eagerly anticipating his upcoming minor league baseball tryout down South with the Chicago Cubs. But then his neighbor and friend Allie Colombo told him that he could line up a fight for him in Holyoke. It seems that Allie, who was in the air force at Westover Field in nearby Chicopee, knew this guy at Westover named Dick O'Connor, who in turn knew Rainault the promoter. Was the ex-GI interested in fighting Epperson in Holyoke?

He was. He had done some boxing in the army and could use the extra cash. So he got the day off from the gas company and took a train across the state, arriving in Holyoke in the middle of the afternoon of St. Patrick's Day. After the weigh-in, the fighter and Allie went over to O'Connor's house, where they were treated to the traditional big steak dinner. Then, following a short rest, they headed for the arena.

Once they arrived, they immediately got into a squabble with Rainault the promoter. It seems that O'Connor had promised Allie that his friend would be paid $50 for his efforts. When they arrived at the arena, though, Rainault was offering only $35. Eventually, Allie and his friend agreed to accept the $35—but only if Rainault agreed to pick up the tab for the boxing license needed in order to fight Epperson. Rainault agreed. The fight was on.

Entering the ring that night in Holyoke, Epperson's opponent certainly didn't look much like of a fighter. He was short for a heavyweight, 5'10" or 5'11" tops. Even though his legs looked like tree trunks, he seemed light for a heavyweight, clearly shy of two hundred pounds. And those arms—oh, those arms. They were short and stubby, unfit for jabbing a rival at long range in the style of the reigning heavyweight champion, the great Joe Louis. On initial appearances alone, it didn't look as if this young boy was much of a fighter. At least he might make a good sacrificial lamb for the local boy, Epperson.

And for a while, the local boy did make good, getting the better of the action for the first two rounds as his rival tossed wild haymakers that missed their mark. But then, toward the end of the second, Epperson's opponent landed several good rights on the jaw that seemed to turn the tide. Forty-two seconds into the third round, Epperson was suddenly knocked out. He had been trying to trap his opponent on the ropes, but his opponent saw him coming, wound up, and threw a mighty right uppercut, seemingly from the floor. Epperson never had a chance. He was knocked through the ropes and out of the ring. The fight, exciting while it lasted, was over.

As it turned out, so was Les Epperson's career as a professional boxer. Years later he would say that he would have had a chance against his opponent had they ever fought again, pointing out that he had a decided edge for much of the first two rounds. But Epperson never fought again after that night in Holyoke. The experience was enough to convince him that he did not face a bright future in the ring. He eventually became a lithographer at a stationery firm in Springfield, Massachusetts.

What about Epperson's opponent? Unlike Epperson, great things lay ahead for him in the ring, far greater than sparsely attended fights in small western Massachusetts cities. He had fought Epperson under the name Rocky Mack, not only to protect his amateur standing but also because it was St. Patrick's Day and the name sounded vaguely Irish. His real name, though, was Rocco Marchegiano. In just a few short years the entire world would know him as neither Rocky Mack nor Rocco Marchegiano but as Rocky Marciano, the heavyweight champion of the world.

The Epperson fight, obscure as it was—it would, in fact, remain undiscovered until late in Marciano's career—was nevertheless a vintage Rocky Marciano fight, foreshadowing his later reign as heavyweight champion in many respects. He won. He won by a knockout. He looked raw and wild before winning. There was some underlying dispute involving money. And his opponent was never the same.

Later, this story line would play itself out again and again in big fights against big opponents in front of big crowds in big ballparks with millions watching on closed circuit television or listening on the radio. But that came later. The beginnings were far more humble in nature.

• • •

In the early part of the twentieth century, Brockton, Massachusetts, was known mainly for shoes. A tough, working-class city of about sixty thousand people located about twenty miles south of Boston, Brockton was filled with a mixture of first- and second-generation immigrants from Ireland, Italy, Lithuania, Poland, Sweden, and other faraway lands, all people who came to work in the shoe factories. Rocco Francis Marchegiano was born in Brockton on September 1, 1923. Shortly after the blessed event, legend has it that his parents received a congratulatory card bearing the imprint of a pair of boxing gloves and the caption "Hail to the Champ."

Rocco's parents, both born in Italy, were part of the more than one million other Italians that came to America during the 1910s. His father, Pierino Marchegiano, hailed from Chieti, a small fishing village near the Adriatic. Shortly after his arrival in America, with World War I in full swing, he enlisted and became part of the American Expeditionary Force in Europe. While in combat, Pierino once received a piece of shrapnel in his cheek that knocked out three teeth. "Didn't bother me, though," he would tell reporters after his son became famous years later. "Spit 'em out and kept going. I'm tough, too."[1]

Back in Brockton after the war, Pierino's long-term health suffered due to the gassing he received during a battle in the Argonne. A small, thin, wispy man who stood under 5'8", his weight dropped to 130 pounds after the gassing. He would remain sickly for the rest of his life, so sick that he occasionally was unable to work in the shoe factories upon his return to Brockton after the war. The fact that he worked on a No. 5 bed laster machine in the shoe factories, one of the toughest jobs in the shop, did not make his health battles any easier. A quiet, dignified man, Pierino Marchegiano carried on the best he could.

Luckily for Pierino and the rest of the family, his wife, Pasqualena Marchegiano, was a pillar of strength. She, too, grew up in Italy, in San Bartolomeo near the city of Naples. Her father, Luigi Picciuto, arrived in America in 1914, and Pasqualena and the rest of the family followed several years later. Shortly thereafter, Pasqualena Piccento (sporting the Americanized version of her last name that her family adopted in the new world) married Pierino Marchegiano. They say that opposites attract, and that was certainly true with Pierino and Lena Marchegiano. While he was reserved, she was outgoing. While he was stoic, she was emotional, with big, brown, expressive eyes. While he was sickly, she was robust, weighing nearly two hundred pounds later in life.

Young Rocco was actually Pierino and Lena's second child. The first had died shortly after birth, and doctors told the young couple that they could have no more children. And, for a while, it appeared that young Rocco, too, might not make it, because he caught pneumonia as a toddler and nearly died. Supposedly, Lena promised St. Anthony (or St. Rocco, depending on the account) that she would give up her diamond engagement ring if her young son pulled through. The son, of course, did pull through—and Lena, as promised, gave up her engagement ring. Years later, the legend goes, the son, now a rich and famous athlete, presented his mother with a new diamond ring.

Around the time that young Rocco beat pneumonia, the Marchegianos moved to a house located at 80 Brook Street in the heart of Brockton's Italian district. Pierino, Lena, and young Rocco lived on the second floor of a modest, two-story, white-frame house owned by Lena's father, Luigi. Very quickly the young family's quarters would become cramped with the arrival of five more children after Rocco—three girls (Alice, Connie, and Elizabeth) and two more boys (Louis and Peter).

Rocky Marciano grew up poor. Money was tight in the Marchegiano family. The Great Depression was on, and although Pierino managed to find work the shoe factories didn't pay much. The family had no bathtub, no running hot water, and no central heat. To stay warm in the winter, the Marchegianos would leave their doors open so they could capture some of the rising heat from the two coal stoves on the first floor occupied by Luigi. For additional heat, the resourceful Lena would constantly keep water heating on the kitchen stove.

Space was another problem. The second floor of the Brook Street house was cramped, consisting of only a living room, a kitchen, and two bedrooms. The three Marchegiano girls squeezed into one bedroom. Pierino and Lena slept in the other along with the youngest boy, Peter. Rocco's other brother Louis (nicknamed Sonny) would often sleep downstairs with his grandfather. Rocco himself usually slept in the living room on a mattress next to the window, which he insisted on keeping open even in the winter.

In other respects, Rocco had an idyllic boyhood. "Even during the tough times, we didn't know we were poor," remembers Sonny Marciano. "We always ate well." There was plenty of family around, too. Downstairs was grandfather Luigi, a big, strapping man who had been a blacksmith in the old country. "[E]verything about him was big," Marciano would recall about his grandfather years later. "He played big, he worked big, he gambled big, he drank big, he ate big, he talked in a big voice." Luigi had a small vineyard on the side of the house, and young Rocco played an active role in helping him make wine, often carrying the heavy crates of grapes down into the cellar and operating the heavy-handled contraption that would mash the grapes. He would later fondly remember the Saturday night outdoor wine parties that his grandfather would host for the other old Italian men in the neighborhood. More often than not the events, which featured the Italian bowling game bocce and the card game *scopa,* would end with alcohol-fueled arguments.[2]

The playground was the center of young Rocco Marchegiano's life. The Marchegiano family home on Brook Street was only fifty yards from the James J. Edgar Playground, where there was always some sort of sandlot baseball or football game going on. When Rocco was a teenager, his family moved from Brook Street to Dover Street on the other side of the playground. The games continued. And Rocco was usually in the middle of them, along with friends such as Izzy Gold, Eugene Sylvester, Nicky Sylvester, Teddy Mason, Connie Cicone, Joe Fidele, Herbie O'Connor, and Allie Colombo. "I always could handle Rocky when he was a kid," his father said. "I spanked him a few times so he remembers that I am boss. He was a good boy and never caused any trouble. He was so crazy about baseball and football, he had no time to join gangs or get into bad company."[3]

By the time he was a teenager, Rocco had become a fine athlete—big, strong, and well-coordinated. His first love was baseball. A stocky catcher with a strong arm and a big bat, Rocco planned on making a career of the game that he loved. In 1937 he began a four-year stint on an American Legion team coached by Brockton car salesman Jack Killory. "Rocky was all right," Killory would recall. "Not a potential big-leaguer, but a good athlete who could hit a ball a mile when he caught hold of it." Father Jeremiah Minnehan, a priest at St. Patrick's Church in Brockton and manager of the CYO team on which Rocco and his pals played, was more glowing in his appraisal of Rocco's diamond skills, calling him "one of the best all-around baseball players I have ever seen," a hard-hitting catcher who could "put that ball down to second base like a bullet." Father Minnehan especially recalled the deciding game of the 1940 Massachusetts CYO championship when his catcher helped St. Patrick's to victory by blocking the plate to prevent the potential winning run from scoring.[4]

The teenaged Rocco Marchegiano was also an accomplished football player. In the fall of 1940, as a sophomore at Brockton High School, he was good enough to start every game for the varsity football team, the defending state champions. It was a disappointing fall for the Red and Black because their twenty-two-game unbeaten streak was snapped and they slumped to 5-4-1. One of the bright spots in the season was the play of the sophomore Marchegiano, who wore number 1 and started every game at center and linebacker. As his coach Charlie Holden would recall, "He was only a sophomore, but he played nearly sixty minutes a game all season. He was a rough, tough, powerful kid of about a hundred and fifty-five pounds who never got tired and never got hurt." The highlight of Rocco's year came on Columbus Day against New Bedford High, when he intercepted a pass and raced sixty-five yards for a touchdown. "I was lucky in that I intercepted the pass over by the sideline and ran straight down the line," Marciano recalled years later. "I needed help, though, and I got it. One guy even blocked out two guys for me. Even at that, however, I didn't score the only touchdown of my career standing up. I was so slow that I was nailed from behind on the one-yard line and fell over the goal line."[5]

Shortly after the conclusion of the 1940 football season, midway through his sophomore year, Rocco Marchegiano suddenly dropped out of school. Several factors played into his decision. The varsity baseball coach at Brockton High laid down a rule prohibiting team members from playing on other baseball teams in the city—and that edict posed a problem for Rocco, who was a fixture on the sandlots and desperately wanted to continue playing for his CYO team. Moreover, Rocco was, at best, a disinterested high school student. "I was never good in school . . . I just didn't care for the books," he would later admit. He was clearly struggling with his studies. "And I thought it was too bad," recalled Holden. "He could have studied. He could have made better marks. He was capable of it. . . . He was very discouraged at the time because of his low marks and the need for making up and boosting his grades."[6]

The major reason he decided to quit, though, was an economic one. Although the depression was beginning to wind down, money was still scarce in the Marchegiano family, with eight mouths to feed and Pierino's shoe factory wages the only real source of income. Rocco had gotten a paper route as a kid. Now he was old enough to get a real job and make some real money to help the family. His uncle, Johnny Piccento, knew of a job that would pay him four dollars a day and urged him to take it. One night at the dinner table, Rocco announced his decision: He was quitting school to enter the work force. Everyone in the family was against it—especially his mother, who greatly valued education. Coach Holden and several teachers also tried to talk him out of it. But Rocco had made up his mind. It was time to go to work.

His first job was a short stint working on a coal truck for fifty cents an hour. He then proceeded to hold a succession of low-paying, manual-labor jobs over the next three years. He worked in a candy factory, mixing candy. He tried the shoe factories but quit when he couldn't stand the smell. He worked in a wire factory. He was a short-order cook in a diner. He also washed dishes, dug ditches, removed snow, landscaped, and delivered beer for a brewery. His fortunes improved slightly after World War II broke out because he landed several plum defense-related jobs, helping clear land for a factory, build a blimp hangar, and construct an embarkation center. Still, Marciano would later refer to his manual-labor jobs as a collection of "dead ends."[7]

On March 4, 1943, the drudgery of manual labor ended for Rocco Marchegiano when he was drafted in the U.S. Army. After completing basic training, he was shipped overseas with the 150th Combat Engineers and stationed in Swansea, Wales. He spent much of the time there helping ferry supplies from the United Kingdom to the beaches of France. He was shipped back home in late 1945 and stationed at Fort Lewis in Tacoma, Washington, until his discharge in December 1946.

He returned home to Brockton and lined up a new job in early 1947, this time with the Brockton Gas Company, shoveling coal and stoking the furnaces for about a dollar an hour. It was during this period that he appeared in Holyoke to fight Epperson. But his attention was on neither the gas company nor boxing. Instead, he was in full pursuit of his dream of a baseball career in the major leagues. Even after he left high school, he had never stopped honing his skills on the ball fields of Brockton. The war had interrupted his progress, but now he was back and ready for the major leagues. In the spring of 1947 he finally got his long-awaited shot: He was invited to try out with a farm team of the Chicago Cubs.

In late March 1947, Rocco and several of his Brockton friends (Eugene Sylvester, Vinny Colombo, and Red Gormley), amid some minor civic fanfare, headed South for their tryout with the Cubs farm team in Fayetteville, North Carolina. Only Sylvester made the grade and stuck. Colombo was cut first. Then, after a month, the Cubs dropped Marchegiano and Gormley on the same day. Unwilling to go home failures quite yet, Marchegiano and Gormley skipped over to Goldsboro, North Carolina, where another Brockton friend, Tully Colombo, was playing with a team in the Class D minor leagues. They failed that tryout as well. At that point, Gormley later said, "We were broke, and I guess we looked like a couple of bums, so we decided to come home."[8]

Many reasons were later proffered for Rocky Marciano's failure with the Cubs. He had hurt his right arm playing ball in the service and could no longer throw as sharply or as accurately as before. His left catching hand may have also been tender, affecting his ability to catch fastballs. And, as Marciano himself later conceded, "The truth is I couldn't hit hard enough."[9] Whatever the reason, Rocco Marchegiano was back in Brockton by late April 1947 with nothing to do. It was then and only then that he decided to turn to boxing.

● ● ●

Actually, he returned to boxing, for by this point in his life Rocco Marchegiano was no stranger to fighting. As a big, strong, tough kid who spent most of his youth on the playgrounds of a rough and tumble city, he had naturally gotten into his share of boyhood scraps. "He was never a pugnacious type kid," recalls Sonny Marciano. "He would not look for trouble. He was very gentle in so many ways. But if, in competition, someone made a gesture that they wanted to fight, then everyone on the team looked for Rocky . . . Rocky was the one who would take care of all the troublemakers."[10]

He played the same role in the service. Once, for instance, while still at Fort Devens in Massachusetts waiting to be shipped overseas, his fellow soldiers in the 150th Combat Engineers drafted him to fight a big Texan who had been hurling daily taunts at men in the company. As Marciano remembered, "This Texan kept talking. You know how those Texans are and everybody was getting sick of his ear-banging and finally the kids jammed up on me. They said I was the biggest guy around and I should shut this Texan up. I tried to get out of it, but they needled me into going in with him."[11] In a makeshift ring and with soldiers surrounding them, Marciano proceeded to knock the Texan out with a big right to the jaw. He had saved his company's honor.

On another occasion, after he had been shipped overseas to Wales, Private Marchegiano stood up to a huge Australian in a pub. "He insulted us at every opportunity," Marciano recalled. "Finally he called me that name no red-blooded man can ignore. I objected and asked him to apologize. He roared another worse insult, got off the bench and rushed at us . . . I had to get him in a hurry or take a beating. I threw a wild haymaker which, lucky for me, landed on his jaw. He went down like a log and stayed on the floor, blood pouring from his mouth."[12] Rocco Marchegiano was starting to believe in the power of his fists.

That belief only grew when he returned stateside in 1945 and began to engage in organized boxing for the first time. Stationed at Fort Lewis, Rocco entered several army boxing tournaments and started to flatten his fellow GIs. He compiled enough wins to qualify for the 1945 National Junior AAU Boxing Championships in Portland, Oregon. He advanced to the finals of the heavyweight division by scoring consecutive first-round knockouts but broke the knuckle on the forefinger of his left hand along the way. He decided to fight in the final anyway. His opponent was Joey DeAngelis from Charlestown, Massachusetts. In the first big fight of his amateur career, Rocco Marchegiano lost a three-round decision. Years later DeAngelis would boast, "Rocky got the dough, but I got the gold medal that shows I beat him."[13]

Around this time, he also made his initial boxing appearance in Brockton. It was hardly a smashing debut. While temporarily home on furlough from the army in April 1946 he squared off against Ted Lester, a tough veteran of the New England amateur wars, at Brockton's Ancient Order of Hibernians Hall. In the third round, an out-of-shape and struggling Marchegiano lost his balance and kicked Lester in the groin. The referee promptly disqualified him and awarded the fight to Lester.

Private Marchegiano was soon back fighting—and winning—at Fort Lewis. He hadn't had any formal training, and he had no style to speak of, but his punch was enough to ensure success. His success in the ring made him a camp celebrity of sorts, but his enthusiasm for boxing as a potential career remained tepid. That skepticism only grew during his trip back to Brockton after his discharge from Fort Lewis in December 1946. On the way home, he stopped in Chicago to visit Joe Sarelli, an old army buddy. Sarelli's father was connected with the fight game and agreed to assess Marchegiano's potential as a fighter. "His father took me to a gym in Chicago's Loop," Marciano recalled. "For three days I hit the big bag and the little bag. I skipped rope and shadow boxed. At the end of the workouts, Joe's father sat down with me. He told me, 'Rocky, why don't you go home and forget about being a fighter. You're too small to be a heavyweight. You'll never make it.'"[14]

Back home in Brockton in early 1947, Marchegiano was perfectly willing to take that advice. For sure, he continued to dabble in boxing, entering an amateur show at the Mechanics Building in Boston, where he scored an upset knockout victory over Red Connolly, a fighter from Dorchester, Massachusetts, with size and a reputation. But Rocco wasn't serious. Even after his victory over Epperson in Holyoke, his attention was fixated not on boxing but on baseball and the Chicago Cubs. By April those dreams had been dashed. He suddenly found himself standing at the first real cross-roads of his life.

* * *

What separated Rocco Marchegiano from all the other former servicemen who returned home and reentered society after the war, content to find an ordinary job and settle down into a life of normalcy? Why didn't Rocco, too, migrate toward a blue-collar existence and a life of factories and bowling nights? Why did he want more? To some extent it was merely old-fashioned ambition. But it was more than that. What really drove Rocco Marchegiano into boxing after his baseball dreams evaporated in the spring of 1947, and what would drive him for the rest of his life, was a singular emotion, simple yet powerful: fear.

Rocco Marchegiano feared being anonymous. As journalist Jimmy Cannon once observed, "Obscurity was all he was afraid of." He clearly was not interested in being another ex-GI, another cog in the wheel, another faceless member of the blue-collar work force. "Rocky, although he was a calm person, he was very restless," remembers his brother Sonny. "And he set his goals, I guess, as a young man. He wanted to be successful. And I think that alone separated him. He was not content just to think about getting a job, getting married, and having a family."[15] Rocco Marchegiano yearned for recognition. He wanted to make a name for himself.

More important, he feared being poor. Much of this stemmed from his father. Poverty had a dramatic and visible effect upon Pierino Marchegiano. As a boy, Rocco would deliver lunch to his father in the shoe factories and see the man he revered standing at the No. 5 bed-laster machine, arms and legs moving, tacks hanging out of his mouth, and sweat dripping from his frail body. His father would tell him, "Be somebody, Rocky. Don't never work in a factory." He would never forget the scene or the advice. Nor would he forget the moroseness that his father would lapse into from time to time or the dreary existence that he often seemed to lead. "He never made any money and he never had any fun," Marciano would later remember. "He was only existing."[16]

In the course of those lunch deliveries, the young Rocco Marchegiano decided that he would not settle for a life in the factories and a row house in the city. As his youngest brother Peter recalls, "He really wanted something better in life. . . . And make no bones about it: it was financial. He wanted some financial success." He wanted money not just for himself but for his family. The fact that he was the eldest son in the family was significant. Rocco Marchegiano grew up in a traditional Italian family where the eldest son was expected to shoulder much of the economic responsibility for the rest of the family. "Rocky was the oldest boy," Sonny Marciano remembers, "and he felt a responsibility to do something. . . . He took that burden on his shoulders. He could handle it." Of primary concern to Rocco was his parents, especially his father. As Sonny recalls, "[H]e also thought, 'How do I make enough money to get my dad out of this?' He knew that it would kill my dad eventually. . . . He wanted the good things in life. I think he wanted it more for my parents than he wanted it for himself."[17]

The need to make money—for himself and for his family—would remain indelibly stamped upon Pierino Marchegiano's eldest son for the rest of his career and the rest of his life, persisting long after he became rich and famous. "The dollar is his God," Marciano's manager Al Weill would later observe. "That is to say, he is a poor Italian boy from a large, poor family, and he appreciates the buck more than almost anybody else. . . . You want to look out for them young broken fighters." As Marciano once told his friend, featherweight champion Willie Pep, "It was rough for me when I was a kid, Willie. It's never gonna be like that again. I'm never gonna be broke now, Willie. Never."[18]

In the years after his discharge from the army, facing a return to manual labor and a lifetime of financial struggle, all of these emotions created a special sense of urgency in Rocco Marchegiano. "The only way was for me to marry some rich women," he recalled to Cannon. "I saw what the factory done to my father and I didn't want it to happen to me. But it looked like I couldn't get away." As he once proclaimed to his family, "I'll *never* work in a shoe factory. I have to find a way out."[19]

His way out, of course, was boxing. In fact, in terms of a career in sports, his only viable avenue out of the shoe factories, his options were dwindling rapidly. He had long ago turned his back on football. Now baseball had turned its back on him. One option remained, however. As he had told his friend Red Gormley during the long train trip back to Brockton from North Carolina after the failed tryout with the Cubs, "The heck with it. I'm through with baseball. I'm gonna get some fights, and you're gonna handle me."[20]

When he returned to Brockton in the spring of 1947, he started to explore the possibilities. As his uncle Mike Piccento would recall, "He come up here and we had a talk and he said, 'Well, Mike, I got nothing left in sports unless I want to play semipro football, but there's nothing left in that.' So then he thought he'd take a chance on fighting." He had no natural love of the ring. But boxing had always loomed as a potential option. When he was a boy he had reportedly told his father, "Pa, some day when I grow up, I'll be heavyweight champion of the world and make $1,000,000 and take care of you and Ma and the kids." Confirms Sonny Marciano today, "He always knew that he was strong. . . . He wanted first to give baseball a shot and he felt that he was going to make it in baseball. But, in the back of his mind, boxing was probably the next thing that he wanted to try."[21]

His ring victories in the army and the amateurs as well as the Epperson victory in Holyoke supplied hope that he could be successful. His friends and family offered encouragement and support. And he had his fears to motivate him. "That shoe leather was something that bothered him," remembers Sonny Marciano. "He didn't like that smell. . . . He certainly knew that he didn't want to work in a shoe factory or digging ditches or anything like that." Indeed, as Rocco Marchegiano told his girlfriend (and eventual wife) Barbara around the time that he turned to boxing, "If I go into the ring, I might amount to something. If I don't, what will I do the rest of my life? Dig ditches?"[22] The prospects terrified him.

●　●　●

So, in the spring of 1947, Rocco Marchegiano reentered the ranks of amateur boxing with a new sense of purpose. Although he kept his day job at the Brockton Gas Company he started to train in earnest. "I guess I realized," he recalled, "that the fight game was my last chance to better myself, and I really worked at it."[23] For the next year, from the spring of 1947 to the spring of 1948, he did work at it, fighting in about thirty amateur bouts throughout eastern Massachusetts. Gene Caggiano, a Brockton mechanic who also was heavily involved in the local amateur boxing scene, served as his manager. His friend Allie Colombo seconded him in the ring.

As an amateur, Rocky Marciano was extremely raw. He would simply flounder around the ring, graceless and awkward, absorbing punishment from his opponent until he saw an opening to land a big one. As Colombo reminisced, "He was crude, but there was one move he would wait for the other fellow to make, and when he made it, Rocky would swing and knock him out."[24] The strategy may have been simple and inartistic but it was also surprisingly effective. He would lose only four fights as an amateur. But his inexperience also led to injury. He knew how to knock opponents out but didn't know how to punch in a way that would protect his hands (which weren't taped properly to begin with). As a result, Marchegiano became a regular at Brockton's Goddard Hospital for treatment of broken or cracked knuckles.

In early 1948 he remained healthy enough to start piling up amateur titles. On February 9 in Lowell, Massachusetts, he won the Massachusetts–Rhode Island Golden Gloves title by knocking out Charlie Mortimer in the third round. One week later, on February 18 and again in Lowell, he won the New England Golden Gloves Championship by scoring a first-round technical knockout of George McInnis, the champion from New Hampshire.

Next came the All-Eastern Golden Gloves Championships in early March 1948 in New York City. His initial bout of the tournament was against Coley Wallace. The highly regarded amateur from Buffalo owned a long knockout string and was being touted as the "next Joe Louis," in part because he bore an uncanny resemblance to the great champion. Wallace entered the ring that afternoon in Ridgewood Grove Arena in Brooklyn an overwhelming favorite over the unknown from Brockton. According to the popular account, Marchegiano shocked the experts by manhandling Wallace for much of the three-round fight. The verdict nevertheless went to Wallace, stunning sportswriters at ringside (with one literally falling off his chair) as well as fans. Jimmy Breslin, then a young reporter on the boxing beat, disputes this account, however. The Pulitzer prize-winner contends that Wallace knocked Marciano down twice and clearly won the fight—and that the reporters who later alleged to the contrary were engaging in a bit of revisionist history. "Were they there or were they making it up?" Breslin asks today, somewhat incredulously.[25] Either way, it was a loss for Rocco Marchegiano—his fourth as an amateur, the others having been suffered at the hands of Joey DeAngelis, Ted Lester, and Bob Girard. He would never lose in the ring again.

Marchegiano rebounded from the loss to Wallace by capturing the New England AAU heavyweight title in late March 1948, beating old friend George McInnis before 4,749 fans at the Boston Arena. What made the victory even more impressive was the fact that he fought against McInnis with an injured left thumb he hurt in his victory in the semifinals of the tournament. After the tournament, doctors discovered that the thumb was broken and estimated that Marchegiano would be sidelined for four to six months. The injury robbed him of a potential rematch with Wallace and a shot at capturing the National AAU title in April, which carried with it an automatic berth on the U.S. Olympic team to compete in London that summer.

The injury also led directly to Marchegiano's decision to turn professional. As he would explain, "It cost me some money to fix the thumb, so I thought I might as well earn some fighting."[26] Moreover, the Brockton Gas Company had laid him off because of his left hand. The choice seemed clear: Either he should become a full-time professional fighter or give up boxing entirely. He chose boxing. In a sense it was inevitable that he would turn professional. Boxing for the sport of it only had limited appeal for Rocco Marchegiano, but it nevertheless represented his last real chance to make a name for himself—and escape a life of poverty.

2 Providence

Al Weill and Charley Goldman were both old-time fight men, and they were both short. That's where the similarities ended. Al was cunning and egotistical; Charley was guileless and altruistic. Al sought the limelight; Charley was happy in the shadows. Al was despised in many quarters; Charley was universally beloved.

Together, however, Al and Charley were a formidable pair, two men quite capable of steering a young fighter with the right stuff toward the top of the boxing world. Weill was the shrewd manager who had the influence to get the right fights against the right opponents in the right places at the right times. Goldman was the trainer who taught the ring techniques necessary for success. By the late 1940s, the Weill-Goldman team had already turned three boys into champions of lighter weight classes. On one June day in 1948 into their lives would walk their fourth and most famous champion: heavyweight Rocco Marchegiano.

The story of how Marchegiano hooked up with Weill and Goldman involves two other fight men, Joe Monte and Eddie Boland. Just around the time that he decided to turn professional, Rocco Marchegiano and his sidekick Allie Colombo went to see Monte, a fighter from Brockton who had enjoyed some ring success years earlier before the loss of an eye ended his career. Monte stressed the importance of getting the right manager. Years before he had relied on a manager from Boston, but the man had lacked the influence to push his career along. He urged the young Marchegiano not to make the same mistake. Boland, a veteran Boston fight man who had seen Marchegiano fight and wanted to help the young fighter along, gave Rocco and Allie similar advice—forget the Boston fight mob and find a New York manager with big-time connections.

It wasn't as if the Boston fight guys were beating down the door for the chance to work with Marchegiano. They had seen the young Brockton heavyweight fight in the amateurs and despite his string of successes came away unimpressed. Neither his physique nor his style marked him as a heavyweight of great potential. As Boston promoter Sam Silverman remembered, "Of all the kids around, Rocky was the most unlikely to succeed. He was clumsy and awkward. He had no stance, no style, nothing."[1] Hometown to the core, Rocco and Allie had tried to interest Jackie Martin, Johnny Buckley, and the other Boston managers who hung around that city's Friend Street gyms. But they weren't interested in Rocco Marchegiano.

So Rocco and Allie set their sights on faraway New York. Boland had mentioned several New York managers who would be ideal for Marchegiano, but the one he recommended the most was Al Weill. Rocco and Allie decided to write to Weill. Allie, not Rocco, was the designated writer and penned a short note boasting of his friend's amateur success and bragging that he would win the title with the proper handling. At the same time, and perhaps more important, Boland also contacted Weill on Marchegiano's behalf. On a Saturday afternoon in June 1948 Weill called Colombo. He had received Allie's letter. Could he and Rocco come down to New York for a look-see?

A few days later the two Brockton boys traveled down to New York. They arrived in the city early on Monday morning and walked around until they could get in to see Weill at his offices on Broadway. Later that morning the kingmaker and his future king met for the first time. After a few perfunctory questions, Weill called Charley Goldman and ordered him to get another heavyweight ready for some sparring. He was bringing the kid from Brockton down to the gym for a workout.

Moments later, at the CYO gymnasium on West Seventeenth Street, Rocco Marchegiano stepped into the ring with Wade Chancey, a big heavyweight from Florida. The prospect from Brockton hardly dazzled Weill and Goldman. "Marciano was so awkward that we stood there and laughed," Goldman later said. "He didn't stand right, he didn't throw a punch right; he didn't block right, he didn't do anything right. Then, all of a sudden, he hit Chancey with a roundhouse right and the big guy went out like a mackerel."[2] Rocco Marchegiano had passed the audition.

●　●　●

It was fortunate that he did so, because Rocky Marciano never would have been champion without Al Weill and Charley Goldman. He may never have even broken out of the ranks of club fighting. He had natural talent for sure, but that talent never would have been properly harnessed without a skillful teacher like Goldman. Moreover, this was an era where a fighter needed more than talent. He also needed a manager who had influence and connections—a manager like Al Weill.

Weill was born in Gebweiler, Alsace, in 1893. At the age of fourteen he came to America to live with relatives in Yorkville, New York. The young Al Weill soon fell into the world he would never leave—boxing—and made a mark for himself on the New York fight scene as both a manager and a matchmaker. Even his enemies—and Weill had many—grudgingly had to admit that he was a shrewd student of styles. He had the uncanny knack of properly assessing the entertainment value of matching one type of fighter against another. That ability served him well when he acted as matchmaker for promoter Mike Jacobs in 1931 and then again in 1937 and 1938. The latter stint with Jacobs occurred just as Jacobs and his organization, the Twentieth Century Sporting Club, were emerging as the dominant promotional power in the sport of boxing, primarily due to Jacobs's close association with the new heavyweight champion Joe Louis. Weill and Jacobs soon had a falling-out, though. It would be nearly a dozen years before Weill found himself near the center of boxing's power structure.

In the interim, Weill continued to distinguish himself as a manager. Here again, his knowledge of styles helped. An Al Weill fighter would usually go into the ring against an opponent with a tailor-made style for his own styles and abilities. Through skillful matching and handling Weill guided three men to the championship of their weight classes: lightweight Lou Ambers in the late 1930s, featherweight Joey Archibald in the late 1930s, and welterweight Marty Servo in the mid-1940s. Ambers was a great fighter, but the reigns of Archibald and Servo probably owed as much to Weill's managerial skill as to the boxers' moderate abilities.

Weill was a manager from the old school. He believed that he—and not his fighter—was the main attraction. Concerning an upcoming fight, for instance, Marciano once mentioned to Weill in passing, "I'm glad I got this match." "You're glad *who* got this match?" Weill retorted angrily. "You think *you* got it. *I* got it. I made this match for you. You ought to pay me for making this match. What are you? You're just the fighter. Without me, you're nothing."[3]

Consistent with that belief, Al Weill demanded total control over his boxers, both in and out of the ring. Weill didn't want them involved with wine, women, or song, and he took steps to make sure they wouldn't give in to those temptations. In the years before World War II, Weill used to house all his fighters in a lodging house near Central Park, placing them on a weekly meal allowance of $5.50 in the form of meal tickets redeemable at a local diner. As A. J. Liebling of *The New Yorker* pointed out, "None of these fighters ever suffered a defeat that could be attributed to high living." After the war, Weill continued to treat his fighters like serfs. "He gave them the proposition when he met them," columnist Jimmy Cannon once wrote of the Weill system. "They would fight with their bodies, and he would think for them with his mind. They could not argue and he would not tolerate any opinions from them."[4]

This is the type of control that Al Weill would successfully exert over Rocky Marciano in the late 1940s and early 1950s. "When I started with Rocky, I declared myself right away," Weill would say. "'Rocky,' I said, 'you got your job and I got mine. You got all you can do to stay in condition and train for fights. I handle everything else.'" Marciano agreed, ceding control of his professional career (and much of his personal life) to Weill. "I was willing to make sacrifices," Marciano later explained. "I wanted more than anything else to be a fighter. Then I wanted to be a good one, and after that a great champion. I accepted my manager's domination."[5]

Perhaps the kindest adjective used to describe Weill was "shrewd." He was always looking to play the angles, to manipulate people and situations. As a result, few in fight circles trusted him. Weill could be charming, even genial, but only when it behooved him to be so. More often his contemporaries found him to be loud, arrogant, rude, and abrasive—personality traits that led *Life* to label Weill the "most cordially hated manager in boxing."

"I didn't think too much of Al Weill," admits Truman Gibson, a lawyer and promoter who worked with Weill at the International Boxing Club (IBC), the promotional power in boxing during the late 1940s and 1950s. "Al Weill knew the boxing business, but he was not an engaging personality. Very blunt. Crude. Crass." Gibson remembers Weill, who was trying to convince a boxer to accept a fight, punctuating his campaign of persuasion by stating, "Well, you have to take that or we'll get a nigger to fight him." As Gibson, who is black, observes, "That in itself was not shocking, but it was not indicative of any engaging personality."[6]

Angelo Dundee, just starting out in the fight game in New York in the late 1940s, also observed the unpleasant side of Marciano's manager. Once, when Dundee was in the process of dropping off something at Weill's office, he became a reluctant witness as Weill berated his stepson, Marty. "He chewed him out," Dundee recalls. "You don't do that in front of people. Chew him out later, not now. He did it right in front of me. To me, that's low." Dundee nevertheless praises Weill as "one tough fight manager." Fight man Lou Duva (who in his more than half a century in boxing has experienced the sport as a boxer, trainer, manager, and promoter) offers a consistent opinion. "You couldn't have a lot of fun with him," he says of Weill. "He was strictly business—and all the business was for himself."[7]

Somehow, his appearance seemed to fit his personality. Weill was a round little man whose expressive face displayed a wide spectrum of emotions, depending on his mood and motivation. As a young man, he had been an accomplished dancer. "He was a terrific dancer," recalls Jimmy Breslin. "He used to go in dance contests when he was starting out. He'd win. He'd push the girl, his partner, out to take the bows and then he'd grab the money and run and go to the next contest." By the late 1940s Weill's dancing days were long gone, as was his svelte physique. A. J. Liebling of *The New Yorker* preferred to think of Weill as portly rather than fat, reasoning, "There is an implication of at least one kind of recklessness about a fat man; he lets himself go when he eats. A portly man, on the other hand, is a man who would like to be fat but restrains himself—a calculator."[8]

He had thick glasses and smoked an ever-present cigar. The grayish pigmentation of his skin was accented by the cigar ashes and smoke that always seemed to envelope him and the gray suits he frequently wore when conducting business in the city. He also had a long-standing penchant for tattersall and velvet vests, which led sportswriters to dub him "the Vest" and "Weskit." They especially liked to make fun of gravy stains that would inevitably find their way onto Weill's vests and suits. New York columnist

Dan Parker, one of Weill's prime tormentors in the press, once joked, "The Vest got all the gravy," referring not only to Weill's stained garb but also his fanatical love of money and his knack for getting it.[9]

Other times, particularly at camp with Marciano, Weill dressed the part of the fight manager—loud jackets, glittering diamonds, and costume jewelry. Once, up in the Catskills shortly before one of Marciano's title fights, Weill went to the airport to greet Harry Markson, one of the bigwigs in the IBC and at Madison Square Garden during Marciano's career. Weill sported green pants, a red shirt, a pink sweater, and a blue beret. Markson, taken aback, joked, "That's the wildest outfit I ever saw." Weill, in a response that seemed to capture his essence, shot back, "Don't tell me how to manage my fighter."[10]

Weill's abrasive, domineering ways became especially pronounced during those times when he occupied a position of power. Some people wear power well. Weill was not one of them. He reveled in it, only further antagonizing his enemies. And in the late 1940s, after years of ups and downs, Al Weill was just reaching the apex of his power, emerging as the matchmaker for the IBC. With his appointment in May 1949 he instantly became one of the most powerful figures in the sport. The IBC was the sole promotional power in boxing, and now Weill was the man most responsible for arranging its fights. That meant that managers, trainers, and fighters had to kowtow to him in order to get a meaningful fight.

Weill would use his enormous power not only to help his own fortunes but also that of his fighter, Rocky Marciano. With Weill presiding over his career, Marciano would never have to worry about getting the big fights. Nor would Marciano have to worry about being rushed before he was ready. "With the wrong manager he'd have been tossed in against better men while his slip was still showing, his crudeness exposed," Arthur Daley of the *New York Times* later praised. "Although Weill never will win any popularity contests, even his legion of enemies admit that he is a very shrewd apple. He hand-picked Rocky's opponents and never overmatched him." Marciano would later admit, "He figured out every move, and he made sure I only met guys he thought I could beat. He knew exactly when I was ready for the next step up. Right from the beginning he handled me perfect . . . I wouldn't have been champ without him."[11]

Nor would Marciano have risen to the top without the yin to Al Weill's yang, trainer Charley Goldman. In the summer of 1948, Rocco Marchegiano had a lot to learn about the rudiments of boxing. For those things, as well as the finer points of life, Charley Goldman was the consummate teacher.

Goldman was born in 1888 in Poland. Like Weill, he immigrated to the

United States at an early age, and, also like Weill, he turned to boxing shortly after his arrival, not as a trainer but as a fighter. A small man who stood just over five feet tall and weighed only a shade over a hundred pounds, Goldman boxed professionally as a bantamweight from 1904 to 1914. Officially, he fought 137 times, but he fought just as many unrecorded bouts and later claimed to have had between three and four hundred pro fights in total (sixty of them against one man, George Kitson). Overall, he had success. In his 137 official bouts he lost just six times. He finally got his shot at the bantamweight title in 1912 when he met champion Johnny Coulan. Alas, the bout was declared a no-decision, and Coulan kept his title.

Two years later, in 1914, Goldman retired as a boxer and became a trainer. He was a natural teacher, and very soon the best managers (including the young Al Weill) were clamoring to hand over their young charges to him. In 1925, however, Goldman left boxing. "I got myself interested in a road-house near Newburgh, New York, and did all right with it, but I wasn't too happy," he said. "I had to get back to boxing. It gets in your blood and there you are."[12] Returning to boxing full time in the mid-1930s, he achieved renewed success training boxers. His training workload typically included between seven and ten fighters represented by various managers. By the late 1940s he had trained four champions: the lightweight Ambers, the feather-weight Archibald, and the welterweight Servo (all Weill fighters) as well as middleweight Al McCoy.

By this time, he had also emerged as a beloved figure in boxing circles. "He was a great, great man," says Dundee, who as a young trainer in New York in the late 1940s and early 1950s counted Goldman as one of his friends and mentors (along with other legendary trainers such as Chickie Ferrara, Jimmy August, and Ray Arcel). As Arcel once recalled, "Charley Goldman was just a perfect man. He was lovely. He was the kind of a man you could actually live with, you know what I mean? And I say that in a sense that he was that friendly. He was that nice."[13]

Charley Goldman was more than just a nice guy—he was a true American original. He was always spouting carefully crafted yet endearing pearls of wisdom about boxing and life, for example, "never buy anything on the street, especially diamonds" and "never play a guy at his own game; nobody makes up a game in order to get beat at it." Such wisdom helped make Goldman a popular member of what was known in the early 1950s as "the fight mob"—an informal and seedy conglomeration of managers, trainers, gamblers, and hangers-on that hung around the fights, the gyms, and the bars in New York. Goldman was one of the more honorable members of the fight mob. Indeed, perhaps his most famous saying was a toast he would give before taking a glass of beer at the Neutral Corner or one of the other saloons frequented by the fight mob: "Protect your honor at all times." As Breslin recalls, "Charley Goldman was a great storyteller at the bar."[14]

Goldman also had definite opinions about women. Once, an attractive actress who wanted to samba with Goldman at a party asked if he was married. "No," Goldman replied, "I'm living ala carte these days." He was, in fact, a confirmed bachelor and categorically opposed to marriage, yet he adored women and was always dating. He called the younger women he dated "cousins" or "adopted nieces." Recalls Dundee, "They were his 'nieces.' Every chick he had, they were his 'nieces.' You gotta love 'nieces.'" Goldman was always scouting for nieces. Once, he attended a Brockton High football game with Marciano. Soon it became apparent that Goldman's attention was wandering. Someone asked, "Don't you like football, Charlie?" The small man in his mid-sixties answered, "Don't bother me. I'm watching them cheerleaders."[15]

For a man entering his senior citizen years, he seemed remarkably young and spry. His secret for defying the aging process? "I don't talk about the good old days," he said. "After all, it's not the good old days, it's the good old youth the old-timers are remembering. And I stay away from most fellows my age. I see them and they complain about rheumatism, and gout, and everything under the sun. I say to myself, 'Hully gee, I'm as old as they are. I'm going to stay away from them or I'll be developing those ailments myself.' To stay young you've got to think young."[16]

He wasn't a wealthy man, earning about only $4,000 a year at midcentury, but he was happy. He lived at Ma Brown's, a West Ninety-first Street boardinghouse noted for accommodating boxing people. Goldman served as both the patriarch and the mother hen for the young fighters who lived there. His room on the second floor was almost a shrine to boxing and filled with pictures of old fighters. It also served as his workshop, where he would mix the various liniments and potions that he would use on his fighters during the day. He would carry the tools of his trade in a small bag inscribed with the initials "Dr. C.G.," a gift from a grateful ex-fighter who had thrived under Goldman's care.

Goldman looked as stylish as he lived. Because he was only about five feet tall, reporters invariably referred to him as "gnome-like." He had a large head and was balding. Atop it he habitually wore a black derby (a "Baltimore heater"). Like Al Weill, he smoked cigars. He also sported thick, horn-rimmed glasses but no jewelry except for a gold ring that his father had given him. As he explained, "People who wear jewelry get stuck up."[17] He also very much looked like the ex-boxer that he was, with cauliflower ears and a mildly warped nose.

His gnarled hands were another badge of honor from his fighting days. He used those hands when he worked with his fighters, for Charley Goldman was very much a hands-on trainer. Explaining his philosophy, he once said, "It don't do no good to tell them. You got to show them." He was a soft-spoken, patient man who rarely raised his voice when working with a fighter. He remained modest about his contributions as a teacher, however. "To say a trainer actually develops a boxer is bunk," he observed. "Sure he can help bring out the best in a fighter, but if the boy hasn't the natural ability to start with, and the willingness to stick to business and work hard, all the teaching and training in the world won't do much good."[18]

Charley Goldman was destined to do the best work of his career with Rocky Marciano. As Dundee says about his fellow trainers in general, "If you look back on a guy's career, you'll see. Certain guys were great with certain guys—like a blend." Goldman was great with Marciano. As a result, claimed Jimmy Cannon, to call Goldman a mere trainer "was like calling Rodin a stone mason. He was one of the great artists of sports, and he created Rocky Marciano. . . . It was the sculptor looking at a block of granite and seeing the statue he would hack of it." Years later, sportswriter W. C. Heinz would similarly remember Goldman as "a great sculptor . . . a stonecutter. A block of granite comes out of the ground and has a certain truth in it. The stonecutter just looks at it and says, 'If I have to make an angel here for the cemetery, I'll make an angel.'" As Dundee says less metaphorically, "He was a genius."[19]

• • •

On that June day in 1948 when he first worked out for Weill and Goldman at the CYO gym, Rocco Marchegiano probably didn't realize that he had found the two men who would make him a champion. Clearly, Weill and Goldman didn't realize that they had found a future heavyweight champion. Goldman, for one, believed that Marchegiano, who said he was twenty-four, was much too old to be getting started in the fight game. (In fact, Marciano was twenty-five, a year older than he had indicated to his future brain trust. He would keep that one year shaved off his official age for the rest of his career.) At that advanced age, how much would he be able to learn?

Clearly, he had a lot to learn. "Al and I have often looked over green kids who thought they could become fighters but I'll eat my derby hat if I ever saw anyone cruder than Rocky," Goldman would recall. The Marchegiano kid also had obvious and undeniable physical handicaps—the lack of height, those tender hands, and, mainly, those short arms. On the plus side, Goldman was impressed with the fact that Marchegiano seemed intelligent, eager, and sincere. As Goldman said years later, "I saw that he had a good body and could punch and I told Weill that maybe I could do something with him."[20]

Weill also wasn't overly optimistic about his discovery (even though he would claim differently later on). At the time, he, too, saw a crude older boy with noticeable physical shortcomings. Still, managers were always looking for a heavyweight with a punch, and for that reason Weill decided to take a flyer on Marchegiano. But his enthusiasm remained limited, for Al Weill, the ultimate control freak and a former dancer of renown, allowed Rocco Marchegiano to waltz all the way back to Brockton, something he never would have let happen had he truly seen greatness.

Weill did make a half-hearted attempt to keep Marchegiano under his thumb. Back at Weill's office on that June day after Marchegiano had flattened Wade Chancey, Weill asked the young heavyweight to remain in New York. He even had a place for Marchegiano to stay (at Ma Brown's with Goldman), although, tellingly, he didn't offer to pick up the fighter's training and living expenses. When Rocco and his friend Allie Colombo balked at the arrangement, Weill quickly turned to Plan B. Was Brockton anywhere near Providence, Rhode Island? It was, replied Rocco and Allie—only about thirty-five miles away in fact. Good, Weill said. He had a couple of friends there who promoted fights and could get Marchegiano some matches when he was ready. In the interim, the fighter could come down to New York from time to time to work with Goldman. Weill had stopped just short of giving Rocco Marchegiano a complete brush-off. There was no written contract, no agreed-upon financial split, no rigid training schedule, and no master plan—just vague promises of some supervised gym work and a few fights in Providence.

It turned out that Providence would be an ideal training ground for the young, raw Rocco Marchegiano. It was near his home in Brockton, which meant that his family and friends would always be there to root him on. It was not a big, impersonal city that would intimidate a small-town guy like Marchegiano. And it was a great fight town. In an era where fight clubs were beginning to close and gate attendance was down all over the country because of the impact of television, fights in Providence continued to draw well. It would be in front of those crowds that Rocky Marciano would serve his apprenticeship over the next three years. Between July 1948 and July 1951 all but eight of his thirty-four bouts would take place in Providence.

The top promoter in Providence at that time was Manny Almeida. In the late 1940s and early 1950s, Almeida offered boxing shows nearly every Monday night of the year at the Rhode Island Auditorium in downtown Providence. Sam Silverman, a legendary Boston fight promoter, joined forces with Almeida in a behind-the-scenes fashion to find fighters, arrange matches, hype the gate, and promote the Monday night shows. Almeida and Silverman were the men Al Weill called in order to line up some fights for his new "discovery."

July 12, 1948, was a warm, steamy night in Providence. On that evening, Rocco Marchegiano stepped into the ring at Rhode Island Auditorium to renew the professional career that he had begun on a lark a year and a half earlier in Holyoke against Epperson. Because it was summer, only 993 fans paid their way into the arena that night. For just $1.25, or $3.50 if they wanted a ringside seat, they got to see the five professional fights featured on the program. The opening bout of the evening was a scheduled four-rounder between Marchegiano and Harry Belzarian. Standing in his corner before the fight, Allie Colombo carrying a bucket alongside, the unknown from Brockton nervously banged his gloves against each other, waiting for the opening bell. Once the fight finally began, Marchegiano made quick work of Belzarian, scoring a TKO in the very first round. For his night's work, he received the princely sum of $40.

Marchegiano quickly became a regular on Monday nights in Providence. He fought eight more times on that night in that city before 1948 was out, plus once in Washington, D.C., and once in Philadelphia. He won them all, of course. What made his future so bright was the way that he won fights. All of Marchegiano's 1948 fights ended in either a knockout or a technical knockout, with only one extending into the third round. He was flattening opponents quickly, and he was flattening them convincingly.

In addition to Belzarian, his 1948 victims were John Edwards, Bobby Quinn, Eddie Ross, Jimmy Weeks, Jerry Jackson, Bill Hardeman, Gil Cardione, Bob Jefferson, Red Connolly, and Gilley Ferron. Most of these men were club fighters eking out a living boxing at small arenas and clubs up and down the East Coast. They were not household names then, nor would they ever be. Later, after Marciano became champion, critics would deride his early opponents in Providence, claiming that they were "a blend of pancake batter and the West Wind" and that Weill was merely trying to manufacture an impressive knockout streak for his new protégé.[21] In fact, Weill had little to do with Marchegiano at this stage of his career. He may have been tracking his progress from afar, but he wasn't handpicking his opponents. It was the New England promoters (Almeida and Silverman) who were making his matches, and although they weren't pitting him against world-beaters—some *were* indeed stiffs—they were regularly sending him into the ring against more experienced fighters.

A few of the opponents also had some talent. In his third fight in Providence, on August 9, Almeida and Silverman matched Marchegiano against Bobby Quinn, a young heavyweight with strong Boston backing, an impressive knockout string, and a growing regional reputation. Twenty-two seconds into the third round, Marchegiano caught Quinn with a powerful right to the side of his head. Quinn was out, stunning the 1,321 in attendance. In his next outing, Marchegiano faced another ballyhooed opponent—Eddie Ross, a heavyweight from Montreal who had won all twenty-five of his professional fights and was regarded as a real prospect in fight circles. In the very first round, Marchegiano nailed Ross with a murderous right to the head that sent his mouthpiece flying and had him out before he hit the canvas. Silverman, who had been skeptical about the Brockton heavyweight up to this point, later said, "When Rocky flattened this boy I knew."[22]

Marchegiano's next fight in Providence, against Jimmy Weeks in late August, established him as a bona fide local phenomenon. He wasn't yet headlining the Monday night cards at the Rhode Island Auditorium, but he was beginning to steal the show. Against Weeks, a veteran fighter of some quality, Marchegiano again scored a first-round victory courtesy of a mighty right. The 1,516 fans were thrilled, hailing the young Brockton heavyweight "as the multitudes used to hail Jack Dempsey," according to *Providence Journal* boxing writer Mike Thomas. "If punching power will do it," Thomas boldly prophesized after the fight, "Rocky Marchegiano may one day become the world heavyweight champion."[23]

Around this time, Rocco Marchegiano changed his name to Rocky Marciano. "Marchegiano" was hard to pronounce and caused nightmares for Providence ring announcer Harold Warman. The local press, too, was regularly butchering his surname, calling him "Marcegino," "Marchegino," or "Marcheginao." Weill, always mindful of a fighter's popular appeal, told his new discovery that he had to adopt a new last name. Would he consider something like Rocky March? Marchegiano demurred; he was an Italian boy and wanted an Italian last name. Then Manny Almeida suggested dropping a few letters, which made the easier-on-the-ears, easier-to-spell "Marciano." Everyone agreed.

It was also around this time that Charley Goldman began traveling up from New York to work in Rocky Marciano's corner on Monday nights in Providence. The news of Marciano's growing string of spectacular knockouts had reached Weill in New York, and although the manager's interest in his new heavyweight remained lukewarm he decided to send Goldman to Providence on fight nights to protect his investment. The veteran trainer first worked Marciano's corner for the Weeks bout. Marciano was ecstatic and told Colombo, "This is it, Allie. We're finally on our way. If Weill sent Goldman, we must be ready for New York."[24]

Goldman was somewhat less ebullient. "He looks like an excellent prospect," he officially told the press after the fight. "He sure can punch. He's a little crude as yet to be sure, but what I like almost as much as his punching mite is his poise. He has a fine temperament, reminds me of Lou Ambers. I believe he'll go far." Privately, though, Goldman still harbored doubts. He told Marciano after the Weeks fight that although he'd do the best he could to bring him along, the boxer still had a lot to learn.[25]

Then again, perhaps Goldman was more optimistic then he let on. Heinz, for instance, remembers interviewing Goldman around that time. When the subject of Marciano's advanced age came up, Heinz expressed concern. "Yeah, Bill," Goldman replied, "but he's got two things that you need today with the heavyweight division: he can punch and he can take a punch." Similarly, Dundee remembers Goldman telling him, "Ang, you gotta come and see this guy." Dundee took him up on the invitation, traveling down to the gym one day to observe Marciano in person. "And in walks this guy—stoop shouldered, slightly balding," remembers Dundee. "Charley described him as a guy with two left feet. But, ooh, how he can punch—right from the beginning."[26]

In that initial spate of fights in Providence, though, Rocky Marciano was still very much the raw, crude product that had auditioned for Weill and Goldman in June. Although he was decking opponents with his powerful right hand, he had no left hand to speak of. He also had no stance, was frequently out of position, and was easy to hit. All of this made for some anxious moments early in his professional career. Goldman would later say that Marciano's toughest professional fights were "some of those early fights he had when he didn't know how to fight. He won them all but I was afraid he would get killed." Lou Duva remembers traveling up to New England to see Marciano in one of his early fights: "He looked like a real rank amateur. He had two left feet, he was falling down, he didn't know really what to do with himself."[27]

●　●　●

Shortly after those initial Providence bouts, Charley Goldman's impact on Rocky Marciano would grow exponentially. At this stage, though, the person making the greatest contributions to Marciano's blossoming career was not a prestigious old fight man but a trusted old friend: Allie Colombo.

Enthusiastic, expressive, and pleasant, Colombo was confident in his friend's abilities and his potential as a big-time fighter. When Marciano decided to turn pro, Colombo gave up his job to work with his friend. Weill tried to push Colombo out of the picture, but Marciano, fiercely loyal to his family and friends, would have none of it. He knew Allie, he trusted Allie, and he wanted Allie to remain by his side. And that's where Allie would stay until the day his friend retired from the ring.

In the beginning, the two friends devised their own training program. They would run through the streets of Brockton every morning, varying the routes and tossing a football back and forth to break the monotony. In the afternoon, Marciano and Colombo would work out at the local YMCA. There, Marciano would hit the heavy bag for hours, topping off his workout by throwing uppercuts underwater in the swimming pool in order to develop arm strength. In time, Marciano and Colombo would stage their workouts at the nearby South Easton estate of Russ Murray, a local sportsman, dog track owner, and fan of Marciano's. There, they continued the regimen they had developed at the Y. They even drafted Marciano's friend Snap Tartaglia as well as his brother Sonny Marciano to serve as sparring partners. "Rocky was brutal even in sparring," Sonny says. "He just didn't know any other way."[28]

The training regimen also involved Rocky and Allie traveling to New York from time to time to work with Goldman in the gym. The first such trip took place in September 1948 after his fifth fight in Providence. Mike Thomas, who had befriended Marciano, dropped him and Colombo off at the railroad station so they could catch the train to New York. They "carried an old battered cardboard suitcase and had shirts wrapped in newspaper," Thomas wistfully remembered years later. "They had in money little more than their train fare to New York. They looked like two lads out of *Huckleberry Finn* on an adventure."[29]

When they didn't take the train, Marciano and Colombo would get to New York by hitching rides from friendly truck drivers. "Once they came down on a fruit truck," Goldman later laughed. "I hope the cabbages on that truck don't look as bad as Rocky and Allie did. They looked like they'd come down to sweep the place up."[30] Other times the Brockton duo would get a ride from Marciano's uncle, Mike Piccento. Later, they would travel to the city in a car that Colombo's father-in-law had given him, a 1935 model on its last legs. They would habitually (and by necessity) stop in Hartford to pour more water into the car's leaky radiator.

Once in New York, they hardly lived in style. They usually stayed at the YMCA on West Thirty-fourth Street, where rooms cost about a dollar a night. The Y was hardly plush, but Marciano and Colombo loved the location—half-way between Weill's office and the gym where they were working out with Goldman and, better yet, close to the hustle and bustle of the big city. The two boys from Brockton would spend most of their free time walking up and down Broadway, soaking in the excitement. They would hang around outside the backstage entrance to producer Mike Todd's *As the Girls Go,* watching the cast arrive for performances and leave after them. Once they spotted Rocky Graziano, the middleweight champion, standing outside a hotel and accepting greetings from well-wishers. Yet another time they saw featherweight champion Willie Pep walking arm-in-arm with a beautiful woman and tailed him for nearly two hours. This was indeed the big time. And Rocky Marciano most definitely wanted in.

For now, though, the hub of Marciano and Colombo's world was not New York but Providence. Legend has it that they would occasionally walk the thirty-five miles or so from Brockton to Providence for Marciano's Monday night fight for reasons of conditioning. They would arrive several hours before the fight with several steaks in hand, carefully wrapped in waxed paper. For a while, Alvina Tartaglia (the sister of Marciano's friend Snap) would prepare the steaks. Later on, either Eddie Beck, who operated a diner and was a fight fan, or Mike Thomas would host the prefight steak dinners for the Brockton heavyweight and his sidekick. No matter who cooked, the men would top off dinner by going over to the Rhode Island Auditorium, where Marciano would quickly knock out another opponent.

As his knockout string lengthened in the fall of 1948, Rocky Marciano became a huge favorite with Providence crowds. Fight fans traditionally like a heavyweight with a big punch, and if nothing else Marciano had a big punch. The fact that he was an Italian American fighting in a city that had a large Italian American community also bolstered his appeal. The fact that Marciano had his own cheering section of friends, family, and admirers from Brockton didn't hurt either. Nicky Sylvester, a close friend and a key figure in his entourage as champion, would recall, "When Rocky had a guy in trouble in Providence, all the Italians from Brockton would stand up and yell, 'Timmmmmmberrr!'"[31]

With all the knockouts, Al Weill finally started to pay attention. Up to that point he had been focusing on the other fighters in his stable and expressing little interest in Marciano. Although he wasn't taking a cut of Marciano's small purses, he wasn't paying Marciano's training expenses either. Marciano was, for the most part, on his own, with Weill limiting his involvement to supplying Goldman on fight nights and passively receiving reports from Goldman and Almeida. Only occasionally would he ask, "Is that kid really that good?" In late September, however, Weill finally saw Marciano fight in person against Gil Cardione in Washington, D.C. It took Marciano just thirty-six seconds of the first round to flatten Cardione, "one of the fastest knockouts in local boxing history" according to the *Washington Post*. Weill was now a believer. He moved quickly to solidify the loose understanding with Marciano, and in early October 1948, when Marciano's record was 10-0, Weill and he finally entered into a written fighter-manager contract.[32]

Weill promptly began boosting Marciano's reputation among the fight mob and looking for opportunities to showcase his new discovery. He soon found a golden opportunity in Philadelphia in mid-December 1948. Joe Louis was about to retire from the ring, but he was still the champion. He was also still the biggest name in boxing—big enough to attract more than seven thousand fans to Philadelphia's Convention Hall for an exhibition against an old rival, Arturo Godoy. Weill got Marciano a spot on the undercard of the main event against a boxer named Gilley Ferron.

The highlight of Marciano's evening came when Weill introduced him to Louis and the future champion got to shake hands with the reigning champion. Otherwise it was a tough night. Weill interrupted Marciano's usual prefight nap in the dressing room to deliver a pep talk that stressed the importance of looking good in front of the boxing bigwigs who had come down from New York. He also urged Marciano to concentrate on Ferron's body. Once the fight began, Weill, working in Marciano's corner for the first time, kept screaming, "To the body, to the body, to the body!" The incessant shouting rattled Marciano, and the more experienced Ferron gave him fits. As Goldman later said, "Rocky didn't know how to get away from a punch. Ferron raised lumps on his head."[33] Still, Marciano persevered, winning the fight in the second round on a TKO after he managed to open a bad cut over Ferron's left eye.

He had won, but he had not impressed. Before the fight, Jimmy Cannon had run into Weill outside the place where the fight mob traditionally gathered in Philadelphia, a restaurant and saloon owned by former fighter Lew Tendler. "The champeen of the world is fighting tonight," Weill had boasted. "Rocky Marciano. Watch and see." But Marciano failed to live up to Weill's advance billing. He looked raw and sloppy, falling forward and once scraping his knees when he tried to punch Ferron. He even broke his right hand along the way, an injury that would keep him out of action for more than three months. Afterward, as they drank whiskey at Lew Tendler's and other Philadelphia taverns, the fight mob had more than a few laughs at the expense of Al Weill and his new "champeen," Rocky Marciano.[34]

Despite his disappointing Ferron performance, Marciano could be proud of his progress and accomplishments in 1948. He had begun the year as an obscure part-time amateur boxer and a frustrated full-time employee of the Brockton Gas Company. Before the year was out, he had won several amateur titles, turned professional, hooked up with two of the best fight men in the business, won eleven straight fights (mostly in spectacular fashion), and established himself as a prospect worth watching in the heavyweight ranks. It had been a good year.

● ● ●

More success followed in 1949. Fighting again almost exclusively out of Providence, Marciano won all thirteen of his fights, running his overall winning streak to twenty-five.

His year began in March against a mediocre fighter from Boston, Johnny Pretzie. The fans of Providence eagerly anticipated his return to the ring after a three-month layoff due to his broken hand, but Marciano disappointed and struggled to a fifth-round TKO. In the wake of the fight, some of his Providence fans began questioning whether Marciano was a legitimate prospect. At least he was now headlining Manny Almeida's Monday night shows and receiving richer purses ($250 for the Pretzie fight) as a result.

After Pretzie, Marciano regained his form by putting away Artie Donato and Jimmy Walls in short order. Then, in early May, he squared off against Jimmy Evans in front of a crowd of 2,775 fans (with thousands more tuning in on the radio). The fight was a watershed for Marciano because, according to Mike Thomas, Evans was a crafty, talented boxer, "far and away the best fighter that Marciano yet has faced."[35] This time Marciano didn't disappoint, winning the fast-paced bout via a third-round TKO. He had never looked better and landed numerous short, sharp punches, including several left hooks (a new weapon in the Marciano arsenal). His knockout streak was now at sixteen.

In his next outing, though, someone finally went the distance with Rocky Marciano. His name was Don Mogard, and his claim to fame was that he had never been knocked out. He kept his streak alive against Marciano. He even made Marciano look bad on many occasions by effectively using his jab and ducking Marciano's long, looping rights. Still, Marciano dominated the fight, winning all but two rounds and receiving a unanimous decision from the judges. After the fight, his knockout streak finally over, Marciano became depressed. Was he beginning to slip? In reality, it was just an off-night against an excellent defensive fighter who specialized in avoiding danger.

It was around this time that a reconfiguration of Marciano's management took place—at least officially. On May 18, 1949, the IBC named Al Weill as its matchmaker. Although the position gave Weill new power in the world of boxing, it also precluded him from managing Marciano and the other fighters in his stable. The New York State Athletic Commission and other sanctioning bodies had a rule forbidding a matchmaker from also managing fighters—and with good reason. Doing so was a clear conflict of interest.

Weill promptly released all the fighters he had been managing except for one—Rocky Marciano. He was unwilling to sever ties with the fighter, who he was now convinced had a chance to go on to capture the heavyweight championship of the world. Weill ripped up their old contract and persuaded Marciano to enter into a new private agreement that maintained their relationship (a document that Marciano later admitted he did not read). Marciano was not disappointed with the development, reasoning that Weill's position as IBC matchmaker would further his career. "We're finally gonna start making some of that big money," he told Colombo. "It's all beginning to fall our way." He not only had increased optimism but also a new manager of record: Al's stepson Marty Weill from Dayton, Ohio, a salesman of jewelry, television sets, silverware, and kitchen utensils. "He's my own son, ain't he?" Al explained. "Why shouldn't I keep it in the family?"[36]

For the next three years Marty Weill would serve as Rocky Marciano's manager, dutifully showing up at his fights and trying his best to maintain the charade. From time to time Marty would deny that he was acting merely as a front for his stepfather. Weill the Elder played his part as well, issuing repeated denials that often bordered on the absurd. Once, for example, when asked when Marciano would fight again, Al replied, "Marty Weill, Rocky Marciano's manager, thinks that it is unlikely that Rocky will fight again this year." In the end, the ruse failed miserably. "We weren't fooling anybody," Marciano would later admit. "Everybody knew my real manager was Al, and he didn't try to hide it. He used to give me orders in front of everybody."[37] Reporters would consistently refer to Al Weill as Marciano's "real manager" or his "off-the-record manager." That Weill was so obviously flaunting the rules and abusing his power only added to his unpopularity in fight circles.

Throughout this managerial shell game Marciano kept winning. During the summer of 1949 he reeled off a string of victories against a succession of journeymen fighters (Harry Haft, Pete Louthis, and Tommy Giorgio). Then, in the fall of 1949, Marciano started to face a tougher caliber of opponent, ring-savvy, experienced boxers who if not viable heavyweight contenders themselves at least had fared well against top contenders. One such fighter was Ted Lowry, whom Marciano fought in early October 1949.

Lowry hailed from New Haven, Connecticut, and knew his way around the ring. Crafty and experienced, he had fought draws with Lee Oma and Lee Savold, two marginal yet ranking heavyweight contenders of the era. His nickname, "Tiger Ted," was a misnomer. Although he packed a good punch, he was less a tiger in style and more what the fight men called, in the parlance of the day, a "cutie." In the ring, he would habitually retreat, retreat, retreat—and then suddenly lurch forward and surprise his foe with a well-placed uppercut followed by a well-timed clinch.

In the Providence ring on that October night Marciano nearly lost for the first time in his career. It was Lowry, not Marciano, who was on the verge of scoring an early knockout, stinging Marciano with two terrific rights in the first round and then rocking him with two mighty uppercuts in the second. By the fourth round, a staggered Marciano seemed only one punch away from being knocked out. But then, inexplicably, Lowry stopped fighting and retreated into a shell despite repeated warnings from the referee to open up and a cascade of boos from the crowd. To many, it appeared that Lowry was deliberately carrying Marciano. Was foul play afoot? Was Lowry getting paid to lose? Or was he merely tiring?

Whatever the reason, a revived Marciano managed to rally in the late rounds even though many of his punches missed their mark by a wide margin or lacked much force. On the basis of his aggressiveness and constant punching, Marciano won a unanimous decision from the judges. Most observers felt, however, that Lowry should have won. Some felt that he *had* won, despite his impersonation of a turtle. As Mike Thomas noted, the bout was filled with "strange developments and questions left unanswered."[38] At the very least, the narrow escape had punctured the aura of invincibility that had arisen around Marciano in Providence.

Marciano recovered from the Lowry setback by scoring two quick and impressive knockouts over Joe Domonic (in what Thomas called "the most spectacular victory of his ring career") and Pat Richards.[39] Then it was time for his second major test of late 1949, this one against Phil Muscato, an experienced heavyweight from Buffalo. Like Lowry, Muscato was a veteran of numerous ring wars. He had won many of them, triumphing over the likes of Oma, Savold, and Joey Maxim (a future light-heavyweight champion). Those victories gave Muscato a national reputation as a quality heavyweight. He was the first "name fighter" Marciano would oppose.

A standing-room-only crowd of 6,775 packed the Rhode Island Auditorium a week before Christmas of 1949 to see if Marciano could successfully step up in class. They found that he could. In registering a fifth-round TKO, Marciano knocked down the game Muscato nine times with powerful overhand rights and deadly left hooks. The bell saved Muscato on two occasions (at the end of the third and fourth rounds), and his display of courage earned him a standing ovation. But it was Rocky Marciano's moment. Thomas, in the lead of his story on the fight, captured the significance of the triumph: "The boxing world, at long last, appears to have the smashing, power-punching heavyweight it has sought."[40]

The Muscato victory at the end of 1949 was a watershed for Marciano. He had begun the year with a reputation as one of the more promising young heavyweights in the nation along with Roland LaStarza, George Kaplan, Harold Johnson, and Phil Berman. Still, there had been much debate as to how far he could go, even in Providence where he was treated as an adopted son. The doubts about Marciano's abilities had persisted into the fall of 1949 and found new life after his performance against Lowry. His convincing win over Muscato, though, silenced the critics and cemented his reputation as one of the best young heavyweights in the country.

Suddenly, respected fight men on the national scene, men such as Dan Florio, Ray Arcel, and Teddy Brenner, were publicly praising Marciano. "He still needs seasoning," Marciano's own fight man, Charley Goldman, told the Providence press in the wake of the Muscato victory, "but he sure has come a long way since his first five fights here."[41] The training ground of Providence had served him well. By late 1949, though, Rocky Marciano had outgrown Providence. He was ready for the big time—New York.

3 New York

In 1950 the unquestioned capital of the sports world was New York City. It was the home of the biggest and best sports columnists—writers like Red Smith, Jimmy Cannon, and Arthur Daley whose syndicated work set the tone and the sporting opinion for the rest of the country in an era where newspapers still trumped television in terms of influence. It was also home to the best teams—the Giants of Leo the Lip, the Boys of Summer in Brooklyn, and, of course, the mighty Yankees—in the sport that was far and away the most popular at midcentury. The fact that the city seemed to host the World Series each and every year seemed only to confirm its status as the mecca of sports.

Like baseball, boxing, the nation's second most popular sport in that era, was centered in New York, as it had been since the days of Jack Dempsey in the 1920s. Stillman's Gym in Midtown was the nerve center of the sport. All the influential promoters, managers, trainers, mobsters, and other assorted members of the fight mob habitually congregated in its run-down, smoky, unwashed environs. And all of the big fights seemed to take place on Manhattan, either at one of the outdoor ballparks (Yankee Stadium and the Polo Grounds) or in Madison Square Garden. To succeed in boxing, a fighter had to succeed in New York. For Rocky Marciano, thrilling the fans of Providence by knocking out a string of boxers, even good ones like Phil Muscato, was one thing; impressing the hardened, cynical critics of New York was another altogether.

Al Weill, a New Yorker to the core, knew all of this. He realized that Marciano's regional success would amount to nothing unless he could duplicate it in New York. But Weill didn't rush his boy into the big time. By the latter half of 1949, Marciano had been fighting professionally for just over a year. He was still very much an inexperienced boxer still learning his trade. It made no sense to rush him onto the big stage while he was still rehearsing. Marciano's impressive victories in late 1949, though, signaled that he was ready.

So Weill turned his young fighter loose on Broadway. First, in early December 1949, he got Marciano a bout on the undercard of the fight between Roland LaStarza and Cesar Brion in the Garden. Marciano destroyed his opponent, journeyman Pat Richards, in two rounds. No one noticed. Then, after sending Marciano back to Providence to decimate Phil Muscato, Weill got serious and matched him against Carmine Vingo in late December 1949 and then Roland LaStarza in March 1950. Although Marciano would win both fights, he would barely pass the audition.

Vingo came first. A native of the Bronx, he hailed from a fighting family and possessed a world of potential. Only twenty years old, he had won sixteen of seventeen bouts. He clearly represented a tough test for Marciano. More than nine thousand filed into the Garden on the evening of December 30, 1949, to see a card featuring several appealing bouts, including the attractive matchup between two young heavyweights who could definitely hit.

And hit each other they did. The fight between Marciano and Vingo quickly became a classic "pier six brawl" with nonstop action that thrilled the crowd. In the very first round, Marciano knocked Vingo down for a count of nine, but Vingo rallied, staggering Marciano on two occasions. By the end of the round, each man was bleeding. The second round was a replay of the first, with Marciano again knocking Vingo down and Vingo again coming back to stagger Marciano, nearly scoring a knockdown in the process. Vingo continued to pour it on in the third round, continuing to outpunch Marciano. And his punches clearly packed some sock. Later, after he became champion, Marciano would repeatedly claim that no man ever hit him as hard as Carmine Vingo did that night in the Garden.

Even though it was still early in the fight, both men were clearly exhausted. They kept punching though. Gradually, it became apparent that the stronger of the two tired men was Marciano. By the sixth round, Vingo was still throwing punches but fading fast. Marciano finally ended matters by dropping Vingo for the third and final time with a short left hook to the jaw. He hit the canvas with a resounding thud and was clearly out. The referee and Vingo's handlers tried to revive the fallen heavyweight from the Bronx, but to no avail. As Vingo remained motionless, the attending physician at ringside, Vincent Nardiello, jumped into the ring. The doctor gave Vingo an injection over his heart and helped him to his feet, but Vingo promptly collapsed, unconscious. After about twenty minutes, and with no ambulance available, Nardiello ordered that Vingo be placed on a stretcher and carried two blocks to nearby St. Clare's Hospital.

Later that night, Carmine Vingo teetered between life and death, lapsing into a coma and receiving the last rites of the Catholic church at the hospital. As news of Vingo's critical condition spread, swarms of boxing people arrived at St. Clare's. Vingo's family was there, of course. So was Rocky Marciano, who came with Allie Colombo and Charley Goldman. He apologized to Vingo's mother, begged Doctor Nardiello to save Vingo's life, and nervously took part in the developing vigil. Officially, Vingo had suffered a concussion of the brain, a contusion and laceration of the brain, and a possible blood clot. No one was quite sure how he had sustained the injuries, though. Was it due to the accumulation of head blows that Vingo had taken during the fight? Was it due to just the last blow, the short left hook that had knocked him out? Or was it due to the fact that his head hit so hard on the canvas after he was knocked out?

Fortunately, Vingo pulled through. Within a few days he had come out of the coma and was starting to show some signs of improvement. By early February 1950 he had been discharged from the hospital and was back home in the Bronx. He remained slightly paralyzed on one side, however, and would never fight again. His boxing career was over. Marciano, who had returned home to Brockton several days after the fight, was relieved but depressed over the near tragedy. Not yet a rich man, he nevertheless reportedly contributed $2,500 to help pay Vingo's hospital bills. The men also became friends. Vingo, in fact, attended Marciano's wedding later in 1950 and also some of his later fights as champion. "Carmine's my friend," Marciano would maintain. "He's forgiven me. If he hadn't, I wouldn't have been able to go on."[1]

But Marciano did go on, next meeting Roland LaStarza in the Garden ring in March 1950. His opponent had been the darling of New York boxing writers for some time. To many, LaStarza represented the second coming of Gene Tunney, the great heavyweight champion from the 1920s. Like Tunney, LaStarza was bright, intelligent, personable, and good-looking. LaStarza fought like Tunney, too, with supreme devotion to the art of boxing and the principles of counterpunching. Like the 25-0 Rocky Marciano, LaStarza was undefeated—and his record was an even more glittering 37-0. As with Marciano, there were charges that LaStarza's streak had been carefully manufactured by sending him in against a succession of "Who's he?" opponents. Still, he was widely regarded as the nation's top young heavyweight.

There were several appealing aspects of the LaStarza-Marciano matchup. For one, the two men had contrasting styles. "He was a puncher, a brawler," says LaStarza. "And I was a boxer. . . . And that makes for the classic fight. A boxer against a puncher."[2] The "boxer versus slugger" theme had intrigued fans since the days of Tunney and Dempsey. The fact that the boxer and slugger were each young and unbeaten offered a fresh twist. Many fans also assumed—correctly as it turned out—that one or both of the young boxers would eventually be fighting for the heavyweight title. Jake Mintz, manager of the reigning champion Ezzard Charles, fueled this speculation when he announced that his fighter would give the winner a title shot in June—if the challenger won in convincing fashion. The two young heavyweights seemed to be gambling it all, not just their respective unbeaten records but also their immediate futures in the heavyweight sweepstakes.

For all these reasons, the LaStarza-Marciano fight generated considerable interest and enthusiasm, especially in New York and the rest of the Northeast. This interest was reflected in the prefight betting, which was the heaviest on a fight in years. LaStarza opened as the clear favorite, but the odds soon began to fluctuate. By fight night, the bout had become a "pick 'em" proposition. More than thirteen thousand fans paid their way into the Garden on Friday night, March 24, 1950, to see which young fighter would continue his advance to the top of the heavyweight division. Fans in twenty-seven other cities (as far north as Boston, as far south as Memphis, and as far west as St. Louis) tuned in on the NBC television network to see the boxer meet the slugger.

This was Rocky Marciano's first certifiable "big fight." And he was nervous. As he told one friend, he wished the fight were on his familiar turf. "In Providence," he said, "I know everybody is on my side. In New York I feel they don't care."[3] At the weigh-in before the fight he appeared nervous, and when he entered the ring later that night he looked drawn and haggard. It was a big fight for LaStarza, too, but he was a Bronx native who had fought many times in New York and had headlined many past shows at the Garden. Rocky Marciano had not. The carnival-like atmosphere of fight night at the Garden was still relatively new to him. As such, he came down with a minor case of stage fright.

Whether it was jitters, or some lingering effect of the Vingo tragedy, or some tentativeness due to the injury to his left hand suffered against Vingo, Marciano wasn't himself in the first three rounds of the LaStarza bout. Curiously, he tried to jab and box LaStarza—and jabbing and boxing were not his forte. LaStarza had little difficulty ducking Marciano's wild leads, counterpunching, clinching, and then scoring in the resulting infighting. Marciano wrenched his back during a clinch in the second round, an injury that hampered his ability to throw lefts for the rest of the fight. About the only positive development for him was that he bloodied LaStarza's nose in the first round. LaStarza's blood would continue to flow for the rest of the contest.

In the fourth round, Marciano finally opened up—and nearly finished LaStarza in the process. After nailing LaStarza with a series of long rights to the head that opened cuts over both of his eyes, Marciano trapped his foe in a neutral corner toward the end of the round and connected with a looping right hook to the jaw. LaStarza bounced against the ropes and fell to the canvas. He was on his knees with one arm draped over the rope at the count of seven when the bell rang, ending the round. Marciano pressed for the knockout in the fifth, but LaStarza survived and may have even won the close round. By the sixth round, the revived LaStarza had fully recovered from Marciano's onslaught, winning the round with his superior boxing.

Marciano started to come on again in the eighth round, rocking LaStarza on several occasions and chasing his wobbly foe from rope to rope. It was, along with the fourth, Marciano's best round of the fight. But referee Jack Watson took the round away from Marciano for hitting low. Marciano won the ninth round when he staggered LaStarza on several occasions, especially in the late going, with a hook. The fighters continued to go after each other in the tenth and final round, pleasing the Garden crowd, which had been yelling most of the way. LaStarza unleashed a two-fisted attack and scored points during the infighting, but Marciano was in command at the end, rocking LaStarza one last time with a mighty left hook right before the final bell.

There was a difference of opinion as to who had actually won the final round, as there had been with several others rounds during the fight. Given all the uncertainty, fans in the Garden and those watching on television eagerly awaited the decision from the judges, and ring announcer Johnny Addie milked the drama for all it was worth. First, he announced Judge Artie Schwartz's card: five rounds for Marciano, four for LaStarza, and one even. Then he announced Judge Artie Aidala's card, which was the converse of Schwartz's: 5-4-1 for LaStarza. It would be a split decision, and Referee Watson's card would decide matters. As an expectant hush fell over the crowd, Addie announced Watson's card: "Referee Watson scores five rounds for Marciano, five rounds for LaStarza. Points: six for LaStarza and nine for Marciano. The winner: Marciano!"[4]

Marciano had won but only because the supplementary point system in New York had decided Watson's card in his favor. It was *that* close. In the ring, after Addie announced the decision, a bruised, battered, and bewildered LaStarza rushed over to the ring announcer and asked, "Did Marciano win?" He had. More than fifty years later LaStarza remains incredulous about the verdict. "I won the fight," he maintains. "There's no doubt about it in my mind." LaStarza is also fairly confident about the reason that he lost: "The fact that his manager [Al Weill] was a matchmaker at the Garden I would say had a lot to do with the decision. . . . That's what I think. That's what everybody thought at the time."[5]

Indeed, many ringside observers in the Garden that night felt that LaStarza had not only won but had also won in convincing fashion. For example, Jesse Abramson, the boxing writer for the *New York Herald Tribune,* called it a "paper thin and exceedingly odd decision . . . Marciano won, but it was a gift." Later, stepping up the rhetoric, Abramson claimed that the decision was "almost universally condemned around the ringside as a miscarriage of justice." Even a member of the New England press corps, which was naturally supportive of the regional fighter Marciano, admitted that it was a "dubious decision."[6]

Whether or not the verdict was justified, it plainly derailed the career of LaStarza. He lost much prestige because of the bout. Even Abramson, one of LaStarza's main advocates in the aftermath of the fight, admitted that he had given "a dull, lifeless performance," fighting in a purposeless fashion and missing numerous opportunities to score against the lunging, wide-open Marciano.[7] In terms of reputation, Rocky Marciano lost as well. Initially, he had been a curiosity to the fight mob. News of his spectacular string of knockouts in Providence had traveled down to New York, but critics at headquarters were skeptical of the glowing reports from the field—particularly given the quality of his opponents. Was Rocky Marciano a real contender, or was he a built-up pretender? The New York critics had adopted a wait-and-see approach.

Now, after Vingo and especially LaStarza, they had at long last seen Marciano in action. They were not overly impressed. Abramson criticized Marciano for his tactics in the LaStarza fight. Why hadn't Marciano pressed his attack and swarmed all over LaStarza with more aggression? For good measure, Abramson claimed that the LaStarza fight exposed Marciano as "a more cumbersome puncher than he had looked against the stiffs on whom he has fattened his knockout average." Matt Ring, the aptly named boxing writer for the *Philadelphia Evening Bulletin*, concurred. Marciano had "an indisputably potent but wildly erratic punch and hardly anything else," he reported. "Watching him pitch those haymakers, one couldn't help wondering if the twenty-four knockouts on his record weren't scored against cigar store Indians."[8]

The fight mob's main problem with Marciano, though, was his awkwardness. Nearly everyone in fight circles felt that Marciano's clumsiness would hinder his climb up the heavyweight ladder. They theorized that he would lose—and perhaps lose badly—if he ever met an accomplished craftsman such as Ezzard Charles or Jersey Joe Walcott. Moreover, this was an era in which boxing men were especially concerned with style. How you won counted nearly as much as whether you won at all. The great champions of the day (Joe Louis, Willie Pep, and especially the great Sugar Ray Robinson) were all supreme stylists, boxers who not only won but also won pretty. Rocky Marciano won ugly. To the purists, he degraded the art and science of boxing.

● ● ●

In reality, by early 1950 Rocky Marciano had already traveled a long way in terms of style—perhaps not far enough for the fight crowd's liking but a long way indeed. The improvement was due to his continuing gym work with Charley Goldman. At the time, the main gym in the city was Stillman's, located on the west side of Eighth Avenue between Fifty-fourth and Fifty-fifth streets. Marciano, however, felt uncomfortable under the bright lights of Stillman's. "I was very clumsy and always making mistakes, and those guys would have laughed at me if they'd seen the mistakes I made," he later explained.[9] Instead, he preferred the CYO gym on West Seventeenth Street, a quieter place with fewer fighters and fewer scrutinizing members of the fight mob. Weill agreed that the CYO gym was a better place than Stillman's to teach boxing to Rocky Marciano.

Goldman made that obscure gym his laboratory. In experimenting with Marciano he was careful not to overshoot his mark. As part of his training philosophy, Goldman believed in preserving a fighter's natural style—and resisting the temptation to try to remake him. Goldman steadfastly adhered to that principle in his work with Marciano. As he told the Providence press early in 1949, "We've got to polish him up, of course, but I'm not going to change his basic style. He either has it or hasn't. We'll soon find out. We'll teach him the tricks he doesn't know. . . . Give me a heavyweight with a punch. It will take time, but I'll teach him the rest. Then it is up to him."[10]

Goldman did, of course, tweak Marciano's basic style, and he shored up his fundamentals considerably. In the beginning, for instance, Marciano didn't know how to stand properly in the ring. The fact that his feet were too far apart hurt him both offensively and defensively. Goldman measured Marciano's stance and found that his left foot was thirty-six inches in front of his right foot. To shorten the stance, Goldman measured twenty four inches of rope and tied it to Marciano's ankles. At first, Marciano occasionally fell while sparring, but eventually he adapted. His stance shortened—and improved.

Goldman improved Marciano's defense in other ways, teaching him how to block punches, slip under jabs, roll with certain punches, and keep his shoulders hunched to protect him when he was on the attack. Equally important, Goldman convinced Marciano to fight less as a "stand-up" fighter and more from a crouch, weaving in with his head low and his hands high, crowding his opponent, and presenting less of a target. As Angelo Dundee remembers, "Charley always told me, 'If you get a short guy, make him shorter. If you get a tall guy, let him stand tall.' Part of my teaching. I'll remember that as long as I live, because it's a good barometer. When you got a kid that short, you gotta let the other guys reach for him." How did Goldman make Marciano shorter? "The legs, the knees, the bend, into the crouch," says Dundee.[11]

In the early years of his career Marciano also needed serious work on his left hand. "You notice, he's a one-handed fighter, relies almost wholly on his right," Goldman told the Providence press. "But you've got to have a left to make the grade in boxing. That's the stamp of a real fighter. That's what we'll work with him."[12] The development of a left jab and a left hook became a centerpiece in the Goldman-Marciano program of improvement. In the gym, Goldman tied Marciano's right hand behind his body so he would become more accustomed to using his left. Slowly but surely, Marciano began to develop a left.

There had never been any problems with his right. From the very beginning, Marciano possessed a looping overhand right that was lethal. His handlers nicknamed the punch the "Suzie Q." Goldman approved of the punch and didn't try to eliminate it from Marciano's arsenal. Despite his awesome power, though, Marciano didn't really know how to punch. Goldman taught him how to speed up his arms and throw more punches. He also taught Marciano how to throw straighter punches. Finally, he taught him how to throw body punches. "You've got to realize that when I took him over he didn't know what a body punch was," Goldman said later. "In the first ten fights I handled him he didn't throw a single one—and I mean not a single one. So I hired a sparring partner for Rocky, and for weeks I had him go in there and not punch once to the head."[13]

Marciano learned all of these lessons slowly. As Goldman explained, "I teach him slow because I want him to feel natural." Any time he would introduce a new wrinkle, Goldman would stop and ask Marciano, "Does it feel natural?" or "Can you hit from there?" Sportswriter W. C. Heinz remembers running into Goldman in Stillman's Gym and asking, "How are you doing with that kid from Brockton that comes down on those trucks?" Replied Goldman, "There's things that I could do. But I'm afraid to do very much. Because if I change his stance and his style so he don't get hit with so many punches I might take something away from his punch."[14]

Goldman was scrupulously careful not to wreck what he saw as the fighter's key strength: his leverage. As he told A. J. Liebling of *The New Yorker,* "He had leverage from the start, and when you teach a fellow like that, you have to go slow, because you might change the way he stands or the way he moves, and, by so doing, spoil his hitting." Confirms Jimmy Breslin, "They saw that the guy was awkward, he had his feet every place, but then Goldman said, 'But we can't do anything to it—anything that disturbs the leverage.' He knew that from the start—do not touch this fucking guy unless we're sure of what's going on with him. Look at the punch! Are you crazy? You don't fix something if it ain't broke."[15]

Overall, Goldman employed what Lou Duva calls "the old-fashioned way of training" to teach Marciano. He also used some innovative techniques. Dundee remembers, for example, that Goldman "had an exercise that he used to make Rocky do. He let him go from a crouching position, like a catcher, and come up and punch while he was coming up—which is very difficult. You try that yourself without even hitting on anything, and it's a stress situation. And Rocky was strong. That's where he got the strength from."[16]

Gradually, all the lessons started to take hold, not just because of the skill and patience of the teacher but also because of the eagerness of the pupil. "Nobody ever was so eager to learn," Goldman later praised. "That made my job easier." By the time of the LaStarza fight, others may have seen awkwardness, but Goldman was beginning to see improvement. "Until he faced LaStarza," Goldman said, "he had never met a real good boxer. I was afraid of that fight. I didn't think Rocky could win it. But when he stood up to LaStarza, trading him punch for punch and actually outboxing him, I was convinced that we had something."[17]

The other half of Marciano's brain trust, pilot Al Weill, didn't share Goldman's optimism. In the wake of the LaStarza fight Weill said all the right things publicly. "We may put Marciano in with Charles this summer, if Charles is still champion, or even with Louis, if Joe intends to come back," he said immediately after the fight. "This kid hits like that atom bomb and he's liable to flatten anyone."[18] Such a match would have been in keeping with Weill's original timetable for Marciano, which called for a title shot in the fall of 1950 or in the spring of 1951 at the latest.

In time, though, Weill came to agree with the New York critics who believed that the awkward Marciano still had a way to go before he could be regarded as championship material. Marciano's pilot revised his timetable accordingly. There would be no title shot or big fight in Marciano's immediate future. At any point after the LaStarza fight, Weill *could* have arranged a big fight for Marciano. Because he had beaten LaStarza, he now had more of a name. He also had a fresh ranking as the ninth-rated heavyweight contender in the world. And, of course, he still had a perfect record, now 26-0. Weill, however, was unwilling to put that record at risk against a top-flight opponent. He had decided to coddle Rocky Marciano.

● ● ●

That Weill could do so was a product not just of his caution but also of his power. Indeed, Weill was in a position to call the shots—and not just because he was Marciano's shadow manager. More important, he was the matchmaker of the International Boxing Club (IBC), the organization that reigned supreme over the sport at midcentury. The heyday of the IBC (1949–57) almost perfectly tracked Marciano's rise and reign, and it supplied the stage upon which he would give all of his greatest performances. The story of the IBC is therefore an important subplot to the story of Marciano.

Ironically, though, the IBC began not with Rocky Marciano but with Joe Louis. As the great champion began to fade from the scene in the late 1940s, so did the man ("Uncle" Mike Jacobs) and the promotional organization (the Twentieth Century Sporting Club) that had controlled the sport for so long. By 1948 Jacobs was in failing health and starting to lose control of the empire he had built and carefully nurtured for the previous dozen years.

For his part, Louis, deep in a financial hole, was looking for a way to exit the boxing scene with his pockets full. As 1948 turned into 1949 he began to look elsewhere, beyond Jacobs, for his farewell gift.

Originally, Louis and his lawyer, Truman Gibson, focused on striking a deal with a man named Harry Voiler, Mae West's former road manager, who had connections with the influential Hearst people in Chicago. After a series of meetings that took place over several months, however, the deal fell apart when Voiler couldn't line up the necessary capital. Louis and Gibson were in South Florida with Louis's press agent Harry Mendel when they finally realized that they would have to look elsewhere. It was then that Mendel said, "I know a crazy guy in Coral Gables that would be interested in a promotional venture." The "crazy guy in Coral Gables" was Jim Norris.[19]

Norris was no stranger to the sports scene. His family already owned three major arenas in the Midwest (the Chicago Stadium, the Detroit Olympia, and the St. Louis Arena). Moreover, Norris and his partner Arthur Wirtz each owned stock in the Madison Square Garden Corporation, the company that controlled the crown jewel of sports arenas, Madison Square Garden. The division of labor in the Norris-Wirtz partnership was clear and effective. Norris was the rich sportsman, the front man with money. Wirtz was the entrepreneur, a real estate expert who had a history of making deals with, among others, the Rockefellers.

In early 1949, Norris and Wirtz met on several occasions with Louis and his men. A plan soon emerged that would give everyone what they wanted—a farewell gift for Louis and the foundation for a monopoly for Norris and Wirtz. Under the plan, Louis would use the vehicle of his existing corporation (Joe Louis Enterprises, Inc.) to sign the four leading heavyweight contenders to exclusive promotional contracts. Louis would then retire as champion and assign the exclusive contracts to the International Boxing Club, a new entity that Norris and Wirtz were in the process of establishing to promote boxing. In exchange, Louis would receive both cash and stock in the IBC.

The imaginative scheme, usually attributed to Harry Mendel, is sometimes referred to as the Mendel Plan. According to Gibson, however, Mendel deserves no such credit. Gibson concedes that Mendel set up Louis's initial meeting with Norris in Florida but maintains that devising such a plan "would be out of his depth." Instead, Gibson alleges that Wirtz was primarily responsible for concocting the scheme during a series of meetings that took place between Wirtz and Gibson. "It was Wirtz," maintains Gibson. "Wirtz was the businessman. . . . It was Wirtz who came to me and said, 'How are we going to do it?' . . . We had a corporation. So Wirtz said, 'If you can get the top four fighters in the heavyweight division signed to your corporation, we'll buy the contracts.'"[20]

Whoever devised the plan deserves some credit because it went off without a hitch and was ultimately effective. In early 1949, Louis signed the four top heavyweight contenders (Ezzard Charles, Jersey Joe Walcott, Lee Savold, and Gus Lesnevich) to exclusive promotional contracts. On March 1, 1949, Louis retired. Then, on March 24, 1949, he assigned the contracts to the IBC. In return, Louis received $150,000 in cash (reportedly, several hundred thousand less than he had originally demanded), 20 percent of the stock in the IBC, and an annual salary of $15,000. Gibson disputes the popular account here as well, contending that Louis received $300,000 rather than $150,000.[21]

With the contracts with the top heavyweights in hand, Norris and Wirtz now made a series of lightning-quick moves to round off their investment. In early 1949 they convinced Madison Square Garden officials to buy out Jacobs's interests (which included promotional rights at the Garden, Yankee Stadium, and the St. Nicholas Arena plus an exclusive contract with the great Sugar Ray Robinson) and assign them all to the IBC. Jacobs, without his health and without Joe Louis, was powerless to put up any resistance. Norris and Wirtz then turned their attention to the Tournament of Champions, Inc., the other major promotional entity in New York. In late May 1949, again operating through the Garden, they bought out the organization and acquired its assets, which included the promotional rights at the Polo Grounds as well as an exclusive contract with middleweight champion Marcel Cerdan. Shortly thereafter, Norris and Wirtz increased their stock holdings in the Madison Square Garden Corporation so that they had more of a direct influence over the company and the famous arena it controlled.

The IBC empire of Norris and Wirtz was now complete. In a period of less than six months a new organization had emerged as the sole promotional power in boxing. It now had exclusive contracts with the best fighters. It had control of the major indoor and outdoor arenas in New York and the Midwest. It had television rights to weekly prime-time boxing programs on the new medium of television. In other words, it had a monopoly that it would leverage to promote thirty-six of the forty-four title fights held in the United States between March 1949 and May 1953. It also had a new nickname: "the Octopus."

After everything shook out, it quickly became apparent that Louis held no real power in the IBC. Mendel also faded from the scene, embittered that he never reaped the rewards of the plan he felt he had devised and brought to Louis. After helping forge the deal that led to the IBC's creation, Wirtz moved on to other deals and receded into the background, content with playing the role of silent partner. That left Norris. Even though he left the day-to-day operations of the IBC to Gibson and others, Norris remained extremely active in the high-level operations of the enterprise. "He was tremendously valuable in terms of persuading fighters, getting fighters, how to pick fighters," Gibson says. Equally important, he was the unquestioned front man for the new organization.[22]

Overnight he had emerged as the new czar of boxing. At first blush he seemed a choice right out of central casting. He came from a sporting family, the son and namesake of a Canadian emigrant who made his fortune in wheat speculation and then later expanded his holdings to include oil, railroads, real estate, and sports properties (those arenas in the Midwest plus the Detroit Red Wings of the National Hockey League). Norris the Younger was also an established sportsman, owning several Thoroughbreds as well as the Chicago Black Hawks of the NHL. He was rich, with an estimated net worth of between $50 million and $200 million. He was relatively young (in his early forties at midcentury). He made a splendid appearance—tall, handsome, well dressed, and with decided savoir-faire. He also seemed to have all the right intentions. In short, he seemed to be the right man to lead his new organization—and the right man to lead the sport of boxing into a new age with new possibilities of television riches and old dreams of million-dollar gates.

Doubts soon cropped up, however. Norris, after all, liked to gamble. (As Gibson remembers, "He had a bet every day of the year on something.") He liked parties. He liked the high life. Most damaging, he liked mobsters. Growing up in Al Capone's Chicago, Norris, like so many others, was drawn to the excitement and glamour of the Mob. As an adult, he became good friends with several mobsters, including "Golfbag" Sam Hunt, a trigger man and head of the "complaint department" for Capone's gang. The race tracks that he frequented around the country led to additional unsavory connections and friendships. As Gibson notes, "That's where Norris met the mob guys, whom he admired greatly as individuals." Echoes Breslin, "Norris was queer for tough guys. He loved them."[23] At the very least, on a purely business level, Norris viewed Mob involvement in certain businesses as a fact of life. It soon became apparent that one of those businesses was boxing and that mobsters would indeed have a prominent place in the new world of the IBC.

In a sense, that hardly constituted earth-shattering news. Mobsters and gangsters had long played a role in boxing, representing both the seamy underbelly of the sport as well as a unique part of its romance and glamour. Poor boxers and struggling fight men from the fringes of society were a natural and easy mark for mobsters, society's ultimate outsiders, especially given that they were all after the same things—action, excitement, and, of course, money. As a result, the Mob had little difficulty infiltrating the sport and helped to promote, stage, and occasionally fix boxing matches throughout the 1920s and the 1930s. Starting in the mid-1940s and into the 1950s, though, the Mob stepped up its involvement considerably, in large part because of the presence of one man—Frankie Carbo.

Carbo, whose real name was Paul John Carbo, boasted a number of aliases, including Jimmy the Wop, the Ambassador, the Superintendent, Mr. Fury, and Mr. Gray. He also boasted a long criminal record filled with assorted bad deeds and transgressions. As a young man in New York in the early 1920s he was charged with felonious assault and grand larceny before finally being sent away to Sing Sing for murdering a taxi driver. A few years later, Carbo was back on the street and participating in the mob wars that raged throughout the country during the Prohibition era. As trigger man for Murder, Inc., he was allegedly the man behind the 1933 murders of Max Greenberg and Max Hassel, two beer racketeers from New Jersey. Carbo was also allegedly the man responsible for the infamous shooting of Murder, Inc. refugee Harry Greenberg in Hollywood on Thanksgiving Eve 1939. (Bugsy Siegel supposedly drove the getaway car.) Carbo was indicted for the Greenberg murder but wiggled away when his first trial resulted in a hung jury and his second trial went south after the key witness fell to his death from a hotel-room window. Carbo may have also been involved in several other mob slayings, including the 1947 murder of Siegel. His lifetime record: nearly twenty arrests, five of them for murder.

As he moved into middle age, Carbo turned his attention from murder to boxing. A muscular, silver-haired man of about 5'8" who liked to wear fine, conservative suits, flash rolls of $100 bills, and live a nomadic life in the fast lane, Carbo was a passionate fight fan. He also saw boxing as a way to make money. As early as the mid-1930s, Carbo started to acquire pieces of fighters, including a string of middleweight champions (Babe Risko, Al Hostak, and Solly Kreiger). He also fell in with Jacobs, exercising influence within the formal corridors of the Twentieth Century Sporting Club as well as the informal environs that surrounded it known as Jacobs Beach. By the close of World War II, Frankie Carbo could boast of a number of substantial interests in a variety of boxers and managers.

Then he got serious. Under Carbo's leadership from the late 1940s until the late 1950s, the Mob infiltrated boxing as never before. Television was the key to the Mob's expanded control, as the new medium transformed boxing from a regional, grass-roots sport to one more national in scope.

Gamblers were suddenly interested in betting on fights not just in their local arenas but at stadiums around the country.

All of this presented Frankie Carbo with an opportunity—and he promptly seized upon it by establishing a well-organized, centralized system of control over boxing. The system featured scores of managers who operated as front men for Carbo, men such as Blinky Palermo, Willie (the Undertaker) Ketchum, Hymie (the Mink) Wallman, Joseph (Pep) Barone, and, significantly, Al Weill. Once a promising fighter arrived on the scene, one of Carbo's managers would quickly muscle in on his ownership, demanding total control or at least a piece of the action for himself—and for Carbo. There were, of course, some managers who worked independently of Carbo. When necessary, however, they, too, were willing to make some sort of accommodation to keep Carbo happy. "Carbo is a killer," said one anonymous manager of the era. "All the managers are afraid of him."[24]

Fear and violence were indeed the linchpins of Carbo's system and the bedrock of his power. If a fighter or manager refused to play ball, he would be quickly frozen out of quality fights—if he were lucky. If he were unlucky, he would be the subject of threats and perhaps even physical violence. Even the famous were not exempt. One night in 1953, for example, an unknown assailant attacked respected fight man Ray Arcel outside a Boston hotel, nearly beating him to death with a lead pipe. Near-tragic incidents like the Arcel beating didn't happen too often—but when they did, everyone in boxing knew about it. More important, everyone in boxing knew that it could happen at any time if they did not submit to Carbo's rule. Unsurprisingly, few dared to resist.

As a result of all this, Carbo earned the title of "the underworld commissioner of boxing." He was an illicit force who had pervasive impact, and his power became such that no big match was made or title awarded without his acquiescence (if not active involvement). Either directly or indirectly, he controlled scores of judges, officials, managers, promoters, and fighters. As David Remnick has correctly noted, it would probably be easier to count the few fighters of the era who Carbo did *not* control rather than try to add up the ones he did, either directly or indirectly. "The fact was that everyone in boxing had had relations with Frankie Carbo in the forties and fifties," Ferdie Pacheco, Muhammad Ali's physician and later a boxing announcer, has observed. "If you knew boxing, you knew at least that much."[25]

Eventually, Jim Norris and Frankie Carbo found each other. Although they had known each other for years from racetracks and other sporting circles, they deepened their relationship considerably in the early 1950s. The impetus may have been a succession of strikes that the guild of boxing managers organized against the IBC in the early 1950s. Norris later testified on Capitol Hill that he found it "necessary to have a certain relationship" with Carbo in order to "get along in the boxing business."[26] In this instance, that meant calling upon Carbo to break the strikes and keep the managers in line. Carbo, recognizing an opportunity to gain a foothold within the formal power structure of the IBC, was happy to comply.

If Norris were a different type of man, he might have taken a different tack and tried to go it alone or even tried, with the help of the press, to expose the Mob's influence in boxing. But Norris wasn't that type of guy. He accepted the fact that "inside stuff" was part of the sport. There was even evidence that he himself had engaged in fixing a fight or two in an earlier flirtation with boxing during the late 1930s. He knew how the game was played, and he wasn't about to change the rules.

Carbo thus became a major player in the IBC power structure. Norris would use him to keep a recalcitrant manager or promoter in line. Or Norris would enlist Carbo to help arrange a key match, with Carbo acting in a role that Norris later described as an "expediter" or "convincer" to help line up fighters such as Jake LaMotta, Tony DeMarco, Willie Pep, and Carmen Basilio for IBC fights.[27] In the formal sense, Carbo never received a dime for his services, although his fiancée, Viola Masters, was added to the IBC payroll in 1954 at the salary of $15,000 per year, presumably to ensure Carbo's goodwill. Then again, Carbo, with his hands in the pocket of numerous promoters and managers, didn't really need to draw a salary from the IBC. What he wanted from the IBC—and what he got—was a foothold in the formal power structure of boxing so his own illicit operations could take place unfettered.

As time went on, Carbo's role in the IBC increased. It got so that Norris hardly made a match—or a decision—without getting Carbo's approval first. As one member of the New York police observed, "When you're talking with Carbo, you're talking with Norris."[28] By the mid-1950s, because of his ironclad ability to control the flow of fighters through managers, Frankie Carbo was effectively running the IBC. The infiltration of the Mob into boxing was complete.

In hindsight, some feel that the underworld's infiltration of the early 1950s fight game was somewhat exaggerated. Sportswriter W. C. Heinz, for instance, believes that the influence of Carbo and other mobsters "was a little bit overblown in the whole context of boxing . . . I think it was greatly exaggerated because it's very difficult to fix a fight, especially an important fight because you're going promise a fighter a certain amount of money but, hell, he could make a helluva lot more if he's champion of the world."[29]

Truman Gibson is even more adamant on the subject. He downplays Norris's relationship with Carbo, maintaining that "the common perception that [Norris spent] every waking moment with Carbo was absolutely untrue." Even so, didn't Carbo have a pervasive influence over the sport? "Believe me, not a chance," replies Gibson. "Nobody ever went to Carbo to make a match. What Carbo did really was, in the parlance of the race tracks, to pass post . . . Carbo, by reason of having been in the fight business in New York, knew the managers. The fighter would never give up anything. The managers would split a purse with Carbo. But so far as making a match is concerned? No."[30]

Gibson therefore regards the notion that Frankie Carbo ran boxing—and the IBC—as preposterous. "He couldn't run anything," Gibson says. "The IBC was a big business." After noting that the IBC's wide scope of operations involved running various gyms and theater clubs, staging two television shows a week, and nurturing young boxing talent, Gibson asks, "How could a bum like Carbo do any of that? It's impossible." Not surprisingly, then, Gibson regards Carbo's reputation as "the underworld commissioner of boxing" as "greatly exaggerated. . . . It makes for nice newspaper reading." Others, however, disagree with Gibson and affirm the popular perception of Carbo as the key man behind the scenes in the fight game of the early 1950s. As Jimmy Breslin says, "He was an ominous figure, and he got what he wanted . . . I don't think he had a small role. As far as the small business of boxing went, he was a big guy."[31]

Later in the 1950s, the overlapping empires of Norris and Carbo would crumble around them amid charges of graft and corruption. In the early 1950s, however, their iron rule went unchallenged. And Al Weill got himself to the center of the new power structure by forging a fast friendship with Norris. Equally important, Weill got along with Carbo. In fact, the two men had a close, long-standing friendship dating from at least the mid-1940s. Norris, Carbo, and Weill were, in fact, a happy trio, so much so that Norris named one of his horses "Mr. Gray" after Carbo and one "Al W." after Weill. Neither horse was "worth a nickel," Norris later revealed.[32] The trio had better luck within the world of boxing, at least until the mid-1950s. Weill clearly enjoyed the power that emanated from his relationships with Norris and Carbo and his job as IBC matchmaker. At the very least it gave him unfettered reign to orchestrate the progress of his prized young heavyweight, Rocky Marciano.

● ● ●

And so, in the spring of 1950, Al Weill, with the power of the almighty IBC behind him, decided to send Rocky Marciano back to Providence. It was the right move. Marciano plainly needed more seasoning. "Folks forget Rocky has been boxing only a few years and has had only thirty-one fights," Goldman would explain in early 1951. "He isn't as experienced as some top-notchers folks ask him to meet. We won't dodge any of them. But we still need time. Rocky has things to learn."[33] By the spring of 1950, Weill had maneuvered Marciano into a good position in the heavyweight ranks. He wasn't about to blow it by rushing him into the ring against a top-flight contender. Weill knew that Marciano might lose such a fight, less because of ability and more because of experience. A familiar place—Providence—would provide that experience.

Later, Weill would receive kudos for his handling of Marciano during this period. As Arthur Daley of the *New York Times* once praised, "Weill practically coddled him as he brought him along with more patience and care than managers usually demonstrate. Weill never let Marciano bite off more than he could chew." At the time, however, many believed that Weill's nurturing was excessive—that he was bringing Marciano along too slowly and selecting his opponents too cautiously. Earl Lofquist of the *Providence Journal* declared in the fall of 1950, "[T]he time for nursing Marciano along like a precious piece of porcelain is now in the past. The guy has either got it or he hasn't . . . Marciano must go to work on the real thing. He already has demonstrated, to the point of monotony, that he can knock over slightly animated punching bags."[34]

Weill had made up his mind, though. In the fifteen-month stretch between his first big fight against Roland LaStarza (March 1950) and his next big fight against Rex Layne (July 1951), Marciano fought nine times, primarily in Providence. A few of his opponents were good heavyweights, some were journeymen, and some were outright stiffs, but not one resembled a top-ranked, legitimate contender. Perhaps not coincidentally, this was the worst stretch of Marciano's career. Sometimes he looked good, other times he looked just okay, but rarely did he look great. He was gaining additional experience for sure, but his career path was no longer moving upward. To some, he appeared to be regressing. At the very least, he seemed to have hit a plateau in his rise to the top of the heavyweight ranks.

His first fight after LaStarza, against Eldridge Eatman in June 1950, was typical. Eatman, no Roland LaStarza, owned a rather unimpressive 14-17-3 record. Still, more than four thousand fans—including some of the top

IBC brass up from New York—filed into the Rhode Island Auditorium to see Marciano resume his career. The fight turned out to be a fiasco. Eatman went down in the third round even though it didn't appear that he had been hit before falling to the canvas. When the referee, Dolly Searle, appeared to signal a knockout by spreading his arms, the handlers for both fighters rushed into the ring and the crowd started to leave the arena, booing all the way. Then Searle cleared the ring and ordered Eatman's handlers to get their fighter ready to fight. (The referee later explained that he had spread his arms not to signal a knockout but a stop in the count because he had believed that Eatman had tripped.) Shortly after the action resumed in front of the bewildered crowd, Marciano quickly ended matters by knocking Eatman out with a right to the jaw. As Eatman's manager knelt over his fallen fighter, he screamed at Searle, "What did you want?"[35]

Marciano's next outing, against Gino Buonvino in Boston, also produced mixed results. At least Gino Buonvino was no Eldridge Eatman. Since coming to the United States, the former champion of Italy had met some quality heavyweights, losing to the likes of LaStarza, Lee Savold, and Nick Barone. The night that he met Marciano at Braves Field in Boston proved to be a surreal experience for all involved, because the fight took place amid a steady drizzle, under poor lighting, and within a ring that was antique and dilapidated. "I'll never forget that night," a bemused Marciano would say two years later. "It was raining and they put the fight on early. And what a ring. It was really small and tilted. I felt like I was fighting uphill all night." The fight itself also proved to be an uphill struggle for Marciano, as he couldn't put away Buonvino until the tenth and final round. Boston writers were unimpressed. Arthur Siegel of the *Boston Traveler*, for instance, declared that the heavyweight field must be "a stinker" if Marciano was a leading contender, because the Brockton heavyweight was nothing more than "a good club fighter."[36]

Marciano plodded on. In September 1950 he faced Boston heavyweight Johnny Shkor in Providence. Using mauling tactics, Shkor managed to open a cut over Marciano's eyelid in the first round. When he reopened that cut in the third, blood started to flow freely. Soon, Marciano's face was awash in his own blood. For a while it looked as if the bout was about to be stopped in Shkor's favor. But Marciano was allowed to continue. He promptly speeded up his attack, knocking Shkor down at the end of the fifth and three more times the sixth, the last of which finally ended the proceedings in his favor. It had been a dramatic, suspenseful, exciting bout. Marciano was now 29-0.

Next came a rematch with Tiger Ted Lowry, the cagey veteran who had lost the strange yet close decision from Marciano the previous October. Marciano wanted to score a knockout to remove all doubts that lingered from the first fight. On the night of November 13, 1950, in front of 7,155 fans (representing the largest gate in Rhode Island boxing history), Marciano failed in his mission as Lowry's style and boxing skill continued to give him fits. Marciano did, however, manage to win the fight handily, capturing a well-deserved unanimous decision. After the fight, Lowry gave tacit approval to Weill's cautious piloting. "I don't want to be critical of him," Lowry said of Marciano. "He's a comer, but I don't think he is quite ready for experienced fighters like Savold, Oma, Walcott, and Charles. I've fought that kind and I know. If I was managing him, I'd wait awhile before firing at the title."[37]

Marciano closed out the year 1950 by destroying a ham-and-egger named Bill Wilson in one round. Then, in a quartet of fights in early 1951, The Rock hit rock bottom. Against Keene Simmons in late January, Marciano was in trouble early before winning—and not before drawing some boos from the Providence crowd for hurling a few low blows. In his next fight, Marciano cruised to a second-round TKO over Harold Mitchell in Hartford. It was hardly a resounding victory, though, given that Mitchell had never won a professional fight in twelve previous outings. Back in Providence, someone named Art Henri managed to last nine rounds with Marciano before succumbing via a TKO. Marciano's next opponent, the equally unheralded Red Applegate, did even better and went all ten rounds before losing a decision.

Through it all, Marciano kept winning—his unbeaten winning streak, after the Applegate victory, was now at thirty-five. Yet his reputation had taken a decided dip. As Lofquist proclaimed during the slump, "Rocky is not going to be the next world champion. Many are beginning to believe that he has been overrated all along. Certainly he has not progressed as expected." What was wrong with Marciano? Lofquist cited the caliber of fighter he was facing: "You'd think the guy was a fragile egg to be kept under glass the way his opponents (LaStarza excepted) have been handpicked. Whether this has been for Marciano's good can be doubted. His improvement over the past year has been slight. But then he has not been fighting anybody from whom he could learn anything."[38]

● ● ●

Several out-of-the-ring developments may have also affected Marciano's performances during this stretch. One such development—a happy one—was his December 30, 1950, marriage to Barbara Cousins. The only child of a Brockton policeman, she had grown into a tall, statuesque blonde. After her graduation from Brockton High School in 1946, she went to work for the telephone company as an operator. In late 1947 the eighteen-year-old

Barbara Cousins met the twenty-four-year-old Rocco Marchegiano (an employee of the Brockton Gas Company and an amateur boxer) at a dance at the Brookville Grange near Brockton. She became his first serious girl-friend, attending all of his amateur fights and then his professional bouts. Shortly after they began dating they became engaged.

It turned out to be a long engagement. For the better part of two years Al Weill succeeded in blocking the marriage. Shortly after the engagement, he reportedly told Barbara, "Rocky's got a career to start and you can help him if he's not married. Why don't you wait a while? I'll let you know when I think it's right."[39] The couple acceded to Weill's wishes for a while. Soon, though, Barbara's friends began to hound her, and she began to hound Rocky, and, naturally, Rocky began to hound Al. Still, Weill refused to budge.

Finally, in late 1950 Weill relented and gave his blessing. The Rev. Leroy V. Cooney married them on December 30, 1950, at St. Colman's Church in Brockton, with nearly eight hundred guests in attendance. Several days later the couple left for a ten-day honeymoon in Miami. The ever-controlling Weill (who, much to Marciano's embarrassment, had given a toast at the reception warning Barbara not to stand in the way of her husband's career) telephoned Marciano several times during the honeymoon. He also summoned Marciano back to New York three days before its end to take a bow at the Ezzard Charles–Lee Oma championship fight at the Garden. Instead of letting Marciano return home to Brockton with his new bride, Weill ordered him to stay in New York to begin training for the Keene Simmons fight that he had booked while Marciano was in Miami. All of this probably didn't help Marciano's frame of mind in early 1951.

Nor did the subtext to the story, the increasingly strained relationship between Weill and Marciano. Money and control were starting to emerge as issues between fighter and manager. Marciano, who would become, in the words of Robert Lipsyte of the *New York Times*, "famously cheap," had met his match in the penny-pinching Weill. "Say you take a trip," recalls Angelo Dundee today. "And Al Weill would say, 'You see so-and-so, tell him to call me.' He didn't want to pay for the phone call." When it came to money, the mixture of Weill and Marciano would often prove to be combustible. As Duva recalls of Weill, "Him and Rocky had a lot of problems over money."[40]

The issue of control, though, was probably more the cause of Marciano's festering feelings of resentment toward his pilot. Weill's daily maneuverings, both before and after the Marcianos' marriage and on a professional as well as a personal level, were all calculated to keep Marciano under his thumb. "It's getting so this guy wants to do all my thinking for me," Marciano told his brother Sonny on his way to the top. "I can't do anything on my own.

He's got his nose stuck into my marriage, my personal friends, and every-thing else. . . . The guy's becoming a real pain in the ass."[41] For the most part, though, Marciano kept silent. That was the price that he had to pay, he reasoned, in order to get to the top. And, in Marciano's mind, it was worth it. He buried his anger—at least for the time being.

An even more distracting development around this time involved a law-suit brought against Marciano by Gene Caggiano, his former manager in the amateurs. Caggiano had been in Marciano's corner for most of his amateur fights, including the string of big victories in early 1948. As his fighter started to pile up amateur crowns, Caggiano moved quickly to pro-tect his investment. On February 27, 1948, he entered into a written con-tract with Marciano that stated that if Marciano decided to turn professional within five years, he would enter into a contract with Caggiano to retain him as a manager. The boxer and the manager verbally confirmed the agree-ment on two separate occasions in March 1948.

By then, though, the relationship between the two men had begun to sour. They were squabbling over money (according to Marciano, Caggiano prom-ised him $100 for headlining an amateur show but produced only $40). They were also in disagreement about the direction of the fighter's career (accord-ing to Marciano, Caggiano told him that he had little chance of making it in the professional ranks). Shortly thereafter, Marciano found Al Weill. He promptly dumped Caggiano. Caggiano discovered that he was out in July 1948 when he read in the local newspaper that Marciano had turned pro under the auspices of Weill. According to Caggiano, when he called Mar-ciano to protest, the fighter told him, "I'll bounce one off your chin," and, "You small, jerk-town manager, I went to New York and got a big wheel."[42]

Caggiano sued Marciano, seeking his share of the approximately $30,000 that Marciano had collected as a pro up to that point as well as a declaration that he (and not Weill) was Marciano's true manager pursuant to the terms of the February 1948 contract. Caggiano later claimed that he received sev-eral threatening letters and telephone calls promising that he would end up in a block of cement if he didn't drop the case. But he forged on. The trial in the matter of *Caggiano v. Marchegiano* commenced on May 22, 1950, in Suffolk Superior Court in Boston, Judge Frank E. Smith presiding. For the next three days, various witnesses (including Caggiano, Marciano, and Char-ley Goldman) offered testimony as to the disputed Marciano-Caggiano rela-tionship. After deliberating for several months, Judge Smith announced his decision in November 1950, ruling in favor of Caggiano. At the same time, though, because the case presented special questions of law, Judge Smith re-ferred it to the Supreme Judicial Court of Massachusetts for further decision.

As the case dragged on into 1951, the episode was plainly beginning to wear on Marciano. His managerial situation was complicated to begin with given the facade of Marty Weill as on-the-record manager and the reality of Al Weill as off-the-record manager. Now his old manager, Caggiano, was pushing to get back into the picture. There were even rumors that Marciano was prepared to quit the ring if he lost the suit and was forced to accept Caggiano. All of this left Marciano greatly disturbed and may have affected his sub-par ring performances throughout the period.

On July 2, 1951, the Supreme Judicial Court of Massachusetts at long last handed down its opinion in the *Caggiano v. Marchegiano* matter. The winner, by decision, was Marciano. In a written opinion Justice Edward A. Counihan held that the Marciano-Caggiano contracts in early 1948 were too indefinite and uncertain to be enforced. Caggiano would later threaten to bring a new court action against Marciano, but he never followed through. The case was over. Rocky Marciano was finally free of Gene Caggiano.

Marciano was relieved and elated at his victory. "It gave me a big lift when I got the news," he recalled.[43] At the time, he needed every psychological edge he could get. In the summer of 1951, Rocky Marciano was getting ready for the biggest fight of his career against the hottest heavyweight in the world, Rex Layne.

● ● ●

To many, Rex Layne evoked memories of the great Jack Dempsey—a big, strapping, brawling heavyweight riding in from the West to take the heavyweight division by storm. Here, they theorized, was the next heavyweight champion of the world, a worthy successor to the throne that Dempsey had occupied three decades earlier. By no means was Layne a finished product. He tended to rely too much on his right hand, seemed rather chunky, and was a bleeder. Nor was he seen as unbeatable. As recently as March 1950, he had lost to someone named Dave Whitfield. Still, in the months leading up to his July 1951 fight with Rocky Marciano, the man with the distinctive windmill style had flashed enough potential to convince many experts that he was the real McCoy.

He came from Lewiston, Utah, where he had once worked as a beet farmer. Like Marciano, he had learned to box in the army. By the time he met Marciano, the blonde, pink-skinned, apple-cheeked Layne owned a gaudy record of 34-1-2 with twenty-four knockouts. And Layne had succeeded where Marciano had failed—he had impressed the New York fight crowd. His main claim to fame was a Garden victory in November 1950 over Jersey Joe Walcott, a highly regarded heavyweight who was a regular in the title mix. Layne had also defeated Bob Satterfield, Cesar Brion, and several other respected heavyweights. Even though he was only twenty-three, he was clearly battle-tested. And he was now a big attraction.

As soon as the Layne-Marciano fight was scheduled for July 12, 1951, in the Garden, experts immediately installed Layne as the clear favorite. In the weeks before the fight, though, the underdog Marciano seemed relaxed and confident as he got ready for the assignment at his first training camp at Greenwood Lake in the middle of the Rumapo Mountains on the New York–New Jersey line, fifty miles outside New York City. "He looked right for my style," Marciano later explained. "He didn't look as though he could do much damage backing up and there's only one way I know how to fight—go forward and keep throwing punches. In order for Layne to be at his best, he's got to do the same." Goldman, too, was optimistic, confident that Marciano could wear down Layne by pounding away at his body. A few hours before the fight, the trainer sidled up to his fighter and told him, "This big farmer is just sent from heaven for you."[44]

The evening of July 12 was steaming hot. Inside the Garden, more than twelve thousand fans gathered to see boxing's new golden boy, Rex Layne, take the next step toward the title. Fans in eight more cities paid their way into movie theaters to see the fight via a new innovation, closed-circuit television. As with Marciano's fight with LaStarza, his match with Layne was a certifiable big fight. In such an atmosphere fifteen months earlier Marciano had been nervous and started off shaky.

There would be no stage fright this time. Instead, the supremely confident Marciano concentrated on carrying out the strategy that he and Goldman had devised. "I decided to fight the first few rounds on top of him," Marciano later explained. "I knew he could outreach me, but that wasn't why I crowded him. I wanted to get loosened up for a few rounds and wanted to get in a few punches from inside before I moved away." The strategy confused Layne, who would remain befuddled throughout the fight by Marciano's changing styles and moves, however awkward. "He fought a perfect fight against Rex," Layne's manager Marv Jensen said after the fight. "He had him figured like Schmeling figured Louis the first time. You got to give him credit."[45]

In the third round, Marciano, as planned, switched gears, moving away from his opponent in order to throw looping, reckless overhand rights. His thunderous blows shattered Layne's bridgework and knocked out a tooth. With a minute left in the third, Marciano buckled Layne's knees with a right to the jaw. Then, in the fourth, Marciano knocked Layne down with a right to the jaw. The knockdown was partially due to a Marciano shove, and

Layne got up right away, unfazed. Still, the touted heavyweight from the West was now in trouble—and everyone knew it.

Marciano's punches to Layne's chunky midsection were beginning to take their toll. Goldman would maintain that "it was body punching that weakened Layne and set him up for the kill." By the fifth round, Layne, his face a bloody mess, was becoming increasingly incapable of resisting Marciano's bull-like rushes. The round ended with Layne staggered, spent, and on the verge of collapse. "I knew I had him in the fifth round," Marciano said after the fight. "I threw a right to the body and I felt the punch hang in the air. I felt him start to go but he clinched and finally the bell rang."[46]

Thirty-five seconds into round six Marciano knocked Layne out. After he connected with a hard right to Layne's jaw, Marciano admitted that he "didn't know what to do. He was gone. I didn't take any swing at him after that right to the head. I knew I didn't have to but I didn't know what was going to happen." What happened next was stunning. Everything seemed to stop. Then, after two or three seconds of suspended animation, with each fighter remaining motionless, Layne began to sink to the canvas with delayed-action effect, slowly at first and then much more rapidly. According to several ringside observers, the falling Layne looked "like an elephant collapsing from a rifle shot" or "a ship sinking into the sea." He dropped to the canvas face forward in a hunched position. Once he hit the floor, he rolled over to his side and curled up. He was out.[47]

The spectacular knockout sent the Garden crowd into hysteria. The fans had been excited throughout, roaring at the action and savageness of the bout. Now, with the electrifying finish, they went wild. In "one of the most tumultuous demonstrations ever accorded a fighter in a local ring," according to the *New York Times* reporter on the scene, several thousand Marciano fans swept toward the ring and cheered for their man. They kept cheering long after Marciano had left the ring and departed for his dressing room.[48]

Amid the melee, hardly anyone noticed Rex Layne. Several seconds after being counted out, he finally came to his senses and was assisted to his corner and out of the ring. Moments later in his dressing room, a disappointed Layne admitted, "His style bothered me. I couldn't get an opening for a clean shot. He hits hard. Not as hard as Louis, but hard. I don't want to take anything away from Rocky—he's good—but I felt logy all night. Couldn't get going. Maybe I've been working too hard and long. I'm going to take a rest. But I'll be back."[49]

Rex Layne never really came back. The fact that Marciano had chilled him on that hot July night shouldn't have necessarily cooled his title chances permanently. But it did. Soon the boxing intelligentsia would label Layne a has-been after he lost to deposed champion Ezzard Charles in the fall of 1951. Although Layne wouldn't disappear entirely from the heavyweight picture—he experienced a minor revival of sorts when he won a questionable decision against Charles in a 1952 return—he never recaptured the momentum that had been his before meeting Marciano. Within a few years he faded from the scene.

If the fight marked the beginning of Layne's gradual decline it also signified the ascendancy of Rocky Marciano. Before the fight, the crowd that hung around Stillman's Gym and various watering holes in New York still had significant doubts about his abilities. After Layne, critics were forced to revise their reviews. They finally accepted Marciano as the nation's premier young heavyweight as well as a legitimate contender for the crown. His appearance on Ed Sullivan's *Toast of the Town* television program only seemed to confirm his newfound fame. Rocky Marciano had arrived.

The Rex Layne bout was the single most important fight of Rocky Marciano's career. The night he met Layne, Marciano's reputation was definitely on the line. "This is a make-or-break fight for him," wrote Mike Thomas in the *Providence Evening Bulletin* before the fight. "This one will determine whether he has the goods to keep going or whether he's just a flash-in-the-pan." With a victory over Layne, echoed Arthur Siegel on the eve of the fight, "Rocky will move into the upper brackets of his business. If he loses, he's just a workingman who may have to wait longer for a chance at the better money."[50] Indeed, had he lost to Layne, Weill and the other powers-that-be may have jettisoned him into a prolonged (and perhaps permanent) exile from the top of the heavyweight division.

No fight was more important in clearing his path to the championship. Even though Marciano had compiled a long string of knockout victories, observed a reporter in the *Washington Post,* they "were over bush-league opposition. Now Rocky has proved he can hit in the majors." His impressive showing meant that Marciano had the showcase victory he needed to stay in the majors, at least for the foreseeable future. With the exception of a few tune-up bouts, there would be nothing but big fights in Marciano's career from this point forward. In addition, as a result of his knockout of Layne, Marciano began to ooze confidence. "That was the one which convinced me that I could win the title," he would recall. "When I beat Layne, I was sure in my own heart that I had a chance to win the title."[51]

The fight was critical for still another reason. By defeating Rex Layne, Rocky Marciano—symbolically and definitively—became the Great White Hope.

4 The Great White Hope

No one asked Rocky Marciano whether he wanted to assume the mantle of the Great White Hope, although that is what he did when he defeated Rex Layne in the summer of 1951. And he would continue to play that role throughout his rise to the title, during his imminent reign as heavyweight champion of the world, and until the day that he retired from the ring in 1956. The Great White Hope would thus become an overarching image and dynamic in his career and his emerging role as the athletic symbol of his age.

Then again, he had little choice in the matter. By the time Marciano arrived on the scene, the role of Great White Hope had long been a permanent (and prominent) fixture on the boxing landscape. The Great White Hope had been symbolically carrying the hopes of the white race, real or imagined, into the heavyweight arena on his broad shoulders since the early part of the twentieth century. In many respects, the history of boxing until that point was the history of the Great White Hope.

Ever since its emergence as a popular sport in turn-of-the-century America, boxing had been a lightning rod for racial tension. The very nature of the sport can evoke a peculiar sort of passion. In boxing, after all, there are no bats, balls, or sticks. There are no teammates. There aren't even any uniforms. Instead, there are simply two men, practically naked, standing in the middle of the ring and fighting with their hands—a stark, one-on-one confrontation in which the man with the superior skill, bravery, and smarts should (and usually does) emerge the victor. During the first half of the twentieth century, when one man in the ring was black and the other man was white, the raw, individualistic essence of the sport often proved to be a racial time bomb.

Times were different, and racism was, in many corners of American society, institutionalized and acceptable. Many whites at the turn of the century believed that the white race, in boxing as in everything else, was scientifically superior to the black race. For this reason white fans feared interracial boxing matches. What would happen if for some strange reason the white man lost to the black man? What would happen to their scientific theories then? And how would blacks interpret—or misinterpret—the result? At the turn of the century, boxing wasn't completely closed to black men. They were allowed to fight for titles in the lighter divisions. They were also allowed to fight each other in the middleweight, light heavyweight, and heavyweight divisions. But they were not allowed to compete for the crown in those heavier divisions, which were the championships that mattered the most. The risk that a black man might capture a big-money title was too great. As boxing historian Randy Roberts has pointed out, "When big men—one black and the other white—fought, white jaws tightened."[1]

There were therefore approving nods all around when the first heavyweight champion of the modern era, John L. Sullivan, announced, "I will not fight a Negro. I never have and I never shall." And Sullivan, throughout his reign (1885–92), never did, even though Peter Jackson from Australia and several other blacks loomed as viable contenders. Sullivan's successor Jim Jeffries (1899–1905) reinforced the color line when he proclaimed, "When there are no white men left to fight, I will quit the business . . . I am determined not to take a chance of losing the championship to a negro."[2] In 1908, however, three years after Jeffries retired, a black man named Jack Johnson captured the heavyweight crown. When news of his triumph over Tommy Burns in Australia trickled back to America, it hardly caused an uproar. The conventional wisdom held that Johnson's reign would be brief—

and that his imminent and inevitable dethroning would symbolically reaffirm white supremacy.

The conventional wisdom was wrong. It soon became apparent that Johnson was a great boxer who would be difficult to dethrone. That he was black made this mere fact troublesome to many whites. What made matters worse was Johnson's persona, for Johnson refused to play by the accepted rules of society. In the ring he was all arrogance, taunting opponents by chattering and smiling and seeming to go out of his way to humiliate them. Outside the ring he lived large. He was a flashy dresser who fancied diamond rings and stickpins. He constantly flashed a broad smile to show off his gold-plated teeth. He spoke with an affected British accent. He drove fast cars. He sipped beer and vintage wine through straws. He adored the nightlife. He was the constant life of the party everywhere he went.

Jack Johnson also liked white women—especially white prostitutes. Several years into his reign he married a white woman named Etta Duryea. After she committed suicide, he married another white woman. As with the other components of his lifestyle, his love life was exceedingly open and public. Johnson, in fact, flaunted his sexuality. As his biographer Randy Roberts has observed, Johnson consciously exploited the ancient "myth of black sexuality" that ascribed lust, passion, and an immoral sexual nature to blacks. He did so by wearing tight-fitting silk shirts, ordering his current companion to run her hands over his chest and back, flashing a lascivious smile, and living a fast life that oozed sex and sexuality in almost every respect. While sparring, he would occasionally wrap his penis in gauze bandages to enhance its size for the benefit of reporters and other onlookers. All of this shocked white America.[3]

Hence the Great White Hope was born. In 1909, with Johnson back in the United States successfully defending his title, white promoters and sportswriters began a desperate nationwide search for a white man capable of unseating the unpopular and menacing black champion. "It was like the search for the origin of the Nile, full of false hopes, preposterous characters, tragic deaths, and excessive newspaper coverage," Roberts has observed. "Indeed, it was a promoter's and manager's dream. All one had to do to build up a gate or a boxer was to mention the magic words, Great White Hope."[4]

Eventually, the search centered on one man: retired champion Jim Jeffries. Was it not incumbent upon him as a white man to shut the mouth of the loud, defiant, black champion and prove, once and for all, that the white race was superior? Novelist Jack London, who in his spare time wrote on boxing for a New York newspaper, declared, "Jim Jeffries must now emerge from his alfalfa farm and remove that golden smile from Jack Johnson's face.

Jeff, it's up to you. The White Man must be rescued." In late 1909, prodded by the press and lured by considerable financial inducements, Jeffries finally yielded to the pressure and agreed to fight Johnson. He was clear and direct about why he was ending his retirement: "I am going into this fight for the sole purpose of proving that a white man is better than a Negro."[5] The fight was set for the middle of 1910 on that most American of days, July the Fourth.

The buildup for the fight was long and considerable, and every move the two fighters made in the months preceding the fight was recorded or photographed. Few sporting events before or since have generated more attention or carried more societal significance. Promoter Tex Rickard successfully cast Johnson as the deliverer of the black race and Jeffries as the hope of the white race. The promotion backfired, however, when the public blew the fight completely out of proportion. Songs disparaging Johnson became popular. Newspaper writers and editors attacked him and the entire black race. Some whites were against the fight even taking place because it constituted an admission of racial equality. Others predicted that a race war would result if Johnson actually won.

By the time the two men stepped into the ring on July 4, 1910, in Reno, Nevada, everything was at fever pitch. Nothing less than the future of Western civilization appeared to be at stake. After Johnson proceeded to destroy Jeffries, winning by a knockout in the fifteenth round, all hell broke loose in America. The fight-related incidents in numerous cities across the land ranged from full-scale riots to isolated slashings and shootings to near lynchings. In all, eight blacks and several whites died as a result of the violence. All the emotions that had built up before and during the fight were finally and fully unleashed—in deadly fashion.

In the aftermath there were the inevitable calls to abolish the sport of boxing. There were also calls for a new Great White Hope. Now that Jeffries had failed, who would emerge to save the white race from the evil Jack Johnson? The press was constantly looking for such a boxer—in vain. Enterprising promoters even organized formal Great White Hope tournaments to play on public sentiment (and make a quick profit). All these efforts failed. Between 1910 and 1915 a succession of Great White Hopes emerged, had their fifteen minutes of fame, and then faded away once everyone discovered that they were somehow deficient.

Eventually, the U.S. government got Jack Johnson, arresting him in October 1912 and subsequently prosecuting for an alleged violation under the Mann Act, which forbade the transportation of women in interstate or foreign commerce "for the purpose of prostitution or debauchery, or for any other immoral purpose." The charge against Johnson was shaky, but the government got its conviction in May 1913. A month later Johnson was sentenced to one year in prison. Rather than go to jail, he promptly fled the country and began a life in exile in Canada and Europe. Two years later, Johnson, having spent most of his money, accepted a fight in Cuba against Jess Willard, the newest Great White Hope to emerge. In the twenty-sixth round Willard knocked Johnson out. Only some believed Johnson's later claim that he took a dive for certain financial and legal inducements. Either way, his long and stormy reign was finally over.

In the twenty-two years following Johnson's reign, from 1915 to 1937, no black man fought for the heavyweight championship of the world. Even after the furor over Johnson subsided, promoters purposely excluded black heavyweights from title fights and other big-money bouts, either for economic reasons (they were convinced that black fighters wouldn't draw large crowds of whites) or personal reasons (they shared the racial prejudice of the time). Not many white fans complained. After Jack Johnson, one boxing historian has commented, "White America would rather have the crown placed in mothballs than worn by a black man."[6]

There was nothing secret about the systematic exclusion of blacks in heavyweight boxing. After he beat Jack Johnson in 1915, Willard declared that he would redraw the color line. White America, anxious to be rid of Johnson's memory, approved. Willard's successor, Jack Dempsey, also remained faithful to the color line, announcing the day after he won the title in 1919, at promoter Rickard's urging, that he would not fight black challengers. The situation remained unchanged as Dempsey reigned into the mid-1920s despite public clamor to give a title shot to Harry Wills, the top black heavyweight of the era. For various reasons the fight never happened. Wills, like other top-flight black heavyweights of the post-Johnson era (Sam Langford, Sam McVey, and Joe Jeannette), languished in obscurity.

Blacks remained on the outside looking in as the heavyweight crown passed from Dempsey to Gene Tunney in the mid-1920s and then to a succession of short-lived, rather ordinary, and definitively white champions (Max Schmeling, Jack Sharkey, Primo Carnera, Max Baer, and Jim Braddock) into the 1930s. Then along came Joe Louis. From the moment he burst onto the boxing scene in 1935 it became apparent that Louis had talent—talent that could not be ignored. His handlers made sure of it. They announced to the press (and the press, with approval, announced to white America) that they had laid down seven rules for Louis to follow. He was never to have his picture taken with a white woman, for example, nor was he to gloat over a fallen opponent. In other words, they established Louis as the anti-Jack Johnson.

The strategy worked, and the color line crumbled. There was never any question that Louis would eventually have a shot at the title. It's not that the times or the racial tolerance of the press and the public had changed that dramatically. Rather, it was a case of the right kind of black man (Louis) coming along with the right kind of backer (promoter Mike Jacobs). So Louis got the big fights. Then, in 1937, he got a title fight against champion Jim Braddock. He won, of course, and began his long reign as champion.

With the emergence of Louis, the Great White Hope came out of his long hibernation. He had not been needed, of course, in the years between 1915 and 1935, given that no black was allowed near the top of the heavyweight division. Now, however, a black man was once again dominating the heavyweights. The call once again went out for a white man to beat him—or so it seemed. In reality, the new era of Great White Hopes turned out to be far different than in the time of Jack Johnson. In that previous age there was a genuine, desperate need to dislodge the black champion. Twenty-five years later, no one felt that way about Joe Louis.

When a well-organized, formal elimination tournament was conducted to find a Great White Hope shortly before Louis became champion, the press and the public reacted with cynicism and little enthusiasm. Only Jack Dempsey's business connection to the tournament sparked some interest. After he became champion, Louis's popularity continued to quash the search for the Great White Hope. As *Newsweek* noted in 1938, and with some irony, "race plays but a minor role" in the new, "less hysterical," search for a Great White Hope. The reason was that Louis "is a respected and popular fighter."[7]

Yet the Great White Hope survived into midcentury, albeit in transmuted form. Although a white man was no longer needed to prove white superiority, a Great White Hope—a white man talented enough to capture the heavyweight championship—was still seen as good for boxing. The reason was essentially economic. Promoters assumed (perhaps correctly) that many fans wanted to see a white man dethrone Louis and would pay to see if it could happen. Black champion versus Great White Hope made dollars and cents; black champion versus black challenger made no sense. The facts are conclusive: Only one of the forty-three men Joe Louis fought before the outbreak of World War II was black.[8] As Louis's reign continued into the late 1940s, the Great White Hope remained alive and well—good for the business (and the box office) of boxing.

• • •

Against this rich historical backdrop, the new Great White Hope, one Rocky Marciano, stepped onto the national stage. He had first been mentioned as the Great White Hope in early 1950, around the time that he met Roland LaStarza. Yet even though he won that fight, he was soon back in the minor leagues of Providence. Instead, it was Rex Layne who emerged as the Great White Hope by virtue of his victory over Jersey Joe Walcott. By the time he stepped into the ring against Marciano on the night of July 12, 1951, the press had labeled Layne as "the new white hope," "the No. 1 'white hope,'" and "a national hope for the heavyweight title."[9]

The events of that fight changed everything, of course, as the mantle of Great White Hope symbolically passed from Rex Layne to Rocky Marciano. Hardly anyone in the mainstream press in the North, Midwest, and West called explicit attention to the transfer, however. In fact, mainstream sportswriters would continue their silence about Marciano's status as the Great White Hope throughout his rise to the title. Even when Walcott, the champion, finally gave Marciano a title shot in the fall of 1952, the mainstream press would keep the issue of Marciano's race under wraps. For sure, many mainstream sportswriters noted the fact that Marciano stood to become the first white man to capture the crown since 1937. A few even dramatized the fact. Al Wolf of the *Los Angeles Times,* for example, described Marciano's challenge as a "crusade to become the first white champion" since Jimmy Braddock.[10] Most sportswriters, however, skipped such heightened rhetoric. What was significant was that many didn't mention the color of Marciano's skin at all. There was no breathless anticipation of recapturing or reclaiming the crown for white America, no suggestion that racial superiority was at stake, and no exploration of the racial dimensions of the fight.

The same would hold true in the press coverage after Marciano beat Walcott to win the title. Many in the mainstream press did cite the fact that Marciano was the first white champion since Braddock—but they did so in passing. Even those who elaborated did so with some sheepishness. For instance, Jerry Nason of the *Boston Globe* noted, "There had not been a Caucasian ruler of the heavyweight in fifteen years. . . . While a man's color was no longer important, only his competence, you felt that it would be a change-of-pace to have a white boy on top after all these years."[11] And, somewhat stunningly, that was about the last time in Rocky Marciano's entire career that someone in the mainstream press from the North, Midwest, or West explicitly mentioned his race.

Sportswriters in southern cities (where racial dichotomies were still an accepted way of life) would be less reticent to highlight the color of Marciano's skin during his rise to the title. Observed Ed Wray of the *St. Louis Post-Dispatch*, "[F]ans are wondering about the white contender . . . Marciano is the first fighter of the Caucasian race to enter the heavyweight picture in recent years, most of his competitors having been supplied by Negro battlers." Added Furman Bisher of the *Atlanta Constitution*, "Marciano is the white hope, for sure, and probably the best heavyweight alive." And Wilton Garrison of the *Charlotte Observer* declared, "Rocky is young and is definitely the new 'white hope,' an animal they've been hunting since Jack Dempsey and Gene Tunney quit . . . we hope he goes far."[12]

Some in the southern press would also take explicit note when Marciano captured the title. In the lead of his postfight column, Bisher trumpeted, "For the first time in fifteen years a white man is heavyweight champion of the world today." But then he quickly reminded readers, "The color isn't significant." Even the precious few who seemed to revel in the crowning of the Great White Hope did so in an understated way. "Every preliminary boy on the card was a Negro," observed Pete Baird of the *New Orleans Times-Picayune* a few days after the Walcott-Marciano fight. "Marciano was the only white boy on the program, but he held up his race's prestige all right."[13] For the balance of Marciano's career, however, southern sportswriters, too, would largely remain silent on the matter of his race.

Perhaps the only segment of the press that was open about the issue was the black press. The weekly black newspapers of the era existed, in large part, to report on race relations. Given this mission, black sportswriters could hardly ignore the color of Marciano's skin. Thus, in the wake of Marciano's victory over Rex Layne, Trezzvant Anderson of the *Pittsburgh Courier* declared, "We have to be honest about this thing! At long last, a 'white hope' has actually hit the fight scene who may lift the highly coveted world heavyweight crown from the brow of its sepia holder." Black sportswriters would also have a strong reaction to the transfer of the title from Walcott to Marciano. The curtain, lamented Joe Bostic of the *New York Amsterdam News*, had finally come down on one of "the most prideful eras of Negro participation in big-time professional sports." The headline in the *New York Amsterdam News* said it all: "A Glorious Fistic Era Comes to a Close."[14]

As Marciano's reign deepened, black sportswriters would be more likely than their white counterparts to place the issue of race at the forefront, advocating for black challengers to get a title shot and then supporting them when they did. A few even took the next step and disparaged Marciano. After Marciano's fight with Ezzard Charles in June 1954, for instance, Ric

Roberts of the *Pittsburgh Courier* contended that the "hacks" were trying to make Marciano into "a living god." He, of course, disagreed. "Aside from his firepower, the Rock has nothing," he maintained, adding that Marciano would have had no chance against Joe Louis in his prime.[15]

Most black sportswriters, however, would treat Marciano with fairness. For instance, Sam Lacy of the *Baltimore Afro-American,* after initially expressing some doubts about Marciano's abilities, was quick to proclaim him "a worthy champion" after he captured the crown. A year later, Lacy reiterated that Marciano was "a true champion. Wipe the mist from your eyes, those of you who think only in terms of Joe Louis, etcetera. While Rocky's no Joe yet (who is?), he's the nearest thing to approach the class of Louis since the Bomber left his bombing in Army khaki." Bostic also came around. In a column entitled "Marciano Ain't No Bum" halfway through his reign, Bostic called Marciano "quite a champion" and instructed readers, "So take the advice of a conservative observer and don't rate the champion as a bum. Because he just ain't, period."[16]

Through it all, many black sportswriters were encouraged by the fact that race was not much of an issue when Marciano fought a black challenger. No thinking black sportswriter welcomed a return to the days when a boxer's skin color evoked the deepest racial passions of fans—for blacks were nearly always losers in that game. Wendell Smith of the *Pittsburgh Courier,* for instance, wrote a column before the first Marciano-Charles fight in which he touched upon Johnson's 1910 fight with Jeffries. "Fortunately, there will be no racial strife connected with this fight," a relieved Smith then noted of the impending affair. "It's strictly Charles vs. Marciano; not white vs. Negro."[17]

● ● ●

It was true. There was "no racial strife" connected with Marciano's various big fights against black men. The political realities of society and sports in the early 1950s demanded such an approach.

On a societal basis, America was enjoying a period of racial harmony during the early 1950s. Although everyday life was plainly no bed of roses for American blacks, it had improved greatly since the 1930s. During the depression, segregation and prejudice had pervaded all aspects of society. In the North, blacks worked menial jobs, lived in ghettos, and did not enjoy complete access to restaurants, nightclubs, and other public places. Things were even worse in the Jim Crow South, where blacks couldn't vote or go to school with whites and were denied everyday privileges and fundamental rights. Moreover, there was little hope that the situation would improve.

Things started to turn around, however, in the early 1940s. World War II was the catalyst. Because the country was fighting a racist enemy, Nazi Germany, it was forced to address its own race problem, which had long bubbled beneath the surface of society. Black Americans like white Americans were being asked to support the war effort, and they did their part both abroad in the military and at home as part of the war economy. To many in the media and in intellectual circles as well, America's racial practices suddenly seemed indefensible on both theoretical and practical grounds.

Many in black America reached precisely the same conclusion. The realities of war helped them achieve a series of victories such as integration of the army's officer training program, enlargement of acceptable duties in the navy, and, more generally, improvement in economic status. These achievements whetted the appetite of blacks for more, and the ideological character of the war stimulated black militancy. Membership in the NAACP soared. The Congress of Racial Equality experimented with nonviolence as a way of challenging Jim Crow. Black leaders used the threat of a march on Washington to pressure Franklin D. Roosevelt to issue an executive order concerning fair employment practices. All told, as historian John Morton Blum has recognized, World War II heightened blacks' self-consciousness and raised their expectations.[18]

After the war, the advances continued, particularly in the political arena. In response to pressure from black leaders, President Harry Truman formed the blue-ribbon Commission on Civil Rights. The commission's resulting report, *To Secure These Rights,* coupled with other principled and political reasons, helped convince Truman to come out strongly in favor of civil rights in early 1948. His program called for anti-poll tax and anti-lynching legislation, fair-employment laws, and an end to segregation in the military. The program was ambitious, and it alienated some southern members of the Democratic Party. When a civil rights platform tracking Truman's program was adopted at the 1948 Democratic Convention, the southern wing bolted and formed its own party, the Dixiecrats, with Strom Thurmond as its nominee for president. In the end, not much of Truman's program was enacted save for a directive ordering the desegregation of the Armed Services. Still, blacks were beginning to establish a political foothold.

For the most part, though, race relations calmed considerably after World War II, largely due to the conservative mood of America. As civil rights historian Harvard Sitkoff has observed, "After more than a decade of rapid, bewildering change, and exhausting battles against the Great Depression and the Axis, the vast majority wanted surcease. Most Americans yearned for stability. They desired harmony. Few had any tolerance for revolutionary proposals, in civil rights or anything else."[19] Blacks were, for the most part, willing to play along with this desire for normalcy. Whatever wartime militancy existed was curbed by the fact that they were sharing in the post-war economic boom. The median income of blacks doubled between 1940 and 1960 as a huge black migration to the North created new opportunities in professional, skilled, and semi-skilled occupations. With more money in their wallets and pocketbooks, most blacks were content to accept slow progress in race relations. The hope was that greater progress was on the immediate horizon.

All of this made it difficult for the black press and civil rights leaders at the NAACP to launch any sort of civil rights revolt. Instead, they worked quietly behind the scenes to launch a legal assault on school segregation, confident that successful litigation would eventually result in immediate improvement in race relations and the death of Jim Crow. They also celebrated the small victories, often coming in the form of a series of "Negro firsts" in a variety of fields. As the NAACP concluded at the end of 1950 after reviewing that year's various accomplishments in race relations, "Some might call these mere straws in the wind, but they do indicate the direction in which the wind is blowing."[20]

Eventually, of course, the wind wouldn't blow fast enough. The key event was the Supreme Court's landmark May 1954 *Brown v. Board of Education* decision, which outlawed the long-standing "separate but equal" facade and mandated school desegregation. At last the patience of black leaders had been rewarded. Now, they reasoned, Jim Crow would certainly die. But it did not. It was instead reinvigorated by the white backlash to *Brown*. The Supreme Court even backtracked a bit, ruling in 1955 that desegregation should occur "with all deliberate speed." Dashed hopes sparked new determination among blacks to fight for their rights in society. When Rosa Parks refused to go to the back of the bus in Montgomery, Alabama, in December 1955, the civil rights movement was on. Significantly, however, Rosa Parks took her stand three months after Rocky Marciano had fought his last fight. In the years when he was fighting, an uneasy yet distinct racial harmony prevailed. It was the calm before the storm—but it was still a calm.

The world of sports—the narrower but equally relevant context for Rocky Marciano—tracked these broader societal trends. In the early 1950s, sports were slightly ahead of the rest of society in matters of race relations. Sports had, in fact, long served as the cutting edge of desegregation. This was primarily due to the triumphs of two men: Joe Louis and Jackie Robinson.

Louis came first. When he emerged in the mid-1930s, the sports world was every bit as segregated as the rest of society. A few black track and field stars (Ralph Metcalfe and Eddie Tolan) had won gold medals at the 1932 Olympics, and a few blacks had made their mark in college football, but the attention lavished on these athletes was minor and fleeting. Nary a black had penetrated the world of professional sports. The new National Football League banned blacks, for instance. Most significantly, major league baseball—by far America's most popular sport—steadfastly maintained its color line. The world of big-time sports was lily white.

The sudden presence of Louis changed all that. He would eventually triumph not just in the ring but in the court of public opinion. Along the way, however, he had to endure an avalanche of abuse from the press. Many sportswriters, for instance, portrayed Louis as a wild beast that had emerged from the jungles of Africa. Even an enlightened sportswriter such as Paul Gallico latched onto the "jungle killer" theme, once declaring that Louis "lives like an animal, fights like an animal, has all the cruelty and ferocity of a wild thing." Other members of the media portrayed Louis as the stereotypical "Southern darkie." New York sportswriter Bill Corum, for example, once wrote that Louis "was born to listen to jazz music, eat a lot of fried chicken, play ball with the gang on the corner, and never do a lick of work he could escape. The chances are he came by all those inclinations quite naturally."[21]

Most commonly, the press used numerous race-based nicknames to describe Louis. "The Brown Bomber" was the most famous and the one that stuck, of course, but there was also the Dark Destroyer, Sepia Slugger, Chocolate Chopper, Dusky Downer, and many others. Such nicknames were partly due to the fact that sportswriters of the era had what Louis biographer Chris Mead has called "an inane passion for alliterative nicknames."[22] Clearly, too, the nicknames revealed that Louis's race remained very much in the forefront.

The tide began to turn with Louis's second fight with Max Schmeling of Germany in 1938. By this point, many were finally beginning to grasp Hitler's true intentions. The fight therefore took on the symbolic importance of fascism versus democracy. Schmeling, of course, was cast as the Nazi superman, and Louis (like Jesse Owens at the Berlin Olympics two years earlier) was cast—and largely accepted—as America's representative. Suddenly, many white Americans began to look at Louis a little differently.

Full acceptance came as a result of World War II. Louis enlisted shortly after the onset of the war. He then made two charitable title defenses for Armed Services relief organizations, donating his purses from those bouts amid much fanfare. Later he participated in propaganda campaigns and morale-building tours for the army. Because of all this, the army awarded Louis the prestigious Legion of Merit for extraordinary service and sacrifice.

Along the way, Louis became a symbol of national unity and patriotism. When he resumed his career after the war the majority of sportswriters accorded him genuine respect as a man of dignity. The widespread acceptance that he, a black man, won from the white public paved the way in due course for blacks in other sports and segments in society. His triumph was complete.

Yet it was subsequently overshadowed—perhaps a bit unfairly but understandably—by the triumph of Jackie Robinson. Among all the "Negro firsts" that black leaders celebrated in the late 1940s and early 1950s, none was more important than Robinson's. Breaking the color line in major league baseball was a significant milepost for blacks—and one that transcended the world of sport. Baseball was, after all, the National Pastime. It was also a sport with a long track record of institutional racism. Scores of people in the front offices, on the fields, in the press boxes, and in the stands were used to seeing the National Pastime as all-white—and they preferred to keep it that way.

In 1947 Robinson underwent a sometimes horrific and definitively heroic ordeal against this combination of forces. He triumphed, of course, and was eventually embraced by all but the most hardened bigots, when, in response to intense pressure, he provided testimony in front of the House Un-American Activities Committee in 1949 renouncing the pro-communist statements issued by entertainer (and former Robinson ally) Paul Robeson. Robinson's triumph was even more significant than Louis's, for it had a ripple effect on all other sports. After Robinson integrated baseball, black athletes, often with considerable personal hardship and heroism, began to trickle into baseball and all other sports. By the early 1950s most baseball teams (but not all) had a few blacks. The NFL, which had allowed its first black players in 1946, also stepped up the pace of integration. Likewise, a trio of blacks (Chuck Cooper, Earl Lloyd, and Sweetwater Clifton) shattered the color line in the fledgling NBA in 1950. The integration of big-time sports was underway.

• • •

In such an atmosphere, sportswriters covering Rocky Marciano were loath to start a race war over a boxing match. As a practical matter, editorial policy precluded many from doing so. It was the policy of the *New York Times,* for example, throughout the late 1940s and early 1950s to keep racial identification out of the news altogether unless it was "germane."[23] Although not every newspaper had a similar policy, most were moving in that direction. As race relations slowly started to change, a new, color-blind style of journalism began to emerge. Moreover, many sportswriters of the era were genuinely fair and kind in their treatment of black athletes, and less enlightened members of the press had toned down their rhetoric considerably since the early days of Joe Louis.

Yet some sportswriters would remain condescending and even occasionally derisive in their treatment of Marciano's black opponents (Jersey Joe Walcott, Ezzard Charles, and Archie Moore) during his title run. They employed the same journalistic techniques they had used early in the career of Joe Louis. Race-based nicknames, for example, remained very much in vogue, although they would decline in frequency and variety in the short span of Marciano's reign from 1952 to 1956. When he met Walcott at the beginning of that reign, many sportswriters had a field day creating nicknames that combined Walcott's color (black) with his age (old). Thus, Walcott commonly became known as Pappy, Pappy Joe, the Old Pappy Guy, and the Grandpappy Guy (even though Walcott was not yet a grandfather). Those with a particular racial bent dubbed him Old Man River or Old Massa Joe. Those without an ounce of creativity referred to him as the Old Negro. Several years later, when Marciano faced Charles, some sportswriters gave Charles race-based tags, such as the Ebony Dude, the Cincinnati Negro, the Ohio Negro, the Rangy Negro, the Cagey Negro, and the Clever Negro. For Moore, the black opponent at the end of Marciano's reign, a sportswriter would occasionally use a racially inspired nickname (the Negro Nomad), but that was rare. By 1955 a color-blind journalistic style was in full force on sports pages.

A few sportswriters in the early 1950s would take a different approach with Marciano's black challengers. They eschewed race-based nicknames but went to great lengths to describe, in graphic fashion, the particular shade of the black boxer's skin. That tactic, too, although far less demeaning than nicknames, represented a fixation on color. To A. J. Liebling of *The New Yorker,* for instance, Walcott was a "great, earthen-hued man," Charles a man of "a fashionable charcoal shade," and Moore a "light-colored pugilist." Liebling was not alone in his fascination with skin color. Other sportswriters noted that Walcott was "molasses-colored." Charles's skin was "ebony-hued." Moore was occasionally described as "Arab-dark."[24]

More derisive treatment would come in the form of stereotypes, another carryover from Louis's era. For instance, in playing up the fact that Walcott was a family man and religious (particularly when calling him something like Old Massa Joe in the process), some sportswriters seemed to be evoking the image of a God-fearing, child-rearing slave on a plantation. Walcott's fighting style also presented a target. He was commonly known as a "cutie," which was part of the boxing parlance of the day and certainly not a racial reference in itself. Some sportswriters, however, used this as a basis to cast him as a stereotypical figure looking to sneak through life. Franklin Lewis, for instance, claimed that Walcott "is in the main a trickster." Likewise, C. M. Gibbs of the *Baltimore Sun* maintained that he possessed "a gift of cuteness by nature."[25]

With Ezzard Charles, it was all about the bass fiddle. Many sportswriters consistently emphasized the fact that Charles played the instrument as a hobby, and along the way some poked fun at him for it, evoking traditional racial images involving blacks and music. Frank Blunk of the *New York Times* once described, at length and with a condescending tone, Charles's search for a hobby. First, Blunk wrote, Ezzard bought a saxophone, which he gave up when he found out that an athlete shouldn't play a wind instrument. Then Ezzard bought a ukulele, which he gave up when he decided that it was silly. Finally, Ezzard found the bass fiddle. "And Ez slaps it and bows it with the best of 'em," Blunk concluded.[26]

Charles became the subject of not only occasional stereotypical images but also coverage that sometimes crossed the line into cruelty with open questions about his courage, armchair psychology, and use of insulting nicknames (Snooks and Ezzard the Gizzard). Mainstream sportswriters in the North, Midwest, and West never couched such abuse of Charles in any racial overtones, but the color of his skin appears to at least have been a factor in the harshness of the abuse and perhaps its existence. The occasional abuse that Charles received from a few sportswriters in the South was easier to link to the color of his skin. After the second Marciano-Charles fight in 1954, for instance, one of Louis's old tormentors, Bill Keefe of the *New Orleans Times-Picayune,* claimed that Charles was "about the poorest excuse" one could find for a challenger. He then dived into a discussion of the anatomical differences between Marciano and Charles. Marciano, Keefe observed, "suffers a big disadvantage, even against white fighters, because of his abnormally short arms; against Negroes, nearly all of whom are blessed with abnormally long arms, poor Rocky needs the courage he has to win a fight from a man like Charles, whose arms are more than a half a foot longer."[27]

Other southern sportswriters would take a different approach, laying off of the black challenger but embracing the white champion, Rocky Marciano. After the first Marciano-Charles fight in 1954, for example, Naylor Stone of the *Birmingham Post-Herald* proclaimed that Marciano "made a magnificent stand and we're still for him, rain or shine, in sickness or health, and sink or swim." A year later, after the Marciano-Moore fight, Stone would admit, "We're glad Marciano won because he's such a nice guy."[28]

What made this remarkable was that Stone was not part of the usual fight crowd. When the champion was fighting in New York or elsewhere, Stone remained home in Alabama. He didn't really know Marciano, yet he openly rooted for him. He did not cite race as a reason, but it is hard to believe that Marciano's skin color was not part of the equation.

● ● ●

If mainstream sportswriters in the North, Midwest, and West also rooted for Marciano—and many most assuredly did—then they largely managed to keep up the facade of journalistic objectivity. Many of those sportswriters nevertheless subtly let readers know that Marciano was the Great White Hope. Early on, for instance, mainstream media outlets consistently remarked upon his huge gate appeal. The *Saturday Evening Post* called him "the biggest boxing draw since Joe Louis." To the *Boston EveningGlobe,* he was "boxing's glamour boy." To one United Press reporter he was "the answer to a promoter's dream."[29] Commenting on Marciano's gate appeal represented a safe way of saying that he was the Great White Hope without actually saying it.

A similar trick the mainstream press employed was to compare Marciano with Jack Dempsey. Marciano was "the second Dempsey," "a poor man's Dempsey," "the new Dempsey," or "the next Dempsey." Television, too, eventually would promote the comparison. The sponsors of *Greatest Fights of the Century,* the program immediately following the televised broadcast of Marciano's first title defense in early 1953, decided to show Dempsey's 1923 fight with Luis Firpo so viewers could make the comparison themselves. There was, in fact, a strong basis for the comparison. Like Dempsey, Marciano was smallish but strong, fought in a bobbing and weaving style, liked to brawl, and scored exciting knockouts. There was also another reason driving the comparison: Jack Dempsey and Rocky Marciano were both white. Comparing the two constituted yet another tacit acknowledgment that Marciano was the Great White Hope.

More important, the fact that Marciano was white facilitated construction of his positive image in the mainstream press. The foundation of that image was a slew of articles that appeared in such general-interest magazines as *Life, Look,* and the *Saturday Evening Post* around the time he emerged as the Great White Hope. That he was the subject of so many profiles can be attributed to the fact that he was a fresh face on the scene. Plainly, too, his race helped make him a cover boy. White sportswriters were operating under the assumption that white readers wanted to read about a white athlete. Perhaps those sportswriters themselves preferred to write about a white athlete. Whatever the reason, they were suddenly writing a lot about Marciano and helping kick-start an all-American-boy image that would make him the symbol of his age.

In contrast, the two black champions who preceded Marciano, Charles and Walcott, enjoyed no such attention during their respective reigns. Instead of reams of copy, they only received a scattered profile here or there. Perhaps that was because Charles and Walcott were widely seen as interregnum rulers. Why build someone up today if he will be gone tomorrow? Or perhaps white sportswriters assumed that white fans were only moderately interested in reading about a black champion. Whatever the motivations at work, neither black champion's image was distributed as widely as Marciano's.

Nor was their image as positive. In remembering Charles and Walcott, Jimmy Breslin proclaims that each was "a lovely guy."[30] Most sportswriters of the early 1950s—even Charles's tormentors among the press corps—would probably have agreed. But they rarely dwelled upon the many good personal qualities the black fighters possessed. Conversely, they appeared fixed on Marciano's personal qualities of spirit and trumpeted them accordingly.

Often the contrast in the tone of coverage was striking. Before the first Marciano-Charles fight in 1954, for instance, Arthur Daley of the *New York Times* spent some time with Marciano at his training camp. They talked about a wide range of subjects, from Marciano's high school football exploits to his love of family. In his resulting columns, Daley relayed all these stories, lavishing Marciano with liberal praise for his forthright nature and modesty. The next day, Daley traveled over to Charles's training camp. The column on that experience was markedly different, consisting of a lengthy analysis of Charles's past performances and an accent on his disappointments. Admitted Daley, "Charles is quiet, reserved and unsmiling by nature. A fellow who has just been subjected to Marciano's overwhelming charm and boyish friendliness couldn't help but be struck by the difference."[31]

The general tone of the coverage Marciano received was far more "up close and personal" than that of his black challengers, which usually emphasized strategy, style, and performance instead. Those elements were, of course, also important in the coverage of Marciano. White sportswriters, however, also took the time to get to know him as a man. Part of this was due to Marciano's friendly, engaging manner, which encouraged such an approach. It was also due to the fact that white sportswriters wanted to get up close and personal with the white fighter. He was, they assumed, more like them and their readers compared to Charles or Walcott. He was someone worthy of getting to know.

Mainstream sportswriters, then, gave Rocky Marciano extra attention, both in terms of how much they covered him (Marciano as cover boy) and, equally important, how they covered him (Marciano as a man with qualities of spirit). He was, in short, embraced. Granted, two black heavyweights of the era (Joe Louis and Archie Moore) were also embraced, although only special circumstances—Louis's enormous talent and heroism and Moore's electric personality—forced sportswriters (and the public) to take a closer look. In many instances they liked what they saw. Daley, for example, adored Louis even more than he adored Marciano, and scores of sportswriters devoted reams of copy (most of it favorable) to Moore before his 1955 fight with Marciano. Plainly, race was not the only variable dictating the treatment of boxers in the early 1950s.

Being a black man did not automatically disqualify you from being embraced, but you had to earn that embrace by being unique. If you were within the realm of the non-remarkable (as were Walcott and Charles, each of whom possessed good but not great talent and an admirable but not charismatic personality), you would receive treatment that was distant and removed. The same rules did not apply to a white boxer like Rocky Marciano. If you were white, you had a built-in advantage.

● ● ●

Marciano's race helped him not just with the press but with promoters as well. His status as the Great White Hope greatly facilitated a rapid rise to the top of the heavyweight ranks. Until then, only a handful of men had scaled the heavyweight heights faster than Marciano did in the late 1940s and early 1950s. It took him only forty-two fights and a little more than four years of professional fighting to get a title shot. His rise was meteoric.

That was not accidental. After his knockout of Layne, the IBC, clearly and openly, started to push Marciano into the title picture. In coverage of his big fights on the way to the title, the press would regularly point out that the IBC wanted Marciano to win. The IBC rooted for Marciano in part because of the color of his skin. Despite Louis's success and eventual popularity, the promotional guidelines of the day still called for white fighters in big fights. White boxers of all classes received better television exposure and were routinely pushed along faster than their black counterparts, even if they happened to possess less talent, ability, or flair. The underlying assumption, of course, was that most white fans preferred white boxers to black boxers—and would be willing to support that preference at the box office.

The racial rules of matchmaking had admittedly loosened a bit. In the years after the war, promoters had finally begun to match Louis against other black men, such as Walcott. After Louis abdicated, the IBC was daring enough to match two black men (Walcott and Charles) for the vacated title. All things being equal, however, white promoters still yearned for a Great White Hope. During Charles's post-Louis reign from June 1949 to July 1951 the IBC continually matched the black champion against mediocre white contenders such as Lee Oma and Freddie Beshore. In other weight classes as well, the IBC banked on the "black vs. white" promotional formula. Sugar Ray Robinson, for example, fought one white man after the other. Given these established rules of matchmaking, it was natural that the IBC would try to steer Rocky Marciano, a white man, toward the heavyweight title. As Truman Gibson of the IBC acknowledges, Marciano's race "was definitely an advantage. Our television sponsors all felt, rightly or wrongly, that a mixed fight benefited the television ratings. Marciano, in a sense, was the Great White Hope and went billed as such."[32]

Although Marciano's status as the Great White Hope clearly played a major role in his rapid rise to the title, two other factors were even more important. The first had to do with his style. Critics may have hated his slugging but awkward style, but fans loved it. When it came to matters of style, promoters listened to fans not critics, because it was the fans who paid the money that lined everyone's pockets. Even black sportswriters acknowledged that a large part of Marciano's promotional appeal was due more to his punching prowess. As Joc Bostic observed on the eve of Marciano's first title shot in September 1952, "The folks with an eye on the dollar feel sure that a change is imperative but, oddly enough, their desire in this direction doesn't hinge entirely on the pigmentation issue. To them the change is needed to get a guy in the saddle who is splashed generously with the intangible called 'color' or flare for the spectacular, which draws the customers through the gates in droves to see a guy do his number." To Bostic, Marciano (like Louis and Dempsey before him) had that type of "color." Still, Bostic didn't completely read race out of the Marciano equation. "The racists hope he wins for another reason, which has no place in the sporting thinking of decent people," he observed. "To them, the question of racial superiority is involved and they feel it's wrong for the minority group, which they feel is inferior, to head up anything that is a test of prowess. . . . But, the less said about such subhumans the better."[33]

Marciano's punch was especially valued at the time because of the comatose state of the heavyweight division. After Louis retired in 1949, big heavyweight fights were limited almost exclusively to long-drawn-out affairs between Charles and Walcott. Between June 1949 and June 1952 the duo fought four times for the championship. Years later, some would fondly remember the Charles-Walcott fights as bouts that "could serve as boxing textbooks, magnificent matchups of two of the cleverest fighters in history."[34] At the time, though, they bored everyone. Long before the merciful conclusion of the Charles-Walcott series the press and public had sounded the call for a new face in the heavyweight division.

Along came Rocky Marciano. With his punch and his exciting style, he was just what people had long awaited. Despite his flaws, Marciano was never boring. His bold, reckless slugging, observed Jesse Abramson, promised "a new heavyweight era following four years of rule by princes of caution." Marciano, Matt Ring of the *Philadelphia Evening Bulletin* theorized, was "a young man with the strength, punch and combative spirit to rescue the world heavyweight championship from the domination of the elderly Jersey Joe Walcott and the aging Ezzard Charles."[35] The IBC was naturally thrilled to find a young slugger who had an exciting style and might bring back a big gate—and it backed him to the hilt accordingly.

Ultimately, though, the biggest factor in Marciano's rapid rise to the top of the heavyweight division had nothing to do with style or race. It had to do with connections. In an era where the influence of the men who backed you largely determined your ring fortunes, Marciano had the most powerful backer of all: Al Weill. Institutionally, Weill wielded considerable power because he was the matchmaker of the IBC. He also controlled (albeit on the sly) a young heavyweight who had some talent and a perfect record to boot. Under these circumstances, Weill would use his power to get his fighter a championship fight. That the fighter in question, Rocky Marciano, had the punch everyone looked for was a bonus. That he happened to be white was also helpful in terms of expediting the process. Regardless of style or race, though, Al Weill's boy was going to get his shot—no matter what.

● ● ●

The advantage Marciano enjoyed with the press and promoters because of his race, however qualified, presumably carried over to boxing's lifeblood—its fans. As Marciano would move toward the title, the press seemed to sense that he was on the verge of being embraced by the masses. Matt Ring called him the "most popular challenger to strive for the heavyweight title in more than a generation." "Rocky Marciano," Franklin Lewis of the *Cleveland Press* predicted, "could be the most popular heavyweight champion since Jack Dempsey. . . . [He] is a plain, everyday fighter. He doesn't stand for anything special, such as race or creed or youth leadership."[36] Lewis's protestations aside, Marciano clearly stood for his race, at least in the eyes of some fans. Also, unlike white sportswriters (who were not in a position to cheer openly for Marciano), white fans had no such shackles. They could cheer for Marciano as loudly and openly as they wished. White people in the early 1950s rooted for their own.

Or did they? For sure, Marciano had fans—many of them. He was, in fact, a crowd-pleaser and favorite. Yet all white fans did not automatically back Marciano merely because he was white. Crowd applause and reaction, however unscientific, was a key barometer. The crowd at the first Walcott-Marciano fight in Philadelphia, for instance, would be evenly divided in sentiment. As Jerry Nason of the *Boston Globe* reassured readers, "The pigment of their skins cut no sentimental yardgoods, either way, in this huge crowd."[37] If anything, more fans were pulling for Walcott, given the fact he was from nearby Camden, New Jersey. The same pattern would hold true in Marciano's other fights with black challengers. If some people cheered for the white champion, others did for the black challenger. Many rooted for Marciano's opponent not because of color but because they liked to back a courageous underdog, whether black or white. Indeed, the two white men who would challenge Marciano during his reign (Roland LaStarza and Don Cockell) garnered crowd support for precisely that reason.

The crowds in the stadiums would not be the only ones to see Marciano fight live. Fans in theaters across the country also watched on the rapidly expanding closed-circuit network. Like those who were there in person, the fans who watched the fight on-screen (most of whom were white) were typically split in sentiment. For the first Walcott-Marciano fight, for instance, crowd support was divided in Los Angeles, San Francisco, and Baltimore theaters. For the first Marciano-Charles fight, fans in a San Francisco theater were strongly pro-Marciano at the beginning of the evening. As Charles made his gallant stand, however, "sentiment switched to his side," reported Eddie Muller of the *San Francisco Examiner.* "Even Marciano rooters tempered their outbursts and we'd venture to say they inwardly hoped Charles would go all the way." At the end of the fight, Charles received a standing ovation from the audience.[38]

The situation was vastly different in the few black theaters on the closed-circuit network. The crowds in those theaters were rabidly for the black challenger. During the first Marciano-Charles fight, for instance, a Baltimore audience made up primarily of black fans cheered Charles as he entered the ring and booed and even laughed at Marciano's initial appearance. Once the fight began, fans urged on their favorite with cheers of "get him Charles" and "come on Charles." When Marciano started to bleed, there was enjoyment. When he started to take control, there were groans. When television announcer Jimmy Powers praised Marciano, there were cries of "oh man, shut up." When Powers remained silent during a Charles flurry, there were cries of "say something, man." And when Marciano was awarded the decision, there was great disappointment all around.[39]

The situation would also be different for Marciano's final fight with Archie Moore. In the months before the title tilt, Moore waged a long publicity campaign targeted at Marciano to get the fight. The campaign involved some belittling of the white champion but was only marginally mean-spirited and had, in fact, a certain underlying humor and good-naturedness. Still, judging by the reaction among the closed-circuit audience, it likely provoked some backlash among white fans across the country. Those in a Philadelphia theater were "heatedly partisan for Marciano," as were fans in a San Francisco theater.[40]

Significantly, fans in theaters in Atlanta, Charlotte, Louisville, New Orleans, and several other southern cities finally added to the closed-circuit network were also rooting for Marciano against Moore. Race certainly helped dictate the intensity of their support. At a New Orleans theater, for instance, the emcee for the evening's festivities evoked a hostile reaction when he predicted that Moore would win. As Bill Keefe reported, "[T]he second he cast his lot with the Negro he became an oratorical suicide—a dead duck as speaker of the house. They wouldn't let him say another word and even booed him. . . . A most partisan house it turned out to be as attested by the fact that every time Bill Corum, the commentator, would say anything favorable for Moore, he in far-away New York, would be drowned out by boos, too." Of course, given Keefe's track record and the fact that he regarded Moore as a "rather fat old Negro," this may not have constituted objective journalism.[41]

The New Orleans incident nevertheless suggests that fans in the South, as opposed to those in the North, probably cheered for Marciano more openly and rabidly, or, more accurately, they were cheering against his black opponent. That had little to do with Marciano and more to do with southern culture, which was still locked into Jim Crow and farther behind the North in terms of racial enlightenment. Many in the South were more inclined to see everything in terms of race, including boxing. In the early 1950s interracial boxing matches were a burning issue in states such as Louisiana and Texas. In 1956 Louisiana even passed a law prohibiting such fights. Many southerners, then, didn't even want to see a white man and a black man together in the same ring. When white and black did meet, they rooted for the white man.

The New Orleans incident also indicates that the racial calm that prevailed when Marciano fought was delicate indeed. Many white people in the early 1950s—southerners and northerners, sportswriters and fans—would accept a black athlete only if he "knew his place." That meant he had to act like Louis, who had won initial acceptance only because he made clear that he didn't want to offend white people and was willing to live by the standards of white society. In other words, Louis projected the image of a well-behaved "colored boy," which was the type of behavior white sportswriters and fans wanted—and demanded—from blacks who sought to play in the big time.

Black athletes who came after Louis followed the blueprint. Jackie Robinson, for example, despite all his competitive fire, turned the other cheek and kept his mouth shut in public (at least initially). This was also certainly true of Marciano's first two black title opponents, Walcott and Charles. They acted like gentlemen, avoided out-of-the-ring escapades, kept their mouths shut, and were respectful and reverential to whites. As Robert Lipsyte of the *New York Times* observes, between Jack Johnson and Muhammad Ali, "for that fifty odd years, if there were black champions, they were honorary white guys." Walcott and Charles fit into that category. Ultimately, though, meeting expectations and knowing one's place only ensured acceptance of a certain condescending kind. As Breslin incredulously notes, "Walcott was a credit to his race . . . Louis before him was a credit to his race. Imagine that? That's what they said."[42]

With all his bluster, Archie Moore would test the boundaries of the "know your place" requirement, and some sportswriters would be uncomfortable with the fact that he was pushing the limits of acceptable behavior. Sam Greene of the *Detroit News,* for example, maintained that Moore had "cheapened himself as a challenger by wanton boasting." Added Furman Bisher, "He is cold and unsympathetic to strangers, doesn't offer Marciano's kind of common touch warmth as a champion. He is merely a guy who has talked himself into the fight and spent a considerable amount of time and words trying to talk Marciano out of it."[43] The backlash wasn't limited to just sportswriters, either. It also swept up many fans, probably including those rooting for Marciano (and against Moore) in Philadelphia, San Francisco, Atlanta, Charlotte, Louisville, and New Orleans movie houses on the night of the fight.

The negative reaction against Moore in some quarters might have been more extreme had Marciano endorsed or participated in it. But he did not. Throughout his career, Marciano, to his credit, avoided playing on racial issues. He never made a snide comment about the color of his opponent's skin, nor did he ever subtly try to raise the specter of a race conflict. Other men in his position might have done so, either because they wanted to capitalize on the prejudice of the public or because they were prejudiced themselves. Marciano, however, wasn't that devious. Nor was he that prejudiced. He enjoyed cordial if not warm relations with all the black men he fought. They liked him and he liked them.

In the final analysis, Marciano probably liked black opponents more than most fans did. Although all white people didn't root for Marciano just because he was white, some most assuredly did. Race at least entered into the equation for many more. It was, after all, the early 1950s and before the civil rights movement. Equality between the races was a foreign concept. Prejudice still prevailed throughout society, and many whites continued to view blacks as second-class citizens and naturally inferior. Given those realities, Rocky Marciano naturally enjoyed an advantage with many white fans. He, too, was white. As Bud Collins (who long before emerging as a tennis authority covered Marciano as a cub reporter) points out, "We've been looking for Great White Hopes ever since Jack Johnson. Certainly [his race] was a factor in his popularity. I think it is for any white fighter, but especially the heavyweight champion—and it had been a long time since Braddock. He was always fighting black guys, and I think there was a racial feeling there."[44]

•   •   •

Ultimately, the effect of Marciano's race on his popularity would have limits. The color of his skin wouldn't ensure his immediate popularity. One year into Marciano's reign, Harvey Breit of the *New York Times* noted that he had "not yet caught fire, nor yet captured the popular imagination. And he may never." Eventually, though, Marciano did capture the public imagination. At the end of his career, most would have agreed when the *New York Herald Tribune* called him "an extremely popular champion."[45] Marciano, however, never attained wild, over-the-top popularity, in part because his reign was so short (less than four years). Had he continued for several more years he would probably have achieved a more stratospheric level of popularity.

Perhaps that would not have happened, however, for several other factors restrained his popularity. One such factor was the IBC. Many in the early 1950s disliked the IBC on the grounds that the organization was controlling, monopolistic, and corrupt. It hardly constituted high praise, then, when reporters called Marciano an "IBC house fighter," "an IBC employee," or the IBC's "glowering favorite son." Many, in fact, thought of him as the IBC's pawn. As Bostic complained after Marciano beat Layne, "Here is a good strong young fighter, who nevertheless has not yet had any real baptism under fire. Still he comes into the Garden as a main eventer and wins a so so victory and is spotted for a shot at the world's championship. How cheap can the title become? . . . [H]e's going to get a shot and that's what counts. And to the hell with the fans." Several months later, after Marciano stumbled to a victory over Lee Savold in early 1952, Bostic would snort, "Marciano looked like a rank amateur and yet they are going to maneuver him into the heavyweight title."[46]

Bostic was hardly alone in transferring his anger toward the IBC to Marciano. Jerry Nason of the *Boston Globe* once noted that there was no "finer young fellow than Rocky Marciano." Still, there was a problem. "Far behind Marciano," he wrote, "stands the somewhat sinister International Boxing Club, and its matchmaker, Al Weill, and an ill-disguised plot to monopolize the sport of boxing through the ancient stratagem of 'owning' all the fighters." Although Nason admired Marciano personally, he admitted that he found it difficult to ignore the fact that Marciano was an IBC house fighter. Others took this a step further and rooted against Marciano because of his association with the IBC.[47]

It was Marciano's connection with Al Weill, however, that really damaged his popularity. As IBC matchmaker, Weill made many enemies among fight managers with his dictatorial ways. The managers exacted their revenge by blasting Marciano in fight circles. Weill was also unpopular among other rank-and-file members of the fight mob—including, most importantly, many boxing writers, who had the power of the pen to influence the public. The writers got back at Weill by harping upon Marciano's awkwardness and the caliber of fighter he had faced in building his knockout string. Some of the ill-will most assuredly spilled over to readers. And, as with the IBC bashers, the Weill haters took out their anger by rooting against Weill's boy, Rocky Marciano. For these people, the fact that Marciano was white could not and did not override their feelings toward Weill.

To the extent that Marciano attained substantial popularity—and he did—it wasn't simply because he was a white man. Marciano had a lot of other things going for him. For one, many people liked Marciano the man. That they did so was due in large part to his image. As we shall see, Marciano came to symbolize his times and embody the precious American Way of Life. And who in the early 1950s didn't embrace the American Way of Life? Moreover, everyone loves a winner, and Marciano won. For that reason alone, many people rallied to his side as his winning streak grew and grew and never ended.

And then there was his style, which not only greatly accounted for his promotional appeal but was also a major factor in his appeal to fans—a factor, in retrospect, that was even more important than race in the Marciano popularity mix. Jimmy Breslin, for instance, believes that Marciano's race "was everything. It always is. Color trumps." Still, Breslin feels that Marciano was popular among fans primarily "because he could knock people out." Similarly, while Robert Lipsyte admits that Marciano's race "absolutely" impacted his popularity, he points to his style as the more important factor. "It was a very manly style," says Lipsyte. "He was willing to take punches to give them. He came straight ahead. He was bull-like. He was powerful." Lou Duva contends that Marciano emerged "because he was white, because he was Italian, but mostly because he was a tough guy."[48]

Furman Bisher points to yet another factor that had an impact on Marciano's popularity: "I think Joe Louis, as far as I'm concerned, was as popular a fighter as Rocky Marciano was. In my eyes, he still is . . . I don't think that we had that much of an issue black/white at that time. As far as I'm concerned, any time that Joe Louis fought anybody, I was pulling for Joe Louis."[49] Like Charles and Walcott, Louis's immediate successors, Marciano never completely escaped Louis's enormous shadow. Although all the tangible benefits of being the Great White Hope in the early 1950s may have put Marciano in a plum position, they didn't guarantee that he would be the apple of everyone's eye.

5 The Uncrowned Champion

For many fans of the early 1950s, the fact that Ezzard Charles and then Jersey Joe Walcott held the title of heavyweight champion of the world was a mere technicality. In their minds and in their hearts there was only one true champion: Joe Louis. The sudden arrival of a new Great White Hope on the scene may have been interesting—particularly given how that dynamic had long played into the career of their man—but it hardly altered that fundamental conclusion.

Louis, of course, had formally held the crown from 1937 to 1949, and during the course of his long reign he had proven himself a great fighter. Many still believe that the best heavyweight on the planet—ever—was the young Joe Louis. In his prime years before World War II, Louis was very much the complete heavyweight. He had it all—a stinging left jab, deadly combinations, a knockout punch, defensive craftsmanship, and a full complement of the necessary intangibles. Once in a while, he would have an off-night and someone like Billy Conn would come close to beating him. He even lost once—to Max Schmeling in 1936. But that was an aberration. Usually, Joe Louis was invincible and indestructible. He was, by all accounts, a great heavyweight champion.

After the war, though, Louis wasn't the same fighter. The years in the service had eroded his skills and dulled his reflexes. At first the decline was barely noticeable, as he beat Conn handily in their 1946 rematch. But then, in December 1947, an obscure journeyman named Jersey Joe Walcott battered Louis around the Garden. Louis won the disputed decision, but the fight was a wake-up call concerning his abilities. He was no longer invincible and indestructible. Louis beat Walcott in a rematch and then retired with his championship in early 1949. Everyone applauded. He had been a great champion but was no longer a great fighter. It was time to go.

There was a problem, however. Joe Louis was broke. Years of careless spending, financial mismanagement, and poor counsel had landed him in a heap of tax trouble. In 1950 the IRS determined that Louis owed more than $500,000 in back taxes. Louis needed money and he needed it fast, so he returned to the ring, agreeing to meet champion Ezzard Charles in Yankee Stadium in September 1950. In his comeback fight Louis showed only a few flashes of the old Louis. Instead, he just looked old. By fight's end, the tubby Louis was bleeding, wincing, and on the verge of being knocked out. The judges awarded Charles a unanimous decision. It was deserved—he had clearly dominated the fight. "I'll never fight again," Louis announced after the bout.[1]

But he did fight again. He had no choice. He was still broke, and he still owed the IRS a lot of money. (Sadly, Louis would never climb out of his financial hole.) In 1951 he was back on the comeback trail, fighting (and beating) boxers such as Cesar Brion, Omelio Agramonte, Freddie Beshore, Andy Walker, Lee Savold, and Jimmy Bivins. For his legion of old fans and admirers—at least those with some grounding in reality—it was sad to witness his slow, sluggish performances. He may have been good enough to beat the mediocre heavyweights of the world, but he had clearly lost much of his greatness. By the fall of 1951 he was still Joe Louis—but in name only.

It is unclear whether Rocky Marciano's pilot, Al Weill, wanted to match his young tiger against Louis that fall. Depending on the account, he either actively sought the match (because he felt that the fading Louis was ripe for the picking) or actively fought the match (because he feared what the old champion might do to his inexperienced fighter). Whatever the case, even Weill had to recognize that it made no sense to send Marciano back to Providence to fight another string of second-raters. After beating Rex Layne in July 1951 and then an out-of-shape and over-the-hill Freddie Beshore in August, Marciano was hot and in the limelight—and he needed to stay there. That meant a big fight against a big name, preferably either Charles or Louis. The field narrowed after Charles lost his championship to Walcott in July 1951. Charles, licking his wounds and waiting for a promised rematch against Walcott, wasn't about to risk his shot at regaining the title by facing the dangerous Marciano. That left Louis.

If Louis made sense for Marciano, Marciano also made sense for Louis. The former champion was in search of a big payday. Ideally, the big-money bout would have involved another crack at reclaiming his lost championship, and for a while that was the plan. Louis was supposed to get a rematch with the champion Charles in September 1951, but that went by the wayside when Charles lost the title to Walcott. Jersey Joe had waited a long time to win the title and was in no hurry to defend it. Shortly after winning the title in July 1951, Walcott announced that he would not fight again until the summer of 1952—and against Charles no less. That meant Louis was frozen out of the title picture until late 1952 at the earliest, although he was in no position to wait—he desperately needed the money. With Walcott and Charles temporarily unavailable as opponents, the new kid on the block, Rocky Marciano, offered Louis the biggest payday. He couldn't afford to turn the fight down.

Still, the Louis-Marciano fight almost didn't happen. Like many people in the fight game, Louis wasn't particularly fond of Weill. In fact, he despised him. The feeling was mutual. As Joe Bostic of the *New York Amsterdam News* observed, "Weill hates Louis with a cold, quiet fury that only good judgment and organizational protocol has prevented from breaking out into the open. Nor does Mr. W appear to Joe as a living reincarnation of Sir Galahad or Robin Hood."[2] A key bone of contention between the two involved Weill's behavior at the Sugar Ray Robinson–Jake LaMotta middleweight championship fight on Valentine's Day 1951. Sitting at ringside, Weill rooted openly and loudly for LaMotta to beat Robinson, perhaps because he had a bet riding on the outcome. Weill's cheering rankled Sugar Ray's close friend Joe Louis, also at ringside for the fight. That Robinson eventually won the fight by a knockout didn't dissipate his anger toward Weill.

He still remembered six months later when the IBC came calling to ask Louis to fight Weill's boy, Rocky Marciano. Louis, instead of accepting the customary even split of gate receipts between the two fighters (which would have resulted in 30 percent for each boxer) demanded 45 percent of the receipts (leaving Marciano with but a paltry 15 percent share). Weill tried to talk Louis down, but Louis wasn't about to listen. Nor did Louis listen to the pleas of Jim Norris, the head of the IBC. So Norris turned to Marciano. He called the young fighter into his office and asked if he would like to fight Louis. Marciano replied that he would. "Well," Norris said, "the only way I can make the match is if you'll agree to take 15 per cent." When Marciano demurred, asserting that he should receive at least 20 percent, Norris told him, "You better take a walk around the corner and think it over."[3] Marciano thought about it and accepted the 15 percent.

The fight was originally set for October 11, 1951, at the Polo Grounds. But this was the autumn of Bobby Thomson and Ralph Branca and the famous "Shot Heard around the World." The unexpected late surge of the Giants tied up their ballpark and forced the IBC to reschedule the fight to October 26 in the Garden. When the baseball buzz finally quieted, everyone began to to concentrate on the fight—particularly on Louis. Boxing writers, columnists, and hangers-on flocked to his training camp in Pompton Lakes, New Jersey, where he was working with trainer Mannie Seamon. They came away impressed. The new Joe Louis, they concluded, looked very much like the old Joe Louis. Like the old days, he looked fit and trim. Like the old days, he looked lethal, knocking out sparring partners on a regular basis. Most encouraging, like the old days, he was putting together his combinations, or as sportswriters liked to call it, "the old one-two." Seamon joyously proclaimed, "He just couldn't get the one-two working before. Now he has it."[4]

Louis seemed to have regained his mental edge as well. He seemed determined to show that he wasn't washed up and that he could, in time, reclaim his throne as heavyweight king. "As long as either Walcott or Charles is champion, I'm going to keep chasing . . . I can beat them," he proclaimed. He was also certain that he could beat Marciano, publicly predicting a knockout. Louis's confidence even shaped the prefight publicity gags. He reportedly walked out of a showing of the Marciano-Layne fight film, declaring, "He can't fight." For his part, Marciano seemed unperturbed when news of the flap trickled over to his own camp at nearby Greenwood Lake. "I don't blame Joe for walking out on the pictures," he joked. "I didn't look good to myself when I saw them."[5]

Publicly, Marciano appeared relaxed and was confident that he would beat Louis. "I only hope that after I beat Louis, the people don't say I beat a washed-up fighter," he told reporters. Moreover, unlike Louis's opponents of yore who would quake at the mere thought of entering the ring with the champion, Marciano seemed unafraid. "It's just another fight," he shrugged. Privately, though, Marciano didn't like what he was hearing out of Pompton Lakes. "Louis really had me worried in advance," he later admitted. "Everyone kept talking about the wonderful shape he was in during his training. He was knocking down sparring partners right and left."[6]

By the eve of the fight the public retained confidence in Louis. He would enter the ring as a 7-5 favorite, and although that was the shortest price ever for a Louis fight, he was still the favorite. The man on the street may have thought Marciano would win, but the boxing intelligentsia backed Louis. Members of the fight mob knew Louis had slipped—that he was, in the words of Jesse Abramson of the *New York Herald Tribune,* a "deteriorated and deteriorating fighter"—but they were encouraged by his training camp performance.[7] He looked better than he had at any point since he originally came back in September 1950 against Charles. For sure he wasn't the Joe Louis of 1938. Perhaps, though, he was the Joe Louis of 1946, the Louis who had been good enough to beat Conn in their rematch—and the Louis who would be good enough to tame the young Rocky Marciano.

They based their belief on Louis's boxing abilities, reasoning that he still had too many skills and would altogether be too much fighter for Marciano. Louis's advantages in reach (nine inches), height (three inches), and weight (twenty-five pounds) would be too much for Marciano to overcome. Louis would use all his years of accumulated ring experience to outsmart Marciano. He would win because he was still, above all, Joe Louis. Indeed, sportswriters and fans had grown up with Louis. They wanted to believe that he was still the dominant fighter of yesteryear. As A. J. Liebling of the *New Yorker* admitted after watching Louis beat Savold in the summer of 1951, "I came away singularly revived—as if I, rather than Louis, had demonstrated resistance to the erosion of time. As long as Joe could get by, I felt, I had a link with an era when we were both a lot younger."[8]

Such nostalgia led boxing writers like Matt Ring of the *Philadelphia Evening Bulletin* to proclaim that "the only way Marciano can win is by accident." Most other boxing writers offered more tempered opinions but still predicted that Louis would win. There were only a few dissenters—most ominously Sam Lacy, the legendary black sports columnist for the *Baltimore Afro-American,* who simply stated, "Joe Louis will be sorry on Oct. 26."[9]

The story line was clear and obvious for the evening of October 26. As Abramson observed, "It is a provocative match—age against youth, experience against stamina, a classic stylist of the ring against relatively raw power, an ex-champion against a possible champion-to-be meeting at the crossroads." As a veteran fight man remarked somewhat less dramatically, "It's a case of how far has the young guy come and how far has the old guy gone."[10] The story line caught on, generating huge interest in the fight. More than seventeen thousand fans in the Garden in addition to a nationwide television audience waited to see whether Louis was really back or whether Marciano would send him back for good.

● ● ●

On the night of October 26, 1951, two men sat around a New York hotel suite. Noticing that it was already seven o'clock, one, Al Weill, said to the other, Charley Goldman, "Wake the man up." After looking at his watch, Goldman replied, "Right." He went into one of the suite's bedrooms and mussed the hair of "the man" sleeping in the bed. "Up, Rocky," Goldman said. "There's work to do." It was time for Rocky Marciano to get up and head toward the arena. It was time to fight Joe Louis.[11]

By the time he entered the ring a few hours later, Rocky Marciano was not only awake but also nervous. He had fought a few big fights in the Garden before, but this was different. This was Joe Louis. As a boy growing up in Brockton, Marciano had idolized Louis. He had even daydreamed of fighting him for the championship of the world. Now he was fighting Louis for real. To Marciano, Louis appeared not only larger than life but also large. "I remember standing in the ring and thinking how big Louis was," he recalled. "I had never remembered Louis being such a big guy. The top of my head seemed to just about reach the bottom of his chin." Waiting in his corner for the opening bell, butterflies churning full blast in his stomach, Marciano looked to his wily old trainer for advice. "Make it a short fight," Charley Goldman counseled. "At my age I can't be runnin' up and down them steps all night."[12]

Marciano nearly carried out Goldman's instructions to a tee. For most of the first round the two fighters followed the age-old custom of feeling each other out. Then, toward the very end of the round, Marciano buckled Louis's knees with a looping right to the jaw. Louis clutched at Marciano, and then the bell sounded. The old champion had narrowly averted disaster. "If I had had just five or ten more seconds, I think I could have put him out of the way," Marciano later said. A shaken Louis returned to his corner, where his trainer Mannie Seamon yelled in his ear above the din of the Garden crowd, "Are you all right? Are you all right?"[13] Meanwhile, in Marciano's corner, Charley Goldman was grinning.

Louis steadied, though. For a while, he even looked like the Louis of old, the Louis everyone wanted to remember. If there was one boxing skill he still possessed, it was his left jab. He used that stinging jab, sprinkled with the occasional right cross, to pile up points in rounds three, four, and five. Marciano was never in serious trouble, but Louis's jabs nevertheless made an impact. "It was like getting hit in the face with a hammer," Marciano would recall. After their hero's shaky start, Louis's supporters swelled with optimism. Liebling later admitted, "When the fifth round ended, marking the halfway point of the fight, I felt that it would be a long way home but that Louis would make it."[14]

In actuality, Louis was beginning to run out of gas. Goldman's prefight strategy had called for Marciano to apply continuous pressure in order to wear the older man down. Marciano dutifully carried out the strategy. As Louis was scoring with his jabs, Marciano was continuing to hurl wild rights of his own. Many missed the mark entirely, but the ones that did land began to have an effect on Louis's arms and body. By the midpoint of the fight, Louis knew he was fading. At one point, after hitting Marciano with a solid jab, he failed to follow up. "He look sort of funny," Louis remembered. "Then, I look down at my right hand to see what happen to it, and it's just hung there and then I know I was an old man in there."[15] Other ringside observers identified the turning point as a fifth-round Marciano punch under the heart that made Louis visibly gasp. From then on, Marciano seemed renewed with confidence while Louis seemed demoralized.

By the sixth round, the tide had plainly turned. "It wasn't that Marciano grew better or stronger; it was that Louis seemed to get slower and weaker," Liebling observed. "The spring was gone from his legs—and it had been only a slight spring in the beginning—and in the clinches Marciano was shoving him around." Marciano's aggressiveness and constant pressure had worn Louis down. His legs were gone. His right hand had been nonexistent from the outset. ("What surprised me," Marciano noted after the fight, "was that Joe didn't have much of a right. They told me he had lost some of his power, but I didn't expect nothing. That's what his right hand was—nothing.") Now his left jabs were beginning to lose their sting as well, in part of because of a hand injury he suffered earlier in the fight. As Louis explained afterward, refusing to make excuses, "I hurt it in the third round. But that had nothing to do with the fight."[16]

By the seventh round, Marciano was in clear command. Comfortably ahead on all the scorecards, the younger man padded his lead by driving the older man to the ropes, shoving him around at will, and nailing him with powerful rights to the head. Louis tried to answer by landing a powerful left hook to Marciano's jaw toward the end of the round. "It was beautiful," Liebling wrote. "It hit Marciano flush on the right side of the jaw, but it didn't seem to faze him a bit. I knew then that Joe was beaten, but I thought that it might be only a decision."[17] Even though he had faded, Louis didn't appear to be in grave danger of being knocked out.

But he was. When Louis began tiring at midfight, his defensive walls started to lower. "He kept dropping his right hand," Marciano said. "I knew I could catch him. His right kept going down and down, little by little." Marciano now had his target as well as the weapon—the left hook he had developed under Goldman's tutelage—necessary to hit that target. As he headed out for the eighth round, Goldman said to Marciano, "Get him now."[18]

Marciano did get him. First he knocked Louis down with a short left hook to the jaw. Louis waited out the count on one knee and then got to his feet, trying to fight back. But he was done. Sensing the kill, Marciano swarmed over him, wild-eyed and open-mouthed. Louis had a temporary reprieve when Marciano missed with a flurry of wild haymakers. Then he connected with two more left hooks that effectively finished Louis. In the dressing room after the fight, Marciano would raise his left hand and proclaim, "I knew this was going to do it . . . that was the baby that did the job." Louis agreed that "it was his left that set me up. That one did the trick." Marciano ended matters with an overhand right. "I saw the right hand coming, but I couldn't do anything about it," Louis said later. "I was awfully tired. I'm too old, I guess."[19]

The final right that put Louis away sent him toppling through the ropes and onto the ring apron, where sportswriters held his head up to prevent him from tumbling further onto press row. Louis tried futilely to get up, but the fight was clearly over. Referee Ruby Goldstein didn't even attempt a count but waved his arms to signal the halt of the evening's proceedings. Louis rolled his head from side to side in bewilderment. The ringside doctor rushed to his side, and it appeared that the old champion might seriously be hurt. After several anxious moments, though, the conscious but stunned Louis finally arose.

The crowd in the Garden that night was a Joe Louis crowd. They were intrigued by the new Great White Hope but not enough to root for him. Instead, they backed the former black champion, who had built up a reservoir of public affection during his long and glorious career. One such fan was a tall, blonde woman sitting near A. J. Liebling. Before the fight, she screamed at Marciano, "I hate him! I hate him! I think he's the most horrible thing I've ever seen." After Louis was knocked out, the woman wept and then booed. Her date said, "Rocky didn't do anything wrong. He didn't foul him. What you booing?" She replied, "You're so cold. I hate you, too."[20]

Others were less extreme but still disheartened by the outcome. They had come in hope that Louis would recapture some of his old championship form. Instead, they ended the evening by saying their final goodbye. Louis was through—and everyone finally knew it. No one had wanted to see his glorious career end with him knocked out, helpless, and dangling over the ring apron. As Arthur Daley of the *New York Times* lamented, "The moment everyone had been dreading finally arrived last night. . . . It had to happen some time and it happened last night."[21]

When it did happen, there was sadness all around. After Marciano knocked Louis down for the first time in the eighth round, Sugar Ray Robinson, Louis's friend, left his seat near ringside and slowly started to make his way toward the ring, almost in disbelief. By the time Marciano knocked Louis through the ropes, Robinson was at ringside, yelling words of encouragement and support. He looked as if he were ready to jump into the ring and help his fallen friend. As the ringside doctor and Louis's handlers tried to revive the former champion, Robinson remained in a state of shock, walking up and down the Garden aisle, shaking his head, and mumbling.

The sadness continued after Louis departed the ring and went to his dressing room. Outside the dressing room, a horde of admirers gathered. One, Josephine Baker, the great singer, stood speechless, her head bowed, waiting to shake Louis's hand. Others in the hallway were weeping. Inside the dressing room the scene was also dreary. Robinson was there, sobbing for his friend. Louis's handlers—trainer Seamon and manager Marshall Miles—were crying openly. Even the hardened sportswriters, scrambling to get postfight quotes to meet their deadlines, were visibly grieving for the fallen champion. Some had lumps in their throats; others were strangely quiet. Only Louis himself remained composed. "What's the use of crying," he said. "The better man won. That's all. Marciano is a good puncher and he's hard to hit. He has a funny style. I'm not too disappointed. I only hope everybody feels the way I do about it. I'm not looking for sympathy from anybody. I guess everything happens for the best."[22]

Rocky Marciano shared in the sadness as well. In the immediate afterglow of victory he had celebrated, jumping for joy, dancing around the ring, clasping and unclasping his hands, smiling widely, and repeating over and over, "I knocked him out! I knocked him out!" As was becoming customary, Marciano's fans from Brockton joined him in celebration, rushing to the ringside and shouting for their hero. Yet as Louis remained sprawled on the ring apron, Marciano began to pace the ring anxiously. Later, in the dressing room, he told the press, "I'm glad I won, but sorry I had to do it to him."[23]

Beneath the official proclamation was genuine sorrow. Louis was, after all, one of his heroes. "Rocky didn't have too many guys that he really looked up to," his brother Peter recalls. "But Joe Louis was one of them." Remembers Lou Duva, "If you wanted to see Rocky cry, see a grown man cry, you should have seen him cry after the fight when he knocked out Joe Louis in the dressing room when Joe had come in," Duva says. "He didn't want to hurt Joe, he knew Joe was done at that time." Marciano would never really shake the feeling of remorse. "To the day he died, Rocky felt awful about beating Louis," Al Falloni, a future business associate of Marciano's, would say years later. "When he was a kid he used to listen to Joe's fights on the radio and Rocky worshipped the guy. He hated to knock him out."[24]

In the days following the fight, attention remained squarely on Louis. "An old man's dream ended," Red Smith rhapsodized. "A young man's vision of the future opened wide. Young men have visions, old men have dreams. But the place for old men to dream is beside the fire." Arthur Daley also saw the fight as a dream—"a strange, unpleasant, nasty sort of dream. Joe Louis, the symbol of invincibility, of dignity, of class and of compelling majesty, had suddenly vanished. Plop! he was gone." Daley mused that perhaps he should be writing about the fighter with the future (Marciano) rather than the fighter with the past (Louis). "But this reporter has been carrying the torch for Joe much too long to start any new flirtation," Daley proclaimed. "It's still love. In this corner Louis losing is more important than Marciano winning."[25]

Eventually, though, attention switched from Joe Louis to Rocky Marciano. Before the fight, Marciano was still an unknown in many quarters. True, he had beaten LaStarza and Layne in legitimate big fights in the Garden. Those fights, though, did not attract nationwide interest but had only caught on in the East. The Louis fight was different. Everyone—east, west, north, and south—paid attention when Louis fought. Now, for the first time, everyone was paying attention to Marciano.

Television helped, too. Marciano had been on television before—against LaStarza in early 1950—but that fight was only broadcast to half the country at a time when a lot of people still didn't own a television set. A year and a half later, far more Americans did own a television. The Louis fight was broadcast not just to the East and points in the Midwest but to the entire country. It was the first important heavyweight fight to be shown on television from coast to coast, with NBC broadcasting the bout on a network of forty-two stations. The result for Marciano was unprecedented exposure to the nation's sports fans.

The Louis victory brought Marciano more than just exposure. As Charley Goldman pointed out, "No matter what happens to him, he's already done the one thing that will always make him a famous boxer. Just as James J. Corbett is remembered as the guy who knocked out John L. Sullivan, Rocky Marciano will always be remembered as the guy who finished Joe Louis." In so doing, Marciano ended Louis's long (albeit recently unofficial) reign as champion. Now Marciano, not Louis, was the "uncrowned heavy-weight champion of the world." Officially, of course, Walcott held the ti-tle. Although he was a very good fighter and a nice story, Walcott was seen as nothing more than an interregnum ruler. In the public's mind, Marciano was now, in the words of Earl Lofquist of the *Providence Journal,* "the uncrowned heavyweight champion of the world, the heir presumptive who will take on the winner of the Walcott-Charles fight for the official title."[26] The official coronation of Rocky Marciano seemed a matter of destiny.

Marciano still had critics, of course. Against Louis, he had been solid, workmanlike, ultimately spectacular, and, to some experts, flawed. As Harry LeDuc of the *Detroit News* proclaimed, Marciano's "ring ability is with-out relation to the science of boxing. . . . The execution was a success, but the executioner lacked finesse." The criticism seemed less meaningful, how-ever, given that Marciano had succeeded Louis as uncrowned champion. Louis himself seemed to endorse his successor. As he told Wendell Smith of the *Pittsburgh Courier,* "He was tough, real tough. . . . He's a good fighter. Better than most people realize. He's strong and young and hard to hit. He was definitely the better man."[27]

● ● ●

By this point in his life, Rocky Marciano was, to a significant extent, still fighting out of fear of the shoe factories. Before the Louis fight, when re-porters asked whether he might choke on the night of the big event, he re-plied, "Look, when I was discharged from the army, I started fighting be-cause I hated the jobs I had before I went into the service. I'm afraid of having to go back and doing some of those same things if I lose to Louis. So natu-rally, I'm not going to choke up."[28]

Now something else was driving Rocky Marciano—the heavyweight championship of the world. The uncrowned champion clearly wanted the crown. "I want to get the title," he told the press on the eve of the Louis fight. "I want to kayo Louis because it will move me closer to the champi-onship of the world. To me, being the champ means everything. It's got everything any guy would want." His tunnel vision impressed Don Dun-phy, the legendary boxing announcer, when the two sat next to each other at a banquet in Buffalo around this time. Dunphy had seen Marciano in the ring a few times and had come away unimpressed, rating him as nothing more than a good journeyman. During dinner, though, Dunphy began to revise his opinion. Here was a young man, he thought, who was intense and supremely confident in his abilities. "Don, I'm gonna win that title," Mar-ciano told him. Dunphy began to believe.[29]

So did Marciano's brain trust, Charley Goldman and Al Weill. "I knew I had the champion the night he fought Joe Louis," Goldman later said. Weill was ebullient but for a different reason. In the dressing room immediately after the fight, Weill pointed at Marciano and said, "There stands two million bucks in cold cash." Weill was in the catbird seat now, and he knew it. Ironically, only several months earlier he had been in a precarious position. There were rumors from New York that the dissatisfied IBC was on the verge of dumping him as its matchmaker. Moreover, the ballyhooed fighter he was managing on the sly had yet to impress in the big time. Then Marciano clobbered Rex Layne and Joe Louis. With those victories, the IBC suddenly needed him more than he needed the IBC. As Gerry Hern of the *Boston Post* recognized, "In one quick move, Weill thus became the top man in the business. He owns the rights to Rocky, and he controls the cards of the International Boxing Club. He's a very big man."[30]

After Louis, Weill wasn't thinking of matching Marciano with anyone—at least for the time being. He knew that the schedule called for Walcott to fight Charles in the summer of 1952, which meant that Marciano likely wouldn't get his title shot until well into 1952. Besides, Marciano had traveled a long way in a short time. He needed a rest. Citing the fact that he had bruised his hand in knocking out Louis, his handlers announced several days after the fight that Marciano would not fight again in 1951.

Then Marciano hit the road, embarking on a long barnstorming tour across America, complete with personal appearances, exhibitions, banquets, and even vaudeville. Much to Weill's delight, the new uncrowned champion proved a good draw. As Matt Ring wrote in February 1952, "They flocked to see him wherever he went. . . . In the last three months, Rocky is believed to have done better business with public appearances than champion Walcott." Marciano, wrote Mike Thomas of the *Providence Journal,* "was caught in whirl of hysteria after his defeat of Louis and he went for the ride."[31]

Around this time he first saw the potential downside of the glare of the spotlight. During an exhibition tour in Maine, Marciano's opponent in some towns was "Pete Fuller." In other towns it was "Tony Zullo." Only it wasn't really Fuller or Zullo (two well-regarded amateurs who couldn't make the tour) but Marciano's younger brother Sonny, who was still a student at Brockton High School. The problem on the Maine exhibition tour wasn't ability—a natural middleweight, Sonny could hold his own in sparring sessions with his older (and bigger) brother—it was appearance. "We looked so much alike," Sonny Marciano recalls today. "When I walked out, you could hear the crowd—they thought at first that I was Rocky." Eventually, the Maine Boxing Commission uncovered the ruse and suspended Marciano for thirty days. He was criticized for engineering the charade and eventually accepted the criticism. "It was a stupid thing to do, and I had no excuses for it," he later admitted.[32] He would remain sheepish about the affair for years to come, regarding it as a black mark on his reputation.

By early 1952 Marciano was ready to return to ring action, and Weill wasn't taking any chances. He didn't want to place Marciano's imminent title shot in jeopardy by sending him against a young, dangerous fighter such as LaStarza, old friend Coley Wallace, or Clarence Henry. According to Lofquist, Weill now deemed Marciano as "bric-a-brac to be kept under glass."[33]

So Weill matched him against Lee Savold. A veteran heavyweight from New Jersey, Savold's career dated all the way back to 1934. Although he had tasted his share of defeat—his record included thirty losses—Savold had also enjoyed some ring success. The high point in his career came in June 1950 when he beat Bruce Woodcock in London for the British championship. In June 1951, though, he lost to Louis in a fight that covered neither man with glory. By early 1952 Savold still had a name but was thirty-five years old, clearly on the downside of his career. To Weill, all of this made Lee Savold an ideal opponent for Rocky Marciano.

Still, when the match was scheduled for Philadelphia on the evening of February 13, 1952, everyone asked, Why? Marciano was entitled to a breather as he resumed his march to the title, but why Lee Savold? A year or two before he would have made a worthy opponent, but now he was plainly washed-up. The public ridicule and cynicism of the impending fight even forced a bizarre public relations move from the Pennsylvania State Athletic Commission, the sanctioning body for the bout. A week before the fight, when both fighters checked in at the commission's office, one of the commissioners, the rotund John ("Ox") DaGrosa, told them, "People are asking me why you two are fighting. You've got to show them why. And it's got to be a good fight, or I'll hold up your purses."[34]

It turned out not to be a good fight. In fact, it was a fiasco. The more than nine thousand fans in Philadelphia's Convention Hall booed and stamped their feet throughout the bout—and with good reason. It was a one-sided travesty. Whether Savold wouldn't or couldn't fight back was an open question; that he didn't was clear. On three separate occasion in the fight—after the second, fourth, and fifth rounds—the referee warned him to start throwing punches. Savold refused to budge, however. He threw only an occasional wild hook, leading some to question whether the fight was on the level. As Hugh Brown of the *Philadelphia Evening Bulletin* observed, the entire affair induced "nausea" and smelled "sourly," worse than the majestic Delaware River "even when standing stagnant under a ninety-eight-degree sun and a lazy southeast wind."[35]

While Savold was impersonating a punching bag, Rocky Marciano was throwing a ton of punches and inflicting much of damage along the way. It was, said Marciano later, "the worst beating I ever gave a guy." In the first round, Savold's nose was bashed. In the second, his nose started bleeding, and his flabby, out-of-shape body turned bright pink. In the third, his lips were split open. In the sixth, his right eye was gashed. "It wasn't a fight," Ed Pollock of the *Philadelphia Evening Bulletin* wrote later. "It was like something you've read about or seen in TV movies . . . a gangster, a Nazi or a Commie working over an innocent victim to get him to confess to something he didn't do."[36]

By the end of the sixth, Savold's manager, Bill Daly, had seen enough. With his fighter now a bloody mess, he leapt into the ring and waived a towel at the referee, signaling the end of the fight. Savold merely sat in his corner shaking his head. Meanwhile, as the referee raised Marciano's hand in victory, the fans of Philadelphia continued to boo. As the razzing went on, the smile on the puzzled Marciano's face grew fainter. Eventually, it disappeared altogether.

His reputation disappeared along with it. Over the course of his career Marciano had a dozen big fights. Among them, the Savold fight was by far the worst. It wasn't that Marciano came close to losing. In fact, he won every round. But, as Gerry Hern pointed out, "Rocky never looked worse, not even as an amateur."[37] Indeed, he may have thrown a ton of punches, but most of them missed wildly. He had no coordination, no timing, and no crispness. Instead, he lunged, sprawled, leaped, and misfired. The low point came in the sixth and final round when Marciano threw a punch that missed so badly that he slipped and fell face first into the ropes. Perhaps it was the effect of the long layoff, or overconfidence, or maybe it was the fact that he had received an injection of penicillin a week before the fight. Whatever the reason, Marciano floundered.

He received a hailstorm of well-deserved criticism. He had been ripped before—and he would be ripped again—but at no point was he ripped more viciously than after the Lee Savold fight. Many mocked Marciano. C. M. Gibbs of the *Baltimore Sun* found it fortunate that the referee stopped the bout "before the customers in the front seats got pneumonia from the wind stirred up by Marciano's missed shots," and Pollock wrote that the bout exposed Marciano "as a wild swinger who couldn't hit an oak tree if it swayed a little in the breeze, but who would keep on trying, nevertheless." Even the New England sportswriters, traditionally friendly to Marciano, piled on. As Clif Keane of the *Boston Globe* declared, "[L]et nobody ever mention Rocky in the same breath with Jack Dempsey—or even Jersey Joe Walcott, for that matter."[38]

Marciano's dismal performance put a screeching halt to the momentum that had been building toward the title. It also created fresh doubts about his abilities. As James P. Dawson of the *New York Times* observed, the appraisal of Marciano "must undergo a revision." Matt Ring declared that Marciano had "forfeited his reputation as a killer of the ring, his stature as a championship contender and his potency as a box office attraction."[39] Around ringside that night in Philadelphia, and at home in living rooms (the fight was televised on CBS), many fans were wondering whether he was really the next champion. Marciano was still in the big-money class of fighters, and he was still the uncrowned champion. Now, however, there were questions. An early shot at the title in June—a hot rumor on the eve of the Savold bout—was now completely out of the question. Rocky Marciano would have to wait.

In the spring of 1952, with the title shot delayed, Al Weill sent Marciano back to Providence one last time to rebuild his tarnished reputation. Marciano got his career back on track by scoring early-round knockouts of Gino Buonvino, the veteran from Italy who had nearly taken Marciano to the limit in their Boston fight in June 1950, and Bernie Reynolds, a decent heavyweight who had captured the New England heavyweight championship and climbed as high as number six in the national rankings in the late 1940s. The knockout of Reynolds was particularly spectacular. "Reynolds actually floated through the air in a horizontal position and his shoulder blades and the back of his heels hit the deck simultaneously," Goldman would recall. According to Mike Thomas, it "probably was as hard a punch as ever was landed in a Providence ring."[40] It was also a fitting farewell to Providence. Rocky Marciano would never fight there again.

• • •

There would be one more fight for Marciano before his crack at the crown—and it was a big one. The setting was Yankee Stadium in late July 1952. The opponent was Harry ("Kid") Matthews, a highly regarded heavyweight from Seattle. Neither Matthews nor Marciano was the real story of this fight, however. That honor fell to Matthews's manager, Jack Hurley. He was the type of character that only the ring seems to produce. A thin, nervous bundle of energy, Hurley was many things—manager, promoter, father figure, old-time huckster, rogue, and man of principle—all wrapped into one. Most of all, he loved to talk, so much so that the British press dubbed him "The Heavyweight Champion of the Word."

Hurley was one of the last of a dying breed—an all-controlling, old-style fight manager—and strictly a one-fighter man. His specialty was finding a boxer willing to accept his control, teaching him the fine points of boxing, selecting his opponents carefully, and then promoting him relentlessly. Hurley most famously employed his system with a lightweight named Billy Petrolle, the popular "Fargo Express" of the 1920s and early 1930s. Then, one day in 1949, Harry Matthews walked into Jack Hurley's life. The son of an Idaho blacksmith, Matthews had enjoyed some success in the ring, losing only three times in seventy outings before meeting Hurley. Financially, though, Matthews was a failure. Because the men he had fought were, for the most part, West Coast nobodies, his fights drew poorly, his purses were small, and he had fallen into debt. Hurley knew that and told Matthews when he agreed to take him on, "You have proven that you are a failure. I have proven myself a successful fight manager. I'm a going concern. If you make it through me it's me making it . . . I'm going to teach you how to fight and publicize you and maneuver you into making matches where we will both make big money. You don't know how lucky you are."[41]

Soon Matthews realized that he was a lucky man indeed. Hurley did everything that he said he would. He made Matthews a better boxer, because beneath all the bluster Hurley was a great boxing teacher. He also carefully selected opponents. "I made sure he didn't fight any great fighters," he said later. "I picked 'em mostly by their styles, guys that had styles just right for Matthews . . . I always picked fighters that really wanted to get in there and fight and lick my fellow, and while they were doing this my fighter was counterpunching and looking great."[42] True to his word, Jack Hurley promoted Harry Matthews. He regularly mailed press clippings about Matthews to sports editors all over the country, a strategy that cost Hurley $6,000 a year but got his fighter's name in the newspaper. He touted Matthews as an all-American boy with a beautiful, loving wife (in fact, Matthews and his wife fought constantly and would later divorce). He called Matthews "the Athlete." He cast him as a dangerous unknown from outside the fight system.

And then, after making Matthews the fistic hit of the Pacific Northwest, Hurley maneuvered him onto the national stage via a televised fight with Irish Bob Murphy in Madison Square Garden in March 1951, with Matthews rallying late to capture the decision. By the spring of 1952 Hurley and Matthews had traveled all the way to the top of the boxing world. Matthews had not lost since 1943, was unbeaten in his last seventy bouts, and had won thirty-five straight under Hurley's tutelage, twenty-eight of which had come via knockout. His overall record stood at an imposing 96-3-6. A natural light heavyweight who Hurley had turned into a heavyweight, Matthews was rated as the number-five heavyweight contender in the world.

It was then that Hurley started to bang the drum for a Marciano-Matthews match, yelping that the IBC was shutting his fighter out of New York while mocking Marciano as "this great star they're keeping in cellophane."[43] Neither the powerful IBC nor the cautious Al Weill wanted the fight, but Hurley managed to swing public sentiment to his side. With the New York State Athletic Commission breathing down its neck for alleged improprieties, the IBC couldn't afford more negative publicity. After convincing the recalcitrant Weill to let his champion-in-waiting Marciano face Matthews the rebel, the IBC caved and offered the match to Hurley. He accepted.

In the weeks leading up to the fight, Hurley's mystery man from the Pacific Northwest baffled the establishment by engaging in what one New York writer called "the most amazing training stint that any fighter ever had for a big bout."[44] Instead of retreating to the mountains as was customary, Matthews trained in New York City, doing his gym work at the CYO and his roadwork in Central Park. Matthews carried his own ring gear to and from the gym and taped his own hands. There was no entourage. There was no team of handlers. There was only one sparring partner.

What made the training routine truly bizarre, though, was the work Matthews did—or did not do—in the gym. After he arrived in New York, he boxed an absurdly low total of nineteen rounds. (In comparison, Marciano boxed more than eighty over at his camp in Greenwood Lake.) On some days, Matthews didn't box at all. On the days he did, he revealed little, concentrating on defense and footwork while throwing few serious punches. The fact that he did nothing in training "has driven the local fight crowd absolutely nuts," reported Jerry Nason of the *Boston Globe*. Explained Hurley, "You don't fight your fight in the gym."[45]

At least Matthews's training sessions made clear who was boss. The fighter didn't make a move or say a thing without asking Hurley's approval first. On one occasion, a reporter asked Matthews if he would like to win the heavyweight crown. He replied, "Better ask Mr. Hurley." When the reporter turned to Hurley in amazement, Hurley pointed out, "See? He has no opinions. Don't need 'em. I got enough for both of us." As Matthews summed up their relationship, "He talks, I fight. He worries, I box. He frets, I relax. It's the perfect partnership."[46]

Hurley very much remained the show in the weeks leading up to the fight. He talked. And talked. And talked. Even the IBC's publicity posters for the fight graphically demonstrated that Hurley was the story. Under the ludicrous billing "The Greatest Heavyweight Bout since Dempsey-Firpo," the IBC placed a picture of Marciano. It also included a picture of Matthews—with Jack Hurley leaning over him. When Hurley asked Jim Norris of the IBC why he had been included in the picture, Norris replied, "Matthews is nothing without you." Numerous newspaper photographs also featured Hurley. One had him dressed in a professor's cap and gown, lecturing the dutiful Matthews. All the ballyhoo led Charley Goldman to ask reporters, "Who are we fighting—Matthews or Hurley?"[47]

On the sizzling hot night of July 28, 1952, more than thirty thousand fans filed into Yankee Stadium to see if all Jack Hurley's words would ring true. They did—for one round. Indeed, in the first, Matthews gave Marciano a boxing lesson. Moving in close and standing toe to toe with Marciano, he eluded Marciano's bombs, countered effectively with his left, and even opened a small cut around Marciano's left eye. "He started faster than I expected," Marciano said after the fight. "He was stronger than I thought, too. . . . He's got a good jab, and he wanted to fight."[48]

Between rounds, Jack Hurley was gleeful. He had devised a strategy that called for Matthews to crowd Marciano (thus cutting off his ability to unleash his powerful, wild swings) and counter with uppercuts while stepping into his punches. The strategy had worked perfectly in the opening round. "The first round was the pattern of the fight," Hurley said after the fight. "Matthews could have gone ten, twelve, fifteen rounds that way and busted up Rocky and maybe knocked him out."[49]

Matthews wasn't the only one with a master strategist, however. Rocky Marciano had one, too, in the diminutive Charley Goldman. Between rounds, Goldman calmly laid out a strategy for Marciano: "Hey, this guy's not running. He's standing right in front of you. Go out there and stand still. Just get right up in front of him and stand still." There was a second part to Goldman's strategy, and it involved Marciano's left hand. As Goldman explained later, "I could see that the guy was trying to counter-punch Rocky to death so I told him to start jabbing and follow through with the jab and then try to hit him with the left hook."[50]

The second round began very much like the first, with Matthews boxing expertly and in command. Then he made his fatal mistake. Between rounds, Hurley had cautioned his fighter not to be afraid and pull back, which would put him in danger of getting in the way of one of Marciano's long-range bombs. Yet that is precisely what Matthews did. Years later, Hurley would maintain that Matthews became frightened when he suddenly realized that he was fighting in front of a big crowd in New York. "Matthews wasn't beaten by Marciano, he was beaten by Yankee Stadium," Hurley said years later. "He was overawed. He would have beaten Marciano in three rounds if they had fought in Seattle."[51] Or perhaps Matthews froze because he was surprised when Marciano, carrying out Goldman's strategy, stood still.

Whatever the reason, in the middle of the second round Harry Matthews definitely pulled away from Rocky Marciano. Marciano had his opening—and the chance to carry out the second part of Goldman's strategy calling for the use of the left jab and then the left hook. He had shaken Matthews moments earlier with an overhand right. Now, with Matthews retreating, Marciano threw an almost playful left jab that sent his rival back even further. He followed with two short, crunching left hooks. Boom! Boom! Just like that, it was over. The befuddled Matthews looked like "a limp rag doll" as he fell in his own corner directly in front of Jack Hurley, who looked helplessly upon his fallen athlete. After the referee counted Matthews out, a jubilant Goldman shouted over and over again in the ring, "I knew he'd fool him with that left jab. I knew he'd fool him." His strategy—not Hurley's—had been the one that had carried the day. As Weill would later crow, "Hurley wanted to be a Swengali [sic] but the strings broke."[52]

As Hurley and his fighter took the long walk down the aisle leading from the ring back to the dressing room, the manager had to endure the taunts of the Yankee Stadium crowd. By the time they got back to the dressing room, Hurley was steaming. "An amateur! You fought like an amateur!" he screamed at Matthews. After Hurley had calmed down, he told reporters, "He pulled back three times and each time he got nailed . . . I gave him the opportunity and he just didn't make it. No alibis. No excuses. He just went amateur on me." A sheepish and tearful Matthews muttered, "I didn't see it coming." After a while, a reassuring Hurley put his hand on Matthews's shoulder. "Well, back West, Kid," he said. "We'll start all over again."[53] Yet there would be no rebirth. Matthews's brief dalliance with the heavyweight title was over. By the mid-1950s he had retired from the ring.

Meanwhile, in Marciano's jammed, chaotic dressing room, the jubilant victor exclaimed, "I can lick anybody I get in there with." He had reasons to be happy. His forty-second straight victory had provided his biggest payday yet ($51,000). More important, his sharp performance provided sweet redemption for his bumbling showing in the Savold fight. The booing he received that night in Philadelphia as well as the criticism he received in the press thereafter had genuinely bothered Marciano. Now, that all seemed ancient history. His triumph over Matthews, admitted Matt Ring, "redeemed in full his abject performance" against Savold.[54]

The Matthews victory also cemented Marciano's reputation as a knock-out artist supreme. From his early days in Providence, he had regularly recorded spectacular, one-punch knockouts. In the big time, against Layne, Louis, and now Matthews, he consistently displayed the same type of firepower. Marciano had no way of knowing how much he would need that punch in his next fight—the long-awaited title shot against Jersey Joe Walcott.

6 Jersey Joe

His real name was Arnold Raymond Cream, but to the world he was known as Jersey Joe Walcott. And by the time he finally crossed paths with Rocky Marciano in the fall of 1952, Jersey Joe Walcott was known. Whenever a big heavyweight fight came around in the late 1940s or early 1950s Walcott was usually involved. In one of those big fights—against Ezzard Charles in the summer of 1951—Walcott had, at long last, become heavyweight champion of the world. One year later, he continued to possess that coveted title. He also possessed a definite public persona.

First and foremost, Jersey Joe was a family man. In an age where the family was held sacred, he had credentials. Growing up in New Jersey (naturally), he was one of twelve siblings. As champion, he remained close to them, particularly his six sisters. He would entertain them during camp, donning a chef's hat and serving Saturday evening dinner to break the monotony and drum up some easy publicity. Walcott also had a wife, Lydia, and six children, who, in 1952, ranged in age from seven to nineteen. In words as well as photographs, the media consistently cast Walcott as a devoted husband and father of six.

Jersey Joe was also a religious man—not just the father of six but "the Bible-thumping father of six." Shortly after he burst into the national spotlight in 1947, he proclaimed, "I am a God-fearing man." Sportswriters now had a theme, and they drove it home religiously, rarely missing an opportunity to cast Walcott in a pious light. It made for a nice story whenever Walcott stole away from camp to attend Methodist services, took a peek at the Bible in his training quarters, or listened to a tape of a sermon between workouts. Walcott was somewhat ambivalent about making his religious beliefs a public matter. "People will think I go to church for publicity," he once instructed IBC publicist Harry Mendel. "Don't put it in the paper. Write up the workout instead." "When the President of the United States goes to church it's news," Mendel replied, "and it's news when the heavyweight champion goes." "It shouldn't be," countered Walcott. "Everybody ought to go to church."[1]

Finally, and perhaps most strikingly, Jersey Joe was an old man. Most believed him when he expressed devotion to his family and his God, but no one believed Jersey Joe Walcott when it came to the subject of age. At the time he first met Rocky Marciano in 1952, he claimed he was thirty-eight. Everyone scoffed. Walcott, some maintained, was at least forty—and perhaps as old as forty-two or forty-four. Among sportswriters, it became sport to try to figure out Walcott's real age. The topic also became prime fodder for wisecracks. "Some say he's thirty-eight, not counting Saturdays, Sundays or legal holidays," joked Frank Finch of the *Los Angeles Times*. Walcott was, according to wire service reporter Bob Considine, "the same age as Jack Benny, thirty-nine."[2] As he surely realized and probably intended, all the speculation and jokes about his age brought reams of free publicity.

Public persona aside, Jersey Joe Walcott was noteworthy because of the strange career that he fashioned. It was certainly bizarre—perhaps the most bizarre in the annals of ring history. He did not take the traditional path to the top of the heavyweight heap. In fact, he was a nobody in boxing for years and years. Only when he was in his early thirties—well past what should have been his physical prime—did he emerge as a contender for the heavyweight crown. And he emerged from nowhere.

Actually, he came from Merchantville, New Jersey, a suburb of Camden, where he was born in 1914 (or so he claimed), the fifth of twelve children in a family that had emigrated from the West Indies. Boxing was in his blood from the beginning. In the 1920s, Merchantville was a popular training ground for black fighters such as Sam Langford. Young Arnold was always hanging around the gym, watching the fighters train. Once he even met Jack Johnson, who arrived three hours late for a scheduled appointment but walked right by Arnold and the rest of the waiting youngsters, two Great Danes in tow. Arnold vowed to himself that if he became a boxer he would not ignore his fans, especially the young ones.

Although Arnold Cream eventually did become a boxer, it would be a long time before he had any fans. His first professional fight was in 1930 against Cowboy Wallace. He made $15, and no one paid attention. That set the tone for the first fifteen years of his career. For the most part, Arnold (first as a lightweight, then as a middleweight, and finally as a heavyweight) fought "coffee and cake" fights for small purses of $10 or $15. Two years into his professional career, he adopted the ring name "Jersey Joe Walcott." There was another Jersey Joe Walcott in boxing lore—a welterweight champion around the turn of the century who hailed from the West Indies (like Arnold's father) and was, in fact, a friend of the Cream family. Arnold thought that the new name might bring him attention. It did not.

On several occasions in the 1930s Walcott came close to breaking through. In 1934 he was working in Philadelphia under the guidance of legendary trainer Jack Blackburn. When Blackburn decided to move to Chicago to take charge of a young heavyweight named Joe Louis, he offered to take Walcott with him to train with Louis. Walcott, though, came down with a case of typhoid fever and had to pass. Two years later, with Louis fighting the big fights and Walcott still laboring in obscurity, Blackburn remembered his former pupil and summoned him to serve as Louis's sparring partner. Walcott did his job—and did it too well. After knocking Louis down during one sparring session, he was summarily dismissed from the camp. Several weeks later at Coney Island, Walcott grabbed some attention by capturing one of the Great White Hope tournaments being sponsored by Jack Dempsey. The attention was fleeting, however, and soon he was once again plying his trade in tank towns.

Walcott's chief problem had little to do with ability. It was strictly financial. In the 1930s, most black heavyweights (Louis excepted) had difficulty attracting financial backing from the managers and promoters who controlled the sport. That meant they rarely fought the big-money bouts that would lead to everything a fighter could possibly want—a big purse, a big ranking, and more big fights with even bigger purses. In Walcott's case, the lack of financial resources also created a more pressing problem: hunger. The depression was on, and money was tight in the growing Walcott family. To supplement his meager fight purses, Jersey Joe took a series of odd jobs—driving an ice truck, digging ditches, carrying a bricklayer's hod, mixing cement, working in the shipyards, and collecting garbage. At one point he even went on relief for $9.50 a week. Although the family scraped by, there was never enough food on the table. Walcott's usual dinner consisted of scrapple, beans, bread, and cabbage—hardly the foodstuff needed to fuel an athletic career. Walcott later claimed that he was literally hungry for more than a decade. "I had the ability to succeed in the ring, but you can't do it with a gnawing at the pit of your stomach," he maintained.[3]

By February 1940 Walcott had finally had enough. After Abe Simon knocked him out in Newark, the weak, hungry, and exhausted Walcott decided to retire. He had quit the ring in frustration several times before. This time he was serious. During the next five years he fought just three bouts, all of them small-time affairs to pick up a little extra money. Instead, he concentrated on his day jobs. He eventually landed a good one, working in the shipyards for $85 per week. By late 1944 he was for all intents and purposes retired, remembered by only a precious few in local fight circles.

Then one night, just before Christmas 1944, Walcott ran into Felix Bocchicchio in a neighborhood poultry store. Bocchicchio was a local businessman and small-time fight promoter. And he did remember Walcott. Was there anything Felix could do for Jersey Joe? Walcott gladly accepted a couple of small loans from Bocchicchio. Then, two days after Christmas, Walcott decided to return to the ring under the management of Bocchicchio. Jersey Joe Walcott had found what he called "my good angel."[4]

Felix Bocchicchio was no angel. His past had included some jail time. He liked to gamble and reportedly had ties with the Mob. To Bob Considine, he was "somewhat sinister." He was not, echoed Furman Bisher of the *Atlanta Constitution,* "the kind of guy you'd appoint as treasurer of the Community Chest." He even looked sneaky, with slicked-back hair, sharp suits, and an ever-present cigarette dangling from his lips. Yet there was no question that Bocchicchio was good to (and for) Walcott. "We've been so close, that I'll do most anything for Joe and he'll do most anything for me," Bocchicchio would say years later. "Joe and I are more than just manager and fighter."[5]

In early 1945, at the ripe of old age of thirty and with some money finally behind him, Walcott returned to the ring. By late 1946 and early 1947 Bocchicchio had moved Walcott onto the fringes of the big time. Walcott was now meeting name fighters such as Elmer Ray and Joey Maxim and for the most part doing quite well. Then, in December 1947, Walcott finally caught his big break when he was matched against champion Joe Louis in Madison Square Garden. No one thought the unknown Walcott had a chance of defeating the great Louis. Yet he almost did. In fact, a majority of observers at ringside felt that Walcott won the fifteen-round decision. So, evidently, did Louis, who at fight's end, before the decision was announced, started to leave the ring as if conceding defeat. "I'm sorry, Joe," he said to Walcott after the decision was announced. One of the boxing magazines of the era, the *Police Gazette,* angrily announced that it was going to recognize Walcott as champion—and then presented him with a jeweled belt to make it official. Overnight, Jersey Joe Walcott had become "The People's Champ" and a national sensation.[6]

He was now at the peak of his popularity and in the upper echelons of the heavyweight division. And he didn't leave. Over the next few years he would get three more title shots. On each occasion he came up short. In June 1948 he lost a rematch with Louis when he was knocked out in the eleventh round. One year later, in June 1949, with Louis recently retired, Walcott faced Ezzard Charles in Chicago for the vacated title and lost in a dreary fifteen-round waltz that invited public scorn. Then, in March 1951, Walcott lost a rematch with Charles in Detroit, rallying too late to win the fifteen-round decision. Despite these title defeats, Walcott kept getting a crack at the crown because his performances were consistently solid. Then again, there really was no one else.

For that reason, in July 1951 Walcott got yet another shot at the title, his fifth overall. Charles hadn't wanted to give Walcott the match, but the IBC felt there was no one on the horizon who was as viable. So they met again, this time in Pittsburgh. And this time Jersey Joe finally seized the day. Fighting more aggressively than he had in his two previous fights with Charles, Walcott set the tone from the outset. Then, in the seventh round, he unleashed a left hook the champion never saw coming. The old king, Ezzard Charles, was dead. The new king was Jersey Joe Walcott. He was, proclaimed *Life,* "history's oldest and most implausible heavyweight champion of the world."[7]

He also proved to be a popular champion. How could anyone root against Jersey Joe? He loved his family. He went to church. He was a gentleman. He was a "Cinderella man" who had triumphed against the steepest of odds. He was, admitted sportswriter Bill Corum, "a hero of mine, as well as so many others who like to believe in dreams." Much of the public rooted for Walcott, rather sentimentally. Even celebrities rallied to his side. Hollywood starlet Joan Blondell, for example, wandered into Yankee Stadium for the second Louis-Walcott fight and decided to root for Walcott because she heard that he had six children and thought she saw him praying in the ring.[8]

Although he was personally popular, doubts persisted about his greatness as champion. By the fall of 1952 his record stood at a slightly less than awe-inspiring 53-16-1. Not all of those losses had come in his food-deprived, tank-town, fighting years. On the eve of Walcott's fight with Marciano, Red Smith pointed out that his record was only 7-5 since he burst into national prominence by almost defeating Louis in December 1947. During that span of time he had only defeated one fighter of note—Charles—and even he was seen as somewhat flawed. "Romantic fancy can picture Joe as a gallant old Horatius standing off wave upon wave of fierce and pitiless youth," Smith wrote. "The records show him standing off a horde of exactly one false Etruscan."[9]

Age was a factor in how people rated him as a champion. Some just couldn't get past it. Observed Smith, "As champion he has been celebrated chiefly as a curiosity, like a whale on a flatcar or calf with two heads." Then there was the issue of caution. To Smith like so many others, Walcott was "a prince of prudence." The critics complained that he danced and pranced but rarely forced the action. His sole title defense before meeting Marciano—against Charles in the summer of 1952—proved once again that Walcott favored a strategy of nonengagement. "Walcott will be in there to do as little fighting as he can get away with," Jesse Abramson of the *New York Herald Tribune* predicted before the Marciano fight. "That's his nature and that's his background in the ring."[10]

In other corners, Walcott had won much acclaim and respect for his ring abilities. He certainly had a distinctive style. He would hitch up his pants, wipe his nose, make crablike feints to either side, and engage in fancy footwork such as a tricky little two-step that was a precursor to the Ali Shuffle. "Walcott is a cutie," declared Arthur Daley of the *New York Times*. "There is no other way to describe him. In his twenty-two years in the ring he has learned all the tricks. He weaves, sidles, shuffles and uses the hit-and-run."[11] This overall ring intelligence and craftsmanship made Walcott a difficult assignment for any boxer—particularly a relatively raw one like the new challenger on the block, Rocky Marciano.

● ● ●

After Marciano knocked out Harry Matthews in late July 1952, everyone wanted to see him and Walcott meet, particularly after three years of nothing but boring Walcott-Charles waltzes. Still, Walcott-Marciano almost didn't happen. Instead, for the better part of three weeks Felix Bocchicchio, Al Weill, and the IBC squabbled over dates, sites, and purses. By early August, talks had broken off, and Bocchicchio was threatening to take Walcott to England to fight. Several weeks later, with time running out on scheduling an outdoor fight (which promised a bigger gate than one indoors), the

IBC was set to abandon the bout. Then everyone came to their senses and realized that they were leaving too much money on the table. They finally agreed on the date (September 23), the site (Philadelphia), and the money (a 40 percent cut for Walcott, 20 percent for Marciano). On August 20, 1952, amid much fanfare at City Hall in downtown Philadelphia, Walcott and Marciano finally signed contracts for the title fight.

In the weeks before the bout, Walcott repeatedly belittled Marciano. Evoking the frequent Marciano-Dempsey comparison, he scoffed, "How silly can they get? He shouldn't be spoken of in the same breath with Dempsey." For good measure, he also declared, "Marciano is an amateur. He wouldn't have qualified for Joe Louis's bum of the month tour. I'll knock him out." Visiting the Walcott camp in early September, Matt Ring of the *Philadelphia Evening Bulletin* noted that Walcott was in "the friskiest mood this reporter ever saw him display." As Walcott said, "I just feel good," also telling Ring that he was worried that working men with wives and children would gamble away their grocery money by foolishly betting on Marciano. All of these statements were very much out of character for Walcott, normally the most reserved of gentlemen.[12]

Meanwhile, Rocky Marciano prepared for his first title fight at a new training camp—Grossinger's in the Catskill Mountains. The Grossinger Hotel was in its heyday in the early 1950s. A well-known entertainment hot spot—the singer Eddie Fisher made his debut there in 1949—it attracted thousands of tourists each year. Team Marciano set up camp away several miles from the plush resort at Grossinger's hilltop, wind-swept airfield. For the next three years, Grossinger's would become Rocky Marciano's office. He would spend many months training there, both before his big fights in the East as well as during the long stretches between fights. "They were all wonderful to me at Grossinger's," he recalled. "It got to be a second home for me."[13]

For now, Marciano was using his new base of operations to get ready for Jersey Joe Walcott. The big news emanating from his camp was the return of Al Weill. Not that he had ever been away, and not that anger had dissipated in fight circles over his shadow management of Marciano. As Sam Lacy of the *Baltimore Afro-American* complained in the early fall of 1952, Weill was "getting away with murdering the ethics of the prize ring."[14] Weill finally stepped over the line at the weigh-in for the Marciano-Matthews fight, though, when he referred to Marciano as "my fighter" in the presence of Robert Christenberry, the new chair of the New York State Athletic Commission. Christenberry took immediate action. You have a choice, he told Weill. Give up your job at the IBC or give up your interest in Marciano. For

Weill, the decision was easy. The IBC job brought power, but managing Marciano offered fame and glory as well as power. On the last day of July 1952, Weill announced that he was quitting the IBC effective September 1 in order to resume management of Marciano.

Officially, Rocky Marciano was happy about the news, declaring, "With Weill back with us, the team is complete." In reality, though, Weill did not make a smooth or welcome reentry onto Team Marciano. A relaxed, happy atmosphere had prevailed in Marciano's camp when he had trained for Layne, Louis, and Matthews in Greenwood Lake. With Weill back in control, that atmosphere vanished. He took charge of everything at Grossinger's, with no one daring to say anything in his presence. He also interfered with the sparring schedule that Goldman had carefully prepared for his fighter. Allie Colombo later charged that Weill "disrupted our camp."[15]

Preparation proceeded on course, however, with Marciano boxing about one hundred rounds to get ready. By the time he arrived in Philadelphia on the eve of the fight, he, like Walcott, was a picture of confidence. After a long car ride from the Catskills, Marciano and his entourage arrived at the Warwick Hotel. Goldman hustled the rumpled boxer through a crowd of reporters, explaining, "I'm sorry, but Rock's got to eat. He had breakfast at 9 o'clock. This is the first time since I knew him that he's been without food six hours. He's dying." That, the reporters figured, was the last they'd see of Marciano until tomorrow. Indeed, it was customary for edgy boxers to stay in seclusion the night before a big fight. But not this time. Instead, after freshening up, Marciano received reporters into his suite and gave an unusual ad hoc press conference, appearing loose, easy, and confident. "None present could recall that champion or challenger ever had made himself so accessible on a battle eve," Don Donaghey of the *Philadelphia Evening Bulletin* observed. The impromptu press conference ended only when Marciano's personal chef, Al Reinauer, poked his head into the room and announced, "Hurry it up, Rock. The steak's ready." With that, Marciano headed off to devour a large steak with garlic sauce.[16]

The next morning—the day of the fight—Marciano did roadwork with his bodyguard, Steve Melchiore, a Philadelphia policeman. "Do you know where you're fighting Jersey Joe?" asked Melchiore. Marciano did not, so Melchiore took him to the cavernous, horseshoe-shaped Municipal Stadium. "This is where you're going to become the world champion," Melchiore said. With that, Marciano teared up, fell to his knees, and recited a silent prayer.[17]

Meanwhile, many bettors also sought divine intervention to help them place their wagers. As Whitney Martin of the Associated Press noted, "The fight really is harder to figure than your income tax, as you can work out a good, practically fool-proof argument in favor of either man, thus leading to utter confusion." It was the type of fight, echoed Wendell Smith of the *Pittsburgh Courier,* that represented "a bookie's gold mine. It is a bout in which every man feels he is betting on a sure winner." More money was bet than on any fight in years. Marciano was officially favored at 8-5 odds, only the fourth challenger in heavyweight history to enter the ring as a favorite. The belief in Marciano reflected, in part, how far his stock had risen among the fight mob. Mainly, though, it reflected skepticism about Walcott—or, more precisely, about his age, with many feeling that he was living on borrowed time. Not everyone in the fight mob agreed, though. "Opinion seems to be pretty evenly split among the boys in the fight mob who hang around Lew Tendler's bar," reported Pete Baird of the *New Orleans Times-Picayune* the day before the bout.[18]

By this point, the city of Philadelphia was agog with excitement. "It's electrifying!" exclaimed the usually reserved Wendell Smith.[19] It was, after all, a fight between the best two heavyweights in the world. It also offered a possible changing of the guard after years of stagnancy in the division. The Walcott-Marciano match stirred the public's imagination more than any heavyweight fight had in years, perhaps even decades. It was just like the old days, with the fight mob and media members streaming into town, jamming the hotels and restaurants. From the outset, ticket sales were brisk. In the end, more than forty thousand fans paid their way into Municipal Stadium to see the fight. Many more around the country (up to 140,000) would watch the bout on the most extensive closed-circuit television network ever. Fifty theaters in thirty-one cities from coast to coast were offering the opportunity to witness the unfolding action live from Philadelphia.

All the fans in Municipal Stadium, and those who watched in movie houses across the country, would not be disappointed. The Walcott-Marciano fight on September 23, 1952, was a classic. It had everything a fight aficionado could want: a surprise early knockdown, an unrelenting pace throughout, multiple momentum shifts, more than a hint of controversy, and a spectacular finish. Those who saw it found it exciting, thrilling, and dramatic. "It was the best fight this ringsider has seen in many years, packed with action, drama and excitement," Arthur Daley reported. Several months after the event, Nat Fleisher, the venerable editor of *Ring,* would proclaim that the Walcott-Marciano fight was the second best of all time, behind only the Jack Dempsey–Luis Firpo thriller in 1923. Even now it remains one of the best heavyweight fights of all time.[20]

• • •

The evening of September 23, 1952, was cool and damp in Philadelphia. The prefight festivities had all the trimmings, and the tension was crackling. In the ring warming up, Walcott looked calm while Marciano seemed to be slightly nervous. Then referee Charley Daggert called both men to the center of the ring for prefight instructions. For more than a minute, handlers for each fighter peppered the referee with questions on rules and fouls. Daggert finally put a halt to the rambling discussion by concluding, with some conviction but little eloquence, "I ask both youse boys to give me no kidney or no rabbit punches. I'm gonna call 'em if I do. I wan' both of yas to give me an honest clean fight. That's all I'm in here to do."[21]

As the anticipation built in Philadelphia and in movie houses around the nation, the rest of the country sat at home, glued to their television sets as they watched vice-presidential candidate Richard Nixon deliver his famous "Checkers" speech, thereby saving his political career. The televised political drama foreshadowed the unfolding ring drama in Philadelphia. It would be a night of surprises and comebacks all around.

The first surprise belonged to Walcott. At the opening bell, everyone expected Jersey Joe to dance out of his corner and away from Marciano. They were wrong. Normally, Walcott was a cautious fighter, but he was confident that he could handle Marciano. As Red Smith once observed, "[W]hen Old Joe believed he had a soft touch he could be a mighty hunter before the Lord."[22] That night in Philadelphia, Walcott confounded the experts. Instead of backpedaling and sidestepping, he attacked. One minute into the round, he connected with a left hook to the jaw that sent Marciano to the canvas.

Up to that point, Marciano had been fighting almost in a trance. Charley Goldman always maintained that Marciano was daydreaming at the beginning of the fight, almost in disbelief that he, an ordinary kid from Brockton, was actually on the verge of becoming heavyweight champion of the world. Over time, Marciano came to agree with his trainer. "[M]y subconscious seemed to take over," he said several years later. "Here I was, face to face with my biggest crowd, my biggest purse and my biggest moment. At last I was fighting for the heavyweight championship of the world."[23]

Now, flat on the canvas of Municipal Stadium and with the fans roaring in shock and excitement, Marciano was finally awake. Somewhat incredibly, it was the first time he had been knocked down in his entire career. "I'd often wondered what it would be like," he said after the fight. "I found out. It sure was nice to discover that I could get up with vision clear." He wasn't hurt. He wasn't even dazed. He was just enraged. Goldman had long instructed him that if he ever were knocked down he should take a count of eight to clear his head. That was the smart boxing move. But Marciano disobeyed his trainer and boxing protocol by arising almost immediately. "I guess I'm only half smart," he joked later. "I got up at four. I was too mad and too surprised to stay down any longer."[24]

The unorthodox rise from the canvas cost Walcott. He had a long-standing reputation as a "poor finisher" and proved that once again versus Marciano. As soon as Walcott scored the knockdown, instead of remaining fixed on Marciano, he turned his back and headed for the neutral corner. When he turned back around to face Marciano, the challenger was already on his feet and ready to fight. Walcott moved in for the kill, but he had already lost precious time. "Before Jersey Joe could close in on him, three seconds passed," Daley wrote. "Opportunity passed with it. The old champion was not to get that close again." Walcott later admitted that he had made a big mistake. "I lost him, I just lost him," he said after the fight. "I should have finished it then but he got away from me."[25] Marciano survived the crisis and was even starting to hurl some of his patented bombs by the end of the round.

Shortly thereafter, the fight began to swing in Marciano's favor. It was becoming a typical Marciano brawl, complete with punches after the bell and other assorted roughhouse tactics. Marciano occasionally looked amateurish but was also starting to score points of his own. More important, he was starting to control the tempo of the fight. "The match now seemed to be following the script more closely," A. J. Liebling of *The New Yorker* observed. "Rocky was slowing him down. The old man would go in a couple more rounds."[26] During the sixth, Marciano shook Walcott with two left hooks and pinned him against the ropes. The end appeared imminent.

Late in the sixth round, however, in a heavy exchange against the ropes, the two fighters accidentally bumped heads. Marciano, coming out of a crouch, banged the top of his head on Walcott's forehead. Almost immediately, blood began spurting from both fighters. Marciano was bleeding from the crown of his forehead, and Walcott sported a severe cut over his left eye. The violent collision changed the fight once again. Suddenly, Rocky Marciano couldn't see.

How had it happened? Did the concoction that Marciano's corner applied to his cut on the top of his forehead at the end of the sixth round inadvertently spill into his eyes? Was it the concoction that Walcott's corner applied to his cut at the end of the sixth that did the damage, somehow making its way onto Walcott's gloves and into Marciano's eyes? Was it, as Charley Goldman and others maintained, the liniment that Walcott's corner applied to his legs and his shoulders throughout the early rounds that found its way into

Marciano's eyes in similar fashion? Or, most ominously, was Marciano blinded because of foul play and deliberate chemical warfare on the part of Walcott's corner (as Marciano later contended, fingering Bocchicchio as the prime culprit)? Despite all the hints and allegations—which lasted for months and even years after the fight was over—the mystery was never resolved.

However it happened, Marciano was clearly in trouble. For the better part of the seventh, eighth, and ninth rounds, he had great difficulty seeing Walcott, blinking furiously and grimacing at times. This, of course, left him extremely vulnerable. Fortunately for him, Walcott had tired and was fighting somewhat cautiously. Although the champion won all three rounds, the blinded Marciano somehow managed to avoid serious danger.

The confusion in Marciano's corner didn't help matters. This was primarily due to the presence of Weill, who hadn't worked in Marciano's corner since March 1949 and whose presence on fight night had always unnerved the fighter. Earlier in the fight, Weill had gotten into an argument with Allie Colombo, which ended with Weill shouting, "Please, please, please, Allie!"[27] Then, when the cut Marciano returned to his corner at the end of the sixth, the excited Weill poured a sponge on top of his head, causing the blood to run down Marciano's face and into his eyes. Now, as the blinded Marciano tried to stay away from Walcott in the seventh and eighth, Weill repeatedly screamed at the referee concerning Marciano's condition. When Ox DaGrosa, one of the officials of the Pennsylvania State Athletic Commission, told Weill to keep quiet or he would have him removed, Weill continued to relay instructions to Marciano via one of his bodyguards in the corner. Before the ninth, Weill left the corner, walked along the ring apron, and got face to face with Daggert, pleading for an investigation of Walcott's hands and shoulders. The referee promptly motioned Weill back to the corner.

Amid all the chaos in his corner, Rocky Marciano was trying to regain his eyesight. Fortunately for him, Freddie Brown (a cut man Weill had hired on the morning of the fight for $50 to work in the corner) was on the case. Between the seventh and the eighth rounds, Brown held Marciano's head back and squeezed a sponge into his eyes. Between the eighth and ninth, he repeated the same procedure. Equally important, Brown remained calm. As Jimmy Breslin recalls, "Freddie Brown saved his ass in the Walcott fight. . . . When he couldn't see, they're all screaming. Weill is screaming, 'You gotta knock him out.' Goldman got nervous, or at least the closest thing to. And they're all screaming at once or something and Freddie just spoke to Marciano, got in front of him and spoke very quietly. I remember seeing him do it. He said, 'Now, listen, you don't have to see. Don't worry about it. Just get your hands on the guy's body so you know where he is and then fucking pound.'"[28]

During the ninth round, Marciano's eyes finally started to clear. With his eyesight restored, he regained the momentum in the tenth, one of the most action packed of an action-packed fight. He landed several good shots to Walcott's body and head and then, right before the bell, crashed a right to his jaw. As Marciano headed for his corner at round's end, Arthur Daley noticed, "he turned his head to look at Jersey Joe, a flicker of emotion on his impressive face for the first time. The look he gave was a strange, quizzical one." Eyewitnesses were also amazed at the older man's stamina. Observed Liebling, "[S]omehow the calculations had gone awry; the old fellow looked further from collapse now than he had six rounds earlier. It might go to a decision, after all."[29]

Walcott continued to amaze in the eleventh and twelfth rounds, winning both handily. Halfway through the eleventh, his best round of the fight, Walcott hit Marciano with a ferocious right under the heart that bent the challenger over, made him visibly wince, and sounded an audible thud around ringside. Walcott proceeded to smother Marciano with a bevy of hard punches, and some felt that only the bell saved the sagging challenger from being knocked out. It was more of the same in the twelfth, with Walcott pounding Marciano and in complete command. By the end of the twelfth, Walcott clearly appeared to be the stronger and fresher fighter. He was clearly thinking knockout.

By this point Marciano looked like he was all through. During the twelfth round he had missed wildly and even appeared rubbery on several occasions. Despite appearances, though, he remained confident. Most saw Walcott as the fresher fighter, but Marciano sensed that the champion was beginning to run out of gas. "I thought he was tiring in the twelfth," he said later. "We were feinting and I expected him to come in, then I felt he didn't want to exchange any more."[30] Still, he was running out of time. His cornermen conveyed the sense of urgency to him, and he himself surely felt it. With three rounds left and Walcott comfortably ahead, Marciano had no real chance of capturing a decision, particularly against the reigning champion in Philadelphia, practically his hometown. To win the fight—and the title—he absolutely, positively, needed to knock Walcott out.

That's precisely what he proceeded to do. As the thirteenth round opened, nothing much was happening. Marciano backed Walcott toward the ropes. Then both men drew back rights and fired. Walcott's only made it a few inches because the faster-firing Marciano stopped him dead in his tracks with a straight right to the chin. "Marciano beat Walcott to the punch," wrote Jesse Abramson. "It was as simple as that." Marciano's punch was short, traveling only a foot, give or take a few inches. To A. J. Liebling, it was "a model of pugilistic concision." As Arthur Daley would rhapsodize years later, "When I was a small boy, I had read about the perfect punch that traveled no more than six to eight inches. I refused to accept so manifestly impossible a premise. Rocky made a believer out of me." Marciano's punch was also powerful. "To ringsiders, the sound of it was frightening," wrote Ed Pollock of the *Philadelphia Evening Bulletin*. "It wasn't the smack of gloves against flesh. It was a crack. Rocky had hit something solid—the jawbone." Observed Liebling, it was, "according to old-timers, about as hard as anybody ever hit anybody."[31]

After Marciano's perfect punch, he threw a follow-up left hook that grazed the top of Walcott's head. It wasn't necessary. Walcott was out. As soon as Marciano's punch connected, Walcott froze, paralyzed. His eyes glazed over, his legs turned to jelly, and he began a slow-motion collapse, hanging onto the middle rope for a bit before sliding down to the lower rope and then all the way to the canvas. To Jesse Abramson, Walcott went down "crumpling all the way in sections like a slow-motion picture of a chimney stack which had been dynamited." And to Red Smith, after sagging on the ropes like "a very weary, rather drunk man does when he leans, arguing, against the bar, supporting himself with elbow on mahogany as Joe was supporting himself," Walcott "went down, sinking slowly by the head like a ship at sea."[32] As soon as Walcott began to fall Marciano raced to a neutral corner, where he waited out the count by kissing his glove. The count was, after all, a mere formality. Rocky Marciano was the new heavyweight champion of the world.

When it was over, Marciano started to dance a jig—but then stopped. "I felt great, but it didn't seem right to show my feelings with Joe lying on the floor," he explained later. (Praised Daley, "That's class, folks. Real class.") Then waves of fans, many of them from Brockton, swept toward the ring to hail the new champion. They charged over press row, stepping on cameras, kicking over typewriters, and sending sportswriters diving for cover. For a while, Philadelphia's finest prevented them from entering the ring, but eventually the police blockade broke and they engulfed the handlers, a revived Walcott, and, of course, Marciano, the man they came to see. No one could remember such a raucous celebration in the ring. And, for one, Sam Lacy questioned the motivation behind it, describing the onrushing mob as "[h]undreds of Marciano well-wishers, plus countless others who obviously had waited fifteen years for this to happen. . . . The demonstration was one surpassing even the wildest expectations in the discovery of the long-missing 'white hope.'"[33]

After fifteen minutes or so, Marciano finally escaped, racing for his dressing room with a group of police clearing the way and his handlers forming a protective vanguard behind him. Once he got there (and then later at the victory celebration thrown back at the Warwick Hotel by a booster named Jimmy Tomatoes), the scene around him remained chaotic and joyous. Meanwhile, Jersey Joe Walcott was trying to cope with the loss of his title. In the ring, after he had revived and realized that he had lost, he wore, in the words of Matt Ring, "a look of such utter sorrow as to wrench the heart." He remained a forlorn figure after he escaped the jam-packed ring and found his way to his dressing room. Sitting on a rubbing table, tears in his eyes and surrounded by crying family members, Walcott was despondent. "I don't remember anything," he said. "He caught me open and that was it. I don't know if it was a right or left. I just don't remember anything . . . I wasn't tired. I felt good. I was setting my own pace, then bang, it hit me. Honest, I still don't know what hit me. I couldn't even try to get up. I still don't remember anything."[34]

So ended the first Walcott-Marciano fight, a bout that Red Smith called "a sweetheart, rough and close and enormously exciting." What made the fight truly great, observed Liebling, were the continuous and almost dizzying shifts in momentum. Walcott had it initially when he knocked down Marciano in the first round. Then it gradually swung to Marciano. Then it swung back to Walcott when Marciano was mysteriously blinded. Marciano regained it in the ninth and tenth, only to see Walcott recapture it in the eleventh and twelfth. And then—finally and conclusively—it swung back to Marciano, with his thirteenth-round knockout of Walcott. "You don't see many fights like that," remarked an admiring Liebling.[35]

If the fight won universal praise, so did the fighters. For Marciano, the fight won him new respect from the fight mob. He had shown, for the first time, that he could take a punch. Even Bocchicchio conceded, "That Marciano really surprised me. I never saw a guy who could absorb a punch like he could. He got hit with some punches which would have knocked a building over and still he stayed in there. Sometimes I wonder."[36] Marciano had displayed courage, guts, and persistence. In the end, of course, he had displayed his formidable hitting power at the moment he needed it the most.

As H. G. Salsinger of the *Detroit News* recognized, "Marciano was the winner but Jersey Joe Walcott was the hero of the fight." It was Walcott's finest moment. In the past, Walcott had won—and sometimes lost—with great caution, but on September 23, 1952, in Philadelphia the prince of prudence slugged. His former critics applauded. Red Smith lauded, "Seldom did he run and never did he flee, as he had done so often in the past. . . . [H]e stood and fought like a man, and not like an old man. It was a magnificent performance, a gory and glorious redemption of a man who had sinned often and grievously by over-caution." Even Marciano chimed in, calling Walcott "a helluva fighter, the best I'll probably ever meet."[37] After he retired, Marciano would continue to cite his first fight with Walcott as the toughest of his career.

● ● ●

Such a classic naturally demanded a rematch—and all principals were willing. From the outset, though, a negative aura surrounded the second Walcott-Marciano fight. It began with scheduling, which the IBC and the rival managers botched. By the time everyone agreed to the date (April 10, 1953), the location (Chicago), and the purses (a 30 percent cut for Marciano and a $250,000 guarantee for Walcott), months had passed and public interest in the fight had cooled. "Every element was present to create a noisy demand for the rematch," Red Smith pointed out. "The fact that the demand has been much more moderate than anticipated simply demonstrates that fight managers are idiots. If they weren't, they'd have brought the bout back, before public enthusiasm had a chance to cool. . . . Instead, the knuckleheads stalled until interest faded."[38]

Then the fight was postponed. In late March, less than two weeks before the scheduled bout, Marciano ruptured several blood vessels in his right nostril courtesy of a punch from sparring partner Tommy Harrison. The injury forced the IBC to reschedule the bout to May 15. Everyone went home—Marciano to Brockton and Walcott to Camden—and whatever interest had built concerning the fight disappeared.

The extra delay also had an impact on the fighters. In training sessions just before the postponement, Marciano had appeared sluggish and lethargic. When he returned to camp in mid-April, the time off had clearly done him some good. He now seemed refreshed and revived. It was a different story with Walcott. Before the postponement he had seemed to be at his training peak. Several weeks later, many speculated that he would have difficulty regaining his form, particularly given his age. His handlers denied the theory. Jersey Joe, they proclaimed, was better than ever and still had his edge. After the fight finally took place, though, Dan Florio, Walcott's trainer, admitted that the delay and training disruption hurt Walcott considerably.

It also hurt interest in the fight, although the rival managers tried to provide a spark by engaging in a spirited and often ridiculous war of words. Bocchicchio took the lead. His primary charge was that Marciano was a dirty fighter. Walcott had lost the first fight, he maintained, because Marciano had given Walcott a head-butt in the sixth round, causing the cut over Walcott's eye (which, in turn, caused blood to trickle into Walcott's eye in the thirteenth, preventing him from seeing the decisive punch that knocked him out). Sportswriters could find no evidence that Marciano had given Walcott a head-butt, but that didn't matter to Bocchicchio. Ten days before the fight he announced that he would request that the Illinois Athletic Commission issue a stern warning against head-butting. With that, Al Weill jumped into the fray. After explaining that he had previously remained silent, trying "to maintain a dignity that goes along with the championship," Weill launched an attack against Bocchicchio: "This is not Philadelphia. The fight is being held in neutral Chicago. And the champ is Marciano, not Walcott. You are not going to dictate the terms and conditions of this rematch. The Illinois commission is fair, and I have every faith in its ability to conduct a fight without help from you."[39]

The interminable buildup and ballyhoo ended when fight night at long last arrived. Few were excited. "It will be a relief to have the Marciano-Walcott return bout fought and finished," observed Harold Kaese of the *Boston Globe*. "For about three months, it seems, the engagement has been ballyhooed incessantly from every conceivable angle. The only celebrities who have not been approached for their views of the outcome apparently are Senator McCarthy, Queen Elizabeth and Arthur Godfrey." The fighters, too, had grown tired of the long wait. Marciano, for example, had been training for the bout since early January. In all, he sparred a total of 225 rounds and logged more than 450 miles of roadwork. "It's been a long grind," admitted Marciano, who rarely complained about the long hours he had to spend training for fights. At least he could look forward to discarding the walruslike mask he had been wearing since mid-April to protect his healing nose. "That mask must weigh about five pounds," he said. "It'll be a relief to fight without it."[40]

He entered the ring an overwhelming favorite to retain his title. The odds were about 3-1, although Chicago bookies reported very little betting on the fight. Most reporters couldn't see how Marciano could lose; in a prefight Associated Press poll, thirty-four of thirty-six picked him to win. He had beaten Walcott before, he now had the confidence of a champion, and— most important—he was facing an even older Jersey Joe. Moreover, an old boxing adage held that "they never come back." Although eight had tried, no former heavyweight champion had ever regained his title. Experts were certain that Walcott would be the ninth to fail in the quest.

Only 13,266 fans—far short from capacity—paid their way into Chicago Stadium to see the fight. The rest of the nation watched on NBC to see if Marciano and Walcott could erase all the negativity by staging another classic. They did not. The fight turned out to be a dud. The first round consisted of Marciano chasing and Walcott retreating and then clinching. With less than a minute remaining in the round, Marciano brushed a left hook against Walcott's cheek and followed that with a short, rising right cross to Walcott's chin that dropped the challenger to the canvas. Marciano's right didn't seem that devastating, particularly to the television viewers. Maybe it was a knockdown punch, but it certainly wasn't a knockout punch. That belief was confirmed when Walcott, after landing flat on his back, heels in the air, pulled himself into a sitting position at the count of two.

As referee Frank Sikora chanted the count, Walcott just sat there, his knees in front of him, his right hand hanging on the middle rope, and his left resting on the canvas. He turned his head toward his corner and then stared back in front of him. Incredibly, he wasn't moving. As Sikora continued his count, Walcott continued to remain motionless save for an almost indetectible twitch or body ripple. To Red Smith, Walcott looked "like a darkly brooding Buddha, thinking slow and beautiful thoughts." To Jesse Abramson, he sat there "like an old man, resting in the park on the grass and reviewing his past life." At the count of eight, a stunned Rocky Marciano said to himself, "This guy's not getting up."[41] He did—but the instant after Sikora had chanted ten. It was too late. Walcott was not only down but also, incredibly, out. The fight was over.

The fans in Chicago Stadium, who had thought that Walcott would get up, were confused. Was the fight really over? When Sikora waved his arms and Marciano's handlers leaped into the ring, they knew. And they booed. Meanwhile, back in the ring, Walcott walked calmly and steadily to his corner. As the catcalls continued to rain over Chicago Stadium, though, he did an about-face. He decided to pick up the theme of Bocchicchio, who in the aftermath kept yelling at the official timekeeper, "He didn't get ten." Walcott, too, started to show outrage. He shot an amazed look at Sikora, banged his gloved hands together, and then flung them down in disgust. He stomped his feet. He looked like he was ready to cry. When Sikora walked over to him, Walcott said to him, "Nine. You only counted to nine." Sikora shook his head. "No, Joe," he replied. "You got a full ten count, the fight's over."[42]

For almost ten minutes Walcott and his handlers continued to rant in the ring. Later, in the dressing room, they continued the verbal assault. "Gentlemen," Bocchicchio proclaimed, "I was robbed in 1948 [*sic*] when we beat Joe Louis, but I never saw no robbery equal to this tonight." Their chief complaint was that Sikora had given Walcott a fast count. "That referee wanted to count Joe out so bad he counted 2-4-6-8," declared Bocchicchio. Walcott chimed in with the absurd allegation that Sikora had pushed him down to the canvas when the count reached seven. Even Dan Florio got into the act. After claiming that his stopwatch showed that Walcott got up at the count of nine, Florio said, "I never saw anything like that. They took the fight away from us, cheated us. That was strictly a fast count. What is this, Russia? When I walked over to the referee afterward, he told me to get out of the ring. What is this, Russia? Can't a man protest in this country any more when he's been jobbed out of something?"[43]

In the days after the fight Walcott and his handlers continued to claim a fast count. In the beginning, some agreed. It had appeared to be fast, particularly on television, where announcer Jimmy Powers, a half-second or so behind the referee's count but wanting to wind up even, sped his count toward the very end. The three-dimensional movies of the fight, however, told the real story. After Bocchicchio filed a formal protest, he and Illinois Athletic Commission officials, with considerable fanfare and more than a bit of absurdity, donned 3-D glasses to watch the fight film, which revealed that Walcott had received a full, audible, evenly spaced count. There was no fast count. The commission summarily rejected that claim as well as the other groundless ones contained in Bocchicchio's protest. Remarked Red Smith, "The referee did not push Walcott down at the count of seven or at any other time. He did not pull a knife on Joe. He did not rap him behind the ear with a banana stalk."[44]

Although Walcott got a fair shake, the essential mystery remained. Why did he just sit there? Why didn't he get up? What happened to Jersey Joe? Theories abounded:

Jersey Joe took a dive. Some immediately suspected that the fight was fixed. Bocchicchio did have some shady connections. Was it possible that he had lined up a sweetheart deal for Walcott to take a dive? Most felt not. As ex-fighter Tommy Loughran pointed out, if the fight had been a tank job, "Jersey Joe would have assumed another posture. He'd have gone down flat on his back or stomach, agonized it a bit, and listened to the full count."[45]

Jersey Joe miscalculated his rise. Another theory held that Walcott wanted to get up and tried to get up but merely miscalculated his rise. If so, the ring veteran made a rookie mistake. An experienced fighter would have gotten himself up on one knee so he could spring up at the count of seven or eight. Walcott made no such move and gave himself no margin of error by attempting to rise from a sitting position. Perhaps Walcott, in the confusion of the moment, lost track of the count. To some reporters, he said that he thought he got up at seven; to others, he said that he thought he got up at nine. "He can't count his years; he can't even count to ten," cracked Red Smith.[46]

Jersey Joe got bad advice from his corner. While he was sitting, Walcott was glancing, at least part of the time, toward his corner, where Bocchicchio was frantically waving with both hands for him to stay down. He may also have yelled instructions at Walcott, although it is unclear whether Walcott could have heard them from across the ring. Equally important, perhaps Walcott's manager couldn't hear the referee's count from across the ring. Bocchicchio later said, "Walcott was O.K., he was watching me for instructions. When I thought the count had reached eight, I signaled for Joe to get up, which you saw he did with no trouble."[47] The miscalculation, then, may have been Bocchicchio's, not Walcott's.

Jersey Joe was knocked out. At first, most weren't overly impressed by Marciano's short, rising right cross that dumped Walcott to the canvas. A notable exception was the referee Sikora, who maintained, "Don't let anybody tell you Walcott didn't get hit. . . . It may not have shown on television, but believe me I was the closest man seeing that punch and it was a knockout punch." After they had a chance to view the films of the fight, several reporters agreed. "It was there. It was perfect," praised Matt Ring. "It was a real good punch, it was inside," Marciano said. "I got a lot of beef behind it, and it hung there on his chin."[48] A few days after the fight, even Florio admitted that his fighter had been hit hard. Perhaps the punch was hard enough to account for Walcott's sitdown in the ring.

Jersey Joe quit. Many believed that Walcott was in a poor mental state going into the fight. As Florio later confirmed, "Joe froze up on us in the last twenty-four hours . . . I tried all day to get him to talk fight—tactics, punches, anything, . . . but he couldn't talk. The guy was through before he went into the ring." In the ring that night in Chicago, once Marciano knocked him down, perhaps all the memories of the Philadelphia punch eight months earlier came back—and perhaps Walcott gave up instead of getting up. As former champion Jimmy Braddock alleged, "The bum quit."[49]

In the end, the answer wasn't clear. Moreover, as Jack Carberry of the *Denver Post* pointed out, "One man knows the true answer. That's Jersey Joe Walcott."[50] A month after the fight, Walcott was still claiming quick count. Years later, Walcott changed his story, claiming that he blacked out late in the count. The mystery, then, remains very much unresolved.

In the aftermath of the fight, one fact was clear: Walcott's reputation was in tatters, at least for the time being. In just 145 seconds, claimed Matt Ring, "Walcott sacrificed the prestige and sentimental favor he had built up with many gallant fights over the past eight years." To Joe Bostic of the *New York Amsterdam News*, it was "the most disgusting exhibition of craven gutlessness in the history of the heavyweight championship division." Walcott's performance stood in striking contrast to his gallant stand in the first fight with Marciano, when he had gone out on his shield. Now, according to Red

Smith, he was going out in "total disgrace." It was sad. "It is hard to believe he would deliberately pass from the fistic scene ignominiously," mused Arch Ward of the *Chicago Tribune*.[51] But he did. Jersey Joe Walcott would never fight again.

Walcott's performance was also responsible for the heavy criticism directed at the fight. Like the fans in Chicago Stadium, fans from around the country were disappointed and angry, jamming the switchboards of their local newspapers to complain about the fight. The press joined the crescendo as well. Baltimore sportswriter Jesse Linthicum claimed that the "bout set boxing back ten years." Philadelphia sportswriter Lance McCurley charged that the fight had been so "nauseating and disgusting and unbelievable" that a congressional investigation of the entire fight game was in order. New York sportswriter Bill Corum simply noted, "This fight, if so it could be called, really was bad. Bad in itself. Bad for boxing. Bad for sports. Bad for this country, which is a sports loving country and where people, in a way, had a right to demand better of Walcott than he gave them last night."[52]

Lost in all the speculation about Walcott's actions and the criticism of Walcott and the fight was Rocky Marciano. In the ring, he had shared the crowd's amazement and disbelief in the sudden end. Had he really won that easily, that quickly? After his hand was raised in victory and he started to file out of the chaotic ring, Marciano heard some boos from the crowd. The boos were for the fiasco of the fight, but they still tarnished his successful defense. Later, an angry Marciano would say of Walcott, "He should have gotten up; I would have."[53]

The few who did pay attention to Marciano in the aftermath of the fight felt he deserved a better fate. He had fought a good fight while it lasted and done nothing wrong. Yet he received little credit for his effort. "I feel very sorry for Marciano today," admitted Franklin Lewis of the *Cleveland Press*. "He's a good boy who prepared in seriousness for the first defense of his crown. He went into the ring last night honest in intent; and he was honest in execution of his labors . . . I only wish Marciano had been permitted to do the job more vigorously, more conclusively, more squarely. He and the customers who paid their way into the stadium deserved a better shake."[54]

No one need have felt sorry for Rocky Marciano. He was still young (twenty-nine). He was still perfect (44-0). Most important, he was now the established heavyweight champion of the world. And he already had the image to prove it.

Part 2: Reigning

7 The Ideal

Long before he became heavyweight champion of the world, the image-makers had been hard at work crafting an official image for Rocky Marciano. His wholesome, all-American-boy persona had started to form as soon as Marciano first burst into the national spotlight with the victory over Joe Louis in October 1951. By the time of his second title fight with Jersey Joe Walcott in the spring of 1953, the image had crystalized and become firmly fixed in print and in the public's mind. It would remain indelibly his for the rest of his career.

That someone like Marciano had such an image was hardly earth-shattering news. In the 1950s it was customary for an athletic hero or a celebrity (as the heavyweight champion of the world, Rocky Marciano was both) to acquire an official public image. That still remains true. What is different today involves the permanence of that persona. Now, because the prime image-making medium is television, which offers such immediacy, and because the media is far more prying, a celebrity's image can change overnight. That wasn't the case in the early 1950s. The prime image-makers of the era were newspaper and magazine reporters, and the images they constructed for celebrities arose in print and had a lasting effect. Moreover, image-makers were far less likely to dig into a celebrity's personal life and change his or her persona as a result of what they found. Once a celebrity acquired an image, it was theirs to keep (barring some public relations disaster, of course).

Marciano's image was fixed through *Life, Look,* the *Saturday Evening Post,* and the other general-interest magazines of the era—all of which, in the infancy of television, retained a prominent role in shaping and conveying popular culture. Then, significantly, newspapers picked up the image, repeated it, and then elaborated upon it for an even larger audience. In the early 1950s, most Americans still got their news and formed their opinions from what they read in the newspapers. In the sports world, too, newspapers still mattered more than television, still coming to grips with how to cover sports. Television rarely provided an "up close and personal" vantage point. The glimpse into personality and character that newspapers provided, however, seemed to stick with readers. When boxing writers, especially the columnists, picked up Marciano's image and made it their own, it became locked in place for the public.

That magazine writers, boxing writers, and sports columnists would help create and then spread an image for the heavyweight champion of the world stemmed from necessity. After all, the best boxers only fought, at most, a couple of times a year. That left sportswriters with a dilemma. The sport's popularity demanded constant coverage, but there was rarely action to write about—stories about sparring sessions and fighters making weight could only take you so far. Sportswriters naturally turned to stories about character and personality to fill lengthy gaps between fights. From those stories, a fighter's image would arise.

By the time Marciano came along, sportswriters had played a huge part in creating and promoting a boxer's image on several notable occasions. In the 1920s they had assisted Jack Dempsey and his press agents in transforming his bad-boy image into a more respectable one. In the end, Dempsey emerged a folk hero in the golden age of sports, and boxing emerged from a troubled past to become a major spectator sport. Then, in the 1930s and 1940s, sportswriters had helped construct the official public image of Joe Louis. As Louis's biographer Chris Mead has pointed out, many sportswriters were aware of Louis's potential social significance as a racial pioneer and wanted to avoid creating a persona that was tantamount to Son of Jack Johnson. Working in harmony with Louis's handlers, they helped forge an image of the fighter that would promote tolerance. He was modest and unassuming. He neither bragged nor gloated. He worked hard. He lived clean. He read the Bible. He saved his money. He was good to his mother. He married a nice black girl. He was, in short, "well-behaved."[1] The image quickly stuck and would remain Louis's public persona for the rest of his life.

What sportswriters had done before they would do again for Rocky Marciano. The image-makers had found an ideal subject. "Here's Marciano," Robert Lipsyte of the *New York Times* observes. "He's solid, he's decent—a good guy in that kind of manly American way."[2] The image that the image-makers proceeded to construct for Marciano would not involve weighty questions of boxing's survival (as with Dempsey) or race relations (as with Louis). Still, the Marciano image was not devoid of broader social and cultural implications. Marciano rose to fame in the early 1950s, a distinctive time in American culture, and his image would mirror and embody that culture.

The 1950s is often remembered as a simple, idyllic decade—or as one writer put it more cynically, "the dullest and dreariest in all our history."[3] To a large extent that was true. Even at the time, not much seemed to be happening—and that's just the way most Americans wanted it. The men and women of this generation had lived through enough crises to last a lifetime—namely, the Great Depression and World War II. With the postwar economy booming, most Americans were ready for a return to normalcy. They were content to revel in a life of bliss, harmony, and prosperity. Beginning in the late 1940s and into the 1950s, they proceeded to do precisely that.

The distinctive popular culture that emerged to fit the tenor of the times is best characterized by one word: consensus. With all the optimism and prosperity in American life, there was no room for dissidence. It simply wasn't tolerated. Everyone was expected to embrace the prevailing vision, beliefs, values, and modes of behavior. As cultural historian Stephen J. Whitfield has pointed out, the sitting president of the era, Dwight Eisenhower, best symbolized this ideal of consensus. Everyone liked Ike. In American society, disagreement and individuality were only welcomed at the margins. Ultimately, conformity was demanded.[4]

The ongoing cold war sharpened those tendencies. With the emergence of the Soviet Union as America's chief rival in the new postwar world, fear of communism—both at home and abroad—gripped the country. This was the age of McCarthyism, with Sen. Joseph McCarthy of Wisconsin leading a witch hunt for communists in the government and in other corners of American society. McCarthyism was about suspicion and fear. Culturally, it also helped lead to what Whitfield has called an "ideology of the United States." As he has observed, "The search to define and affirm a way of life, the need to express and celebrate the meaning of 'Americanism,' was the flip side of stigmatizing Communism."[5] Thus was born the American Way of Life—a set of values and a corresponding standard of behavior that was good, proper, and uniquely nationalistic.

As the antidote to communism, the American Way of Life took the ideal of consensus to a new level. And it was everywhere. It made its way into history textbooks, which treated the American Way of Life as stable and entrenched. It was extolled in popular literature, magazines, newspapers, and films. It also played itself out in the nation's living rooms—every night—through the new medium of television. Nowhere was the American Way of Life portrayed more powerfully and with such lasting effect. In a 1950s sitcom family, as David Halberstam has pointed out, there were no marital problems, no parent-child problems, no health problems, no economic problems—in fact, no problems whatsoever. Instead, everything was happy, upbeat, and optimistic. Game shows (embracing capitalism) and cop shows (embracing the criminal justice system) also reflected a basic belief in the American Way of Life, culture of conformity, and society of goodness. It was all about truth, justice, and the American Way.[6]

The sports world embraced and reflected the American Way of Life as well. As Mead has pointed out, sport has always served as "a signpost" of American society and has played a "peculiar and central role in our culture."[7] That was certainly true in the early 1950s. In particular, the American Way of Life found living embodiment in one of the leading sports heroes of the day: Rocky Marciano.

In constructing an image for Marciano, sportswriters derived the basic elements of his persona from the basic tenets of the American Way of Life. The fact that the new heavyweight champion of the world actually possessed many desirable qualities made their job easier. Along the way, of course, they also embellished and invented still other qualities so he would even better fit the ideal. Whether all of this was a conscious exercise is difficult to ascertain. Either way, the image-makers seemed to be saying, "Here is a man who represents the best that our country has to offer. Here is a man for our time. Here is a man of our time." Rocky Marciano, therefore, came to symbolize the culture of consensus and conformity, the way Americans saw themselves (or desperately wanted to see themselves) in the early 1950s.

▼ ▼ ▼

The ideal man of the early 1950s was, at heart, a family man. He was married, of course, and he loved his wife. He had children, of course, and he loved his kids. "Fifties Man" was completely devoted to his family; it was the absolute center of his existence. He was a picture of domestic bliss. Think of Jim Anderson arriving home at the end of the day, a smile on his face and a newspaper tucked under his arm, ready to kiss his wife and help sort out any pleasant mess that the kids had caused during the course of the day.

Rocky Marciano was, the press continually reminded the public, a family man through and through. He was, first and foremost, a faithful husband. His wife Barbara became an integral part of his persona. Often, newspapers would report on her attendance at his big fights, accounts sometimes accompanied by photographs that detailed her reactions while the fight unfolded. And the press was charmed. To the *Boston Globe,* Barbara was "tall, blonde, wholesome; looks like a girl who lives in your home town." To the *Chicago Tribune,* she was a "winsome wife" who had the "graceful figure and walk of a professional model, belied by a school girl complexion."[8] She also was a good wife, standing behind her man and sharing in his dreams. Her husband's career came first, even if it involved long stretches of time away from home.

With such an attractive, supportive wife, was it any surprise, the image-makers noted, that Rocky preferred to stay home with Barbara rather than hit the nightlife of Broadway? When he did take in shows, he did so only when Barbara was firmly by his side. The Marcianos made an attractive couple, he the famous yet down-to-earth husband, she the glamorous yet wholesome wife. After Bill Keefe of the *New Orleans Times-Picayune* had dinner with the couple during their visit to his city in 1953, he remarked that Rocky looked like an ordinary, successful salesman, doctor, or businessman who had with a "charming and refined wife" properly in tow.[9]

Rocky Marciano was not only a devoted husband but also a doting father. On December 6, 1952, boxing's first couple had their first child, Mary Anne. The new father, who always wanted a big family, was crazy about his new daughter. "He's a wonderful father," Barbara told the press in the fall of 1953. "He gets up early just to change and bathe the baby, and he loves it." Around the same time, the package became complete when the Marcianos moved into a nine-room, $35,000, brick, fieldstone, and clapboard ranch house on the fashionable west side of Brockton. Barbara immediately started a garden, explaining, "Rocky likes a lot of fresh vegetables and I like the flowers."[10]

The house with the white picket fence sealed it: Rocky Marciano was "a devoted family man." Barbara and Mary Anne, Tim Cohane of *Look* reassured readers, were Rocky's "pride and joy." Charley Goldman also got into the act, observing, "One worry I had with some fighters that I've never had with Rocky is the bright lights. He's wrapped up in his wife and their new baby and his family back in Brockton, Massachusetts."[11] Marciano even won a "Sports Father of the Year" award in the spring of 1953. If testimonials and awards weren't enough, the press supplied visual images as well. Magazine profiles of Marciano would invariably include a picture of him with Barbara and/or Mary Anne, and newspapers would habitually run pictures of the happy family at birthday parties or vacations. Even the dream house made it into a few pictures.

Ultimately, and perhaps most powerfully, Marciano projected the image of a family man. In an interview with Arch Ward of the *Chicago Tribune* in the fall of 1953, for example, he couldn't stop talking about Mary Anne and showing off a nicely framed photograph of his daughter given to him by Barbara. In other prefight interviews with Ward and sportswriters such as Arthur Daley of the *New York Times,* he would complain about how long he had to spend in training camp away from his wife and daughter, how much he missed them, and how he was looking forward to seeing them again after the fight. Like the ideal man of his age, he was fixated on family.[12]

Fifties Man was also a loyal creature. He had to be if he wanted to survive in society, for no quality in the age of McCarthyism, spy rings, and blacklisting was more critical. Loyalty was the hot issue on Capitol Hill throughout the era as the House Un-American Activities Committee investigated the loyalty of a parade of witnesses, from low-level government workers to glamorous Hollywood types. To avoid being called to the carpet, Fifties Man had to demonstrate his loyalty at all times.

Rocky Marciano was unfailingly loyal in several key respects. He never forgot his parents, for instance. He paid off the mortgage on their house and bought them a washer, dryer, freezer, and other newfangled appliances. He insisted that his father retire from the shoe factories. He sent his parents on a dream vacation to the old country. And he kept his parents involved in the fabric of his life as heavyweight champion of the world. His father, for instance, became a fixture in his training camps. Pop Marciano (as he was often called) was a beloved figure in the champion's entourage, mixing his son's "health cocktails" and tossing his Italian salads. IBC press agent Ben Bentley later recalled Marciano telling the rest of his entourage, "This old man smelled shoe leather long enough. Now he smells the roses." The press noted all of this with approval, because how you treated your parents mattered greatly in 1950s society. As Pierino Marchegiano noted, "He is loyal to his father. Being champion of the world is one thing. But being loyal to your family is another."[13]

Marciano was also loyal to his friends. When Marciano hooked up with Weill, for instance, his new pilot wanted to jettison Allie Colombo. But Marciano insisted that he remain on the team. Nicky Sylvester and others from the old gang in Brockton also continued to have a presence in the life of the champion. He plainly liked having them around. Again, the image-makers approved. Marciano "likes to surround himself with old friends from Brockton," Al Hirshberg of the *Saturday Evening Post* observed with admiration. Despite his fame, lauded Wilton Garrison of the *Charlotte Observer*, he remained "the kind who will do anything for a friend."[14]

Finally, and most powerfully, Marciano was loyal to his hometown. He was, at bottom, a hometown guy, someone who "had the typical American town upbringing," according to Joseph C. Nichols of the *New York Times*. When he attained fame and glory he naturally became the hometown hero. The people of Brockton, Massachusetts, proceeded to shower the hometown hero with love and support. They always bet heavily on the Rock, for example. When he won, they won. "A lot of working people in this town are a lot better off because of Marciano," one Brockton resident told sportswriter W. C. Heinz. "There are families that have suddenly moved into brand-new homes. The man is a factory worker, and everybody knows what he makes. They say, 'Where does he get the money to buy a house like that?' It's obvious. He's been betting on Rocky."[15]

In addition, thousands of Brocktonians attended each of Marciano's big fights. They suddenly found themselves, however vicariously, in the big time. Those who stayed behind also shared in the excitement. Brockton on a Marciano fight night pulsated with electricity. Thousands of people would gather on Main Street to listen to fight updates piped in from loudspeakers hanging from the town's newspaper office. Everything else in the city would come to a complete stop; factories would shut down, and the movie theaters would be empty. "When Rocky fights on TV, the streets are deserted," an editor of the Brockton city newspaper told Heinz. "You can look the length of Main Street and not see a soul."[16]

Until Marciano won, that is. When that happened, Brockton usually went into bedlam. Celebrations were especially raucous on the nights he beat Louis and Walcott for the first time. People honked car horns, formed informal motorcades, snake danced, waved banners, and mobbed Marciano's regular hangout, the Ward Two Memorial Club. On each occasion, newspaper accounts compared the celebration to New Year's Eve. And, on each occasion, as well as after his 1951 victory over Rex Layne and his 1956 retirement, the people of Brockton followed up by throwing Marciano a parade, complete with all the trimmings. The largest, after the first Walcott fight, drew more people (between sixty and a hundred thousand, depending on the estimate) than had turned out for President Roosevelt and President Truman's previous visits to the city—and with good reason. Shoes may have put Brockton on the map, but Marciano gave the city its identity.

If Brockton loved Rocky Marciano, Rocky Marciano loved Brockton right back. His ties to the town were strong and unquestioned. His home remained in Brockton. Most of his friends were people from Brockton. In the ring, he even wore an old robe with the colors (black and red) of Brockton High School. The press once again approved. To Arthur Daley, Marciano was a "homebody who still prefers hanging out in the corner drug-store in Brockton to risking bedazzlement by the bright lights of Broadway." As Tim Cohane observed, "Never has sport known a greater romance than this one between the gladiator hero and his home town."[17] He was indeed the Brockton Blockbuster.

Fifties Man was not only loyal but also had healthy respect for authority. On an individual level, that meant respecting your elders, the men and women who had guided the nation through the Great Depression, World War II, and on into prosperity. On a societal level, that meant respecting those institutions of authority—from the army to the FBI—which preserved that prosperity and safeguarded freedom from the evils of communism. Just a decade later, millions of young people would challenge, buck, and ultimately reject authority. Not Fifties Man. He followed orders and toed the line.

Rocky Marciano respected authority. That was evident in his relationship with his parents, especially his father. As Jim Jennings of the *Philadelphia Sunday Bulletin* observed, "The champion reveres and respects his dad, whose word is law to the titleholder." The true authority figures during his career, however, were not his parents but his handlers, Al Weill and Charley Goldman. To the press, it made sense to have two veteran fight men give the orders. The press also approved of the way that Marciano obeyed. "Part of Rocky's success is due to his willingness to follow orders, without asking questions—a virtue other fight managers would like to see more of in their tigers," Marshall Smith observed in a 1952 *Life* profile. "Rocky is willing to leave the heavy thinking to others, and in his camp it is done by two very sharp minds." Smith went on to characterize Weill and Goldman as the brains and Marciano as the brawn. "It is a mutually benevolent arrangement for all three," he concluded. "Without Weill and Goldman to think for him, Rocco Francis Marchegiano would probably still be digging mains for the Brockton gas company."[18]

Others were less insulting in praising Marciano's respect for the authority of his handlers. Tim Cohane noted approvingly that Marciano "accepts unquestioningly any chore or instruction from Weill and Goldman." Echoed Arthur Daley, "Fortunately for Al Weill, Charlie Goldman and other members of his Joint Chiefs of Staff, Rocky is the world's most obedient fighter. If Weill told him to eat steel shavings to develop strength, Rocky would eat 'em." Even Marciano himself recognized his willingness to toe the line, telling *Time,* "You gotta take orders, you know."[19]

Along the same lines, the ideal man of the early 1950s was patriotic. He loved America and the lifestyle, prosperity, and freedoms that it had to offer. Perhaps he had even risked his life to protect those freedoms by serving his country in World War II or the Korean War. When the latter "conflict" finally ended in 1953, peace returned to America. Yet with the ever-present and ongoing threat of communism, there was still need for patriotism. Fifties Man was ready to answer the call.

Rocky Marciano's patriotism was not in question. Like many of his contemporaries, he had served his country during World War II, and sportswriters didn't let readers forget it, particularly around the time of his first big fights against Roland LaStarza, Layne, and Louis. They would routinely point out that Marciano was an "ex-GI." He was, Jesse Abramson declared, "one of those war products every one expected to come out of the service in droves." Paul Zimmerman of the *Los Angeles Times* noted that "[j]ust as World War I produced a world's heavyweight champion, Gene Tunney, World War II gets credit for giving the new title king, Rocky Marciano, to the fistic game."[20]

Although references to his military hitch faded after he became champion, Marciano continued to earn his patriotic stripes in other ways. In 1953, for instance, when he fought Walcott in Chicago, Marciano reached out to several former Korean War POWs. One was Vincent D'Andreo of Swampscott, Massachusetts, who upon release from captivity immediately asked if Marciano was still champion. "If that boy could have me in mind after all that privation he sure can come to see me fight," Marciano announced to reporters. "I'll see that he gets a ringside seat."[21] Marciano plainly had his priorities well in order.

Those priorities included religion and, again, Marciano's image tracked the ideal. Fifties Man was for God as well as for country. He approved when the words "one nation under God" was added to the Pledge of Allegiance in 1954 and when Congress adopted the national motto "In God We Trust." Evil communists, after all, were godless. Good Americans were not. Fifties Man believed in God and, just as important, believed in the institution of religion as part of the American Way of Life.

Rocky Marciano was a God-fearing man. Sportswriters frequently hailed him as "a religious man" and "a devout Catholic." His mother, observed Bill Liston of the *Boston Post*, "has guided the new champion in the teachings of his religion." Confirmed Tim Cohane, "The Catholic faith is deeply ingrained in him."[22] As with Jersey Joe Walcott, sportswriters trumpeted Marciano's attendance at Sunday mass during his training camps. They also reported when he would sneak away in the anxious hours before a big fight to find solace in a chapel or a church. His other visible demonstrations of faith—falling to his knees in his dressing room and praying to St. Anthony before the first fight with Walcott, covering his chin and hands with St. Jude's oil while in his corner and waiting for the start of that fight, and reading *The Confessions of St. Augustine* before his fight with LaStarza in the fall of 1953—all made for splendid copy as well.

Likewise, the press heralded the fact that Marciano regularly kept the company of priests. If he wasn't buying a television for a priest from Brockton (who, unfortunately, tumbled off a stage and broke his leg while installing the gift), he was playing golf with a priest from Denver. Or he was helping a priest from Carbondale, Pennsylvania, with a parish benefit. Or he was, most notably, opening a community center and going to lunch with Cardinal Spellman of New York. When Spellman remarked to reporters that Marciano was a former CYO boy, he was revealing nothing new to members of the sports world. They had long regarded Marciano as a religious man.

Fifties Man also retained a refreshing sense of innocence. He was filled with optimism about life and its possibilities despite the Great Depression, World War II, and other crises he had endured. He was not cynical. There was no trickery or deception about him, and he was pure as the driven snow.

Here again, the heavyweight champion of the world measured up. Rocky Marciano was an innocent man. As Harvey Breit of the *New York Times* observed, Marciano could look "astonishingly innocent" and ten years younger than he actually was because he was "totally without deception, totally without guile." Consider his actions the night he won the title from Walcott in Philadelphia. At 3 or 4 in the morning, after the celebrations had died down, the new champion, unable to sleep, went outside and walked around Rittenhouse Square. He was stunned that the big city was still bustling. "There were a lot of people on the streets then," he later told reporters, eyes wide.[23] Plainly, Rocky Marciano was still a bit in wonder of it all.

The fact that he personified clean living only added to his innocence. Sportswriters often reminded readers that Marciano neither drank nor smoked. They liked the fact that, when asked by the host of a party in Brockton what he wanted to drink (scotch, rye, or bourbon), Marciano replied, "If you don't mind, I'll take an apple." Marciano was even, in the words of Red Smith, "pure of speech." As Tim Cohane revealed, "His grammar is not quite so pristine as that of President James B. Conant of Harvard, but it is pleasantly free from profanity. Rocky decided to give up swearing when he was in the Army." There was no doubt that he was, as *Life* proclaimed, "a clean-living boy."[24]

Even one of Marciano's few acknowledged "vices"—food—was refreshing. The press loved to talk about how he loved to eat. Marshall Smith called him the "knife-and-fork champion of the eastern seaboard. Rocky often devours two steaks with all the trimmings, and then stuffs his pockets with cookies and bananas to tide him over." The toughest task for Charley Goldman, added Cohane, was to "keep his tiger from building a between-meal snack into an infinity-course dinner. Steaks, chops, roasts, spaghetti—it's all the same to Rocky." A picture in his 1956 autobiographical serial in the *Saturday Evening Post* said it all about the purity of the "vice." There, on the front porch, was Rocky and his best friend Allie, eating cake and ice cream.[25]

As an outgrowth of his innocence and purity, the ideal man of the early 1950s worked hard at his trade or craft. He believed in a dollar's pay for a dollar's work. He also believed that those that worked hard got ahead and reaped life's benefits. Fifties Man considered the high national standard of living, as well as the many glorious achievements of capitalism and big business, as the ultimate vindication of the American Way of Life.

Again, Marciano fit the bill. He had an unmatched work ethic in his chosen field. Proclaimed Tim Cohane, "No man in the history of athletics could have subjected himself to a more sustained Spartanism than The Rock did." To Arthur Daley, Marciano brought an "austere, sackcloth-and-ashes approach of a monk" to his training. Similarly, Jimmy Cannon observed that Marciano trained "like a man practicing a holy ritual." As Charley Goldman once said to Marciano, "I've been in this boxing business fifty years, and I've never seen anyone like you yet. Work. Work. Work. Train. Train. Train. Sometimes, I suspect you're not even human."[26]

It wasn't just the long hours he put in at training camp that impressed the image-makers. It was also the way he went about it. In the fall of 1953, Harvey Breit noted that "like an earnest sixteen-year-old, he is always trying to improve himself. It is not the Boy Scout approach either. Improving himself has become an instinct with him and it is something to marvel at."

In the fall of 1955—before Marciano's last fight—he was still trying to improve. As he watched Marciano train, Saul Pett of the Associated Press observed, "He said nothing, never smiled. . . . His eyes remained earnest. It was more the look of a schoolboy struggling with a long division problem."[27]

Because it was built on attitude and a desire for self-improvement, Marciano's work ethic was distinctly American. "I actually enjoy training," he once revealed. "Here's the way I look at it. If I opened up a grocery store and bought a lot of canned goods, I'd be out hustling try to sell those goods and be a success. But fighting is the only work I know and I want to put the same effort and hustle into it that I'd put in the grocery business or any other kind of business. I want to be the best." To Charley Goldman, "Rocky must be something like this golfer, Ben Hogan. I read how Hogan will shoot a fine score and then go out and practice for a couple of hours. Rocky is exactly that way." Marciano, concluded Harvey Breit, "is the classic American story: work and win."[28]

The ideal man of the early 1950s was also a decent one, and Rocky Marciano was, in the words of Jimmy Cannon, "a kind and decent man." To Daley, he was "inherently a decent, righteous and truly wonderful guy. . . . His innate decency and wholesomeness shine through in a dedicated glow." That decency was reflected in his modesty, which consistently dazzled sportswriters. Early in Marciano's reign, Stanley Woodward begged him to "remain the same unfresh kid you are now after you have been recognized as the greatest of all heavyweight champions." He did. As Whitney Martin observed toward the end of his reign, "We never cease to be amazed at the humility of Rocky Marciano . . . [he] treats everyone if they were the celebrity and he the awed little guy." To Prescott Sullivan of the *San Francisco Examiner,* Marciano was "probably the humblest of heavyweight champions."[29]

Equally important, Marciano was friendly. To Daley, Marciano possessed an "innate friendliness." Observed Bob Cooke of the *New York Herald Tribune,* "He reminds you of a great, friendly collie from the kennels of Albert Payson Terhune." Even Marciano's ever-present smile seemed to crave acceptance and welcome a friendly conversation. "It is the grin of a shy fellow happy to be recognized, at last, as a member of the gang in good standing," observed A. J. Liebling of *The New Yorker.*[30]

Beneath the friendly exterior, revealed the image-makers, lurked a gentle man. Jim Murray of the *Los Angeles Times* called Marciano "the gentlest athlete I have ever known." Besides his behavior toward children, anecdotes supplied the evidence. Once, Marciano, jogging by a golf course in Brockton, stopped to pick up a stray golf ball in the street. The enraged golfer berated him. Marciano just handed over the ball and went on his way. On another occasion, while filing out of Franklin Field after watching a Notre Dame–Penn football game Marciano bumped another fan, who threatened to flatten him. Again, the heavyweight champion just shrugged it off. Boston sportswriter John Gillooly contended that "[t]here never was a gentler giant. . . . Outside [the ring] you could, if you suddenly went stark silly, slap him across the face and receive nothing but a verbal rebuke in reprisal." More metaphorically, Harvey Breit called him "a lamb in lion's clothing."[31]

All of this made Rocky Marciano an immensely likable man. In an era that cultivated and cherished conformity, to be liked by one's peers was of no small significance. As Marciano said, "I like to be liked." If that was his goal, he succeeded. Sportswriters would invariably tell readers that the heavyweight champion of the world was a nice, pleasant, and likable guy. To Hugh Brown of the *Philadelphia Sunday Bulletin,* he was "probably the world's most agreeable fellow." To Arthur Daley, he was "as easy to know and like as the freckle-faced kid down the block."[32] Once again, Marciano fit the mold of the idyllic Fifties Man.

There was one quality to the ideal that was perhaps more important than any other. The ideal man of the early 1950s was, at bottom and above all, a simple man. There was little that was complicated or complex about him. He liked a simple lifestyle filled with simple pleasures, and it didn't take a lot to make him happy. He left nothing hidden, pulled no punches, and was satisfied with his lot in life. In the Age of Simplicity, a simple nature was most assuredly a virtue.

To the image-makers, Marciano had that virtue in spades. He was, proclaimed *Time* in 1952, a "simple, good-natured fellow." Some cast his simplicity in a condescending light, particularly at the beginning of his reign. As Marshall Smith put it, "In a profession that is not distinguished for its nobility or its ethics, he is a real live edition of the comic-strip champion, Joe Palooka: unassuming, clean-living, not too bright, a humble guy with a heart of gold who uses his God-given strength to slay ogres and flatten city slickers."[33]

Ultimately, though, most came to admire Marciano's simplicity. Take Arthur Daley, for example. After Marciano won the title from Walcott, Daley proclaimed that Marciano's greatest charm was his "utter simplicity." A year later Daley observed, "Rocky's boyish enthusiasm and naturalness contribute immeasurably to his appeal." Halfway through Marciano's reign as champion, Daley gushed that every visit with the champion was a "refreshing experience. . . . There's no sham or pretense to him and that's why he is one of the most captivating personalities in the entire realm of sports." Then, toward the end of Marciano's reign, Daley was enraptured with the fact that

Marciano seemed thrilled that Boston Red Sox centerfielder Jimmy Piersall had asked whether he would mind if someone took a photograph of them together. ("Gee, would I mind?" Marciano said to Daley. "It was an honor for me to have my picture taken with a player like Jimmy Piersall.")[34] Daley remained charmed by Marciano's simplicity to the end.

He was hardly alone. Bill Keefe declared, "He has the plain old personality that clicks . . . Rocky Marciano is a typical American—the plain type that's satisfied with himself and with the sphere he moves in." To Harold Kaese of the *Boston Globe,* he was a man of "simplicity and sincerity." "His personality, like his ring technique," Red Smith remarked upon Marciano's death in 1969, "was marked by simplicity. He was unaffected, warm, straightforward."[35]

The final word on Marciano's image belongs to an unlikely source. Al Weill was not the mushy type. Even he, however, had to admit, "Rocky is the sweetest man I've ever met."[36]

● ● ●

A family man, loyal, respectful of authority, patriotic, religious, innocent, pure, hard working, decent, modest, friendly, gentle, likable, simple—the ideal man of the early 1950s was all these things. And so was Rocky Marciano, at least according to his official public image. To some extent the qualities the image-makers enmeshed in the ideal of Marciano are timeless ones that have been valued in every era. They were truly cherished in the early 1950s, however, and often at the expense of charisma. Marciano, in fact, possessed a certain charisma, but that didn't matter much to the image-makers. They wanted their heroes straight down the middle. The type of image they constructed for Marciano was filled with idealistic qualities and devoid of any sort of individualism. Now such an image might seem corny (if not somewhat sickening). At the time, it was enviable.

But was the image accurate? When Marciano retired from the ring in 1956, W. J. McGoogan of the *St. Louis Post-Dispatch* proclaimed, "All the good things said about Marciano are true."[37] To a certain extent, McGoogan was correct. Much of Marciano's image was grounded in fact. He really was good to his parents. He was extremely loyal to everyone who knew him. He respected authority. He was probably as patriotic as the next man. From outward appearances, Marciano appeared to take his faith seriously. He really didn't drink or smoke. Clearly, no one worked harder. Modest, friendly, and likable—Marciano was all of those things. There was a certain significance to the stories and anecdotes that image-makers repeated over and over. In addition to helping shape Marciano's image, they also spoke volumes about Marciano the man. In most respects, then, image did match reality.

In a few respects, however, it did not. Here again, the man mirrored the decade, simple at first glance but somewhat more complex beneath the surface. As David Halberstam has noted, the 1950s were neither simple nor dull. Beneath the happy facade, seeds of change were being planted and beginning to sprout. All this change—involving racial, sexual, and other cultural and political mores—would emerge in full-bloom during the 1960s. The early 1950s, then, were not that clear-cut.[38]

The same holds true for that cultural icon of the early 1950s, Rocky Marciano. He had a certain complexity, part of which took the form of peccadilloes and another part that was evident in his distinct—and human—character flaws. Marciano's image, however, sacrificed complexity for conformity. As a result, his image suffered from some invention, some embellishment, and a few glaring omissions. For instance, the image-makers took some liberties in claiming that Marciano was a model family man. For sure, family meant a lot to Marciano. He was exceedingly close to his parents as well as his siblings. He also was devoted to his wife, at least at the beginning of their marriage. (They would drift apart after he retired.) By all accounts and at all times, he was crazy about his daughter. The fact was, however, that Marciano spent hardly any time at home. When he wasn't in training, he was constantly traveling around the country and the world making personal appearances, racking up more than a hundred thousand miles as champion.

Along the way, he missed a lot. When Barbara gave birth to daughter Mary Anne in Brockton, Rocky was in California making personal appearances, unable to get home until a week later. When Barbara, vacationing with friends in Mexico, had a miscarriage, Rocky was in training for the first Charles fight and didn't find out until later. When Barbara developed a glandular condition, Rocky was on the road and, again, didn't find out until later. During his career, Marciano didn't spend a lot of time on the home front. He and Barbara estimated at the time of his retirement in 1956 that he had spent just 152 days at home over the previous four years.

On several occasions, Marciano seemed to concede that he didn't fit the prototype of a family man. For instance, in September 1953 he told Arthur Daley (who seemed to serve as his father confessor for such matters) that he had been home only twenty-six days since the birth of his daughter in December 1952. "Gosh, she doesn't even know me," Marciano said. Marciano once told Daley that although he didn't like spending so much time in camp away from the family, "that's the price I have to pay. And, I might add, I have no regrets." At the end of his career, he felt considerable guilt about all this, admitting, "I wasn't much of a husband and father."[39] Marciano was probably being hard on himself. Still, the fact persists that the prototypical 1950s family man would have probably limited his time in camp, and definitely on the road barnstorming, in order to spend more time at home. Marciano made no such choice. He may have been devoted to his family, but he was not a true family man, at least in the idealistic early 1950s sense.

Sportswriters also embellished Marciano's simple nature. He wasn't as simple as portrayed during the Age of Simplicity. For sure, his tastes were simple, but he also liked the limelight. After he had a taste of it, he didn't want to go back to his ordinary existence. And he never did, even after he retired. Marciano liked the good life. He also liked the action of the fast lane. After he rose to the top of the sports world, he never would have been comfortable in returning to Brockton and hanging around the corner drug store.

Lifestyles aside, there was an unexplored side to Rocky Marciano's psyche. Although he wanted to become a boxer and then a champion for all the traditional reasons (fame, wealth, and glory), what really drove him was fear—fear of poverty and fear of obscurity. The image he acquired during his career, however, didn't address those factors, or any other psychological component for that matter. What made Rocky Marciano tick? What drove him to work so hard? Why did he so desperately want to succeed? The image-makers of the 1950s were largely unconcerned with such questions, and if they knew the answers they weren't telling. Among the many thousands of stories written about Rocky Marciano during his career, only a precious few addressed psychological dimensions. They weren't seen as part and parcel of a proper image. What lurked beneath the surface in the Age of Simplicity—and with Rocky Marciano there was plainly something bubbling beneath his one-dimensional image—was conveniently glossed over. Surface simplicity, however, was fair game and harped upon accordingly.

Then there were the omissions from Marciano's official public image. One character trait that altogether failed to qualify for that image was sportsmanship. The omission was, in one sense, curious given that sportsmanship was at the heart of the American Way of Life. Nothing was more quintessentially American than to play fair and square, yet it was strangely missing from the image of that living embodiment of the American Way of Life, Rocky Marciano.

And with good reason: Marciano hardly exuded tremendous sportsmanship in the ring. From his early days in Providence, he fought rough-and-tumble. That sometimes involved hitting below the belt, hitting on the break, or hitting after the bell—all of which were illegal. After he hit the big time,

Marciano retained his roughhouse tactics. In fact, they would often become major subplots of his title bouts. In the wake of the fouls, he typically drew jeers from the crowd and stylistic criticism from the press. When asked about the infractions, Marciano typically offered excuses or claimed ignorance. He also claimed that the flak greatly bothered him. Yet the fouls persisted.

Part of the reason was stylistic. Marciano was wild, awkward, and out of control, and a fighter with that type of style is bound to land some errant punches. But Marciano probably could have curbed many of the fouls had he wanted. He did not. They remained a problem to the end of his career. Ultimately, he may not have intended to foul, but he also had no intention of altering the roughhouse style that produced those fouls. In the ring he always cared more about the end than the means. The necessity of winning trumped whatever remorse he felt for fouling.

In any event, most sportswriters, in addressing Marciano's character, didn't mention his recurring departures from the ideal of fair play. Of the few who did, some denied the allegations outright. For instance, Arch Ward once asserted that Marciano was "regarded as one of the cleanest fighters in the business," which was clearly not the case. Others apologized for Marciano. Yes, they admitted, he was rough, but he wasn't dirty because he didn't intend to foul his opponent. Instead, those sportswriters praised the sportsmanship he displayed when he felt miserable after beating Louis and Walcott. "What's the matter with me, anyway?" Marciano asked Arthur Daley after one such occasion. "Not a thing, Rocky," wrote Daley in reply. "Not a thing."[40]

The most glaring omission from Marciano's public image, however, was his bizarre obsession with money. For better or for worse, the fixation was one of the most striking aspects of his personality. Yet the image-makers largely ignored it. Occasionally, they would slip in a cute reference, noting that Marciano was "not an easy spender" or that his "appetite improves if someone else is paying the check." They might drop a humorous quip from one of his handlers (Goldman had joked that "[h]e wouldn't spend a nickel to see an earthquake"). Or they would put a positive spin on things and call Marciano "a thrifty gladiator" or "a thrifty fellow."[41] Taking that a step further, some image-makers maintained that he was willing to spend when the chips were down. Others trumpeted the fact that he had given money to Carmine Vingo after their near-tragic fight in late 1949. And, of course, they noted that he was generous with his family and friends.

Frugality and generosity skirted the issue of Marciano and money, though. Marciano was bitter about money. He often thought he was being short-changed, whether by Al Weill, rival managers, the IBC, or others in the boxing world. Sadly, he was often right. Because of various circumstances and machinations beyond his control, his purses (especially for the Louis fight and the second Walcott bout) were sometimes far smaller than they should have been. He also didn't see much of those purses. By the time all those who had a piece of the Rock were taken care of—some combination of Weill, Allie Colombo, and perhaps others—Marciano may have been left with a relatively small percentage of his own winnings. As Bud Collins of the *Boston Globe* notes, "Rocky must have been chopped up deeper" than the typical fighter in that regard. Moreover, unlike fighters of the past, Marciano was not reaping the benefits of regular million-dollar gates and a low income tax rate. "I should have come along during the Tunney-Dempsey period," he said in 1952. "Whenever I think of the $1,000,000 Tunney got for the second Dempsey fight my palms itch. And to think he paid hardly any income tax."[42]

More than anything else, though, Marciano was strange about money. He was obsessed with making it—in cash, not checks. He was determined not to spend it, exhibiting a cheapness in certain areas that far exceeded the boundaries of ordinary frugality. He was also hell-bent on keeping it and hiding it in all sorts of strange places throughout the country. It was only after his career concluded, however, that stories about Marciano and money began to leak out. The fixation was more evident in his postretirement years, when Marciano was finally free from the clutches of Weill and the endless training grind—and finally free to demonstrate personality traits that may have been partially hidden when he was fighting and forging an all-American-boy image. One does not develop a fixation on money as strong as Marciano's was overnight, however; certainly, it was present in some measure during his fighting days. Sportswriters of the early 1950s chose not to report it, however, and omitted it from the image they constructed for him.

In the final analysis, Marciano's pristine image belied the complexity of the man behind that image. It also set him up for a fall from his pedestal. No one could have possibly lived up to the too-good-to-be-true image that image-makers of the early 1950s constructed, and Rocky Marciano did not. He, like everyone else, had character flaws and eccentricities. He was, in short, human.

● ● ●

In the spring of 1955, toward the end of Marciano's career, Curley Grieve, the sports editor of the *San Francisco Examiner*, claimed, "Millions of words have been written about Rocky Marciano without one knock against his character or habits."[43] It was true. Although many criticized Marciano the fighter, no one criticized Marciano the man. When it came to matters relating to Marciano's personal character, sportswriters accentuated the positive and eliminated the negative.

The reason they did so, on a practical level, was in part due to the excellent relations that Marciano enjoyed with them. At the beginning of his rise to prominence, the raw Marciano was somewhat taciturn with the press. Eventually, though, he grew at ease with sportswriters. He also recognized their importance to his image, which he was well aware of and jealously safeguarded. Muses Collins, "I think early in his career somebody had gotten to him and said, 'These guys, these newspaper guys, you've got to talk to them.' And he was pretty good at it." As Robert Lipsyte remembers, "He seemed sweet and modest in his press conferences. He was approachable. He was certainly an accessible man. He was a nice man." Jimmy Breslin contends that Marciano used his personal charm, which was considerable, "to cater to sportswriters. Oh, the worst!" Does Breslin think sportswriters realized that Marciano was consciously charming them? "They don't know fucking anything. He would do it to them again today."[44]

It wasn't that Marciano was good for a juicy quote. In fact, he preferred questions that could be answered with a simple yes or no. Rather, it was in the way in which he treated questioners. He developed the habit of answering sportswriters directly and by name ("Gee, Hank, I'm not sure"). Praised Franklin ("Whitey") Lewis, star columnist of the *Cleveland Press*, "This fellow has mastered the trick of the personalized approach. Even reporters have a slice of ham in their dinner pails and they, too, love being first-named by big wheels." When Boston sportswriter Bill Liston arrived at Marciano's training camp in California before the 1955 fight against Don Cockell, for example, Marciano leaped to his feet, smiled, shook Liston's hand, and said, "Bill, how are you? It's good to see you. How's everything back home? Are any of the boys coming out to see the fight?"[45] Marciano was also patient with the press. He would answer any question, however silly. Once, after a fight, he even let one nosy scribe pinch open a cut above his eye and peer into it.

If there was a problem between Marciano and the press, it was the ever-controlling Al Weill, who draped what one reporter called "a Havana-curtain" around Marciano that occasionally blocked unfettered access to the champion. Yet Weill was smart enough to take care of star columnists such as Arthur Daley of the *New York Times* and Arch Ward of the *Chicago Tribune*. Daley, for instance, always received special access, whether in the form of a surprise long-distance call from the champion, a private interview on the porch of the champion's training quarters, or a special visit to Marciano's hotel suite after a fight. "Before every major bout he would unfailingly invite me to dine with him at the battered old farmhouse on the edge of the Grossinger airport where he trained . . . I got to know him pretty well," Daley confessed years later.[46] Not coincidentally, Daley—the top sports columnist on the top newspaper in the country—always gave Marciano great press.

Ward received special access of a different sort. According to Breslin, Weill told Ward, "You eat breakfast with him every morning of a fight. That's your contract." So, on the morning of each of his title fights, Marciano ate breakfast with Ward. They had a "pact that the procedure will be followed as long as he retains the title," Ward proudly told readers.[47] (After Ward died in 1955, Marciano kept the tradition alive before his final fight with Archie Moore by eating breakfast with Ward's son Tom.) The "breakfast with the champion" columns were unremarkable, however. After reveling in discovering the location of Marciano's top-secret prefight hideaway, Ward would describe what the champion ate for breakfast and other mundane matters. Still, the breakfasts served their purpose. Ward was the most powerful columnist in the Midwest, and he became one of Marciano's staunchest supporters. Like other sportswriters, he grew to love him.

No one, however, loved Rocky Marciano more than Franklin Lewis. Unlike Daley and Ward, Lewis had no national influence or special access to Marciano. He was also somewhat of a curmudgeon. Nevertheless, he adored Marciano with a love that only deepened through the years. In 1952, for instance, Lewis informed readers, "To refute any whispers that he is anything except a nice, a very nice guy, let's begin with the premise that he is, period." A year later, he gushed, "There isn't a newspaperman I know who would ever attempt to embarrass Rocky orally. We like the guy. We like to talk to him. We get square replies." He continued to express his love for the rest of Marciano's reign, writing columns with headlines such as "Visit with Champ Makes Work Pleasure" and "A Guy Just Can't Help Liking Rocky." Many sportswriters felt similarly, so they gave Marciano great press. As Breslin says, "Nobody ever got better."[48]

That Marciano had such a positive image was also due in large part to the nature of sportswriting—and hero-making—during the 1950s. Many sportswriters of that era traced their roots to the 1920s and the "gee-whiz" school of sportswriting. Its founder and lead practitioner was Grantland Rice, whose famous lead on the Four Horseman of Notre Dame became the signature example of the style. Rice and his disciples wrote in hyperbolic, overblown, florid prose, complete with allusions to the Bible and Greek mythology. They also routinely turned star athletes into larger-than-life heroes with the qualities of Greek gods.

Although the gee-whiz style was starting to fade in the early 1950s, it still remained a heavy influence on most sportswriters. Arch Ward, for instance, was a modified gee-whizzer. He would never criticize sports personalities. Instead, he would befriend them and then wield his considerable power to further their careers. Arthur Daley also represented the new generation of gee-whiz sportswriters. He refused to write about people he didn't like and was decidedly positive about those he did. Red Smith—less a gee-whizzer and more noteworthy for the wit and elegance of his prose—once admitted that he and other sportswriters were "guilty of puffing up the people they write about." Smith liked to quote a plea that his editor, Stanley Woodward, once made: "Will you stop Godding up those ball players?"[49] Even the 1950s sportswriters who had no gee-whiz strain to their style—such as Jimmy Cannon, passionate, romantic, and tough—saw the world in terms of white hats and black hats. They were not reluctant to build up the white hats.

Marciano, of course, wore a white hat. The modified gee-whizzers (like Ward and Daley) glorified him, leading to such lines as one that appeared in *Time:* "To hero-hungry fans from Brockton and across the nation, Rocky is . . . Hercules, Ivanhoe, Paul Bunyan. He stands for the comforting notion not that might makes right, but that might and right are somehow synonymous."[50] Sportswriters who fell outside the gee-whiz tradition (like Smith and Cannon) were less deifying but also accentuated the positive in Marciano. Sportswriters of all types and styles built an image for him. They weren't interested in exposing his dark side or any extracurricular escapades. Instead, they were interested in building him up in larger-than-life fashion. They succeeded.

The way we now treat and view sports heroes is markedly different, of course. Observes Furman Bisher of the *Atlanta Journal Constitution,* who began to write about sports right after World War II and has yet to stop, "If Babe Ruth were alive today and playing baseball, and lived the lifestyle that he lived, he'd probably be vilified. All of his bad habits would become public. That was the difference. None of us knew any of the athletes' bad habits in those days. Very rarely. It had to be very sensational before we ever heard anything of that nature." Even if they did know, Bisher and his contemporaries were content to look the other way. Bisher, for instance, remembers writing many columns about Marciano, and none mentioned the specific flaws Bisher knew he possessed. "It was a kind of respect we all gave athletes in those days," Bisher observes. "We did not pry—we were not there to reveal his glitches and his bad habits." Recalls Collins, "When I first started covering baseball, you knew what guys were doing but you didn't write about it. It was just one of those things." With Marciano, too, the athlete's personal life remained his own business. "It did and I'm glad it did," declares Collins.[51]

Why do we now probe deeper and seem to delight in trying to knock heroes from their pedestals? The socioeconomic differences between media members and athletes play a significant role. In the Age of Simplicity, sportswriters and the athletes they covered made the same type of money, often lived in the same neighborhoods, and drank together in the same bars. As a result, sportswriters received access and were willing to play along with the game of image-making. "These guys always knew what was going on," Robert Lipsyte says. "And just as long as they were winking to their colleagues that 'We do know,' it was cool. And the rubes out there, their audience, well, they didn't deserve to know. They were not part of this deal. We were all in this together. Well, that's no longer the case. I don't think their feeling is that we're all in this together. The schism between athlete and journalist is just too wide." According to Lipsyte, that current gulf makes today's image-makers more willing to unearth the flaws in their heroes. "If you don't have access to 'the hidden fears of Kenny Sears,' these kind of inside stories, then the only way that you can act out your own competition in journalism is by coming up with shit and shooting these guys down."[52]

Others believe that the quality of the journalism today is markedly better. W. C. Heinz cites some of the journalists of the 1930s, 1940s, and 1950s—a boxing writer who wrote about "the lightweight champion from Panamania" because a press release had referred to him as "the Panamanian lightweight champion" or a police reporter who believed other reporters when they told him that the Magna Carta was "the rug from Buckingham Palace." For Heinz, the writers of yesteryear weren't nearly as intelligent or as talented as today's journalists. And then there's the issue of the athletes themselves and what Lipsyte calls "the racial divide. Most of your prominent athletes in the major sports are black, and the journalists are still white." Jimmy Breslin is more blunt: "They're all black today, so of course they try to pick them apart. Marciano was a white hero."[53]

Finally—and perhaps most significantly—there is the effect of television. As Collins observes, "We've become a tabloid culture. . . . You've got all this twenty-four-hour news going around all the time. You can never shut it off. And everybody is trying to beat everybody else to see who can get the dirtier stuff. And I find it sad and reprehensible." Echoes Bisher, "Everybody's trying to rival television—or, if you do something like that, sooner or later you wind up on television. And for some reason or other, people seem to think that winding up on television is more important than going to heaven—because you get to TV first."[54]

Television has changed the basic rules of the image-making game. After all, it provides today's fan with instant exposure to athletic heroes. There is less need to recount a hero's exploits in the newspaper the next day, because everyone has seen them the night before on television. There remains, however, need for further analysis and insight. Before television and sports formed their marriage, the key questions concerned what athletes did and what they stood for. With television, the key question is now why athletes do what they do, whether on or off the field. Before television, image-makers could afford to be reverential. With television, they are forced to be skeptical and probing.

Rocky Marciano was, in a sense, lucky. He wasn't placed under a microscope, nor was he subjected to the type of prying coverage that might have unearthed his flaws. Instead, he benefited from the journalistic canons of the day and acquired an image that was more superhuman than human.

* * *

At his camp at Grossinger's several days before the first fight with Jersey Joe Walcott, Rocky Marciano met with a priest. "That boy is no ordinary prizefighter," the impressed priest later told a friend. "He is one of the most dignified, straightforward people I have ever met in my life. The people of the world should be informed of this boy's character and personality. Because if they knew him as I do now, he will become one of the most highly-regarded personalities in the history of sports."[55]

The priest was wrong. Even though sportswriters informed the public "of this boy's character and personality"—repeatedly—Rocky Marciano failed to become "one of the most highly-regarded personalities in the history of sports." For sure, he had many fans. Some even revered him. And there is no question that he was definitely a popular champion. Yet despite all the tremendous qualities he possessed (and despite the fact that he was cast from day one, in the words of Shirley Povich of the *Washington Post*, as a "lovable sort of character" and "the All-American boy of the heavyweights"), he was never wildly, over-the-top popular.[56] In a sense, then, his image ultimately failed him.

The prime reason for that failure was, again, television. In the early 1950s, television was becoming increasingly more important in terms of its ability to convey ideas and images. It was also rapidly dominating other forms of media. In 1950 (the year that Marciano had his first big fight against Roland LaStarza), there were only 3.1 million television sets in America. By 1955 (the year that Marciano had his last fight against Archie Moore), there were thirty-two million television sets in America. In five short years television had grown from a novelty item owned by a few to a household staple owned by nearly every family in America.

Marciano wasn't a complete stranger to the new medium. During his rise and reign, he regularly appeared in America's living rooms in guest stints on Ed Sullivan and other variety shows. In addition, four of his big fights (Roland LaStarza in 1950, Joe Louis in 1951, Lee Savold in 1952, and the second Jersey Joe Walcott fight in 1953) were on free television. With the exception of the Harry ("Kid") Matthews fight in 1952, all of Marciano's other big fights were on closed-circuit television in movie theaters across the country. Closed-circuit television was a bold and controversial venture for the IBC. It was also successful. Whereas Marciano's fight with Rex Layne in 1951 appeared in just eleven theaters in eight cities (attracting an estimated audience of approximately thirty thousand), his fight with Archie Moore in 1955 would appear in 133 theaters in ninety-two cities (attracting an audience of approximately four hundred thousand). Although the growth was considerable, the combined audience for Marciano's closed-circuit bouts (approximately 1.25 million people) was small by today's standards, and the exposure wasn't the same as on free television. Still, it was significant.

The print media, not television, was responsible for Marciano's image, but the exposure he received on free and closed-circuit television nevertheless had a definite effect on that image. What the print media built up, the electronic media partially and inadvertently tore down. As Chicago sportswriter George Strickler once observed, "You can't build the heroes today the way you used to. In 1924 you could write about Red Grange or the Four Horseman, and they were very romantic figures, big heroes. Very few people saw them, but everybody could read about them. . . . Today, with television, a guy comes along and in one afternoon, in one game, sixty-four million people see him. When you see a player, in the flesh or on television, it takes a lot of the romance out of it."[57]

That is precisely what happened with Rocky Marciano. Sportswriters had constructed a larger-than-life, romantic, idyllic image of the new champion, and fans read about it. Then they saw Marciano fight on television. Although they saw a somewhat dominant champion, they also saw someone with flaws (wildness and crudeness). For these fans, the image that had arisen in print may not have been completely debunked, but it was at least counterbalanced. The superhuman whom they read about looked human on the screen. Previous heavyweight champions such as Jack Dempsey and Joe Louis didn't have to contend with the demythologizing effect of television. Films of their fights were occasionally shown after the fact but did not offer the immediacy of television. The images that had arisen in print concerning their heroic deeds continued to carry the day.

Television, then, took the romance out of Rocky Marciano. The image that many fans retained of him was of the dynamic, dominant-but-flawed brawler they had seen on television, not the static, larger-than-life hero they read about in newspapers and magazines. The rules for image-making had changed, and even image-makers didn't know it.

8 The Ugly Duckling

When Rocky Marciano and Roland LaStarza first met in the ring back in March 1950, both were young, up-and-coming fighters, and the future had appeared bright and wide open. That future had become a reality for Marciano. It had eluded LaStarza. Marciano had a big-time, well-connected manager who had gotten him the big fights and then pushed him into the title picture. LaStarza did not. Instead, his career went nowhere until the fall of 1953, when Marciano, at long last, granted LaStarza a rematch.

The mere fact that LaStarza had to wait so long for a return engagement bothered him immensely. Indeed, before their first fight, Al Weill had supposedly promised LaStarza that he would get a rematch if Marciano triumphed. After Marciano's narrow victory, however, Weill changed his mind. He was interested in sending Marciano back to Providence for more seasoning and then maneuvering him into big fights against big names. He was no longer interested in Roland LaStarza. Besides, Weill may have been harboring a grudge against LaStarza's manager, Jimmy ("Fats") DeAngelo, for slamming a door in his face after the fight. Whatever the reason, the rematch failed to materialize.

Not that LaStarza and DeAngelo didn't try. They would appear at nearly all of Marciano's big fights, like spurned guests begging for an invitation to the party. By the time of the Marciano-Walcott rematch in the spring of 1953, LaStarza was still pursuing Marciano. With Marciano now champion and with a few recent big wins in his own back pocket—primarily, a victory over Rex Layne—LaStarza stepped up his campaign. The press, which was struck by Weill's lack of fair play in refusing to grant a rematch, had long been sympathetic to LaStarza's plight. Now he began to leverage that sympathy as never before. In early 1953 he wrote an article for *Sport* in which he tried to justify the rematch by analyzing the scoring of the first fight. He prepared a formal written challenge to Marciano. And he was there, of course, with DeAngelo in tow, when Marciano and Walcott squared off in Chicago Stadium.

This time the guests who had been shut out of the party for so long finally managed to snag an invitation. After the second Marciano-Walcott fight in May 1953, Weill had originally planned to keep Marciano on the shelf for the rest of the calendar year. That fight was such a fiasco, however, that Weill agreed with IBC head Jim Norris that a fall defense was in order— for the good of boxing and for the good of his fighter. The leading candidates for the next shot at Marciano were Ezzard Charles and LaStarza. Many felt that Charles was more deserving because he was the more accomplished fighter. Then again, Charles was old hat. As LaStarza argued, "Sure I'm the most logical contender. I deserve the shot ahead of Charles because he had his chance last year with Walcott and missed out."[1]

Eventually, Weill decided in favor of LaStarza. Marciano's pilot was dead set on having the fight take place in New York. Although Charles was far better known on a national level, LaStarza (a local boy born, bred, and still living in the Bronx) would draw there. Then there was the matter of talent. The experienced, crafty Charles loomed as a tough opponent for Marciano— tougher than LaStarza. As Wendell Smith of the *Pittsburgh Courier* explained, "Marciano has little to worry about in the case of LaStarza. . . . There is no intent here to imply that Marciano is afraid of Charles. He isn't. It's just that he wants the easy guy first. Why grab a lion when you can sock a kitten?"[2]

With his long but belatedly successful campaign finally over, Roland LaStarza now found himself in the chips. He was going to get another shot at Marciano. He was going to get a shot at the heavyweight crown. He was going to get his first big payday. And he was finally going to step out of the shadows. After the fight was scheduled for September 24, 1953, in the Polo Grounds, people finally began to take a closer look at LaStarza. What they saw was anything but the prototypical boxer.

He certainly didn't have the name of a boxer. Real fighters had names such as Tony, Joe, Sugar Ray, Kid, and, of course, Rocky. LaStarza sported the first name of Roland, which was, observed W. C. Heinz in the *Saturday Evening Post,* "more appropriate for a poet or a painter than a prize fighter." To Hugh Brown of the *Philadelphia Evening Bulletin,* it denoted "the sensitive, the lover." Somehow LaStarza managed not to acquire a nickname. Nor did he ever acquire the traditional trademarks of a boxer—a flattened nose, warped ears, or a scarred face. Instead, he was a good-looking man who was almost movie-star handsome, with dark-brown hair and flashing brown eyes. With his sleek body, he looked more athlete than boxer. According to one reporter, he "reminds you of a streamlined Notre Dame halfback."[3]

He also didn't live like a boxer. Out of the ring, most boxers, at least in image, tended to be either a solid family man (like Walcott or Marciano) or the swinging toast of the town (like Joe Louis or Sugar Ray Robinson). LaStarza was neither. Instead, he still lived with his parents in a small, clean, apartment in the Bronx. He didn't hit the nightclub scene in New York, although he would occasionally go dancing at a Bronx roadhouse or at the annual dinner dance of the Roland LaStarza Social Club started by his admirers. About the only offbeat parts of his persona were a passion for flying his open-cockpit stunt airplane and a rather strange set of ring superstitions: not brushing his teeth for several days before a fight, not allowing anyone to kiss him the day of the fight, and having his father rub his back with a rusty nail in the runway before entering the ring.

Nor did LaStarza carry himself like a typical boxer. Most fighters mumbled their words, swore profusely, or butchered the English language with double negatives and the like. Not Roland LaStarza. He was pleasant, personable, well mannered, and had a mild disposition. His intelligence plainly set him apart from other boxers. LaStarza had attended college at City College of New York, where he took physical education classes and also played varsity lacrosse. He left CCNY after two years when he was drafted into the army and never went back to graduate. No matter. He was "the college man" or "the college-educated boxer," someone, sportswriters constantly reminded readers, who was highly intelligent and mentally superior to his peers.[4]

Given all that, his contemporaries had a hard time figuring out how LaStarza ended up in the ring in the first place. It was hardly a case of manifest destiny. The son of a hard-working immigrant couple that ran a small, immaculate, grocery store and butcher shop in the Bronx, the young Roland showed no instinct for fighting. "Rollie was always the timid one," his father told Heinz. "He always afraid to hurt anybody."[5] Eventually, though, his older brother's interest in boxing drew Roland into the ring. Like Marciano, LaStarza was a natural athlete who adapted his talents to boxing. He used those talents to win several amateur titles before entering the army in 1945.

When he got out of the army in the summer of 1947, he decided to make a go of it as a professional. He hooked up with DeAngelo, who had been managing boxers for a long time but with only limited success. DeAngelo was a nice, honest man who was personally respected and had many friends; he also fell outside the boxing power structure. In other words, he was the anti-Weill, and LaStarza adored him. "He's like a father to me," LaStarza said. "I couldn't ask for a better manager. There isn't another manager [who] would do for his fighter what he's done for me."[6] Indeed, DeAngelo personally borrowed money on several occasions to pay expenses and keep LaStarza's career afloat. He also considered selling his interest in LaStarza, realizing that the fighter would be better served with a manager who had the influence to move his career along faster. LaStarza, however, insisted that DeAngelo stay at the helm and direct his rise up the heavyweight ladder.

For a while that rise proceeded at a good pace. By the late 1940s, LaStarza was headlining fight cards in the Garden and had earned a reputation as the nation's premier young heavyweight—and a potential champion of the future. Then, in March 1950, he suffered his first defeat at the hands of Rocky Marciano. His career promptly came to a screeching halt. He continued to win regularly, but none of his victories were over big-name opponents. He even lost bouts along the way to two mediocre heavyweights, Dan Bucceroni and Rocky Jones. The fact that LaStarza beat them both in return matches did little to reverse his sliding reputation. Then, in February 1953, LaStarza suddenly reemerged in the title picture by beating Layne, who was on his last legs but still had a name. LaStarza and DeAngelo parlayed that victory into the title shot with Marciano.

At the time that he signed to fight Marciano, LaStarza's overall record stood at an impressive 53-3. Many experts held him in an esteem commensurate with that record. He was, after all, a purist's delight, with textbook footwork, form, and style—a superb defensive fighter who could pile up points with clever counterpunching. Just as many, however, criticized LaStarza for being too cautious, timid, and mechanical. Some speculated that his college background hurt him and that he thought too much and relied too little on instinct. LaStarza admitted that he thought before acting in the ring. He also confessed to a lack of killer instinct. And he received barbed criticism as a result. Nearly half a century later, he would admit that the criticism was fair. "There was some truth to it," he says. "You know, I never really wanted to hurt anyone."[7]

At the time, LaStarza's handlers—DeAngelo and trainer Dan Florio (who had also trained Walcott)—tried unsuccessfully to make him want to hurt someone. Fans wrote to him as well. "A lot of them say the same thing," he revealed to Heinz. "They tell me I've got to be mean and vicious." He was, some felt, most effective in those moments when he was aroused, abandoning his precious boxing style and simply flailing away. But that didn't happen often enough for some, who wondered whether something was missing from his makeup as a fighter, especially compared to a fighter such as Marciano. "I liked him as a person," Heinz now says. "He was a nice kid. He was polite. But he wouldn't be a foxhole buddy. And Rocky would be."[8]

LaStarza was nevertheless convinced that he could take the title away from Marciano in their rematch. Looking back at their first fight, he proclaimed, "I am as sure as income taxes that I beat him." In the weeks leading up to their return fight, LaStarza was outwardly confident that he could do it again. "I'm going to win," he said. "I can outbox him and I can outsmart him . . . I may stop him or even knock him out. Probably stop him because he cuts badly and his eyes close up." LaStarza's verbal assault also included some disparagement of his old rival's abilities. "They say he's improved," LaStarza declared. "I ask you, how can a crude fighter like Marciano improve? Furthermore, where does everyone get the impression that he's a superman? Just because he's champion?"[9]

All of this was part of the normal prefight patter to hype the gate, and Marciano probably recognized it as such. But when LaStarza also told reporters that Marciano was bound to get "soft in the head" or "punch-drunk" as a result of all the blows he was taking, Marciano became genuinely enraged. "It bothered him when he saw a fighter who spoke in 'dose' and 'dems' and acted not intelligent," remembers Marciano's brother Peter. "It bothered him terribly. So, the one thing that would really bother Rocky is if someone called him 'punchy.' That would be worse than putting a sword through his heart." LaStarza maintains that he meant nothing by the comment—and that Marciano wasn't really angry at the time. "What it was," he remembers, "is Al Weill says, 'We'll talk this up, get a good fight going, call each other names.' So I called him—I don't know what it was— I said, 'He will get punch-drunk if he keeps on taking punches.' Who the hell wouldn't get punch-drunk if he kept on taking punches? Rocky, at the time, right after the fight, he said, 'You shouldn't have said that. I didn't like that. That wasn't nice.' But then later on, when we met later on, he realized that it was to build up the fight. Hell, I would have called him everything to build up the fight."[10]

Marciano didn't really need the extra motivation. He was, after all, getting a chance to erase the only real asterisk on his perfect record. If he had haunted LaStarza since that Friday evening in March 1950, so had LaStarza haunted Marciano. When sportswriters or fans wanted to tarnish Marciano's record or question his abilities, they would always cite that fight prominently. As Marciano revealed in late 1952, "The fight was on television and I still bump into people who think I lost. Why, I don't know." It had become, in the words of one sportswriter, "the skeleton in Rocky Marciano's fistic closet." Now he had a chance for redemption. "Beating LaStarza is the only thing I have to do before I'll ever be able to fully appreciate being world's champion," he said on the eve of the fight. "Until I do that, I won't be satisfied."[11]

Most observers figured he would do just that. He entered the ring an overwhelming 6-1 favorite, with most predicting a Marciano knockout in the middle rounds. Very few gave LaStarza much of a chance. The prefight buildup was bland, centering around the tired yet reliable "boxer vs. slugger" theme. Several evoked analogies to Tunney and Dempsey, with the college-educated, stylish LaStarza cast as the former and the working-class, rough-and-ready Marciano cast as the latter. Still, the fight caught on. Aided by perfect autumn weather, it became a box office success. More than forty-four thousand fans flocked to the Polo Grounds (as well as those in forty-five theaters in thirty-four cities on the coast-to-coast, closed-circuit network), paying to see the old rivals renew hostilities.

● ● ●

The fight turned out to be a good heavyweight clash, long on tension but short on thrills. It also followed a clear linear pattern. For the first six rounds, LaStarza had his way. He impressed with his overall boxing style and defensive skills, avoiding Marciano's crowding and traps with clever footwork. He was less cautious than usual, scoring with jabs, hooks, counters, and combinations. Although he never had Marciano in any sort of trouble, LaStarza scored points and built up a slight lead on the judges' cards. "He was better than I expected," Marciano admitted after the fight.[12]

Meanwhile, Marciano was stumbling. He tried to score the haymaker that would result in a quick knockout but never came close. He managed to land some punches, open a cut near LaStarza's right eye, and even win a couple of rounds, but he looked awkward and clumsy in the process. He looked even worse when he kept fouling LaStarza. A head-butt in the second round was followed by hitting on the break and after the bell in the third, which was followed by low blows in the sixth and seventh. The infractions drew repeated warnings from referee Ruby Goldstein and a cascade of boos from the crowd. Afterward Marciano explained, "I didn't do it on purpose; LaStarza knows I didn't."[13] Indeed, LaStarza dismissed the fouls as unintentional and a natural by-product of Marciano's roughhouse style. For the most part, ringside observers agreed.

In the seventh round, the tide turned, with Marciano driving LaStarza into corners and steadily bombing away. He later speculated that a left hook he landed to LaStarza's body in that round might have marked the turning point. "That one really hurt him because I heard him grunt, and after that he lost all his zip," Marciano said. Months after the fight was over, LaStarza concurred that the decisive blows had come in the seventh: "He gave me two terrific belts to the body and I was done." Marciano's switch in strategy also helped turn the tide. As he later explained, "I saw I wasn't getting anywhere trying for the one big one, and I was afraid of falling behind on points, so I switched to left hooks and inside combinations instead of gunning for his head."[14]

At the same time, LaStarza began to tire. By the tenth round, he would be completely exhausted. The fact that he had come into the bout several pounds underweight didn't help. "I was too light for that fight," he maintains. "I had worked too hard. I worked for three months in the summertime for that fight and it killed me . . . I was losing weight, losing weight, working hard—and of course I was worried." The problem, LaStarza says, was that DeAngelo had a heart attack during training camp and "couldn't watch me too much and my trainer, Dan Florio, he ruined me. He worked me to death. I was ready for that fight two months before the fight took place. And Dan Florio—I've never said this before now—but Dan Florio worked me to death. He killed me." In fact, LaStarza says he received an anonymous telephone call after the fight, presumably from gamblers. He recalls, "They wanted to pay a visit to Dan Florio and teach him a lesson for ruining me for that fight." LaStarza, who believes there was no malicious intent on Florio's part in overworking him, strongly told the voice on the telephone to back off.[15]

Unfortunately for LaStarza, he was unable to convince Marciano to back off during the fight. The onslaught continued. Always moving forward while unleashing a barrage of crunching punches—some of which continued to miss but many of which found their mark—Marciano battered LaStarza throughout the eighth, ninth, and tenth rounds, opening cuts on his nose and inside his mouth. By the ninth round, LaStarza's face was lopsided and he was spitting blood. It got to the point where each Marciano punch would spray droplets of LaStarza's blood onto press row. "That second fight he destroyed me," says LaStarza today. LaStarza's prefight comments about being "punchy" probably gave Marciano even more fury than usual. "When he got into the ring against LaStarza, he really went in there with a vendetta," Peter Marciano remembers. "He wanted to really and truly punish him. He didn't even really want to knock him out. . . . He wanted to really punish him. And, after the fight was over, he felt badly about it."[16]

For Roland LaStarza, it became a fight for survival. Unable to muster the strength to throw many punches of his own, he concentrated on retreating and trying to hang on. No one would have blamed him had he quit. But he didn't—and as a result earned a heap of acclaim from the crowd, the press, and even his opponent. "I was surprised he stayed up so long," Marciano said after the fight. "I've never seen a gamer guy. I hit him with everything I had and even though I missed a lot I got in some real good licks, too." He said a similar thing to LaStarza's father when the latter, somewhat oddly, burst into Marciano's postfight shower in order to shake hands with his son's naked conqueror.[17]

Marciano finally put LaStarza away in the eleventh round. A long, powerful right to the jaw followed by a solid left hook and a couple of glancing rights sent LaStarza crumpling backward through the ropes and onto the ring apron. He pulled himself up at the count of five. Goldstein, the referee, forgetting that the mandatory eight-count rule was not in effect, wrongly continued the count until nine and then foolishly allowed the fight to continue. Marciano waded in and resumed his furious barrage with a dozen unanswered punches. LaStarza was now completely defenseless—a fact that Goldstein at last recognized by stepping between the fighters, steering Marciano away, and leading the wobbly LaStarza back to his corner. One ringside observer thought he saw LaStarza mutter "thank you" when Goldstein finally put a halt to the battering.[18]

Moments later in his dressing room, LaStarza seemed relieved that the fight was over. He answered reporters' questions with politeness and ease. He didn't seem terribly upset. He even joked with the physician attending his many wounds, the ubiquitous Doctor Vincent Nardiello, "He really busted me up, didn't he, Doc?" He also liberally praised Marciano. "He's a great champion," LaStarza kept repeating. He also proclaimed, "He's definitely a better fighter than when I fought him before—5,000 percent better."[19]

● ● ●

Roland LaStarza was right. Rocky Marciano had improved greatly as a fighter since 1950. That wasn't anything new to members of the fight mob. They had seen Marciano improve from big fight to big fight—from his tentative showing in the first LaStarza fight, to his more assertive showings against Layne, Louis, and Matthews, and then to his heroic performance against Walcott in their first fight. As Franklin Lewis of the *Cleveland Press* observed before the LaStarza fight in September 1953, Marciano "still misses punches, dozens of them. But he follows rights with lefts and lefts with rights. He doesn't find himself tangled in the ropes nearly as often. He bobs and weaves while trying to work in close to his opponent. He seems to have changed his style—for the better—ever since the first Walcott fight."[20]

Several months later, the ultimate expert on Marciano the fighter, Charley Goldman, seemed to deliver the final report when he said, "Rocky has improved in each fight. He now does by instinct what he used to do by memory." When Marciano (who was present when Goldman issued his report) jokingly asked if that meant he didn't have to think anymore, Goldman replied, "You'd better do some thinking in the ring, because my days as a Svengali are over. You're on your own now."[21] It was a joke, but it was also true. For sure, Marciano would continue to improve at the margins after LaStarza. His peak fight was probably his last one, against Archie Moore in 1955. At the time he fought LaStarza, though, Marciano was essentially a finished product in the ring.

That was fortunate because his strengths and weaknesses as a boxer and his greatness as a champion were starting to be assessed as never before. The critical reviews were decidedly mixed. Everyone conceded that Marciano had improved since he first emerged on the national scene in 1950, but many felt he hadn't improved enough. As a boxer, he retained a few fundamental flaws that some experts found impossible to ignore.

The LaStarza fight exposed perhaps Marciano's greatest flaw—his wildness. In the course of the fight he missed numerous punches, often by ridiculous margins. At one point in the tenth round he threw a right that was so wild it knocked him off his feet, although a wet spot on the canvas also contributed to the slip as well. All of this made him look like a "confused bull," according to *Newsweek*. To Hugh Brown, the haymakers Marciano tossed and missed were punches "that an Elks Club preliminary boy would have been properly ashamed of." To Bob Considine of the International News Service, Marciano missed so many punches "that if their power had been harnessed it could have lighted Omaha, Neb., for two years."[22] Much of the problem was in the way Marciano misfired punches. Often when he missed, he missed by a wide margin. He was like a slugger in baseball who strikes out a lot. When he connected—bang! When he didn't—whiff!

When he wasn't looking for a home run, Marciano's style was to charge his man, get inside, and try to land a combination or a flurry of punches. To his critics, that only highlighted another flaw: his lack of a jab. The strategy of standing outside and trying to lower his opponent's defenses by flicking a jab wasn't in accord with his physical attributes. Marciano's reach was only sixty-eight inches, one of the shortest in heavyweight history. He usually gave away between five and ten inches in reach to an opponent, which would have made it difficult for Marciano to employ a jab effectively. This shortcoming, however, didn't doom him in the ring; he managed to inflict plenty of pain without a smooth jab. Still, many held it against him. This was a generation weaned on Joe Louis's jab, which was as elegant as it was powerful. A fighter without such a jab was seen as incomplete.

Then there were his defensive abilities (or lack thereof). Part of what bothered the experts was his poor footwork, which, observed Whitney Martin of the Associated Press, "consists of moving forward in a direct line to a point where he is within cannonading range." Even Goldman conceded, "Certainly Rocky's footwork is not ideal."[23] As a result of this and other fundamental flaws, many in fight circles criticized Marciano's defensive abilities. Often that criticism came in the form of the words "easy to hit." At other times the phrase "wide open" was the label hung on Marciano. Either way, some believed that Marciano didn't defend himself with enough skill.

Marciano's wildness, lack of jabbing, poor footwork, and questionable defensive abilities all contributed to an overarching weakness: his general awkwardness in the ring. The LaStarza fight vividly illustrated the type of biting criticism that Marciano received throughout his career for his ring style. Jimmy Cannon proclaimed that his performance "exposed the champion as an ignoramus at his trade," and Jesse Abramson of the *New York Herald Tribune* echoed that the fight exposed Marciano's "boxing crudities" once again. Marciano, agreed H. G. Salsinger of the *Detroit News,* was "still a crude fighter."[24]

Crude. That was the word critics used most often to lampoon him. As Whitney Martin declared in 1954, "He's still crude to the point of being ridiculous at times."[25] The fact that long stretches of time occurred between his title fights didn't help. Marciano was the type of fighter who needed to fight often to stay sharp. After he became champion, however, he fought only twice per year—once in the spring and once in the fall. As a result, he often suffered from "ring rustiness." He usually looked his worst at the beginning of fights before rounding into better form as the bout progressed.

The fact that Marciano was such a poor gym fighter was also a contributing factor. Many members of the fight mob formed their opinions of boxers based on how they looked in training, not how they looked in the ring. If Marciano appeared crude in the ring, he appeared really crude in the gym. All his glaring faults seemed to show up during workouts. Reporters snooping for a story were always writing about how bad Marciano looked during sparring. Even his handlers knew it. Once, after a particularly heinous workout, Goldman stated, "Same old Rocky. He always looks bad in training, and he always wins." Added Marciano after that same workout, "I guess I been looking bad."[26]

In retrospect, the "crude" label was somewhat unfair to Marciano because it was dictated greatly by physical appearances. He certainly didn't have the classic proportions of a heavyweight that might have made him look more graceful. He had short, stubby arms, and his thick legs resembled "inverted tree trunks." His muscles, although superbly conditioned, appeared fleshy rather than cut. As A. J. Liebling of the *New Yorker* observed, "His body has no Grecian graces; he has big calves, forearms, wrists, and fingers, and a neck so thick that it minimizes the span of his shoulders."[27] Significantly, Marciano was both short (5'11") and light (about 185 pounds) for a heavyweight. All told, he appeared small and tough, not tall and smooth like Joe Louis or Muhammad Ali.

To a large extent, however, it was true—Marciano was crude. Even if he had classic body proportions, he still would have seemed primitive based on the way he fought. To Jimmy Breslin, Marciano could be "a sheer fucking caveman when he fought. He was out of the fucking stone age." As Ezzard Charles declared, "He's crude, I'd say . . . just plain crude." Marciano knew he was crude. Once Red Smith asked if he resented the charge. "I don't resent it because I am crude," Marciano replied. "I'll never be a finished boxer."[28] Although the "crude" label began to bother him more later in his reign, try as he might he could never escape it.

● ● ●

The harping on his crudeness and his other weaknesses tended to overshadow Marciano's many strengths as a boxer, which in some instances were underrated and in others were unmatched. First and foremost, he had the punch. As 1952 opponent Bernie Reynolds once noted, "He had amazing strength. Any time Marciano hit you, he could hurt you. He didn't do much flicking; every punch was a knockout punch." Adds LaStarza about his erstwhile opponent, "His strength was his greatest strength." Although Marciano's arms were short, his hands were unusually large. His short but wide fingers made his fist look like a boulder. And when the fist landed, it felt like a boulder. The key to it all, though, maintains Angelo Dundee, were his legs: "The power of Marciano was from the lower extremities. He had big legs. He was a catcher. And he was able to sorta give a spring-type of motion. It's all with the knees, actually. You see a little bend of the knee and then you pivot and let your shots go. That's where the power comes from. And Rocky had that power. . . . The strength of his legs served him in great stead his whole career."[29]

To many, Marciano's punching ability was so formidable that it overrode his stylistic weaknesses. "Crude? Maybe so," mused Al Wolf of the *Los Angeles Times*. "But the atom bomb that hit Hiroshima was relatively crude, too, in the light of later developments and refinements. Yet it was vastly more powerful than anything which went before. Maybe that applies to Marciano, too." By the time he became champion, Marciano had atomic power with either hand. "He used to have just one equalizer, the right hand," noted Goldman in early 1953. "Now he's got two, the right and the left."[30]

Yet just around that time, Goldman gambled by tinkering with Marciano's punch. The problem, as Goldman saw it, was that Marciano's stance was leaving him too wide open. So Goldman decided to shorten the stance. Although the change made Marciano a better boxer because it tightened his defense, it also changed the way he punched. With a shortened stance, he was forced to throw shorter, snappier punches. He also started to put those punches together more often in combination style. He continued to throw his patented long, looping rights, but he didn't go for the home run nearly as much. As Keene Simmons, one of his former opponents and a frequent sparring partner, said in 1955, "There've been some changes in him. A slugger like Rock doesn't turn into a boxer but he no longer tries to murder you with one punch the way he used to. He now throws combination of punches. They're much shorter but just as powerful."[31]

All of this brought about a change in the way his fights ended. During his rise and early reign, Marciano had knocked out rivals with one or two devastating punches. The LaStarza fight in September 1953 signaled a switch in the way he put away opponents. With his power now harnessed, Marciano's knockouts would henceforth result from an accumulation of punches rather than any one or two punches in particular. To Red Smith, that made Marciano a "pick-and-shovel" fighter: "He keeps swinging that pick with all his might, chopping at the hard pavement without apparent effect, until all of a sudden the asphalt crumbles away and there is only the soft earth underneath." Budd Schulberg of *Sports Illustrated* compared him to "a hydraulic drill attacking a boulder."[32]

Not everyone approved of the change. After the LaStarza fight, Marciano's critics and even some of his supporters began to wonder what had happened to his famed one-punch prowess. Later in his reign, as Marciano continued to use the hydraulic drill rather than the atomic bomb to beat opponents, Gerry Hern of the *Boston Post* declared, "The Rock may never again be the fighter he was against Walcott. Age and a changed style may have taken away some of his superb talent for punching. Perhaps, in making him a smart boxer, his management has taken away his terrific punching power. In shortening up his punches the management may have shorted out his power."[33]

In reality, Marciano's punches still hurt—a lot. Freddie Brown, Marciano's cut man on fight nights, maintained in early 1953 that "nobody yet realizes how hard Rocky hits. . . . The guy paralyzes you. He hits you with something that looks like a little tap when you sit out in the crowd, but the guy who gets hit shakes right down his legs." Confirmed 1954 opponent Ezzard Charles, "Rocky numbs you all over. Wherever he hits you, he hurts you; on the arms, the shoulder, the neck and the head." Even the many Marciano punches that went astray and didn't land clearly on target took their toll. As Pete Baird of the *New Orleans Times-Picayune* recognized in 1955, "He doesn't hit in vital places with any accuracy, true, but in his style of fighting, punching on arms, elbows and shoulders is most effective . . . while Rocky is boxing only a little, the other fellow isn't boxing hardly at all. His arms hurt him. His head hurts. Everything hurts. He wants the fight over."[34]

That was, in fact, Marciano's plan. "His theory in boxing was similar to hockey players," recalls Peter Marciano. "You know the theory that if you keep throwing the puck at the net something's going to go in? . . . His theory was the more punches that you throw, the more chance you have of winning a fight. And he always believed in the theory that you get more tired receiving a punch than throwing a punch." Echoes Lou Duva, "Rocky would wear you down, wear you down, wear you down. No style, but he would wear you down. He wasn't a Fancy Dan or anything like that. He was never a good boxer. He was a slugger. He would wear you down and then eventually knock you out."[35]

Ultimately, of course, Marciano's record is the most convincing evidence. Rocky Marciano fought forty-nine times as a professional. Only Don Mogard, Tiger Ted Lowry (twice), Roland LaStarza (in their first fight), Rex Applegate, and Ezzard Charles (in the first of their two 1954 fights) managed to take him to a decision. In the remaining forty-three bouts, Marciano concluded matters with a knockout or a technical knockout. His punch almost always carried the day.

Marciano could take a punch as well. That ability first received widespread acclaim the night he beat Walcott for the title. Many maintained that the punch that put Marciano on the canvas in the first round would have knocked out most heavyweights. Marciano, though, got right up and persevered—not just until the end of the round but for the rest of the night as Walcott continued to dole out punishment. "Few heavyweights have ever taken more," H. G. Salsinger wrote of Marciano's resilience that night. Echoed Charley Goldman, "I can't think of when a guy absorbed more bombs on the head and body and still came back to win."[36]

For the rest of his reign Marciano would time and again display his absorption powers. Marciano, W. J. McGoogan of the *St. Louis Post-Dispatch* once observed, "absorbs punishment like a sponge and brushes aside whatever physical pain he feels." Eventually, some recognized that his powers here were rare. As Jesse Abramson acknowledged in 1955, "Marciano can take a punch possibly better than any heavyweight before him, or anyway as good as the best."[37] Again, his record is instructive. Only a few times in his career was he staggered or in trouble. In his forty-nine fights he was only knocked down twice (against Walcott in their first fight and then against Moore in 1955). He was never, of course, knocked out as he drove his way to victory after victory.

His incredible stamina enabled him to keep driving. During their 1953 fight, for example, as LaStarza grew more tired, Marciano grew stronger. "He never seemed to tire," marveled the exhausted LaStarza after the fight. This would remain the pattern for the rest of Marciano's career. As a fight progressed, his foe would become worn out while Marciano relentlessly kept up (and often stepped up) the pace. Arthur Daley called Marciano a "perpetual motion punching machine." "It's like fighting an airplane propeller," Archie Moore said. "The blades keep whirling past your ear and over your head."[38] To some extent Marciano was born with that natural stamina. To a larger extent, however, he developed stamina through constant exercise and conditioning. And it is here that all credit must go to Marciano.

He accepted the strict training regimen imposed by his handlers. "He trained like a monk, really," says Heinz. Month after month, Marciano would work at Grossinger's, often in virtual isolation. Until late in his career he was almost completely cut off from his wife and daughter while in camp, with no visits and only nightly telephone calls and occasional letters allowed. In the two weeks before the fight Marciano would stop calling and writing, and the isolation became almost complete. "I haven't read a sports page or any mail in ten days," he complained several days before his first fight with Walcott. "I get the newspaper every morning but the sports page is cut out. No mail. That's turned off, too. It's like a monastery, I can't keep in touch with the world this way." Explained Goldman, "He's got to get his rest and peace and keep his mind free."[39]

Marciano went about training for a fight with vigor and passion. Even potential moments of relaxation became opportunities to push himself physically. Duva remembers visiting Marciano while he was training at Greenwood Lake early in his career. "He would have me take a walk with him," says Duva. "All he kept doing was bending down, picking up pebbles, and throwing him into the lake there. I said, 'The hell with that.' I finally got smart and started going with him with a bicycle. I wasn't going to keep bending down with him." To Dundee, "Nobody worked like he worked. He worked like it was a vendetta."[40]

When he wasn't working, Marciano was also serious about eating properly and getting his rest while in camp. "What was good for the body, he wanted," observed Shirley Povich. "What wasn't, he rejected. No smoking, no drinking, no night life, ever, because he had work to do." Marveled Goldman, "He's always thinking about his condition. If I happen to forget his celery and carrot juice just once, you'd think he was going to die. If a friend comes up to see him at 9:28 at night—it doesn't matter if he's his best friend who came from two thousand miles away—Rocky still goes to bed at his regular time, at 9:30."[41]

Marciano even largely abstained from sex during his fighting days because he had heard that it took something away from a fighter. Heinz remembers a story that used to make the rounds among sportswriters. According to the story, once, during training camp, some of the people around Marciano sent camp visitor and Hollywood bombshell Jayne Mansfield into a room where Marciano was—alone. The objective of her mission was obvious. Mansfield nevertheless (and perhaps somewhat incredibly) failed, emerging from the room after a while and saying only, "What is he, crazy? He didn't want anything to do with me."[42]

Marciano also remained focused and worked hard on those occasions between fights when he wasn't in camp. At home in Brockton, he and Allie Colombo would run, hike, do calisthenics, play handball, or swim at the YMCA. Proclaimed Goldman, "No athlete ever—ever—was as self-sacrificing as he was, even to the point of overdoing it . . . even when he was not training, every day—I mean every day, too—he'd take a long walk. Even if he comes to your house for a vacation, he'd bring along an old pair of pants and shoes so he could take his walk." His body, observed Harvey Breit of the *New York Times,* was "the alpha and omega in Rocky's life, and his instinct that it should be so appears sound. Rocky's body is to him what armor is to a tank."[43]

In a sense, Marciano exercised for the sake of exercising. "Look, a guy with a bankroll has got something, right?" he once posited. "A good-looking guy's got something, right? Well, a guy with a good body, he's got something too. I always wanted to have strength—more than the average guy. It makes you feel proud. As a kid I always admired guys with muscles." Even in those early years, Marciano was willing to work hard to get that type of body. His brother Sonny remembers waking in the middle of the night to the sight of his older brother kneeling and lifting a chair over his head repeatedly. "He was always exercising," says Sonny. He kept exercising as an adult. Peter Marciano cites the little things his older brother did while training—breathing in a special way because he believed it got bad air out of his lungs or attaching a ball to the drawstring of a lamp and following it for hours because he believed doing so strengthened his eye muscles. "He was almost to a point of being—I hate to use the word—mental," recalls Peter. "He constantly, constantly wanted to better himself."[44]

Marciano made clear on several occasions, however, that he exercised and sacrificed not just out of preference but also from necessity. "My occupation is fighting and it is an extremely exacting profession," he once noted. "I must be at my physical peak every time I defend my championship." As he elaborated on another occasion, "I like to train. I always thought that fighting mainly was condition; to be able to go ten, fifteen rounds at a high speed requires good conditioning and that makes a big difference with a lot of fighters. Some fighters have ability, but they don't condition themselves properly. I always try to condition myself the right way. It's no effort for me. I enjoy it because I know it'll be helpful to me."[45]

The hard work, training, and sacrifices were all helpful. They gave Marciano an abundance of confidence. "Rock," Peter Marciano remembers asking, "how does it feel to just be the shape you're in?" Marciano thought for a second and then said, "How does it feel? It's an amazing thing to know when you get into the ring that you're never going to get tired." More tangibly, Marciano's conditioning had direct bearing on the outcome of his bouts. He "won fights largely on condition" maintained veteran sportswriter Harry Grayson. That conditioning, agreed Abe Attell, a former featherweight champion, gave him "the stamina to keep attacking no matter how much punishment he was taking or had taken, and no matter how long the fight was going. He won on pace as well as punch." As Jesse Abramson concluded in 1954, Marciano was "the most superbly conditioned fist fighter who ever lived."[46] That assessment was neither hyperbole nor an unusual viewpoint.

A less recognized point concerned Marciano's defensive abilities, which by 1953 were vastly improved and vastly underrated. Experts who claimed that Marciano was "easy to hit" or "wide open" were wrong. He may have looked that way on some occasions but in reality he was a tough man to dent. Part of the reason for that was the exaggerated crouch Marciano used in the ring. Part of it was also the defensive skills he possessed. "He ain't easy to hit as they say," Goldman contended in 1952. "Rocky rolls under punches and he weaves under punches. . . . He protects his belly by blocking punches with his elbows." Later, in 1955, Goldman pointed out, "We've had to sacrifice some of his punching power—remember how he used to bring up his right hand that we call his Suzy Q punch from the floor—to tighten up his defense. Yeah, he has a defense, more than most people appreciate. He has learned to block punches and roll under them and with them."[47]

LaStarza, when asked in what area Marciano had improved the most between their two fights, replied, "In defense. It was harder to get at him." According to Dundee, "Rocky was very a deceiving guy. He [Goldman] taught Rocky so well that he used to slip on punches. . . . He was not that easy to hit. He had that misconception. He used to slide on you, he would stick you with that jab much, much better than anybody realized." How smooth did Goldman make Marciano? "He got him so smooth—forget about it," says Dundee. "He got him so where he was slick." Jimmy Breslin agrees that Marciano was "a lot cuter than they thought he was. He didn't get hit as much as it looked. He didn't get hit that much at all. . . . He was pretty cute."[48]

The fact that he was so awkward made him that much more difficult to hit. Whitney Martin of the Associated Press, while asserting that Marciano was crude and easy to hit, admitted that "the very awkwardness of his bobbing, weaving attack makes him a difficult target." Some of his opponents attested to how difficult it was to penetrate the awkward Marciano. "He fools you," Keene Simmons once said. "When you look at him from outside the ring he seems easy to hit but if you're in the ring with him you find this isn't the case. His head is bobbing and he's crouched low, so low in fact that you can't get a clear shot at him." Echoed LaStarza, "Rocky fools you. He doesn't take as much punishment as it seems. He looks easy to hit inside but he isn't."[49]

An even more unheralded advantage created by Marciano's awkwardness in the ring had to do with tempo. Many of his opponents went into the ring with a strategy. Few were able to execute. "It is impossible to think, or to impose your thought, if you have to keep on avoiding punches," observed A. J. Liebling. Recognized Paul Zimmerman of the *Los Angeles Times*, "Marciano never lets the other fellow set the pace or fight his style." Perhaps the lone Marciano opponent to succeed in dictating the pace of the fight was Jersey Joe Walcott in their first fight. Otherwise, Marciano always fought the type of fight that he wanted—a fast-paced, action-packed brawl. As 1955 opponent Archie Moore later confessed, "He doesn't let you fight your fight." Freddie Brown put it another way, "It is not like football. Rocky never gives you the ball."[50]

While some of of Marciano's ability to control tempo had to do with his determination and stamina, it also had much to do with awkwardness. It was difficult for an opposing fighter to find a rhythm against Marciano. He came at you with an odd style, and he was thoroughly unpredictable. "He has a peculiar way of fighting," Charles once observed. "You get out of the way of a right and your jaw catches a left. He feints with his fists and he feints with his feet. And too often you can't see where the punches are coming from." Added Moore in the wake of their 1955 fight, "[H]e kept changing the speed and rhythm of his propellers. That threw me off."[51]

To enhance all he brought to the ring physically and stylistically, Marciano possessed a host of mental qualities that also contributed to his greatness as a fighter. One such intangible was focus. Marciano once revealed that he tried "to forget all about the other fellow until you face him in the ring and the bell sounds for the fight." What struck Allie Colombo was his lack of anxiety in the weeks leading up to a fight. "Rocky never asks any questions about the guy he's going to fight," Colombo said. "All he wants to know is the time and place. In some of his earlier fights he never even knew the name of the guy he was going to meet until he was introduced to him in the ring." On the day of a fight Marciano was famous for remaining relaxed, nerveless, and almost detached. He was, Goldman observed, "absolutely without tension before a fight."[52]

Once in the ring, of course, Marciano became all business. He fought with what Shirley Povich called "a wonderful singleness of purpose as a prize fighter." Marciano's cool, unruffled manner before and during a fight once led Goldman to say, "He goes in for a fight like I go in for a glass of beer." He also brought a certain meanness to his trade. "Rocky, when he stepped into the ring, was a mean, mean man," Peter Marciano recalls. "Outside the ring, if he were walking down the street and someone accidentally bumped into him, he'd be the first one to say, 'Excuse me.' . . . Once he got into the ring, his whole personality changed."[53]

At the same time, however, he remained poised. He had, praised Liebling, both "presence of mind" and "a good fighting head," critical qualities given that he rarely entered the ring knowing exactly what he planned to do. "We don't have a strategic campaign for a fight," Marciano once noted. "We pick up as the fight goes along. It all depends on how the other guy fights. He might not fight the way you expected him to and that might upset you." When Marciano needed to make adjustments during the fight—such as in the LaStarza bout when he stopped going for a home run and started to concentrate on the body—he made them. When Goldman ordered a specific strategic plan of attack—such as in the Matthews bout—Marciano followed orders. It may not have always looked like Marciano knew what he was doing in the ring, but he usually did. "I said he may look crude," Charles once clarified to a reporter, "but that he was always thinking. He's a good thinker in that ring, and a good puncher, too."[54]

Marciano also had confidence that often bordered on arrogance. Jimmy Cannon pointed out the discrepancy in his personality. Outside the ring he was basically a humble guy from Brockton who couldn't believe that he was the champion of the world. Inside the ring, however, he "accepted the myth of his own invincibility." Red Smith noticed that as well. Once, Smith asked Marciano what he was thinking about after Walcott knocked him down in their first fight. "Nothing," Marciano replied. "But going to my corner after the bell I thought, 'This old man knocked me down. He might do it five or six times tonight. This could be a tough fight.'" Smith believed the response was telling. "There is the clue," he wrote. "If he were knocked down five or six times, it would be a tough fight. A tough one to win, that is. There's no such thing as losing." Confirms Peter Marciano, "When he went into the ring . . . he knew, no question, that he was going to win the fight. It was a question of what round."[55]

Perhaps his greatest strength, though, mental or physical, was his determination—and Rocky Marciano seemed to know it. Early in his reign, when asked whether great fighters had a common denominator, Marciano answered with a single word: "Determination." Others agreed that determination was his hallmark. Weill and some boxing writers labeled it his "will to win." Allie Colombo put it another way. "Losing," he said. "He was afraid of losing."[56]

However it was labeled, Marciano's determination paid off in the ring. Praised Jesse Abramson, "He can drive himself mercilessly. He can wade through a bucket of blood—his own—and batter though all kinds of adversity to conquer his foe." Even his fellow boxers recognized Marciano's determination. When asked his opinion of Marciano after watching him fight, Archie Moore replied, "I tell you what impressed me most. I was impressed by his determination to win." Floyd Patterson, Marciano's successor as heavyweight champion, went even further: "He was the most determined heavyweight I have ever seen in my life. That man got in the ring and there was no way he was going to lose. . . . Determination is based in the mind. How far can you go? What is your limit? With Marciano there was no limit."[57]

Decades later, Marciano's determination still remained legendary among the men who covered him. As Bud Collins points out, "It was through dint of really a big heart, ambition, and ability to work hard that characterized a lot of his fights because he got beat up by a lot of guys but he kept wading in and wading in. And he wouldn't settle for defeat. He was extraordinary. People get talent mixed up sometimes. I think that's a talent—to stay with it . . . I think he had a great talent with his heart and his desire." As Breslin says, "He was a tough bastard."[58]

● ● ●

When he reigned as champion, Marciano's various physical and mental strengths as a boxer were recognized in varying degrees. They also led to an aura of invincibility. Most of Marciano's contemporaries—even his critics—didn't think he would ever lose. Toward the end of Marciano's reign, Jack Hand of the Associated Press admitted that the press and the public had long regarded Marciano "head and shoulders above the division."[59] That was true, and the odds proved it. Marciano was an underdog in the Rex Layne fight and a slight underdog in the Joe Louis fight. After that, he was always the betting favorite, usually prohibitively so. In later years, long after his career was over, Marciano somehow acquired a reputation of being an underdog (perhaps because his screen alter ego, Sylvester Stallone's Rocky Balboa, was one). Rocky Marciano was no underdog, however. His contemporaries always expected him to win, and, of course, he always did.

At the time of the LaStarza fight in the fall of 1953, even though many of his contemporaries were starting to view him as invincible and unbeatable, not everyone believed that he was a great champion. Many experts found his performance against LaStarza to be disappointing and remained unwilling to proclaim his greatness. Several months later, John Lardner of *Newsweek* admitted, "The public and the boxing experts are reluctant—and I think rightly so—to accept Marciano as another Dempsey, Jeffries, or Louis just yet."[60] Although with each fight after LaStarza more and more people would accept Marciano as a great champion, he would never succeed in winning over everyone. There were holdouts and doubters to the very end.

All the while, critics and supporters both kept harping on his flaws as a fighter. The positive spin on that theme came in stories about how much Marciano had improved his stance, his defense, and his accuracy. "All this may be true, probably is true, but it never was said before about a heavyweight champion of the world," Red Smith would observe in June 1954. "Ordinarily, when a man wins the title it is taken for granted that he has reached his peak. Improvement is not expected, or even considered possible, because he is already the best." One year later Smith remained amazed at the lack of respect Marciano had earned from members of the fight mob who kept harping about his improvement. Smith attributed "the myth that he's still a preliminary boy" to Marciano's appearance, his modesty, and the backlash against Al Weill. As Smith pointed out with some amazement, everyone seemed to forget that Marciano was the heavyweight champion of the world—and one who had a perfect record at that.[61]

Joe Louis was the main reason that public acceptance of Marciano as a great champion was slow and never universal. Marciano's generation had grown up watching and reading about the majesty of the great Louis, whose reign ended only three years before Marciano's began. Comparisons were natural, particularly given that the rising Marciano had met the fading Louis on his way up. Marciano suffered from the comparisons. In contrast to the Louis everyone remembered (in his prime), Marciano looked like an amateur. He may have been just as effective, but he had none of Louis's stylish elegance. Louis was a graceful swan. Marciano was an ugly duckling.

To Charley Goldman, Marciano was like another great but unorthodox athlete also in his prime in the early 1950s. "Maybe Rocky is not very fancy," Goldman said in 1955. "Let's be honest, he's never going to be. But I see baseball and I see Yogi Berra and he isn't fancy either. He's never going to be. But he can throw the ball and swing that bat and he gets nice results and that's what Rocky does, too."[62]

In the final analysis, his contemporaries didn't give Marciano his proper due as a great fighter. In a sense, their opinion of him as a fighter was the flip side of their opinion of him as a man. If they overrated him as a man by giving him a larger-than-life, too-good-to-be-true image, they underrated him as a fighter by constantly harping upon his flaws and failing to recognize his many great attributes in the ring. Rocky Marciano was, warts and all, a great heavyweight champion.

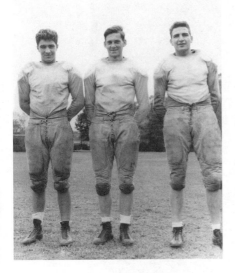

The teenaged Rocco Marchegiano (left) poses along with two other Brockton High football hopefuls around 1940. Young Rocco's athletic dreams centered on football and especially baseball, not boxing. (Stanley A. Bauman)

December 1948: Rocky Marciano at the dawn of his professional career—raw, hungry, and packed with power. (Stanley A. Bauman)

December 1949: In the aftermath of his first big victory in Madison Square Garden, Marciano's defeated opponent Carmine Vingo lapsed into a coma and teetered between life and death. Here, Marciano (with black eye) prays for Vingo's recovery. While his prayers were eventually answered, Vingo would never fight again. (Stanley A. Bauman)

December 1950: Marciano and his bride Barbara Cousins on their wedding day. She would become a key element of Marciano's all-American-boy image. (Stanley A. Bauman)

1950: The hometown hero shares the secrets of his growing fistic success with fellow Brocktonians. (Stanley A. Bauman)

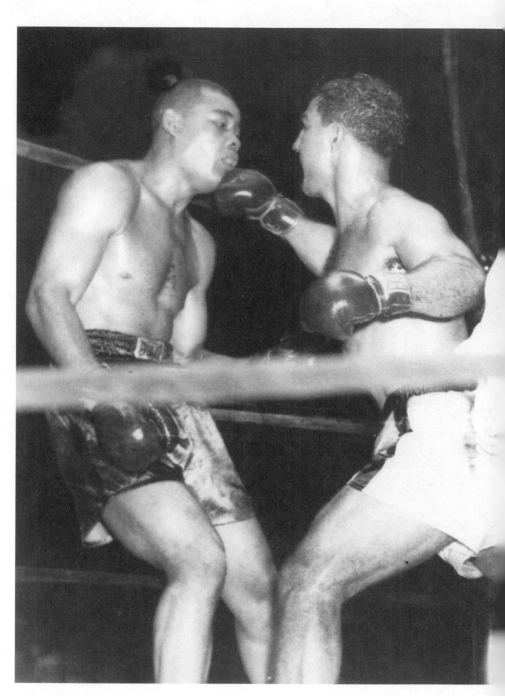

October 26, 1951: Marciano finishes Joe Louis's evening in Madison Square Garden, ending the great champion's final comeback and seizing the title of "uncrowned champion" in the process. (Stanley A. Bauman)

In the aftermath of a victory, a battered Marciano stands amid some of his handlers, including the diminutive trainer Charley Goldman (front left), the ubiquitous Allie Colombo (directly behind Marciano), and the hanger-on Chick Wergeles (right). (Stanley A. Bauman)

July 28, 1952: Under the tutelage of masterful trainer Charley Goldman, Marciano developed some underrated defensive skills. Here he eludes a punch from Harry Matthews in Yankee Stadium on his way to earning a second-round victory—and a shot at the title. (Stanley A. Bauman)

In the hours leading up to his long-awaited title shot against Jersey Joe Walcott in September 1952, Marciano walks the streets of Philadelphia flanked by the two most trusted members of his entourage—father Pierino Marchegiano and sidekick Allie Colombo. (Stanley A. Bauman)

Image-makers of the era constantly praised Marciano's loyalty to his family, friends, and hometown. Here Marciano, ever the loyal son, shows the sights of Philadelphia to his father before his title bout with Walcott. (Stanley A. Bauman)

September 23, 1952: Normally a "prince of prudence," champion Jersey Joe Walcott surprises everyone—including challenger Rocky Marciano—by taking the offensive. (Stanley A. Bauman)

Later that night, behind on points in the thirteenth round, Marciano lands the classic punch that brings an end to a classic fight—and makes him heavyweight champion of the world. (©Bettmann/CORBIS)

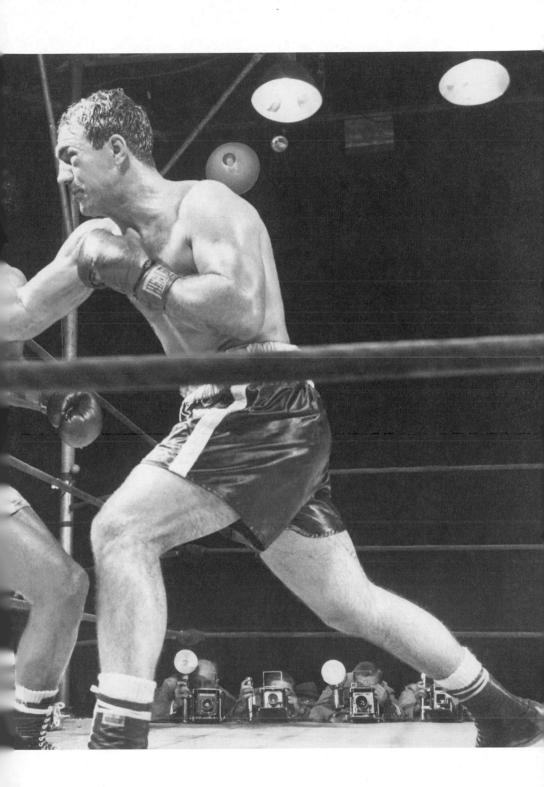

WILDERMUTH

Whenever Marciano won, there was bedlam in Brockton. Here, Marciano's mother Lena Marchegiano (holding a picture of her son) and a legion of loyal fans celebrate another big Marciano victory at his hometown hangout, the Ward Two Memorial Club. (Stanley A. Bauman)

June 1953: With an image that tracked the idealistic qualities of the American Way of Life, Marciano came to symbolize his era. Here he is at the White House visiting with another powerful symbol of the Age of Simplicity, President Dwight D. Eisenhower, along with fellow Italian American hero Joe DiMaggio. (©Bettmann/CORBIS)

September 24, 1953: As a pure puncher Marciano had it all—powerful arms, powerful legs, and remarkable leverage. Here he uses all of that to punish Roland LaStarza in the Polo Grounds. (Stanley A. Bauman)

In a typical scene, Marciano patiently caters to the press while manager Al Weill (left) whispers into his fighter's ear and desperately tries to maintain control of the situation. (Stanley A. Bauman)

Lena Marchegiano serves her son a heaping bowl of spaghetti and meatballs. Image-makers during the Age of Simplicity often drew upon this type of photograph to point out that Marciano was an all-American boy—and most definitively Italian. (Stanley A. Bauman)

September 17, 1954: With his crown suddenly in jeopardy because of a dangerous cut on the tip of his nose, Marciano doggedly pursues his challenger, the enigmatic Ezzard Charles, across the Yankee Stadium ring. The end for Charles would come moments later via an eighth-round knockout. (Stanley A. Bauman)

As the heavyweight champion of the world, Marciano felt a strong sense of social responsibility. Here he greets a throng of adoring youngsters. He reportedly never refused an autograph. (Stanley A. Bauman)

September 21, 1955: In what proved to be his final fight, Marciano unleashes his customary fury to shake his courageous challenger, the charismatic Archie Moore, in front a packed house at Yankee Stadium. (Stanley A. Bauman)

9 The King and His Kingdom

Rocky Marciano's return engagement with Roland LaStarza in the fall of 1953 signaled a return to the kingdom of heavyweight championship boxing. Following Joe Louis's retirement in 1949, heavyweight championship fights had lost much of their luster. Too often, they featured cautious craftsmen like Walcott and Charles in front of moderate crowds in places such as Detroit, Pittsburgh, and Philadelphia. Although Marciano's first two title fights in Philadelphia and Chicago had brought back much of the glamour to the heavyweight championship scene, there was still something missing—the carnival-like, big-event atmosphere that was uniquely New York's.

Before the fall of 1953, New York had not hosted a heavyweight championship fight in almost three years—and that bout had been a dispirited affair between Charles and journeyman challenger Lee Oma. The excitement was finally back when Marciano met LaStarza. It was just like the old days, with the fight mob arriving from around the country and arguing in bars and in front of the Garden. On fight night, more than forty-four thousand fans went uptown and jammed into the Polo Grounds to watch champion and challenger duke it out for the most coveted title in the world of sport. Everything was right again. The kingdom of heavyweight championship boxing had been restored.

There is no such kingdom today. Occasionally, a major heavyweight fight will come along that will capture the public's fancy, and when it does some fans might pay $30 or $40 for the privilege of watching it on pay-per-view. A few—boxing's last true believers—might even travel to Las Vegas to attend the event. But after the fight has come and gone the average fan forgets about boxing for a year or so until the next appealing bout comes along. Other events on the sports calendar—the Super Bowl, the World Series, and March Madness, for example—command far more interest and passion.

It wasn't always that way. In the early 1950s, heavyweight championship boxing was, in the words of Jimmy Breslin, "another world than today."[1] The reason was, naturally, the popularity of the sport itself, which dated back three decades. After the turbulent reign of Jack Johnson, the sport had really taken off in the 1920s with popular champion Jack Dempsey. With his flair and personality, Dempsey gave his sport acceptance, headlines, and million-dollar gates. By the time he and his chief rival Gene Tunney retired in the late 1920s, boxing had become the second most popular professional sport in the nation behind only baseball. Boxing took a dip in the early 1930s with a string of unspectacular champions and questionable decisions tainted by the influence of organized crime but then returned to prominence in the 1930s and 1940s with Joe Louis. By the time Marciano came along, boxing remained America's second most popular sport.

There was little else, really. The National Football League had established a foothold but had not succeeded in attracting a widespread following. The National Basketball Association was still in its infancy—a rinky-dink league operating in rinky-dink places such as Rochester, Syracuse, and Fort Wayne. The National Hockey League had only six teams and attracted little interest outside of Canada and a few American cities. College football and college basketball were essentially regional sports. Golf and tennis also had fans, mainly among the country club set but not on any widespread basis. A few isolated events, such as the Kentucky Derby and the Indianapolis 500, commanded attention, but they were, after all, single-day events that came and went quickly.

Boxing, then, had little competition on the sports pages. In terms of fan support and interest, it was well behind baseball but comfortably ahead of everything else. The heavyweight division was boxing's crown jewel. Fights in other divisions drew interest, for sure. But the division everyone cared about the most was the heavyweight division, and the fight everyone wanted to see the most was a heavyweight championship fight. It was a highlight of the boxing year and the sports year as well. "Top sports classics in the United States are the Kentucky Derby, the World Series and a heavyweight championship fight," Wilton Garrison of the *Charlotte Observer* declared in 1955. "They are hard to match in drama, pathos, action, excitement and thrills."[2]

Some rated a heavyweight championship fight even higher. On the eve of the second Walcott-Marciano fight in the spring of 1953, Jack Carberry of the *Denver Post* asserted, "It's fair to say that a world's heavyweight title fight commands greater public attention than any other event in the athletic world—including the World Series, its nearest rival." Similarly, Shirley Povich of the *Washington Post* maintained in 1955 that a heavyweight championship fight had an excitement and "emotional wallop" that no other sporting event (even the World Series) could match. "I always will believe the emotional tides run higher in the setting of a world heavyweight championship prize fight than at any other spectacle," Povich contended.[3]

In reality, the "emotional tides" began to run well in advance of fight night. A heavyweight championship fight in the early 1950s had a lengthy, enormous buildup that today's fan would find odd and perhaps even hilarious. The buildup consisted of endless and often trivial talk about the upcoming fight, linking liberally mixed opinion and fact, truth and fiction. More important, the buildup followed a set pattern with familiar elements. It was, in short, a ritual.

The ritual began three or four weeks before the fight when boxing-beat writers would descend upon the training camps of the fighters. They faced a daunting task. As Harold Kaese of the *Boston Globe* once pointed out, "Without a doubt, one of sports' dullest spectacles is that of a fighter training for a bout." An average day at training camp consisted of the fighter doing some roadwork in the morning and some sparring in the afternoon—hardly earth-shattering, newsworthy stuff. Yet everyone wanted to read about the upcoming fight. The problem was that the public was hungry for information, but there was nothing to feed them. Boxing writers resolved the dilemma by producing what Jerry Nason of the *Boston Globe* called "twenty tons of unstrained type tripe."[4]

Much of the "type tripe" focused on trivialities. How did the boxer look while sparring? Was he in shape? How much did he plan to weigh for the fight? Did he have any new wrinkles to his style? Did he have a game plan?

What was his state of mind? What did he think of his opponent? How was the gate moving along? The answers to these questions rarely made for interesting copy, but the boxing beat writers had no choice—they had deadlines to meet. For several weeks the public was served a steady diet of bland stories concerning sparring performances, weights, and gate predictions.

To spice up their daily dispatches, the boxing writers would routinely and habitually turn to several reliable sources. One such source was the boxing champions from yesteryear, who would invariably visit the camps of both fighters a few weeks before the bout in order to issue what A. J. Liebling called "the customary Delphic prediction."[5] The favorite "touring and predicting" former champions in the early 1950s were Jack Dempsey, Joe Louis, Jimmy Braddock, and, after he retired in 1953, Jersey Joe Walcott. The trick here was to get the former great to praise and then pick the underdog in order to hype interest in the fight and, ultimately, the gate. When Marciano defended his title, many former champions fell in line with the custom and picked his underdog opponent.

Then there were the medical examiners. A prefight medical examination of a fighter offered few thrills. Of course the fighter was in shape—he had been training for several months and was at the peak of his physical condition. Boxing writers, desperate for information, filed such stories anyway. A week before the second Walcott-Marciano fight in Chicago, for example, the Illinois Athletic Commission administered medical examinations to both fighters. Unsurprisingly, Walcott and Marciano passed their physicals. The man on the scene from the *Chicago Tribune* nevertheless informed readers that "the rigid tests" had created a tense atmosphere. He then breathlessly reported that Walcott had a "blood pressure of 128 over 80, pulse of 66 before exercise, and 72 after activity. His respiration was 10 and 16 after exercise. Marciano's blood pressure was 128 over 78, his pulse 60 and 66, and his respiration 10 and 16."[6]

The examination would become considerably more interesting if Dr. Vincent A. Nardiello were involved, as he was for all of Marciano's title fights in New York save for one. In his mid-sixties, Nardiello had been around the sport of boxing for years and was the original "fight doctor" long before Ferdie Pacheco claimed that title as part of Muhammad Ali's entourage in the 1960s and 1970s. Nardiello served as the dean of medical examiners for the New York State Athletic Commission (NYSAC) as well as a staff doctor for Madison Square Garden. He was also regarded as the IBC's "house doctor" and was ringside as the attending physician for most of the IBC's big fights in New York.

As part of his duties, Nardiello would visit the camps of both fighters a week or so before a big fight to administer medical examinations. And he would do so with no small measure of enthusiasm. Four days before the Marciano-LaStarza bout, for example, he gave Marciano an examination at Grossinger's as members of the press looked on. Marciano kept up a steady stream of chatter and looked almost amused as Nardiello examined him "almost like a scientist encountering a new specimen." After the examination was over, the elated Nardiello gushed, "The guy don't need a doctor. He's in the finest condition of his career." The good doctor also lauded, "He's everything a fighter should be."[7]

When it came to glowing medical reports, Nardiello didn't play favorites. On the day after he examined Marciano, he paid a visit to LaStarza's camp in Greenwood Lake. His one-word verdict: "Superb." Questions nevertheless persisted about Nardiello's objectivity. He had long enjoyed a special, personal relationship with Marciano; in fact, he had served as Marciano's personal physician on the night the boxer won the title from Walcott in Philadelphia. Because of that, the NYSAC considered bypassing him as ringside physician for the Marciano-LaStarza fight. Nardiello responded with outrage. "I am also personal physician to LaStarza and personal physician to almost every fighter who comes this way," he declared. "Are you doubting my integrity now?" Nardiello got the assignment. For the rest of Marciano's career, Nardiello would continue to gush over the champion's condition, proclaiming that he was in "terrific condition" before his first fight against Ezzard Charles in 1954 and then in "perfect" condition before his fight against Archie Moore in 1955. The press never seemed to tire of the glowing medical reports.[8]

Ultimately, however, boxing writers scrounging for a story got the most help not from soothsaying former champions or feel-good fight doctors but from the press agents of the promotional organization of the day, the IBC—and particularly from the IBC's ace publicist Harry Mendel. Short and fat, Mendel was an old-time publicity man who had a flair for the sensational and, occasionally, the absurd. After promoting six-day bicycle races in Chicago, he found a real home for his talents in the boxing world. He forged a close relationship with Louis during Louis's long reign in the 1930s and 1940s, acting not only as his press agent but also as an adviser. It was Mendel who helped give Louis the idea of hatching the IBC upon retirement. The organization then quickly eased Mendel out of the picture—a fact he remained bitter about for the rest of his life. But he forged on with his ballyhoo, handling publicity in camps for all the major fighters of the era.

By the early 1950s, Mendel had become the best ballyhoo man in the business. He was, in the words of Bob Cooke of the *New York Herald Tri-*

bune, "an incongruous publicist" and "a bundle of ballyhoo" who wrote "preposterous paragraphs." Mendel would do everything in his powers to try to get boxing writers and the public to forget about everything else and focus on a fight. And Mendel's powers were considerable. In the weeks before the fight, a stream of press releases would issue from his inventive mind. Cooke claimed that he could find a story in the mundane fact that a boxer had ham and eggs for breakfast. He was, in the words of Arch Ward, "the little fellow who makes the biggest noise on the boxing front."[9]

From 1952 to 1955 Mendel was directing that noise against Rocky Marciano. For each of Marciano's seven title fights, he was the IBC press agent assigned to the training camp of his opponent (Walcott in 1952 and 1953, LaStarza in 1953, Charles in 1954, Don Cockell in 1955, and Moore in 1955). Occasionally, however, Mendel faced some difficulty with taciturn challengers reluctant to say anything cocky or controversial about the champion. Before the second Walcott-Marciano fight, for instance, Mendel griped to reporters, "I have trouble getting Walcott to talk to me let alone anybody else." But the clever press agent overcame that obstacle and whipped up some frenzy nevertheless by engaging in a war of words with Murray Goodman, the IBC press agent assigned to Marciano's camp. As part of his counter-offensive, Goodman wanted to release a song he had composed entitled "Don't Cry, Joe." When that old pillar of ethics Al Weill found out, he told Goodman, "Don't you dare put that out under Rocky's name. We don't use those tactics."[10]

Mainly, Harry Mendel made up quotes. Even a discerning reader sometimes couldn't be sure whether a training camp quote came directly from Marciano's challenger or from the vivid imagination of Harry Mendel. At other times it was clear that a fighter's quote was a whole-cloth invention. Before the second Walcott-Marciano fight, for instance, Harry Stapler of the *Detroit News* recognized, "Mendel has quoted Walcott in wordy statements that would do credit to an Oxford professor, let alone ex-longshoreman Jersey Joe." Mendel once had Ezzard Charles saying of Marciano, "He's faking those nosebleeds so I'll go for his nose." The comment was patently absurd. As Kaese noted, "Marciano has all he can do to fake a punch, let alone fake a nosebleed."[11]

It was with Roland LaStarza, though, that Harry Mendel really hit his stride. LaStarza was a college man, thus providing unprecedented inspiration for Mendel's creativity. He had LaStarza quoting Robert Burns and saying such things as, "Napoleon had his Waterloo, Samson had his Delilah and by the same reasoning Marciano has his LaStarza." Mendel also had LaStarza issuing the following analysis: "Let's look at the other side of the ponsasanorum (the ass's bridge, as this algebraic formula is known). Add up youth, skill, speed and confidence, balance it with a better-than-fair punch, and even the guys who didn't go to college can tell you that's a pretty good combination against punch, everything being relative."[12] LaStarza was, in other words, Harry Mendel's muse.

If words weren't enough, Mendel would occasionally resort to cheap publicity stunts. Perhaps his most infamous came several days before the second Walcott-Marciano fight. Fueled by Mendel, Walcott and Bocchicchio had repeatedly claimed that Marciano was a dirty fighter who had illegally butted Walcott during their first fight. Then Mendel decided to drive the point home—with a goat. As reporters and photographers looked on, Walcott climbed through the ropes while someone simultaneously lifted a goat into the ring. Walcott then got down on one knee and started to push the goat in the face in the hope that it would deliver some head-butts in return, thus providing a vivid demonstration of Marciano's alleged tactics. Alas, the goat didn't cooperate and refused to butt back. Later, Mendel even wanted to bring it to the weigh-in on the day of the fight. IBC officials wisely vetoed the idea.

This particular stunt produced some backlash toward Mendel and the buildup campaign in general. Why, Jerry Nason asked, did Walcott submit to "that insulting gymnasium pose with the goat"? To Nason, the entire smear campaign against Marciano had gone too far: "For me, this one-sided name-calling contest has cheapened what is, with the World Series, sports' most staturesque event—a match between two men who have been champions." He felt that the "synthetic circus 'buildup'" in Chicago had also damaged Marciano's reputation and integrity. "Sorry for the soap-box session, kids," Nason concluded. "I just got heated up by this try out here to cheapen a pretty fine young guy."[13]

Red Smith, the great columnist from the *New York Herald Tribune,* also frequently tried to chop down what Mendel and his counterparts at the IBC tried to build up. Before the second Marciano-Walcott fight, for instance, he remarked with disgust, "Just now public attention is focused on a battle between a decent, attractive young man who may be the finest one-punch hitter who ever lent excitement to the sport, and a Bible-reading old pappy guy who is a ring-tailed marvel by all known physical precedents. With a showpiece like this on display, how does the mob respond? With snide insults, epithet and innuendo." On another occasion, Smith observed that the buildup had "achieved a pungent and heady fragrance unattainable by any sports event save a fist fight for the heavyweight championship of the world."[14]

At the other end of the spectrum were the sportswriters who praised Mendel for supplying the drivel. Before the Marciano-LaStarza fight, for instance, Arch Ward praised Mendel for doing "a masterful job of building up LaStarza in the public prints." Those old enough to remember the big-budget publicity campaigns launched by promoter Tex Rickard in the 1920s sometimes even complained that the ballyhoo for Marciano's title fights was lacking. As Prescott Sullivan of the *San Francisco Examiner* lamented before the first Marciano-Charles fight in 1954, "The whole operation has been handled as if no one cared. Reports from the respective training camps of the two principals have been brief and colorless and hardly worth the printing. . . . The late Mr. Rickard fashioned 'Battles of the Century' out of far less material, but then he knew how to do it. To his successors, ballyhoo is a lost art."[15]

The vast majority of sportswriters, however, benignly endorsed Mendel's work by incorporating most of it (except for his outrageous pieces of publicity) into their stories, on the sly and without attribution. For most sportswriters, someone like Harry Mendel was a godsend. With nothing exciting to report from training camp, his fiction at least added some sizzle. Besides, boxing writers depended on the success of the sport (especially the success of heavyweight championship fights) for their livelihoods. They wanted to cover big fights and needed to cover them in order to justify their jobs. Boxing writers therefore found themselves aligned with the IBC and its press agents in pursuit of a common goal: to interest fans in the fight, so much so that they would buy a ticket. It was almost like a conspiracy against the public, with sportswriters and promoters joining forces to create a big gate through an extensive buildup. They needed people to pay to perpetuate the kingdom of heavyweight championship boxing.

● ● ●

By the eve of the fight, every fact had been unearthed, every prediction made, every angle beaten to death—and everyone was generally talked out. As Red Smith observed before Marciano's 1955 fight with Moore, the ratio of words to punches in boxing was "at least a million to one, maybe a billion to one . . . so little action spawns so much talk. . . . Talk, talk, talk. It goes on for weeks and weeks, in the training camps, in bars and restaurants and living rooms and in the newspapers." Still, the talk continued. "Between heavyweights, a big championship fight has something that compares with nothing else, not even the World Series," noted Jerry Nason on the eve of the first Marciano-Charles fight in 1954. "It buzzes at the bars, on the streets, in the hotel lobbies. The combatants involved achieve the rating of personal acquaintances to all who discuss them. Bellhops quarrel over their man with a vehemence reserved for defending family honor. Every man (and some women) is an expert on the 'big fight.'"[16]

The volume only increased when the fight mob—what Red Smith once called the "bizarre, clamoring, contentious, motley mob"—hit town several days before the fight. "Old champions and managers and gamblers and hangers-on and hoodlums and hustlers and patrons of the fancy have filled the hotels and restaurants," Smith reported before the first Walcott-Marciano title fight in Philadelphia. "They throng through the lobbies, gather in knots on the streets, assemble in noisy swarms and Lew Tendler's saloon and chop house, the traditional meeting place of the fight mob in this town."[17]

The fight mob may have been seamy, but it also brought a certain romance and glamour to the scene. As Franklin Lewis of the *Cleveland Press* relayed to readers on the eve of the first Walcott-Marciano fight in Philadelphia: "Fight night. The guys and the dolls. The moochers and the well-heeled . . . Lew Tendler's place a madhouse, inside and on the sidewalk in front. Wonder why they make skirts so tight at the knees a dame can't step over an old mutuel ticket? Gray suits and blue suits, mostly. And blue suedes. . . . Tinhorns with small bankroll and big mouths telling how much they got down on the fight. The creeps, they don't have the right change for a sawbuck."[18] Mickey Spillane, that master of 1950s pulp fiction, would have been proud.

To the end, boxing writers maintained their rituals, and the final few days were the most ritualistic—and most trivial—of all. Newspapers would run one last "tale of the tape" comparison accompanied by large still-shots of both fighters. And sportswriters would tick off, one last time, the final betting odds, the gate projections, and the probable weights of the fighters. They would dwell on the weather forecast. They would reveal exactly when and how the fighters planned to get from training camp to the city. They would speculate on each fighter's whereabouts the night before the fight. They would describe each boxer's day-of-the-fight breakfast. And they would divulge each boxer's planned afternoon-of-the-fight meal, which for all fighters at all times centered around a big steak.

The final prefight ritual was the weigh-in, which was usually held at noon on the day of the fight. As A. J. Liebling of *The New Yorker* observed, "The weighing-in before a heavyweight fight is completely irrelevant, since the men do not have to make any stipulated weight. It provides photographs and new leads for the afternoon newspapers, however, and has a social function . . . giving all visiting journalists and milling coves, active or retired, a place of rendezvous where they can exchange autobiographical notes since the last fight."[19] A weigh-in rarely produced anything newsworthy. Still, sportswriters had to file their stories. Who looked more fit? Who seemed more nervous? Did they even look at each other?

Once it finally arrived, fight night had its own set of rituals and its own special brand of excitement. As a *New York Herald Tribune* reporter noted in 1954, "Normally there is something about a heavyweight championship fight crowd that makes it different from any other sporting event, even a World Series throng; something indefinable in the surrounding atmosphere, something which makes the spirits glow and the adrenalin flow."[20] Part of the atmosphere was due to the celebrities who would flock to a heavyweight championship fight. They still attend big fights, of course, but not in droves. Moreover, they are often not A list celebrities. When Rocky Marciano fought, the crème de la crème of sports, entertainment, and politics would come to watch.

Gen. Douglas MacArthur, for example, attended all four of Marciano's title fights in New York. New York governor and near-president Thomas Dewey was at ringside for the first Marciano-Charles bout. Secretary of State John Foster Dulles breezed in for the Marciano-Moore fight. Humphrey Bogart sat in the press row for both of Marciano's title fights in 1955. He was studying for the role of a press agent in a film, *The Harder They Fall,* although the whiskey he placed on the work bench for one of the fights presumably had little to do with his preparation. Bogie's wife Lauren Bacall was also present at the Marciano-Moore fight. Frank Sinatra attended several of Marciano's bouts, accompanied at one of them by his then-wife Ava Gardner. Milton Berle, James Cagney, Danny Thomas, Rosemary Clooney, Dagmar, Eddie Fisher, Debbie Reynolds, Don Ameche, Bob Hope, Jimmy Durante, Perry Como, Red Skelton, Jackie Gleason (who wore a pink suit to Marciano-Moore), Gregory Peck, George Raft, Walter Winchell, and Ed Sullivan—they all came to see and be seen at Rocky Marciano championship fights.

Also present and accounted for when Marciano fought were former and present greats from the boxing world—Joe Louis, Sugar Ray Robinson, Carmen Basilio, Kid Gavilan, Joey Maxim, Two Ton Tony Galento, Max Baer, and Jack Dempsey. They got to take bows in the ring, one of many cherished rituals in the final moments before the fight. It was a sport of sorts to judge the fight-night attire of the galaxy of champions. For the first Walcott-Marciano fight, for example, Hugh Brown of the *Philadelphia Evening Bulletin* awarded Robinson "sartorial honors with an entirely fresh ensemble, consisting of green, red and black plaid jacket, with lapels of sable satin, a marcelled hair-do, and a brand-new nose with not a dent to mar its beauty."[21]

The drama built during the introductions of the old fighters, playing of the National Anthem, introduction of the fighters, and instructions in the middle of the ring. These rituals are still followed, of course, but they had a different effect then. "The delay before an epic fight is always tantalizing," observed Budd Schulberg of *Sports Illustrated* in his account of the Marciano-Moore fight. "Most of the spectators have been waiting for the fight all week, talking it up all day, betting it, masterminding it, until they have brought themselves to an exquisite peak of anticipation."[22]

Then the ring was finally cleared, leaving the fighters alone at long last, waiting anxiously for the opening bell. To many, this was the most exciting moment of all. The significance of the moment, claimed Schulberg, "presses on the crowd and it falls silent, grave. The stadium seems to hold its collective breath." For Shirley Povich of the *Washington Post,* the final few seconds before a heavyweight championship fight began were the most exciting of the entire sports year. "It's that sequence just before the fight after the referee has told the champion and the challengers and their handlers that he has no more to say to them except to come out fighting when they hear the opening bell. Then, each to his own corner. . . . Never yet have I seen one sneak a look at the other. It's part of the unwritten code. The bell does sound, and dreams begin to collide. Around the ringside tummies are doing flips. The tensions come off a bit after the first blow is struck. It amounts to a release."[23]

The excitement of a title fight not only gripped people like Povich, who were lucky enough to be on the scene, but also people across the country. Everyone was interested in being part of a heavyweight championship fight. Some called their local newspapers for the result. Others went down to the local movie house to watch the fight on closed-circuit television. Still others listened on the radio. One such fan was a young boy in Kentucky, Cassius Clay. Years later he would tell *Sports Illustrated,* "One night I heard Rocky Marciano fighting on the radio, and all the excitement! 'The heavyweight champion of the world!' 'Marciano hit him with a left!' 'Marciano connects with a right!' 'Now the champion of the world comes out!' And it sounded so big and powerful and exciting. Here I was, a little Louisville boy riding around on a bicycle, no money, half hungry, hearing about this great man, Marciano."[24]

Nostalgic sportswriters of the early 1950s would sometimes pine for the Dempsey-Tunney era and the early days of Louis, when the world seemed to come to a complete stop when two heavyweights fought for the title. Much of that old-time glamour and romance, however, carried over to the age of Rocky Marciano. There were, of course, a few exceptions, notably his 1955 fight with Don Cockell (which bombed at the gate in far-away San

Francisco) and his second title fight with Ezzard Charles in the fall of 1954 (where the excitement was strangely missing). Marciano's other title fights, however, had a distinct "big-event" feel about them. In particular, his first title fight with Walcott and his last one against Moore each crackled with tension and excitement—and illustrated that the kingdom of heavyweight championship boxing was alive and well.

● ● ●

Every kingdom needs a king, of course, and in the early 1950s that king was Rocky Marciano. He was more than just the lead actor in the drama of a heavyweight championship fight, however. Rocky Marciano was "the heavyweight champion of the world." The title—the status, really—meant something special in the early 1950s.

That had been the case for some time. Even before the turn of the century, men had coveted the crown. It was, after all, the top prize in the top division in the entire sport of boxing. The title really acquired symbolic significance and supremacy in the sports world during the reign of Jack Dempsey in the 1920s. Dempsey set a whole new standard of behavior for the man who held the title. One part of the Dempsey formula involved a lifestyle of wine, women, and song—living it up on Broadway, making the rounds at New York nightclubs and speakeasies, buying drinks for the house, and tipping liberally. As Jimmy Cannon maintained years later, heavyweight champions "should go down streets with people following them and crowds coming up on their feet shouting when they enter a fight club. It ought to be plenty of money rolling in and fast action and the excitement of true fame."[25] The other part of the Dempsey code involved a certain responsibility. Even though he could theoretically lick any man in the world, the heavyweight champion of the world was supposed to spend his time out of the ring in a classier, more gentle way. After all, the king owed something to his subjects.

After Dempsey, the crown itself became more important than the king who happened to wear it. It was the status of the heavyweight champion of the world (not the man himself) that bestowed fame, glory, riches, and prestige from the sports world and society at large. The man fortunate enough to own that title could reap those benefits, but only while he held the title. Once he lost it, everything automatically passed to the new champion. Because of the power of the crown, the title "the heavyweight champion of the world" came to occupy a supreme status atop the sports world. Only a handful of baseball icons could rival his fame.

This remained true in the early 1950s, although some luster had clearly worn off the crown. The heavyweight champion still sat on "the most coveted, most romanticized throne in the world of sport," in the words of W. C. Heinz. The crown he wore was still what Red Smith called "the most glittering bauble in sports." In the early 1950s the heavyweight champion of the world was still royalty.[26]

He was even more than that. He was a mythic archetype. As Robert Lipsyte of the *New York Times* points out, historically many have viewed the heavyweight champion of the world as the "epitome of American manliness—the toughest man in America who also evokes our feelings about what a man should be like." According to Lipsyte, Louis and Marciano each neatly fit the image. "People kind of knew he [Louis] was fucking every white woman in Hollywood, but he was willing, at least for cosmetic purposes, to once again follow through these feelings, these attitudes of what a manly heavyweight champion should be. And Marciano was the best at that. Whatever he might have been, it didn't really matter. It was the image."[27]

Marciano himself seemed to grasp the power and significance of the throne. "When I fought Joe Louis, I thought it was the biggest thing of my life, but a bigger thing came along the night I fought Joe Walcott for the title," he told Shirley Povich in 1955. "That made the difference, the title. Louis was more famous than Walcott, but he didn't have the title. If I could beat Walcott, I knew I would get the title. The title was always in front of my eyes." The morning after he had won the title, Marciano lay awake in bed, thinking about the significance of his new title and status. "It was then that I finally realized that I was the guy who could beat any man in the world with my fists," he recalled. "It was then that I made up my mind that I would never do anything to disgrace the title. I sorta felt that I was privileged to hold it and it scared me a little bit, the more I thought about it."[28]

Marciano willingly and enthusiastically played the part of the heavyweight champion of the world in all respects, both in and out of the ring. Every king, for example, needs a court, and Marciano had his. Comparatively speaking, his entourage was smaller than that of several other contemporary champions such as Sugar Ray Robinson. It was certainly smaller in number and noise than entourages that would surround future champions, such as the traveling road show that accompanied Muhammad Ali. Still, Marciano was surrounded by his own curious collection of fight men, hangers-on, and other assorted characters.

The key men in Marciano's entourage were, of course, Al Weill, Charley Goldman, and Allie Colombo. Marciano's father and friends from Brockton such as Nicky Sylvester also held places of honor. Beyond that, there were people who had defined functions. There was Al Reinauer, the personal chef who had the temperament to befit a man of his profession. ("Utensils," he once proclaimed to a scurrying hotel staff. "I must have proper utensils to prepare his food.") There were bodyguards such as Capt. Louis Capparelli, the deputy chief of traffic with the Chicago Police Department, and Philadelphia police sergeant Steve Melchiore. There was Soldier Farr, who served as greeter, good-will ambassador, and court jester. Then there was Chick Wergeles, an old friend and patron of Weill. It wasn't clear exactly what Chick did, though. Technically, he was identified as Weill's man of affairs or Weill's attaché, with responsibility for hiring Marciano's sparring partners. More jokingly—and perhaps more accurately—sportswriters dubbed Wergeles as the "vice president in charge of reading the newspapers" or "the man who holds Al Weill's coat."[29]

And then there were the hangers-on, those who did nothing for the champion but somehow landed in Marciano's training camps. Perhaps the most famous was Jimmy Cerniglia, a wealthy Atlanta tomato packer occasionally referred to as the "Florida Tomato King" (which was odd because he hailed from Georgia) or the "tomato king of the U.S." He was, praised Jerry Nason, "a guy who has parlayed the lowly tomato and a smart twist for business into a lot of bucks."[30] When he was in Marciano's camp, Cerniglia was known as Jimmy Tomatoes. He first became friends with Marciano when he won $21,000 by betting on him in the Rex Layne fight. When Marciano faced Walcott in Philadelphia, Jimmy Tomatoes again bet heavily on the Rock. To protect his investment, he was a constant presence in Marciano's training camp before that fight. He later showed his gratitude by springing for a big post-fight party in the ballroom of a Philadelphia hotel; everyone aligned with Marciano attended.

During training camp, Marciano's entourage helped the champion create a life that had a distinct flavor. As Harvey Breit of the *New York Times* observed after a visit in 1954, "It has autonomy, life is lived there as anywhere else, chores and jobs and recreation are integrated. . . . There is a planned routine and a crisp bustle and a crackling vitality. . . . The atmosphere is one of getting a job done and living as decently as you can while getting it done, and having a simple confidence that it will get done well." The life, however, was also surreal, contrived, and temporary—and Marciano knew it. As he would occasionally caution companions in camp, "Some day this ship's gonna reach port, gang, and that's as far as we go together."[31]

Marciano's entourage also included, by extension, fellow celebrities whom he befriended. He and Ted Williams, the other Boston sports icon of the era, became good friends, for example. As a token of their friendship, Williams gave Marciano his cap, which Marciano proudly wore around camp. On another occasion, Marciano visited Williams at his apartment after a Red Sox night game. Williams immediately took out two quarts of ice cream, one for him and one for Marciano. After the ice cream was gone, Marciano asked, "When do we eat?" Williams replied, "I never eat anything except ice cream after a game." Marciano immediately left to seek steak and spaghetti. He reportedly never felt the same way about ice cream again.[32]

Other celebrities also hung with the Rock, often visiting him during training. Before his fight with Archie Moore in 1955, for example, two of the premier golfers of the day, Cary Middlecoff and Jimmy Demaret, showed up at Camp Marciano, as did five members of the New York Yankees (Hank Bauer, Elston Howard, Don Larsen, Andy Carey, and Frank Leja). Eddie Fisher and Debbie Reynolds, one of Hollywood's power couples at the time, also visited Marciano while he was preparing for Moore. On another occasion, Marciano was taking a walk with Jerry Lewis when Lewis asked, "Do you realize what you are, Rock? You are the boss of the world—the whole world."[33] As now, a mutual admiration society existed between sports stars and entertainers.

Marciano even associated with the high and mighty from the political arena. He was one of forty-three sports figures invited to the White House in June 1953 to have lunch with President Dwight Eisenhower (Al Weill somehow managed to get himself on the guest list as well). The next day, newspapers across the country ran a photograph of Ike jovially admiring Marciano's clenched fist as a bemused Joe DiMaggio looked on. The picture would provide material for Marciano's stock banquet speech. He would tell of returning to Brockton shortly after his visit with the president and walking past a couple of old pool-hall cronies. "Look at old Rocky," they said. "Stuck up ever since he got his pitcher taken with DiMaggio."[34]

●   ●   ●

Marciano hobnobbed with celebrities because he was a celebrity himself. The title "heavyweight champion of the world" automatically granted him that status. Certifiable proof of his celebrity came in the form of frequent postfight appearances on America's cultural barometer, Ed Sullivan's Sunday evening *Toast of the Town* television program. In addition, immediately after the second Charles fight Marciano flew from New York to Los Angeles to appear on NBC's *Colgate Comedy Hour* hosted by Eddie Fisher and featuring Louis Armstrong and Peggy Lee among others. In the summer of 1954, he and Ezzard Charles were the subjects of Edward R. Murrow's *Person to Person* show on CBS. Marciano was deluged with fan mail after the appearance, as he was throughout his reign.

Besides the numerous television appearances, Marciano attempted to cash in on his celebrity status by barnstorming. Between fights he was constantly on the road. He boxed exhibitions. He refereed wrestling matches. He made personal appearances. He gave banquet speeches. In fact, as the athletic symbol for the Age of Simplicity, he was an ideal speaker for church groups, youth groups, and similar organizations. Characteristically, he worked hard at honing his speaking ability. His speech sometimes began with a joke: "When I started in the fight game, I was very nervous at dinners like this. So I would say I wasn't much of a speaker but that I could lick any one in the house. I don't say that any more. My manager tells me that when I fight I've got to make money."[35] For some reason, the joke often brought down the house.

Al Weill made sure that the champion was paid for every speech, every appearance, and every movement. As Tim Cohane of *Look* noted in 1955, "Weill has industriously hustled him around the country to squeeze every possible dime out of the championship." Marciano's customary fee for an appearance was $3,000. In the beginning, he felt sheepish about collecting the money. "Three grand, three grand for the things I say," he would moan. The guiltless Weill would respond, "Don't be a big fish. They want to hear you, leave 'em pay to do so, you are the champeen."[36] Marciano eventually lost his reluctance.

Weill even made sure that Marciano made money when he trained. At Grossinger's, Marciano's stomping grounds when he fought in the East, Weill would charge a dollar to those who wanted to watch Marciano train. He often collected the money at the door himself, in front of a stand stocked with Marciano souvenirs. The same held true when Marciano trained in Holland, Michigan, for the second Walcott fight and Calistoga, California, for the Cockell fight. The way those two small towns embraced Marciano indicates the power and majesty of the crown he wore.

The residents of Holland, a small, immaculate, friendly town known for its tulips, are primarily of Dutch origin. Marciano quickly became a phenomenon there as he trained on the grounds of the Holland Furnace Company. The townspeople became so smitten that they named a new tulip in his honor. "The Marciano" was red and black, the colors of Brockton High School. Marciano returned their affection by coming back the day after the fight to help host Holland's annual Tulip Time Festival.

Calistoga was similarly awed by the presence of the heavyweight champion of the world. Shortly after Marciano decided to train there for his 1955 fight against Don Cockell, Ken Hively, the chief of police, declared, "[T]he entire Napa Valley considers the appearance of the heavyweight champion in our area the greatest thing that's ever happened."[37] Residents threw Marciano a huge welcoming dinner and made him honorary chief of police; Weill was named honorary mayor. Later, as Marciano trained at the Napa County Fairgrounds, Hively collected tickets at the door while the mayor tended bar. The town couldn't offer Marciano a tulip, but it did present him with a special orange-and-black silk robe with the words "Rocky Marciano—Calistoga's adopted son" emblazoned on the back.

Whenever or wherever Rocky Marciano traveled, he did so in style. He received VIP treatment and was treated as royalty. He was, after all, the heavyweight champion of the world. "It's the one little word 'champion' that I miss," Charley Goldman said after Marciano retired. "It's a great thing. It can *do* things. It opens doors for you. It gets you the plane reservation when all the seats are sold. It gets you the best suite in the biggest hotel in town. And every place you go, people want to do something for you or give you something, like a shirt or a tie or a suit. When they do that they think they're part of the champion, I guess."[38]

Marciano's travels and appearances gave the champion a chance to meet his public. From the beginning, he seemed to recognize that he was more than a mere ambassador. He carried the responsibility that went with being the heavyweight champion of the world. Ironically, he may have learned that lesson as a boy when he saw Jack Dempsey, the man who defined what it meant to be heavyweight champion. "I wanted to be like Dempsey in smiling and acknowledging all the greetings," Marciano recalled shortly after winning the title. "He made you feel that he knew you, that he was happy to say hello even though you were just a punk kid like I was then. I felt that I knew him and the way he smiled and talked made me feel that he knew me, too."[39]

Marciano followed suit when he himself became champion years later. H. G. Salsinger of the *Detroit News* was not the only reporter to point out that "he loves children and would spend all his time signing autographs for them and doing card tricks for them if his manager and handlers did not interfere." As Bud Collins recalls, "He was a good guy and always very obliging. . . . He wouldn't refuse autographs and he was very glad when people approached him." Marciano claimed that he never refused to sign an autograph. "You see, all my life I've liked people—and especially the ones who don't have too much," he explained to one reporter. "Your hand gets awful tired at times signing all sorts of cards, programs, etc., but it goes with the championship and, as I say, the sight of a little disappointed face sticks with me for days and nights. Of course you wonder why so many young-sters want autographs from a person who gets prominent, but that's the American way of life and I've never heard of any better way."[40]

Most agreed that he wore his crown well. In that sense Marciano reminded many of the great Joe Louis. Marciano, Jimmy Cannon lauded, "is a kind-natured man. He accepts the responsibility of being a champion and acts like one. . . . He is an intelligent guy and enjoys the homage all champions know. But he doesn't take advantage of his position. Only Joe Louis in my time had this grace." He was, echoed Budd Schulberg, "a champion in the classic tradition. Like Joe Louis he has innate taste and graciousness. As is often true of fighters, his ring manners, which are not too couth, have noth-ing to do with his social manners, which are gentle and warm-hearted." Jerry Nason claimed that no heavyweight champion, even Louis, had "kept faith with the championship as Marciano has. He has enormous pride in it and his conduct has been willfully governed by it."[41]

For sure, Marciano found the role of being heavyweight champion of the world to be suffocating on occasion. He had little time for himself or his fam-ily, and fans always seemed to be around, occasionally intruding into his private time. There was also a surreal isolation to it all. "In a sense, the heavy-weight champion of the world leads one of the loneliest existences on earth," Bob Addie of the *Washington Post* observed in 1956. "He's not a man; he's a symbol. There's something vastly intriguing, even to civilized people, about a man who can lick anybody in the world. A heavyweight champion is closely guarded, almost like the President of the United States."[42]

For the most part, though, Marciano relished being heavyweight cham-pion of the world. He explained why on several occasions:

September 1953: "Being champion is a thrill . . . I haven't been champion for long but it does something to a guy. It makes you surer of yourself, gives you more confidence and—well, someone once described it to me as offering you a spiritual exhilaration. Those are fancier words than I'd ordinarily use my-self but they seem to fit the situation perfectly and I'm not too proud to bor-row them."

September 1955: "It's everything. You lose the title and you lose people's re-spect and admiration and, of course, you lose money. It would hurt—it would hurt a lot—to find a guy who could lick me, you know? So far, I haven't. And I don't think I will for awhile. That's important, you know? I mean knowing you can lick anyone in the world. It's the kind of confidence a guy needs."

January 1956: "That's what's nice about being champion—to be accepted and liked. Tomorrow I'm going to have dinner with the governor. It makes you feel proud to be accepted with these fine people. They admire you and have a lot of respect for you and they're interested in you. The young kids look at you and say, 'Gee, he must be the strongest guy in the world, he could lick anybody; whatta tough guy; look at his muscles; look at his hands.' . . . They only think of strength and muscles and toughness. They don't know that the nicest part is that people like you."

Or, as Marciano said on another occasion, "What could be better than walking down any street in any city and knowing that you are the champion?"[43]

Marciano, who feared poverty and obscurity, clearly liked that feeling. In 1955, toward the end of his reign, he told Curley Grieve of the *San Francisco Examiner* that his greatest thrill was not any particular knockout but rather a moment before one of his fights with Ezzard Charles in 1954. He was entering Yankee Stadium an hour or so before the fight, walking up the ramp to his dressing room with a police escort. As a crowd gathered around, the police cleared way, and the lead sergeant yelled, "Make way! Here comes the champ!" At that moment Marciano thought back to his rise from virtual nobody to champion. "It was just like a movie," he recalled thinking. "The best movie I ever saw." He turned to his faithful sidekick Allie Colombo and said, "Al, what a contrast! And just two and one half years ago we had to hitchhike to New York on a truck." Marciano called the moment "the unsurpassed thrill of my life."[44]

●　●　●

Shortly after Rocky Marciano retired in 1956 the kingdom started to crumble, and the king started to lose much of his power. One reason for the swift decline of heavyweight championship boxing was the corresponding rise of other spectator sports in the latter half of the 1950s. When Marciano first rose to prominence at the beginning of the decade, baseball was boxing's only real competition on the sports pages. That began to change after he retired. Several sports, particularly professional basketball, benefited from the influx of black athletes. By the end of the 1950s the NBA had superstars such as Bill Russell, Wilt Chamberlain, and Elgin Baylor, and the game was obviously better because of their presence. The same was true of college basketball and college football, each of which had started to become national in scope.

The biggest change in sports during the late 1950s concerned professional football, and the reason was, of course, television. In the 1958 NFL championship game the Baltimore Colts beat the New York Giants in a televised overtime thriller, the "Greatest Game Ever Played." Pro football had arrived in America's living rooms. In terms of spacing, pace, and action, pro football proved ideal for television. By the late 1950s, television technology had improved dramatically, and advertisers were seeking to tap into the buying power of sports fans. The stage was set for the sport's rapid growth. Soon the NFL (and after 1960 an exciting upstart rival league called the American Football League) was attracting scores of new fans. By the end of the 1960s, pro football had become America's leading spectator sport. All the growth came at the expense of older, more established sports such as baseball and particularly boxing (which, like football, relied on violence for part of its appeal).

The primary reason for the sudden decline of heavyweight championship boxing, though, was internal. In the latter half of the 1950s, the sport of boxing fell apart as the synergistic empires of Jim Norris and Frankie Carbo came crashing down around them. A primary problem concerned a declining product. In the Mob-fueled regime of the IBC, neither the fighters nor the fights seemed quite as good. That was due in large part to television, which had always been a staple of the Norris-Carbo cartel. Boxing was, indeed, ideal for the early days of television, when the underdeveloped technology required simple sports with simple angles and when there was overall need for cheap programming to fill the airwaves. Norris and his men were more than happy to fill the programming void, supplying the fights for several prime-time weekly boxing programs that appeared on the various networks. As a result, boxing enjoyed a new and more widespread popularity in the early 1950s—at least for the short term.

In the long term, however, the exposure (or, more accurately, overexposure) backfired. Television damaged gate receipts, particularly at the local level. Why would a fan go out and pay a few dollars to watch a couple of local kids fight when he or she could sit at home and watch a big fight in a big arena for free? Perhaps more important, television destroyed boxing's grass-roots institutions that had long been critical in producing quality fighters. Amateur boxing, for instance, lost much of its standing in the early 1950s. Moreover, the small fight clubs that had previously served as a training ground for young fighters vanished almost overnight. In the era of the IBC, young fighters long on flair but short on experience and fundamentals were rushed onto the screen, often well before they were ready. The fans eventually caught on, and skepticism about the sport started to grow.

A spate of questionable decisions in the early and mid-1950s hardly helped matters. This was nothing new for boxing. Boxing had always had its seamy side. Historically, the press had turned a blind eye on those aspects of the sport. This may have been due to the fact that sportswriters saw the seamy side of boxing as perversely providing some of the sport's glamour. Or perhaps the benign neglect was due to regular payments and special favors that the IBC (and predecessor organizations such as the Twentieth Century Sporting Club) may have provided to boxing writers and columnists in order to ensure their silence. Then again, many in the press legitimately took a "boys will be boys" attitude toward the criminal influence in boxing. The belief was that mobsters had a somewhat benign and rarely destructive effect on the sport.

By the mid-1950s, though, the funny business began to stink as never before, and some sportswriters could no longer ignore the stench. They finally began to expose boxing's scandal-ridden underbelly. *Sports Illustrated,* for instance, declared three months after its debut in 1954 that "Boxing's Dirty Business Must Be Cleaned Up Now." For the balance of the decade, the magazine kept up its crusade against the shady elements in boxing, making Norris a particular target of investigation and ridicule. A growing number of influential sportswriters, such as Dan Parker of the *New York Daily Mirror,* joined the call for a wholesale cleanup of the sport.

The government was already on the case. The first blow came from the New York State Athletic Commission, an unlikely source given that, too often, state sanctioning bodies had steadfastly stayed out of the way of Norris, Carbo, and company. The NYSAC struck its blow at an unlikely target, the managers' guild, which operated under several different names in the early 1950s but was, throughout, dedicated to the sole purpose of lining members' pockets with more money. The guild was not a formal part of the IBC and represented a major thorn in Norris's side through much of the early 1950s. It was part of the status quo power structure of boxing, however. Then, suddenly, it was gone. In December 1955 the NYSAC, under the leadership of reformer Julius Helfand, denied recognition of the guild in the state of New York because of its deceptive practices and "malevolent influence" on boxing. Helfand ruled that any manager who had not resigned from the guild by mid-January 1956 would have his state license revoked. When Norris (after some arm-twisting from Helfand) unexpectedly aligned with the NYSAC, the guild's resistance to Helfand's decree quickly collapsed. Within a few weeks it was dead.

Perhaps Norris joined the forces of good against the evil guild in an attempt to cast the IBC in a favorable light. If so, the about-face was too little and came too late, for the IBC was in a heap of legal trouble. Its problems began in 1951 with, ironically, manager Jack Hurley, who blustered so loudly about the injustices being perpetrated against his fighter Harry Matthews that he convinced three U.S. senators from the Pacific Northwest (Harry Cain and Warren Magnunson of Washington as well as Herman Welker of Idaho) to call for a congressional investigation of the IBC.

Nothing ever came of the matter on Capitol Hill, but it did raise eyebrows at the U.S. Department of Justice (DOJ). In the fall of 1951 the DOJ tasked a grand jury with investigating the practices of the IBC. By March 1952 the grand jury had developed enough evidence to enable the DOJ to file an antitrust suit against the IBC, alleging it had established a monopoly in violation of the Sherman Act. The IBC was granted a reprieve in February 1954 when a federal district court dismissed the DOJ's suit. Boxing, it held, was like baseball, subject to the antitrust exemption (a legal theory that the National Pastime would successfully use until the mid-1970s to block free agency). Less than a year later, in January 1955, the Supreme Court reversed the decision, ruling that boxing was subject to antitrust laws. The suit was back on, and the IBC was in trouble.

The trial took place in the spring of 1956, around the same time that IBC favorite son Rocky Marciano announced his retirement. About a year later, in March 1957, Justice Sylvester J. Ryan of the U.S. District Court for the Southern District of New York announced his decision. He ruled against the IBC, finding that the organization was guilty of monopolizing championship boxing and carrying out a conspiracy in violation of the Sherman Act. Worse yet, the decree Justice Ryan handed down in June 1957 included a number of time-phased measures that all but dismantled and dissolved the IBC in the name of restoring fair competition. The IBC's days were numbered.

The IBC, of course, appealed to the Supreme Court. As he waited and hoped for a reversal, Norris desperately tried to regroup. In April 1958 he relinquished the IBC presidency to long-time lieutenant Truman Gibson for purposes of public relations. Nothing really changed, however, because Norris continued to call the shots from behind the scenes and also continued to do business with Carbo in an attempt to maintain control of boxing. The sport was beginning to slip from Norris's grasp, however. He couldn't find a way to get the heavyweight title away from Cus D'Amato, manager for Floyd Patterson, who had taken either a principled or a pragmatic stand against the IBC, depending on one's point of view. Then, in January 1959, the Supreme Court upheld Justice Ryan's ruling. It was the death-knell for the IBC.

Even then, Norris refused to give up. In the wake of the Supreme Court's decision, he set up new corporations, National Boxing Enterprises and Title Promotions, Inc., both under the nominal leadership of Gibson, to promote championship fights. He also continued his quest to regain control of the heavyweight crown. Along with Carbo and others, Norris established ties to leading contender Sonny Liston. Then, after Ingemar Johansson beat Patterson to capture the title, Norris entered into an ill-advised scheme with a man named Bill Rosensohn, setting up yet another corporation to leverage Rosensohn's alleged influence over Johansson. In the end, that scheme failed, as did all of Norris's desperate measures. In the fall of 1960 Jim Norris, defeated and with his reputation in tatters, finally stepped away from the sport he had ruled for so long. In self-defense, Norris pointed that he had inherited and not invented Frankie Carbo. He also proclaimed, "I don't want to be sacrilegious but I would say that even if Cardinal Spellman got into boxing, in two weeks he would be a discredited man."[45]

At least Norris escaped conviction. Frankie Carbo was not quite as fortunate. Frank Hogan, a New York County district attorney who had long made organized crime his target, had stayed on Carbo's case for years, watching and waiting to unearth the evidence he would need for an indictment. In 1958 he finally got that evidence via wiretapped conversations. Several months later, in the summer of 1958, a grand jury issued a ten-count indictment against Carbo based on his undercover management and matchmaking activities. Carbo promptly went into hiding and successfully remained a fugitive from justice for almost a year. In May 1959, however, the police finally tracked him down in Hayden Township, New Jersey. Five months later Carbo pleaded guilty to three counts against him and threw himself on the mercy of the court. He was subsequently sentenced to two years of jail time in Rikers Island, New York.

It was merely a harbinger of things to come. On the other coast of America, federal lawmen had already started proceedings against Carbo, Gibson, and several others. Gibson maintains that the man who precipitated the probe was Robert Kennedy, who was then trying to bust the rackets and Jimmy Hoffa in particular. Gibson and company entered the Kennedy-Hoffa crossfire during the famous Cheasty trial in the summer of 1957, when Hoffa faced seemingly insurmountable charges. Hoffa's top lieutenant, Paul Dorfman, had once helped Gibson and the IBC find its way out of a labor mess in Detroit. Now Hoffa had his own legal troubles, and Dorfman asked Gibson to repay the favor by sending Joe Louis on an all-expenses-paid trip to Washington, D.C., to serve as a character witness for Hoffa. Gibson had an even better idea for Louis's participation. "Don't pay anything," he told Dorfman. "Don't pay his hotel room. Don't pay for anything. But have him at the trial for a week. And when the jury files out, have him talk to Jimmy doing whatever." That's exactly what Louis did in full view of the mostly black jury that was to decide Hoffa's fate. Many later criticized Hoffa's lead defense counsel, Edward Bennett Williams, for engineering the episode, although Williams vigorously denied any involvement.[46]

In any event, the ploy worked, and, much to Kennedy's shock and dismay, the jury acquitted Hoffa of the charges. Several weeks later the FBI paid

a visit to Gibson, who subsequently signed an affidavit explaining the reasoning for Louis's participation at the trial. "That infuriated Mr. Kennedy,"
remembers Gibson. "And that was the end of the ballgame so far as we were
concerned, because he was well-known for carrying deep-seeded grudges
against anybody connected with Hoffa. . . . After that, they started with the
long-drawn-out arrangement for the trial in California."[47]

They quickly found what they needed in California in the form of a
botched conspiracy to extort a share of the earnings from the managers of
welterweight champion Don Jordan. In September 1959 the government got
indictments against Carbo, his chief associate Blinky Palermo, Gibson, and
several others. In May 1961 the government got its convictions. The resulting
penalties were severe: a twenty-five-year sentence for Carbo, a fifteen-year
sentence for Palermo, and a five-year sentence for Gibson that was suspended
in light of his distinguished government and legal career.

The Carbo-Norris era in boxing was officially over, but it was hardly for-
gotten. All of the scandals, investigations, lawsuits, and convictions had weakened the integrity of boxing and shaken the public's faith in the sport. To the
extent that any faith was left, it was destroyed by the hearings that the Sen-
ate Antitrust and Monopoly Subcommittee conducted under the leadership
of Sen. Estes Kefauver in December 1960. Over the course of eight days,
thirty-six witnesses paraded before the committee, including Norris (who was
permitted to testify in a closed session due to his poor health) and Carbo (who
evoked the Fifth Amendment twenty-five times in order to stonewall the committee). In the end, nothing ever came of the hearings. The bills Kefauver
subsequently introduced in Congress that proposed a national boxing commission under the wing of the DOJ failed for one reason or another. But the
damage had been done as a long litany of abuses, excesses, and corruption
from the previous decade was finally, fully, and officially detailed.

Boxing, then, entered the 1960s as a mere shell of its former self. In December 1960 *Sports Illustrated* proclaimed that despite boxing's long and
sordid history, "there are reasons to believe that public skepticism about the
wholesomeness of the sport has never been deeper than it is today." Six
months later, the magazine observed that boxing, in less than a generation,
had gone from "an exciting sport to a perverted and sadistic racket."[48] In
other words, the sport had imploded.

● ● ●

Boxing has never really recovered from the scandals of the 1950s. The impact that the sport has had on its fighters has only accelerated its decline.
That, proclaims Jimmy Breslin, is why the glamour is gone from boxing:

"Everybody you see that fought . . . who brought great compliments out of you as you stood and applauded, every one of those fellows is punch-drunk or dead—dead early." One incident in particular rattled Breslin, an encounter with former middleweight champion Rocky Graziano in P. J. Clarke's, a New York saloon, in the late 1960s or early 1970s. The men had lived in the same neighborhood in Queens and known each other fairly well. As Breslin recalls, "I hadn't seen him in a couple of years . . . I'm sitting there in the daytime. He walked in at 1 o'clock in the afternoon. He squinted. Then he walked up to me in the bar. He looked at me and he says, 'Do I know you?' I didn't know what to say. And he said, 'Didn't we fight in Cleveland?'" After walking away for a stretch, Graziano came back to Breslin, shook his hand, and said, "Oh, I know you." The encounter understandably saddened Breslin. He no longer watches boxing. "I can't look any more," he says. "I've had it. I've seen too many cases." To many fans today, boxing is what Lipsyte calls "a sport that has absolutely no moral justification."[49]

Boxing, of course, still has its fans, but it's not the same. Since the mid-1950s there have been dozens of heavyweight championship fights. Few, however, have possessed the crackling excitement and old-style glamour that was present in the days of Rocky Marciano. The heavyweight crown has also lost much prestige and standing. Being "the heavyweight champion of the world" still means something—a lot, in fact. It just doesn't mean quite as much. Holding the crown no longer automatically places you atop the sports world. Instead, the heavyweight champion of the world has slipped in the pantheon of sports stars. He is no longer royalty.

What about Muhammad Ali, who was heavyweight champion for intervals during the 1960s and then the 1970s? Ali's fame was certainly greater than Rocky Marciano's. No boxer—arguably, no athlete in the history of sports—enjoyed the worldwide fame of Ali. But Ali never followed the Dempsey code for being the heavyweight champion of the world, as so faithfully adhered to by Louis and Marciano. Instead, he invented his own standard of behavior for a modern superstar athlete with international appeal. As Robert Lipsyte, who cut his teeth in journalism covering the young Cassius Clay, observes, Ali "led sports out of the crucible of character and into the world of entertainment, where it had always secretly been. . . . He was post-modern before there was modern."[50]

Ali's fame was due less to his connection to the tradition of heavyweight championship boxing and more to his own magnetic personality. The fact that he held the heavyweight title at various intervals helped put him in the spotlight but was ultimately incidental to his fame. The reason he fought in big, glamorous fights (and no fight crackled like the first Ali-Frazier fight) was not institutional but personal. He—not the institution of heavyweight championship boxing—supplied the electricity. Ultimately, Ali was a political and social force that transcended his sport (and all sports for that matter). His individual brilliance and charisma did not restore the kingdom of heavyweight championship boxing but merely obscured the fact that it had crumbled years before. That fact became evident once he faded from the scene in the early 1980s.

Marciano, then, was the last man to derive his fame from the institution of heavyweight championship boxing. As it turned out, although no one knew it at the time, he was the last of a dying breed.

10 Ezzard

Ezzard Charles puzzled people. Perhaps that is why he never won the acclaim that should have been his when he reigned as heavyweight champion
of the world from 1949 to 1951. Instead, he became the most enigmatic,
misunderstood, and ill-treated boxer of his generation. By the time he met
Rocky Marciano in the summer of 1954 in a quest to reclaim his throne,
Charles was still vainly chasing respect.

What made all of this particularly sad was the fact that Charles seemed
to have it all. "Charles is a boxer in the classic meaning of the word," praised
Gerry Hern of the *Boston Post*. "He slips punches, he blocks and parries.
He hooks to the head and body. His footwork is worthy of the professors
of the field. He moves fluidly. He takes calculated risks. Whatever he does
in the ring, he does well."[1] Because he was small for a heavyweight and was
more of stinging, cutting type of hitter rather than a bludgeoning one,

Charles received some minor criticism for his lack of knockout power. But that was nitpicking. Most of his contemporaries conceded that he was a well-rounded, highly skilled boxer with speed, flexibility, and smarts.

He had a fine set of qualities outside of the ring as well. He was a family man with a wife and a child. He was a clean-living man. He was a religious man who served as an usher at his local Methodist church in Cincinnati. He was a handsome man whose appearance hadn't suffered due to his wars in the ring. He was a well-dressed man who wore tasteful suits, conservative in cut and color. He was a successful young capitalist who had purchased several homes and businesses in the Cincinnati area. He was a good citizen who was a member of several upstanding organizations (the Owl Club, the Progressive Club, F. A. Masons). He was even something of a Renaissance man, with wide-ranging interests in music, reading, poetry, and oil painting.

Charles's personality was as admirable as his lifestyle. He was tactful. He was generous. And he was exceedingly modest. "He dislikes talking about himself or his experiences, detests bragging or showing off on the part of others, seems to take small pleasure in his ring accomplishments," observed W. C. Heinz in a profile he wrote about Charles for the *Saturday Evening Post*. "Among fist fighters he is a true Ferdinand the Bull." Reporters also found him to be personable, poised, intelligent, and even fun-loving. In training camp, he played his bass fiddle or practiced card tricks and hypnosis on members of his entourage. "Outside the ring, Ezzard was all quiet class," Red Smith maintained years later. "He liked people. He laughed easily and often. He could talk with warmth and humor."[2] Charles may have lacked personal magnetism, but he possessed a quiet nobility that certainly befit the crown he had once worn.

Yet there was something missing. Personally, he was hard to get to know, even for those closest to him. "I've never known a fighter like him," observed Ray Arcel, one of Charles's trainers during his short reign. "I wake him up in camp and we go out on the road. It's six o' clock in the morning, and I say to him, 'How did you sleep last night?' He says, 'All right.' Maybe he didn't sleep all right, but he won't complain to anyone, and that's the extent of our conversation." On another occasion, a reporter asked Charles if he were excited about the prospects of making history by becoming the first man to reclaim the heavyweight title he had lost. "I don't know," Charles replied. "I don't care about history." Concluded his profiler Heinz, "It is possible that no one really knows Charles well. . . . He seldom gives vent to deep feelings, even when among his best friends."[3]

He could be as strange as he was distant. Take his marriage to his wife Gladys, for instance. They were wed in December 1949 in the home of a friend, but he swore everyone to secrecy in order to kept the marriage hidden from the public. Thereafter, Ezzard continued to live with his grandmother and great-grandmother while Gladys continued to live with her parents. Charles only revealed the existence of the marriage after the couple had a daughter in February 1951. As he later explained, "I just thought it was best to live apart, my being an athlete and everything, but when the baby came, my wife insisted that people should know we were married. I tried to tell her that it didn't make any difference what people knew—that she knew she was married—but it's better now, and I sense the responsibility more."[4]

Charles also acted strangely when he defeated Walcott to capture the heavyweight title in June 1949. Even though he had just won the richest prize in sports, Charles didn't seem excited at all. Several hours after the event, he and a friend slunk away from the postfight celebration. They ducked into a Chicago nightclub, where Charles wore dark glasses and made every effort to conceal his identity. Soon, however, people began coming up to their table and asking, "Aren't you Ezzard Charles? You sure look like him. Didn't you just beat Walcott tonight?" Charles tried to deny his identity, and his friend tried to help by introducing Charles as "Bob Harris," a bass player from Springfield, Ohio. Eventually, Charles's cover was blown, and the two men left the nightclub. The next morning, one of his handlers awakened Charles and asked, "Feel any different bein' champeen of the world?" Charles responded simply: "Nope."[5]

It was his behavior in the ring, however, that truly mystified his contemporaries. One of his handlers, Arcel, once lamented, "He is like a good horse which won't run for you." The press and public agreed. Charles was, claimed Jesse Abramson of the *New York Herald Tribune,* "a man of curious moods insofar as his ring adventures are concerned." To Abramson, even though Charles seemed to have it all he lacked one critical ingredient: "concentrated drive." Echoed Arthur Daley of the *New York Times,* "Charles had size, strength, speed, skill and a reasonably solid punch. His physical attributes were many. It was the inner man who always was a doubtful factor." Like so many others, H. G. Salsinger of the *Detroit News* thought of him as "an enigma."[6]

Several fights in Charles's past were particularly mystifying to sportswriters and fans. One was his fourth and final fight with Walcott in June 1952. For the better part of eleven rounds, it appeared that Charles would recapture the title he had lost to Walcott a year earlier. But then, with a slight lead in points, Charles went into a shell and stopped fighting. "I miscalculated, I guess," he explained later. "I thought I had so big a lead that it was idiotic to take chances." Walcott rallied to retain his title by a close decision. Charles didn't seem too upset, noting, "I thought I won, but I'm not complaining."

Everyone else did, however. The title had been there for the taking, yet Charles refused to take—and they couldn't understand why. Reporters charged that he had "failed to give his total effort" and had lost because of "his own faintheartedness." The bout, *Time* asserted, proved that Charles was "clearly the most reluctant challenger in heavyweight history."[7]

Because of this type of performance, sportswriters habitually delved into Ezzard Charles's mental state. It was an era where there was reluctance to analyze the psychological drives behind an athlete's performance, but sportswriters couldn't resist when it came to Ezzard Charles. As Harold Kaese of the *Boston Globe* observed, "Charles is the most psychoanalyzed fighter ever to enter a championship bout. The sanctuary of his soul has been ruthlessly invaded by men who may not know a complex from a steam shovel, in an effort to determine what makes him so cautious, and if he might not—for just once—act boldly."[8]

The focus of the armchair psychology centered on his caution. Marciano had faced opponents before, such as Walcott and LaStarza, who were regarded as too cautious, often to their own detriment. When it came to caution, however, Ezzard Charles topped them all. Some called him a "reluctant dragon," and the description seemed to fit. When opportunities presented themselves, he fought with a "cautiousness bordering on timidity," according to Matt Ring of the *Philadelphia Evening Bulletin*.[9]

Many cited his intelligence as the reason. As Wendell Smith of the *Pittsburgh Courier* noted, "Ezzard is far above the average fighter with respect to intelligence, one of the smartest in ring history." As Smith also noted, however, Charles thought too much in the ring. To Arthur Daley, he was "much too intelligent and imaginative for his own good. This attitude wraps a shield of caution around him." Hugh Brown of the *Philadelphia Evening Bulletin* had the impression that Charles was "an introvert, a fellow who lies awake at night thinking too much." Agreed John Lardner of *Newsweek,* "His temperament is thoughtful . . . Charles reflects as naturally as other men sweat."[10] To fight men in the early 1950s, such introspection was clearly not a good thing.

Others believed that Charles's caution was due to the simple fact that he lacked a killer instinct. Many criticized him for that, especially given that Charles had showed true greatness on those rare occasions when he did turn tiger in the ring. H. G. Salsinger and others attributed his failings here to his natural personality and, somewhat comically, to musical ability. "They say he was never meant to be a fighter," Salsinger observed. "As a boy he took violin lessons and showed considerable talent." That became his reputation—someone who, in the words of Whitney Martin of the Associated

Press, supposedly had the "soul of an artist and was too sensitive and imaginative to put his heart into the cruel business at which he made his living."[11]

Perhaps Charles lacked a killer instinct because he had once killed. It happened in February 1948, when Charles was just beginning to emerge on the national scene. In front of more than eleven thousand in Chicago Stadium, Charles met Sam Baroudi, a young but promising light heavyweight. In the tenth and final round, Charles knocked out Baroudi. The finish was decisive but not devastating, and there was no reason to think that Baroudi was in any sort of physical danger. But he was. He didn't revive after he hit the canvas. Later that night, Baroudi died. A coroner's jury later returned a verdict of accidental death, exonerating Charles of any blame. Still, Charles was, understandably, devastated. He wanted to quit the ring, but his manager, friends, other fighters (such as Henry Armstrong), and even Baroudi's father talked him out of it. Before long he was back fighting. Many felt, however, that the Baroudi death had left a permanent scar on Charles's psyche and ring style and that he now pulled his punches and refused to go for a decisive knockout for fear of another tragedy. As Charles admitted, "You never forget something like that."[12]

His background offered other clues to his psyche and ring performances. Ezzard Mack Charles was born on July 7, 1921, in Lawrenceville, Georgia, the only child of a trucker, William Charles, and his wife Alberta. When Ezzard was only five, his parents divorced. His father moved north, and his mother went to Atlanta. Young Ezzard was shuttled off to Cincinnati to live with his grandmother and his great-grandmother, both of whom were deeply religious. "She kept after me about the Bible and kept after me about praying," Charles later said of his grandmother. "She was always telling me to live clean. She believed that clean living people have courage and don't get scared of anything. I never had time to go wrong."[13]

As a boy he was eventually drawn to boxing. He came to idolize comic-strip heavyweight Dynamite Dunn and real-life boxers Young Stribling and Joe Louis. The defining experience that lured him into the ring, however, came when eleven-year-old Ezzard met Kid Chocolate, a junior lightweight and featherweight champion of the early 1930s. Chocolate drove into Ezzard's neighborhood in a big touring car and stopped at a candy store, where a crowd quickly gathered around him. Ezzard heard someone ask Chocolate how many suits he owned. "Man, I got a suit for every day in the year," Chocolate proclaimed. "I got 365." When he heard that, Charles recalled, "I said to myself, 'I'm gonna be a fighter and have clothes like that.'"[14]

From the beginning, then, he was in it for the money (and the clothes), not the love of the ring, and he would always retain a businesslike approach to his trade. As he once explained, "Fight night is a man going to work . . . it's just a job." The attitude showed in his ring performance, which was often cool, detached, and dispassionate. "There's nothing to get mad about," he reasoned. "You're trying to lick a man and he's trying to lick you, because that's the business."[15] Charles wasn't all that unique; many boxers were in the sport not for love but for money. He was, however, an extreme case.

His talent was evident from the moment he stepped into the ring. As an amateur in the late 1930s, he won all forty-two of his bouts. Fighting first as a welterweight and then as a middleweight, he captured amateur titles in the Golden Gloves, the Diamond Bells, and the National AAU. In 1940, while he was still in high school, Charles turned pro under the management of a trio of Cincinnati sportsmen. More success followed as he reeled off twenty consecutive victories to start his career. His promising career had hit a plateau, though, by the time he was drafted into the army in the summer of 1943.

He would later regard the thirty-three months he spent in the military as a turning point. A disciplinary incident—plus the harsh realities of life as a soldier—seemed to mature him. "It was while I was in the service that I took stock in myself," he recalled. "I had tried taking the easy way out as far as fighting was concerned and saw it didn't pay off. Now, in the Army, I realized what it was like again when I wasn't making big money."[16] The maturity showed when he returned to the ring after his discharge. Now fighting as a light heavyweight, Charles registered victory after victory, winning twenty-nine out of thirty from early 1946 to mid-1949.

In 1947 Charles also got a new manager—a bald, excitable, lovable rogue named Jake Mintz. He was a former boxer, dime-store operator, carnival worker, dance champion, and constable who financed his way into the business end of boxing by winning a craps game. He started out as a promoter, then became a booking agent for Charles, and then began to represent himself as Charles's manager as he traveled around the country, lining up the fighter's matches. This was, of course, unfair to Charles's original managers. They sued but eventually agreed to sell out to Mintz and partner Tom Tannas.

The rise of Mintz helped Charles. He was a colorful character who played well with sportswriters, in large part because he was a notorious butcher of the English language. (Once, when asked whether Charles would make a good champion, he said, "My predicament is that Charles will make you mastricate your words.")[17] More important, Mintz had the gumption to push Charles into the national spotlight. Until that point, no one—particularly in New York, where he fought just twice before 1949—knew much about Charles. Soon, however, he began to be mentioned as a possible successor to Louis.

Much to his surprise, the IBC tabbed him to meet Walcott in June 1949 for what was facetiously billed as "the approximate heavyweight championship of the world." Before the fight, both the state of New York and Great Britain announced they would refuse to recognize the winner as champion. Even more damning, it became clear that a large portion of the public wasn't ready to accept the winner either. To most, there was only one true champion, Joe Louis, and neither the aged Walcott nor the unknown Charles qualified as a worthy successor. The fight was labeled as a "stinkeroo" before it was even staged, and the bout lived up to its billing. In front of just twenty-six thousand fans in Chicago's Comiskey Park, Charles and Walcott staged what even the usually chipper *Life* called "one of the dullest heavyweight fights in history."[18] The crowd booed throughout the later rounds and until fight's end, when Charles was declared the winner. Mintz supplied the evening's only excitement by fainting as the verdict was announced.

In the end, Charles reigned for two years and successfully defended his title eight times. Along the way, however, he failed to receive the full acclaim and idolatry that usually traveled with the heavyweight title. Instead, he received criticism. As Earl Lofquist of the *Providence Journal* noted toward the end of Charles's reign, "Charles does not fit the bill. Whether he is underrated, as most observers contend, or overrated as a few of us believe, is an academic question. The sad reality is that he does not fire the public imagination." Some sportswriters, who liked Charles personally, argued that he was much better than his reputation. Others, however, were extremely critical and frequently cruel, referring to the champion by his childhood nickname of Snooks or the derogatory Ezzard the Gizzard.[19]

Perhaps he never won complete respect as champion because he typically won "with skill and finality but with no flash of fire," in the words of Red Smith. Or perhaps, Smith mused, it was because "he never quite accepted himself as heavyweight champion of the world. . . . Chances are Ezzard never realized that it was his reluctance to assert himself that conditioned the public attitude. Neither in the ring nor out of it did he ever play the role of boss to the hilt." Others also focused on the way he carried himself as champion. "Ezzard never assumed the dignity and confidence that go with the mantle," Arthur Daley maintained. "He acted as if he were an imposter, a small boy masquerading in false purple." Added H. G. Salsinger, "The public did not believe in him and he generally looked like a man who did not believe in himself."[20]

That he was not a popular champion plainly bothered and frustrated

Ezzard Charles. "Maybe, maybe I'm not big enough," he once mused. "I don't look very big in street clothes. Maybe they expect the champion to be massive and look like a killer." He also lamented, "I don't know what I have to do. No matter how many times I win, or how easily I win, I don't know whether the public will accept me." Charles also once compared himself to a famous author who didn't receive acclaim until he stopped writing. "I guess I'm like Stephen Foster," he said. "They won't appreciate me until after I'm gone." Heinz, who liked Charles, recalls that Charles had "an inferiority complex."[21]

Respect even managed to elude him when he defeated Louis in September 1950, the high point of his two-year reign. Charles had dreaded the fight because Louis was his boyhood idol. (He still had a boyhood scrapbook he had kept on Louis.) Yet the fight presented Charles with opportunity to gain recognition from the state of New York, erase the stigma of having captured a vacant title, and prove himself to the public. Charles was frustrated again, however, when his convincing victory over Louis failed to translate into respect and acclaim. Instead, many berated him for failing to score a knockout (some ringside observers speculated that he held back out of respect for his idol). Others disliked Charles because he had beaten the popular Louis. Somewhat incredibly, Charles's popularity diminished further.

Ultimately, Louis himself was the primary reason the deck was stacked against Charles from the beginning. Charles was the man who had followed the great Louis as champion, and nothing he could have possibly done would have let him escape that huge shadow. Much of the public would have directed scorn at any successor, let alone someone who dared to defeat Louis when he tried to reclaim his throne. "I finally figured it out," none other than Rocky Marciano recognized about Charles years later. "People just didn't want to see Louis lose. It wasn't Ezzard's fault. He had simply come along at a time when a blood-hungry public couldn't appreciate him."[22]

Most were relieved when Charles lost his title to Walcott in their third fight in July 1951, thus bringing an end to his short and rather lifeless reign. For the next three years, until he met Marciano, Charles floundered, losing to Walcott in a rematch and then to the likes of Rex Layne, Nino Valdes, and Harold Johnson. His days as a leading heavyweight contender appeared to be over. But Charles still had friends in high places—namely, Jim Norris, the head of the IBC. Norris encouraged Charles to forge on. He had appreciated his willingness to defend often, and according to the IBC's wishes, during his reign as champion and wanted to repay the favor with another title shot. Significantly, Al Weill, too, fell in line. "I promised Jake Mintz and Tom Tannas that I would take their fellow," he revealed after the LaStarza fight. As 1953 turned into 1954, Charles sealed the deal by defeating two "name opponents," Coley Wallace and Bob Satterfield. The IBC rewarded him by arranging a title bout with Marciano in June in Yankee Stadium. "This is the chance of a lifetime," Charles proclaimed.[23]

• • •

In truth, it was his last chance—and everyone knew it. Charles seemed determined to take advantage of it as he trained for the bout at Monticello, several miles away from Marciano's camp at Grossinger's. He had been studying films of Marciano's fights and claimed that he had been working on a plan to beat the champion for eighteen months. He also seemed confident that he could hurt Marciano, reasoning, "Nobody has a steel chin."[24] He was sparring with his customary skill and seemed more relaxed than usual, spending much of his down time glued to the McCarthy–U.S. Army hearings on television.

This, then, was the "new Charles," a more focused and passionate fighter who had a fresh, unburdened mental determination to go along with his established physical skills. Not everyone bought that story line, however. Some believed that Charles was washed-up. It wasn't his age (thirty-two) as much as the many years he had spent in the ring (seventeen). He had, after all, been fighting since the late 1930s. In that long span of time he fought forty-two times as an amateur and ninety-seven as a professional. Some speculated that all the fighting had finally taken a toll on Charles. As Franklin Lewis of the *Cleveland Press* concluded, despite all the talk of the "new Charles," he was merely a fighter who was "over the hill physically."[25]

Meanwhile, over at Grossinger's, the same old Marciano was training with his usual zeal. Or was it the same old Marciano? The champion, typically the picture of relaxation before a big battle, appeared irritable. There were even alarming reports that he had lost his appetite. (Marciano denied the rumors, adding, "I don't know how the story ever got started that I was a big eater.") He was, in fact, overtrained. He arrived at Grossinger's shortly before Christmas 1953 and never really left. By the time the fight finally rolled around in June 1954, he had been preparing for nearly seven months— an absurdly long time even by his own spartan standards. The long grind had made him edgy. The fact that his family had received several threatening letters only added to his jitters. As camp wound down, Marciano seemed to regain to his form and customary mental frame. Two days before the fight, he looked ferociously sharp in a secret workout. "He looked great, didn't he?" crowed Weill to one of the few reporters on hand.[26] Still, doubts lingered.

As the fight approached, Harry Mendel and the rest of the boys at the IBC were in a quandary. They couldn't get the fighters to act mean toward one another. The problem, observed Shirley Povich of the *Washington Post,* was that Marciano and Charles were "nice guys" who "don't know how to talk tough, hold no rancor toward each other." Before the fight, Charles proclaimed that Marciano was "as nice a fellow as ever entered the ring." Not everyone approved of the lovefest. "Neither has uttered a threat or cast a menacing scowl," complained Prescott Sullivan of the *San Francisco Examiner.* "Their gentlemanly conduct is laudable in its way, but unless this thing is to be decided on the basis of politeness, with Emily Post as the referee, it seems to us they ought to start getting sore."[27]

This isn't to say that Mendel didn't orchestrate some controversy, getting Charles's camp to complain ahead of time about Marciano's penchant for fouling. Joe Louis also tried to take one for the team, declaring after he observed Charles mixing it up with sparring partners, "Charles is training all wrong. . . . He ain't going to mix with Marciano, is he?" (Charles labeled Louis's remarks as "crazy.") Most outrageously, Weill accused Mintz of stealing a "classified" film of the first Walcott-Marciano fight from Weill's secret files. "They're studying it to use against us in the big fight," Weill complained. "It ain't right."[28]

There was little need for such theatrics. This was, after all, an appealing fight with two established and familiar fighters of high quality. Still, Marciano was the clear favorite at odds ranging from 3-1 to 4-1. Jesse Abramson was one of the few who came out for Charles, reasoning, "Skill has mastered brute strength in the ring before, and may do it again tonight . . . it is the conviction here that Charles has the skills, the flexibility, the reach, the speed, strength and cunning to beat the short-armed Marciano to a decision."[29] Only a few others picked Charles to win, but many gave him at least a legitimate chance based on his overall skills and the fact he was a cutting type of hitter (with Marciano clearly having the tendency to cut).

The question was, of course, whether "the new Charles" would really bring some determination into the ring. Charles, observed Wendell Smith, "must realize that he cannot afford to be gentle and merciful in this one. He must exhibit the fiery enthusiasm of a savage, the cruel instincts of a jungle beast. He cannot be kindly, tender or dispassionate." As Abramson stated, "The burden of proof is on Charles."[30]

● ● ●

On the unseasonably cool night of June 17, more than forty-seven thousand fans packed Yankee Stadium to see whether Charles would meet that burden. They were joined by an estimated two hundred thousand fans watching in sixty-one theaters in forty-five cities on the closed-circuit television network as well as millions more listening in on the ABC radio network.

The large and exuberant crowd was treated to a brutal, savage fight that went the full fifteen rounds. There was sustained intensity, mounting tension, and suspense throughout. It was, Paul Zimmerman of the *Los Angeles Times* declared, a "bout that must go down in history as one of the most bitterly fought in heavyweight ring history." Wilfrid Smith of the *Chicago Tribune* agreed, proclaiming it "a brawl the like of which modern pugilism seldom has seen." As Smith also observed, "The bout was not etched in distinct lines. It was painted in broad sweeping strokes. It was painted in red."[31] In fact, the bloody affair unfolded in three neat acts, much like a Greek drama.

Act I consisted of the opening four rounds, and it clearly belonged to Charles. From the outset he was, in the words of Abramson, "cool, poised, the master," mixing stinging left hooks to the body with sharp right leads, right counters, and well-timed combinations. This was all part of Charles's "secret plan," which called for him to pound Marciano's body with hooks and jabs in an attempt to wear down the champion's incredible leg strength, from which he derived so much of his punching power. It was a sound strategy. Charles also scored when he went for Marciano's head. In the first round, for instance, he bloodied Marciano's nose. He also connected with a sharp, downward chopping right to Marciano's head that stunned the champion, if only for a fleeting second. Charles failed to capitalize, however. "That first round chance never came again," he lamented after the fight.[32]

Meanwhile, Marciano was floundering, perhaps because he took longer than usual to warm up. "Maybe the long layoff bothered me," he admitted after the fight. "I started awfully slow—slower than usual."[33] The champion looked bewildered, blinking his eyes and shooting several quizzical looks at his opponent. He was lunging, trying unsuccessfully to get the fast Charles to stand still. He was also, of course, throwing punches, most of which missed their mark. He landed a few, but Charles continued to carry the fight.

It was more Charles in the fourth, his best round. As Marciano continued to flail away with little success, Charles stepped up the pace of his attack. And that attack yielded results when Charles inadvertently capitalized on an old wound Marciano had suffered way back in his Providence days at the hands of Johnny Shkor. A powerful right cross from Charles shortly after the fighters broke from a clinch resulted in (and reopened) a nasty, crescent-shaped cut over Marciano's left eye. His blood immediately began to flow and would continue to do so for the balance of the drama.

Act 2 of the fight, which covered rounds five through eight, marked the resurgence of the bloody yet unbowed Rocky Marciano. In these four rounds, Charles remained effective and at times masterful. It was Marciano, though, who began to dictate the tempo of the fight, and he did so despite the dangerous two-inch-long, one-inch-deep cut over his left eye. "With a cut like that, you got to be nervous," Marciano's cut man Freddie Brown later said. "A quarter of an inch further in and it would of run like a faucet." Between rounds, Brown worked frantically to stem the flow of blood. His triage work was, by all accounts, superb. Still, no repair job could prevent Charles from reopening the cut, which he continued to do with his marksmanship. The blood continued to cascade into Marciano's eyes, plainly bothering the champion on an intermittent basis. "Maybe three or four rounds there were times where I couldn't see out of it for half a minute or a minute so I'd circle around until I could see," he revealed after the fight.[34]

Ultimately, the real significance of the cut over Marciano's eye lay in the fact that it helped bring about a change in Charles's strategy. Early on, he had concentrated on the body with great success. Now, however, Charles had a very visible and very bloody target. He started to go for it, reasoning that the fight might be stopped if he were successful. At the same time, Charles started to neglect his original target, and the change in strategy made him less effective. "I went crazy for that eye and forgot to fight my own fight," Charles would admit later. "That was the turning point."[35]

At the same time, Marciano finally started to warm up. Perhaps the rust finally wore off. Or perhaps the sight and taste of his own blood served as a wake-up call. Or perhaps it was the fact that, in the words of Jimmy Breslin, "He truly liked to fight." Whatever the reason, Marciano finally got going in the fifth round. To prove he was his old self again, he even hit Charles after the bell, drawing boos from the crowd. In the champion's corner between the fifth and sixth rounds, Charley Goldman urged his fighter to throw caution to the wind and revert to type. "He's blocking those left hooks . . . so forget about them from now on and start throwin' an overhand right," Goldman told Marciano. "You've got to punch your way out of this fight."[36]

Marciano started to do just that in the sixth round, which some ringside observers called one of the greatest in heavyweight history. About a minute into the round, Marciano connected with a short hook to the jaw that stopped Charles in his tracks and "made a sound like a steamroller passing over a soupbone."[37] Now Marciano smelled blood—and not his own but that of Ezzard Charles. For the better part of the next minute he poured it on, chasing Charles from one end of the ring to the other while unleashing a steady, rapid-fire, and furious stream of unanswered lefts and rights. The avalanche of punches wobbled Charles, but he managed to stay on his feet. After Marciano finally tired enough to halt his barrage, Charles even fought back at the end of the round, nailing Marciano with a left to the jaw. Even though Charles steadied over the next few rounds, the tide had plainly turned.

It was now a Rocky Marciano type of fight, fast-paced and brawling. There was even the customary chaos in the champion's corner, primarily in the person of Al Weill. Several months earlier, Weill had undergone a gall bladder operation and lost thirty pounds as a result. He was now under doctor's orders to keep his blood pressure under control, and in the first four rounds he did manage to keep his emotions in check. By mid-fight, however, Weill could contain himself no longer. He let himself go, urging Marciano on so vociferously that he elicited repeated warnings from a New York State Athletic Commission official camped near the corner. At one point, Weill screamed repeatedly "give him the one-two," which was ironic given that Marciano didn't have a one-two. The annoyed official finally turned to Weill and said, "Shut up, or I'll give you the one-two."[38] Things were indeed back to normal.

In the third and final act of the drama (rounds nine through fifteen), Marciano won the fight. He did so with a nonstop, unrelenting barrage of punches that Charles somehow absorbed without hitting the canvas. Charles survived crisis after crisis and was seemingly on the constant verge of collapse. On several occasions, as his knees buckled or he started to stagger, the reporters at ringside would scream, "There he goes!" But he stayed on his feet, however unsteady, and occasionally even fought back. Eventually, his courage won the crowd over, and the cries turned to "stay up, stay up, Charles!"[39] Somehow, he complied.

By this point, Marciano's punches were not only rocking Charles but were also beginning to make a definite impact on the challenger's appearance. Over the course of the last half of the fight, Charles's right eye gradually closed and his lower lip became split and swollen. Most strikingly, a curious lump the size of an egg (later diagnosed to be a blood clot) suddenly appeared on the left side of Charles's jaw in the late rounds. It was a lump "that suggested he had a mouthful of pingpong balls," noted Red Smith. Generally, as Cal Whorton of the *Los Angeles Times* reported, "Charles's face took on the appearance of a grotesque mask." To Hugh Brown, it looked as if five trucks had rolled over Charles, followed by a bulldozer and a steamroller. Observed A. J. Liebling, "His face—rather narrow, with a high, curved nose—changed in shape to a squatty rectangle as we watched; it was

as though he had run into a nest of wild bees or fallen victim to instanta-
neous mumps."[40]

The most damaging injury to Charles, however, was one that had no visible effect. At some point—probably in the eighth or ninth round, although
no one (including Charles) was sure—Marciano hit him in the Adam's apple. "I was doing okay until then," Charles explained after the fight. "But
for two rounds after that blow I had a hard time breathing. Then when I
did manage to get my breath back I wasn't as effective as I had been." Echoed Charles's trainer Jimmy Brown, "If he hadn't been hit in the Adam's
Apple, he would have won. That punch took all the life out of him. He
couldn't swallow." Perhaps that is why, according to Red Smith, "[t]here
were times when Charles, sitting in his corner, looked as though he wanted
to cry with discouragement and pain."[41]

Still, Charles carried on. In fact, a few of the judges awarded him the
twelfth round as well as the fourteenth. Going into the final round, though,
Marciano had established a comfortable lead on the scorecards. Marciano's
cornermen were still nervous. As he headed out for the final bell, they told
him, "Win this one or we blow the fight." One last time, Marciano poured
it on, and in the final minute of the final round the weary and exhausted
Charles finally dropped his guard. Then Marciano—incredibly, for the first
time in the fight—managed to pin Charles on the ropes. He proceeded to
hit him with everything that he had left, hurling dozens and dozens of unanswered punches at the battered challenger. "I thought I almost had him
at the end," Marciano admitted later. So did everyone else. Yet the groggy
Charles managed to hang on until the final bell in what Paul Zimmerman
called "a closing stand [that] will go down in ring annals as one of the greatest of all time."[42]

Moments later, ring announcer Johnny Addie announced the verdict. The
winner, by unanimous decision, was Marciano. Some sportswriters claimed
that only a great final kick in the last few rounds had won it for Marciano.
Others speculated that had Charles somehow managed to muster enough
strength and win the final round, he (not Marciano) would have been declared the victor. In reality, it wasn't that close. All three judges gave Marciano a clear edge in rounds. And all three gave him an even more decisive
advantage on points, the supplementary (and in this case more accurate)
indicia. No one disputed the scoring, with the odd exception of Joe Louis,
who criticized both the decision and the refereeing. To everyone else, Marciano had plainly won.

The first Marciano-Charles fight is remembered—when it is remembered—as one of the better heavyweight title fights of all time. Many saw it

that way then, although others were more tempered in their reactions. Liebling, for instance, wrote, "It had been a hard fight but not a great one, in my opinion, because there were none of the sudden changes of fortune that mark a great one, as in the first Walcott-Marciano match."[43] Liebling was right. Marciano's first fight with Charles was not as great as his first fight with Walcott. It was nevertheless a very good (and nearly great) heavyweight title fight.

Even though he was the victor in a classic battle, Marciano received some criticism. *Time,* for instance, titled its article on the fight "Bumbling Champ." He was, Cal Whorton declared, "still a crude piece of fighting machinery." Others criticized Marciano for failing to score a knockout. He himself saw flaws in his performance. A few months later he recalled, "I did plenty things wrong, but mostly I was over-trained and stale and had to fight myself into condition." As a result, Marciano would label it "my worst fight."[44]

In general, though, Marciano received praise for his effort. Red Smith, for instance, alleged that "Rocky had to make his best fight to win" and in doing so exhibited his hallmarks, "his incredible indifference to pain and the numbing force of his punch." Smith also praised Marciano for his "other powers, which he had never before used so ably and with such effect," his inside punching and his combinations. Likewise, Whitney Martin of the Associated Press called it his finest fight because he displayed strength, "unswerving determination and confidence," and "a body conditioned to withstand anything for an endless period of time." As Matt Ring noted, Marciano was "no Dempsey for ferocity, no Tunney for finesse, no Louis for deadly combination hitting, but as they used to say about the British Empire—he can sure muddle through to success." Al Weill put matters more succinctly: "He was great when he had to be great."[45]

Most thought that Charles was even greater. As Wilfrid Smith observed, "Charles unquestionably offered the greatest fight of his long career . . . Charles was the man who rose to greater heights." Against Marciano, he had removed all doubts about his determination and will to win with what Wendell Smith called a "gallant, heroic, violent bid. . . . Here was a man who had lost the battle but won the respect of everyone. . . . Here was a man with great dignity, courage and unrivaled spiritual and mental strength."[46] No one—even his few ardent supporters in the press—had said that about Charles before the fight. Now, everyone was saying it. In defeat he had finally gained some of the acclaim and stature he never attained as champion.

Armchair psychological evaluations continued, of course, but now the diagnoses were positive. Whitney Martin, for instance, labeled it Charles's "finest hour" because he had showed that "he could submerge his imagination and kindly nature and allow the primitive brute that is in every man to rise to the surface." Others sheepishly sought to make amends for their past doubts and for belittling his ring character. The day after the fight, for example, Franklin Lewis wrote an open letter to Charles that began, "So much of us owe you an apology, fella, and I'd feel pretty much like a first-rate louse if I didn't chip in. We had you pegged all wrong. We never dreamt you'd be great or magnificent or, of all things, valiant, up there in the Bronx last night."[47]

"Marciano is not the best fighter I ever fought," the heroic Charles said in his dressing room after the fight. "In fact, I don't think he beat me. I think I won the fight." Charles also rated Marciano a notch below his old foe Walcott. "He's strong and throws a lot of punches, but he didn't give me as tough a fight as Walcott did. In fact, all of my fights with Walcott were tougher. He didn't hurt me as much as Walcott did." (Strangely enough, Marciano in his dressing room quite independently noted that Charles "didn't sting me like Walcott did.") Charles also made clear that he would seek a rematch. "I want him again," he said.[48]

● ● ●

In the immediate afterglow of his gallant performance, many felt that Charles indeed deserved another chance at Marciano. Fortunately for Charles, Al Weill was one of them. He had been exploring the prospects of matching Marciano with British champion Don Cockell in London, but he immediately shelved those plans after the fight. "[T]he match in this country is Ezzard Charles," proclaimed the patriotic Weill. "Charles is the man the fans want to see. And Charles is entitled to the return."[49] The IBC hastily arranged a rematch for September 15, 1954, in Yankee Stadium.

By early August, the fighters were back in their training camps and preparing for the rematch. After his first fight with Charles, Marciano had recognized the perils of a long training grind. "My best fights were when I fought three times a month back in Providence," he reasoned after the fight. "I'll never go that long in camp again. Six weeks is long enough."[50] Even if he felt differently, there really wasn't enough time to become overtrained—the bout was only six weeks away. In the end, he boxed a total of 112 rounds amid a camp atmosphere that struck some observers as somewhat overconfident.

Meanwhile, at Kutscher's Country Club in nearby Monticello, Ezzard Charles was studying and learning from the films of his first fight with Marciano. He had, he told the press, made several mistakes the first time out. "I know what they are and I won't make them again," he said cryptically. On other occasions, he maintained that he could have jabbed and countered bet-

ter and could have even been in better shape. "I saw some things while looking at the movies," Charles said. "I know you have to fight him in close. You
can't hurt him going away."[51] Charles was confident that he could successfully apply what he had learned to his strategy this time around.

He was practically alone in that belief. Marciano would enter the ring an
overwhelming favorite among the boxing writers (thirty-eight of thirty-nine
in one poll picked him to win) and the bookies (who established him as a
6-1 favorite). Many asked why the IBC was staging the rematch in the first
place. The questions had begun several days after the first Marciano-Charles
fight. For instance, W. J. McGoogan of the *St. Louis Post-Dispatch,* after
conceding that Charles had certainly earned another crack at Marciano,
added, "[A]fter thinking it over, you wonder what Charles could possibly
do in September or any other time that he did not do on June 17. He fought
a wonderful fight, possibly the best of his career of about seventeen years,
and still he was beaten to a pulp by the younger, stronger champion."[52] As
the rematch drew near, others found themselves asking the same kind of
questions. How could Charles possibly do better this time around? How
could he possibly win?

None of this helped the buildup, which was hampered to begin with by
the fact that the few obvious angles had been exhausted the first time out.
In desperation, Harry Mendel and company turned to some familiar sources.
Joe Louis, for instance, declared several days before the fight, "Marciano is
one of the finest fellows I know, but he has to follow orders from his corner. And his handlers tell him to fight foul." Al Weill, the obvious target of
that statement, gave his best on another front, claiming that robbers had
stolen more than $6,000 in cash, jewelry, and fight tickets from his Man-
hattan office. Although the thief later sent Weill a letter returning the jewelry and some of the tickets, the rest of the tickets and the cash remained at
large. Many were, understandably, skeptical about the entire incident. Of
course, Mendel invented asinine statements that he attributed to Charles,
for example, "When I went in to the Marciano fight, I admit I started out
with doubts in my mind. . . . Now there aren't any doubts in my mind. Win,
lose or draw, I'll fight like I know I can. I'm no longer the Lord Jim of boxing. I'm no longer the sea captain who deserted his ship."[53]

Ultimately, however, all efforts failed, and the fight failed to spark public
interest. Several days before the event, Al Wolf of the *Los Angeles Times*
noted that the bout was "one of the best-kept secrets in sports." Added
Prescott Sullivan, "If the International Boxing Club had deliberately set out
to keep it a secret it couldn't have succeeded in doing a better job. Presumably, the principals are aware of the impending engagement, but it has tak-

en almost every one else by surprise. The lack of fanfare in connection with the event has been positively deafening."[54]

To make matters worse, stormy weather postponed the fight for two days. On the evening of September 17, the weather finally cooperated. Only 34,330 fans trudged into Yankee Stadium, however, a crowd far below the original gate projections. In large part because of the disappointing turn-out, the usual crackling atmosphere was absent. "There was none of this first-night stuff of standing up, looking around and waving 'yoo-hoo, dar-ling' at no one in particular in the hope that a wandering camera lens would record the scene," observed Everett B. Morris of the *New York Herald Tri-bune*. "And if there were any celebrities, actual, would-be-or-been in the turnout, they were discreetly inconspicuous. There weren't even any ermine-wrapped dolls to distract attention from the ring."[55] Still, it was a heavy-weight championship fight, so the crowd in the stadium (as well as fans watching in seventy theaters in fifty-one cities and listening on CBS Radio across the nation) paid attention.

● ● ●

It turned out to be a surprisingly dramatic fight that supplied one of the defining moments of Marciano's entire career. But that came at the end. Before that point the September sequel was a plodding affair that lacked the nonstop action and excitement of the June original. The first round set the tone. There wasn't much action; caution carried the day. At least, however, Charles seemed confident and determined to battle. He won the round by landing a couple of clean shots to Marciano's jaw. His strategy was clear: He was swinging all-out in selected spots in an attempt to score a quick knockout. As he returned to his corner between rounds, he told his trainer Jimmy Brown, "He's a sucker for a right."[56]

But in the second round the fight turned—and Charles's confidence dis-appeared—when Marciano connected with a body blow. "I hit him a hard right hand under the heart in the second round, he grunted and I knew I had him," he explained later. Seconds later, Marciano did something he had failed to do during the course of fifteen rounds in June: He knocked Charles to the canvas courtesy of couple of rights to the jaw followed by a flurry of punches. Down on all fours, Charles looked dazed and quizzical but got up quickly at the count of two. Marciano moved in for the kill, but Charles escaped, fought back, and survived the round. "I should have finished him then," Marciano would admit, "but I was overanxious."[57]

Suddenly, Charles was no longer the same fighter in terms of confidence or determination. When he arose from the knockdown, maintained Arthur

Daley, "he arose a different man." For the rest of the fight, according to Daley, Charles "reverted to type, maneuvering with a caution that bordered on timidity. He was an octopus who used all eight arms to block Rocky's punches or hold then in a frenzied clutch. Rarely did he strike back and when he did, he threw a punch half-heartedly as if he didn't dare open up his defenses for an instant." It was, declared Budd Schulberg, "the more familiar Charles, the Charles of the spiritless road shows with that old trouper Jersey Joe, Charles the Ferdinand who wished they would open the gate because he really didn't want to hurt anybody and he didn't want anybody to hurt him."[58]

Because of Charles's return to caution, the fight settled into a dull, somewhat listless pattern for the next four rounds. Marciano would chase and try to land as many blows as possible. Some would miss, others would connect. Meanwhile, Charles would mechanically clinch, clutch, grab, hold, and retreat, firing only an occasional punch or two. On a few occasions he would rally and show some signs of life, but then he would retreat into his defensive shell. The extra weight Charles had put on in hope of scoring a knockout didn't help him. "He wasn't moving as fast as in their first fight," Shirley Povich reported, "and Rocky had a slower target."[59] But Charles's cautious tactics also made it difficult for Marciano to fight his kind of fight. Only occasionally did he manage to break through and stagger the challenger. The fight's plodding pace continued.

About the only spark came from Marciano's constant fouling. On several occasions, he hit Charles after the bell and landed a low blow. The fouls elicited repeated warnings from referee Al Berl as well as catcalls from the crowd. They also eventually aroused the ire of Charles, who was infuriated when Marciano hit him after the bell in the fifth round and fired back a couple shots of his own. After the fight, a calmer Charles dismissed Marciano's multitude of fouls by muttering, "Guess that's just the way he fights." Marciano proclaimed innocence. "Yeah, I guess I did hit him a couple of times after the bell," he admitted. "But, honest, I didn't hear it. Just once I heard it. That was after he hit me after the bell."[60] In any event, the fouls didn't hurt Marciano on the judges' scorecards. By the end of the fifth round he was comfortably ahead and appeared on his way to an easy victory.

Then a funny thing happened. Ezzard Charles almost won the fight. As the two fighters emerged from a clinch toward the end of the sixth round, Marciano was suddenly sporting a nasty cut at the tip of his nose, a deep vertical gash starting in his left nostril and extending upward. No one was sure how it had happened. Some attributed the cut to a Charles hook or uppercut. Marciano claimed he had caught Charles's elbow while they were clinching. "Charles was lower than myself," he said. "We turned around to pull away and it was that elbow that did it." However it happened, the impact of the cut was clear—and dramatic. Almost spontaneously, Matt Ring observed, Marciano "began blowing a spray of blood from the tip of his nose." The nose, thought Red Smith, was split "like a walnut so it dripped blood like rain from the caves: in a steady, menacing pattern." Marciano later said, "It bled like anything. I knew something was wrong because the blood was running like from a faucet."[61]

Suddenly, Marciano was in trouble. Before the fight, conventional wisdom held that the only way Charles could win was to cut the champion so badly that the fight would be stopped. And now Charles had cut Marciano—badly. After the sixth round, Charles's jubilant corner instructed him, "Go to work on the nose." Meanwhile in Marciano's corner, Freddie Brown hurriedly worked on the cut. Brown had proven his value before, particularly in the first Walcott fight and the first Charles fight. Now he proved it again. At the end of the sixth, Marciano, Brown recalled, looked "like he's got two noses both bleeding like it was water out of a faucet. Rocky don't know he is cut; he thinks it's just a bloody nose. But I never saw a cut like that before. Rocky's cool and so am I. Between the two of us, we get him fixed up." The repair job didn't stop the flow completely—the cut was far too severe for anyone to fix it totally—but it did buy Marciano at least a couple of rounds. Later, several praised Brown for giving Marciano the time to retain his title. Weill said in the dressing room as he pointed to Brown, "There's the guy who saved it for us."[62]

Going out for the seventh round, Marciano wore a makeshift orange patch on the tip of his nose, a device Brown had hastily applied for protection. Charles quickly knocked it off. With the cut now bare, Charles sniped for the nose. Still, Marciano won the round as he continued to force the action and land the most blows. By round's end Charles was staggering. It was Marciano, though, who was in the real danger because of the cut. Between rounds, with their man gushing blood, his handlers were in a panic. As Marciano headed out for the eighth, Weill nevertheless instructed him to continue to pound Charles's body.

Marciano wisely ignored the orders. Instead, he decided to go not for the body but for the head—and a knockout. As he later explained, "I was spilling too much blood, and they might have stopped it. I like my title too much to lose it on account of a little blood. I don't knock 'em out in the body. I knock 'em out on the chin." His sense of urgency was well-founded. Because of the cut, many believed that the fight was a round or two away from being stopped. Charles later said, "If they had let me, I think in two more rounds I would have beat him. He was cut up pretty bad." According to legend, the ringside doctor, who was closely monitoring Marciano's cut, was on the verge of halting the proceedings. And, legend has it, referee Al Berl went over to Marciano's corner before the eighth and told him, "Rocky, that's a terrible cut. I'll let the fight go another round, but then I'll have to stop it."[63]

Much of this is, in fact, legend. The cut was bad for sure, but few at ringside that night reported that the bout was in danger of being stopped. Even more significant, the man who had the authority to stop the bout—Dr. Alexander Schiff, the ringside physician—revealed several days later that he had no intention of calling a halt to the proceedings. "I wouldn't have stopped it for the cut," he said. "This was a championship fight. Even though in twenty-nine years of treating boxers I had never seen the nostril torn right through, I knew Rocky was not too hurt to continue with a cut of that type."[64] Even if the fight were not in imminent danger of being stopped, however, the cut did not bode well for Marciano. If the fight went much further, he would surely have begun to lose points on the scorecards on the basis of appearance. Perhaps at some point the fight would have been stopped, particularly if the blood cascading from the cut started to affect his vision. In other words, if Marciano didn't want to flirt with disaster, he needed a knockout.

He got one. Just as he had when he needed to in the first Walcott fight, Marciano rose to the occasion. The eighth round began with a Charles rally that opened a small cut over Marciano's left eye. The new wound only made Marciano accelerate his pace of attack even further. As he later explained, "After Charles cut me a second time, all that blood made me nervous. Didn't you see where I started to fight harder?" Marciano's renewed determination paid dividends. The payoff began when a flurry of punches punctuated by a right to the jaw sent Charles down sideways. He was up at the count of four, but the fight was over. As Marciano recalled after the fight, "I knew I had him then. The rest was easy. He had no more defense."[65]

The end came courtesy of a fresh Marciano barrage punctuated by three consecutive right-left combinations. "You'll have to tell me what hit me in the eighth," Charles said after the fight. "I just didn't see 'em coming." Marciano later characterized this flurry as "merely window dressing. He was out on his feet." Once he hit the canvas, Charles pulled himself into a sitting position and waited out the count. A split second after the referee counted ten, he leaped to his feet. But it was too late. Charles "grinned in a sickened and relieved way," walked over groggily to congratulate Marciano, and whispered, "Nice fight, Rocky."[66] At 2:36 of the eighth round, the fight was over.

Many felt that Charles could have beaten the count. "I was slow getting up," he admitted, "but I wasn't really hurt." Few, however, castigated Charles. Wilfrid Smith called it an "intelligent decision—if he made it wittingly—to call it a night." Jesse Abramson added, "The feeling here is that Charles had come to a dead end. He knew it, every one in the house knew it. No one blamed Charles for not getting up. The spirit that enabled him to take triple the punishment without falling once in the June fight was missing. Even if the spirit was willing, the flesh was not. He was fighting a hopeless fight, anyway, in a hopeless way."[67]

For winning what Red Smith called "neither a great fight nor a dull one," Marciano received generally positive reviews. Although some felt that it was not one of his sharper nights, others maintained that he looked much crisper than he had in his first fight with Charles (Marciano agreed, declaring, "I felt much better and sharper than last time"). A few went even further, proclaiming it "his finest performance." Years later, some would regard the fight as one of his greatest and one of the defining moments of his reign, mainly because he had displayed, in the words of Jerry Nason, his "indomitable persuasion to win."[68]

Ezzard Charles, however, lost much of the acclaim he had gained only three months earlier. A whole new set of questions arose concerning his state of mind. Why had he fought so cautiously? Was he too tense from the postponement? Was he haunted by the beating he suffered in June? What was he thinking when he got knocked down in the second? Why didn't he try harder to capitalize on the promising cut on Marciano's nose? Did he have the right attitude? Did he quit?

Charles had puzzled people throughout his career, and he continued to puzzle them at its end. And this was the end. In his dressing room, the unmarked, smiling, and almost cheerful Charles said all the right things—that he didn't find Marciano as tough this time around, that he still thought he could beat Marciano, that he planned to continue, and that he wasn't through. As Arch Ward and scores of others noted, however, the fight constituted Charles's "fistic obituary."[69] It was his third shot at reclaiming the title he lost in 1951. Everyone knew that he was unlikely to receive another chance, particularly given his age and the poor performance against Marciano. Charles would never approach the top of the heavyweight division again. He would keep fighting, although with little distinction, for a few more years and then retire.

At the time, though, Charles didn't realize that his second encounter with Marciano would be his swan song. After the fight, in his dressing room, Charles asked one of his handlers, "When do I fight again—for the championship, I mean?" The embarrassed handler replied softly, "It may take some time, Ez. It may take some time."[70] There was always a certain sadness to Ezzard Charles.

11 The Italian Hero

For his next title defense in May 1955, Rocky Marciano took the heavy-weight championship out of New York and to the West Coast to fight British champion Don Cockell in San Francisco. Despite the cosmopolitan over-tones, though, few paid attention. Among Marciano's seven title fights, this was the only one that failed to generate much in the way of public interest.

The source of the apathy was his opponent. Not much was known about Cockell, and the limited stream of information that had trickled across the Atlantic hardly dazzled anyone. His ring history was one problem. In sev-enty-two fights as a professional, Cockell had lost ten times. Several of his defeats had come at the hands of obscure opponents, and five had come via knockouts. His record didn't exactly shroud him in invincibility. Nor did his appearance awe anyone. Simply put, Don Cockell was fat. Although he was only about 5'10", he weighed around 210 pounds. He had rolls of fat around his waist, his legs were thick and flabby, and his arms and hands appeared to be fat and soft.

A former blacksmith who had taken up boxing in 1946, Cockell began his career as a light heavyweight. In the early 1950s, and after a couple of resounding defeats, he took some time off, packed on thirty-five pounds, and began fighting as a heavyweight. Despite his new, overstuffed appearance, he enjoyed immediate success, reeling off ten victories in a row before meeting Marciano. Along the way he captured the Heavyweight Championship of the British Empire, a dubious title but a title nonetheless. More significant were Cockell's three victories over Harry Matthews and his 1954 triumph over Roland LaStarza in London, which had all the earmarks of a hometown decision but nevertheless qualified as a big win. By the spring of 1955, Cockell was ranked as the number-two heavyweight contender in the world behind Nino Valdes of Cuba.

There was some talent behind the ranking. Despite his flabby appearance, Cockell possessed speed and quickness. His hands were particularly fast. He also had a good left jab and could take punches in return. Marciano had never seen him in action but proclaimed, "LaStarza told me he was a good fighter and I'm taking Roland's word for it." Al Weill was more reverential. At the time of the contract-signing in February 1955, he pulled one reporter aside and whispered, "I wouldn't try to fool you. This guy is terrific. He's a killer. You know, he's got the killer instinct. You know me. I wouldn't give you a bum steer."[1] Most were convinced that Weill was doing precisely that, however, and few viewed the impending Marciano-Cockell battle as a full-fledged championship fight.

Instead, it was widely cast as a test run for Marciano's nose. After the second Charles fight, a Los Angeles doctor named Henry Ruben had performed plastic surgery on the badly split nose. Now, all that remained was a tiny scar and a minor national obsession. In March 1955, for example, *Life* ran a story entitled "Most Famous Nose in Sport," which featured large before-and-after photographs of Marciano's nose as well as an image of Weill examining the nose with the aid of a magnifying glass. Despite all this attention Marciano put on a brave public face. To another reporter, however, he confessed, "It's my big worry. I think about it a great deal. Every day after I get through boxing I look into the mirror to see whether the slit is redder or wider."[2]

Weill was worried, too—enough that he wasn't about to send Marciano into the ring against a heavy-hitter like Valdes or an accomplished sharpshooter like Archie Moore. Instead, the ideal opponent for the champion's rebuilt nose was a boxer who had some credentials but neither the power nor sting to inflict heavy damage—someone against whom Marciano could afford to gamble if the nose did fail to hold up. Cockell fit the bill on all accounts. He was, noted Budd Schulberg of *Sports Illustrated,* "a manufactured opponent, hand-picked by Al Weill as the least menacing of the heavyweight contenders."[3] Only Marciano's nose, conventional wisdom held, gave Cockell a real chance at dethroning the champion.

Given those odds, the usual prefight buildup sputtered. The British and American press corps tried their best to rescue the dire situation by engaging in a sustained and spirited international war of words. The Americans had fired the first shot at the contract-signing in New York in February. Cockell's appearance there was the first time that most U.S. sportswriters had laid eyes on the flabby British champion—and it got their creative juices flowing. Arthur Daley, for instance, proclaimed that Cockell "bestirs memories of the Fat Boy in Charles Dickens' 'Pickwick Papers.'"[4] Sportswriters throughout the country started to churn out nicknames: Dumpling Don, Fatso, the Glandular Globe, the Waist of Time, and the Battersea Butterball. The British champion seethed.

When Cockell arrived in San Francisco for the fight, though, he was treated like a visiting dignitary, with California Gov. Goodwin Knight and others on hand to welcome him to the city. International peace was seemingly restored. It wasn't. British boxing writers had latched onto the story and weren't about to let go. They had noticed when the Americans joked about Cockell in February, and they hadn't liked it. One leading British sportswriter, Peter Wilson, characterized the American treatment of Cockell as "a big sneer campaign that must be the most devilish attack ever directed at a British champion."[5] Two months later, they still remembered American insults as they arrived in California for the fight. They came ready to engage in verbal warfare.

It was nationalistic pride as well as good business. The Marciano-Cockell fight was a big event in England. No British heavyweight, after all, had fought for the world title since 1937, when Tommy Farr had unsuccessfully challenged Joe Louis. Moreover, Cockell was a popular champion in Britain. His countrymen called him "Our Don." Although Americans had a laissez-faire attitude about the most recent Marciano defense, Fleet Street treated the fight as a matter of the utmost importance. And the press desperately needed headlines.

It got them by not just defending Cockell but by attacking the entire American boxing establishment. In the weeks before the fight, British dispatches were filled with wild and lurid tales of gamblers, blonde bombshells, and conspiracies. At one point the British even claimed that a plot was afoot to poison Cockell before the fight. In reality, none of the fifteen or so British writers on the scene in California actually believed that Cockell would win. Many of them, however, were convinced that their man wouldn't receive a fair chance in America.

Marciano was the focal point of their coverage. The British press portrayed the champion as a brute, a tool of sinister forces, and, mainly, a rule-breaker. As British sportswriter Desmond Hackett wrote, "I feel depressed, appalled. No man could live with this ruthless mauler who tears up the rules book as viciously as he rips up any one who challenges his right to share the same fight ring." Echoed Peter Wilson, "I do not think Don Cockell has the remotest FAIR chance of beating Rocky Marciano. . . . It's like a bowman of Olde English trying to combat a Sherman tank. . . . This could be the dirtiest fight of all time."[6]

The Americans fired back, of course. The British, some complained, possessed an annoying air of superiority. How dare they paint such an insulting picture of the American champion, the living symbol of the Age of Simplicity? As Red Smith proclaimed on the eve of the fight, "It may not be necessary to tell American readers that the picture of Marciano thus created is a monstrous and deliberate falsehood. It is difficult to tell the truth without appearing to wave the flag, but the simple truth is this: Rocky Marciano is not a foul fighter. He is as clean and decent and genuine and honest as any man in sports, and you could not find a more level guy in any field."[7]

Despite all the nationalistic passion, the savvy fans of San Francisco never warmed to the bout. On the night of the fight, only about fifteen thousand paying customers trickled through the turnstiles at Kezar Stadium. Attendance was also down in movie theaters around the country, leading Wilfrid Smith of the *Chicago Tribune* to label the bout "the financial flop of recent pugilistic history."[8]

The fight itself didn't qualify as an artistic flop, but neither did it get anyone's pulse racing. Although it had its share of action, it followed the predictable pattern that Marciano had established in several previous title bouts. As usual, the rusty Marciano, fighting off eight months of inactivity, started off slowly in the first several rounds. Soon, though, he was carrying the action and battering Cockell with repeated body blows. On several occasions between rounds Cockell became nauseated from the punishment he was absorbing.

The end almost came in the eighth round when Marciano hit Cockell with a steady and furious barrage of shots to the body and head, most of which went unanswered. To the amazement of the crowd, Cockell remained standing. Seconds before the end of the round, though, Cockell finally fell. As the round ended, he was jackknifed over the middle rope. Only the bell had saved him. The appreciative crowd gave Cockell a standing ovation for his gallant stand. The ninth was anticlimactic. With a storm of punches, Marciano first knocked Cockell down for a count of seven and then again for a count of five. He waded in again to resume his attack against the defenseless and obviously dazed Cockell and even unleashed two more blistering punches before referee Frankie Brown officially stopped the bout at fifty-four seconds of the ninth round.

In the aftermath, British sportswriters lavished praise on their national hero. Peter Wilson, for instance, proclaimed that "the high and the mighty" were rising "in a kind of primeval mass sympathy and acclamation" for Cockell, who had displayed "[t]he kind of courage which refuses to bandage in front of the firing squad" and "[t]he driving urge which made men die rather than surrender to Everest." The Americans were only slightly less dramatic. Cockell's performance was, declared Joseph C. Nichols of the *New York Times,* "one of the most inspiring exhibitions of gameness in the history of heavyweight championship competition." Even Marciano joined in. "He's got a lot of guts," he said after the fight. "He took it, he took everything I had and he kept standing up. He's an underrated fighter. I don't think I hit anyone else any more or often or harder, maybe Ez Charles the first time, but I don't think so."[9]

Even though he had won convincingly, however, many critics panned Marciano's performance. Why had he taken so long to dispose of Cockell? Had he lost his one-punch knockout power? How could he be so wild? How could he be so awkward? *Time* called Marciano "as clumsy as any champion since Carnera." Agreed Arthur Daley, "Marciano is the best amateur ever to win the world professional championship." Marciano himself later admitted, "That was a very bad fight. I wasn't sharp, and I knew it. . . . He's better than rated. But I had trouble finding him. Shortest man I ever fought. Couldn't use my overhands that I like."[10]

Marciano's performance also gave the British fresh ammunition for another attack on the champion. During the fight, Marciano, employing his usual roughhouse style, hit Cockell twice after the bell. He butted Cockell on several occasions. He also hit him with a few low blows. Most vividly, he hit him when he was down on one knee as he was falling during the first knockdown in the ninth round. Marciano had excuses for all of the infractions, of course. He was also apologetic. "On my wife and baby, I don't do one of those things knowing I do it," he said.[11]

The British weren't ready to entertain excuses or apologies, however. For several days after the fight London newspapers hurled a stream of bitter charges against Marciano for his roughhouse tactics, all in front-page, tabloid style. Eamon Andrews declared that Marciano "never read the rule books; he played a different sport from the one Cockell was taught." The *Evening News* observed, "Marciano may not be the greatest world champion ever but he is certainly the dirtiest. In an English ring he would have merited disqualification half a dozen times." A few went a step further, portraying Marciano not only as a rulebreaker but also as some sort of savage animal. Peter Wilson, for instance, said that Marciano fought "like a gorilla, except that a gorilla does not eat meat, and Marciano is the most carnivorous fighter I have ever seen." Even the staid *London Times* couldn't resist, calling Marciano "the rugged, dark 'killer'" who "went for the kill like a tiger."[12]

As Budd Schulberg of *Sports Illustrated* humorously noted, the episode proved that "even in these days of NATO and Anglo-American brotherhood, the revolutionary war crackles on." More seriously, the war of words revealed the cultural differences between the British and Americans, both as to boxing and in general. "It may have something to do with the difference in cultures," Schulberg added. "The British would seem to be more 'civilized,' while we still have one foot in the backwoods. Or, in Rocky's case, it would be more apt to say, in the jungle."[13] Cultural differences aside, the international war of words surrounding the Marciano-Cockell fight proved that nationalism in the post–World War II world could still rise to a fever pitch, even over something as sporting as a boxing match. The world was far less connected than now, and where you came from meant everything.

• • •

Rocky Marciano could have verified that fact long before his 1955 fight with Don Cockell. It wasn't the first time that the forces of nationalism and ethnicity had an impact on his career. He was an Italian American, and in America in the early 1950s ethnicity didn't just describe people, it helped define them. Marciano's ethnicity was a key part of his identity. The press saw him as an Italian. Fans saw him as an Italian. And, significantly, Marciano saw himself as an Italian.

He was hardly unique in that regard. For decades before the 1950s many Americans thought of themselves in terms of their own ethnicity. That was particularly true of the European ethnics whose families had arrived from Italy, Ireland, Germany, Poland, and Scandinavia in the late 1800s and early 1900s. For many, assimilation into American society was slow in coming.

Before World War II, ethnicity rivaled race and class as a prime source of social, economic, and cultural differentiation. Part of the reason for that was self-determination. European ethnics in the prewar era tended to remain wrapped in their own insular worlds. As historian Richard Polenberg has observed, "It was by no means unusual for a person's entire life to be encompassed by the ethnic community, for his social world to be defined by it. The parochial school one's children attended, the church at which one worshiped, the stores in which one shopped for groceries, the clubs to which one belonged, the circle of friends one saw—all might be ethnically exclusive, or largely so."[14] Before the war there were numerous foreign-language movie houses, newspapers, and radio programs as well as scores of churches, coffee houses, and halls that supplied places for entire ethnic communities to gather on a regular basis.

This was, to a certain extent, socially beneficial and almost romantic, but there were also many downsides to the ethnic mores of the era. Often, it would dictate where people lived and what they did for a living. To be Italian in New York City, for instance, was to probably live in the South Bronx and perhaps repair shoes; to be Irish was to live in Manhattansville and likely be a mill hand. Much of this was, for sure, a stereotype. In general, though, European ethnic groups were in residential, occupational, and economic straitjackets and generally did not have the educational opportunities necessary to shed them. They remained inside their cocoons in large part because they remained on the outskirts of society, looking in.

That was certainly true of Italian Americans, who generally found life more difficult than their fellow European ethnics. Between 1900 and 1920 more than three million Italians emigrated to the United States, including Rocky Marciano's parents. They hardly won immediate acceptance from those "old stock" families who had been in America for centuries. Instead, they were met with hostility and hatred, perhaps best typified by the emotions that surrounded the trial and then execution of Nicola Sacco and Bartolomeo Vanzetti in the 1920s. Resistance toward Italians continued to block their assimilation into American society well into the 1930s, and along the way several strong and primarily negative stereotypes arose about them. Some saw them as passionate and exotic. Others saw them as gangsters, usually within the milieu of organized crime. Others saw them as stupid. And still others saw them as dark and greasy. Under the prevailing racial code of the day, many in the American Protestant establishment didn't consider Italians to be "white people" at all.

A May 1939 *Life* cover profile that featured Joe DiMaggio, the legendary centerfielder for the New York Yankees, vividly illustrates that largely stereotypical and negative sentiments toward Italians continued to linger before the war. Even though the author of the piece, Noel F. Busch, generally praised DiMaggio's skills and personality, he noted that DiMaggio did not "wear himself down by unreasonable asceticism. In laziness, DiMaggio is still a paragon." Busch also reassured readers that DiMaggio "speaks English without an accent and is otherwise well adapted to most US mores. Instead of olive oil or smelly bear grease he keeps his hair slick with water. He never reeks of garlic and prefers chicken chow mein to spaghetti."[15] By the time he retired in 1951, DiMaggio had become the quintessential American hero. Shortly thereafter he even got the girl—the blonde Marilyn Monroe, symbol of sex and all-American beauty. By then no one spoke of DiMaggio in terms of olive oil, garlic, or bear grease. What happened?

As with race, World War II was the turning point for societal attitudes regarding ethnicity. Richard Alba has recognized that the war was "a watershed for European ethnics" because a variety of factors "served to fluidify the boundaries separating ethnics from old stock groups." Some of this was due to the mobility that the war demanded. Many Americans, of course, went overseas to Europe or the Pacific. Those who stayed at home were also on the move from city to city and town to town, seeking lucrative national defense jobs. Many were former European immigrants who had previously remained in ethnic cocoons. As Polenberg has maintained, "The sense of ethnic attachment, which drew support from the fixed social structure of the immigrant community, waned as wartime mobility disrupted old neighborhoods."[16] With smaller communities to serve, the institutions that had previously kept them together, such as foreign-language newspapers and radio programs, declined in number and impact.

The war also had an immense effect on the way Americans viewed nationality and ethnic differences. The war demanded complete loyalty and national unity, and ethnicity, which promoted differences, flew directly in the face of mandated solidarity. To win the war, European ethnics could no longer stand on the outside looking in but had to become part of the team. *Time* observed that the group of American men on one mission "sounded like the roster of an All-American eleven. . . . There were Edward Czeklauski of Brooklyn, George Pucilowki of Detroit, Theodore Hakenstod of Providence, Zane Gemmill of St. Clair, Pa., Frank Christensen of Racine, Wisconsin, Abraham Dreiscus of Kansas City. There were the older, but not better, American names like Ray and Thacker, Walsh and Eaton and Tyler. The war . . . was getting Americanized." Hollywood reinforced the new melting pot. As one critic pointed out, the composition of military units in movies was "invariably composed of one Negro, one Jew, a Southern boy, and a sprinkling of second-generation Italians, Irish, Scandinavians and Poles."[17] In war novels as well, more recent European ethnics were seen as the equals of those with "old stock" origins. Suddenly, European ethnics belonged.

In reality, ethnics were not completely on equal footing, at least in terms of socioeconomic opportunity. But in the years after World War II that slowly began to change. Italian Americans, like other European ethnics, no longer had to battle widespread discrimination. They began to receive new occupational and educational opportunities. Like other Americans, they shared in the economic boom. They also shared in the massive postwar flight to the suburbs, an exodus that further weakened the strength of traditional urban Italian American enclaves such as the North End of Boston. By the early 1950s, "assimilation" and "melting pot" were the jargon of the day. There was, according to Polenberg, a "declining sense of ethnic awareness in the nation as a whole."[18] Ethnicity as a social, economic, and cultural force was gradually beginning to recede.

• • •

Ethnicity, then, like race, was very much at a crossroads in the early 1950s. This was reflected in the career and person of the athletic symbol of the Age of Simplicity, Rocky Marciano. He very much thought of himself as an Italian American. His upbringing was, after all, steeped in Italian traditions and customs. The elders who raised him—his parents as well as his maternal grandfather, who lived in the same house as the Marchegiano family—had all spent their formative years in Italy before arriving in America. Naturally, their ethnic awareness was acute, and it spilled over to Rocco, the eldest member of the next generation.

Several traditions of the Italian family ethos carried over to the Marchegiano family in the New World, such as the general presumption that family interests should take precedence over individual ones. There was also a specific belief that children should make an economic contribution to their families as soon as possible, even at the expense of schooling. Young Rocco, of course, dropped out of high school for precisely that reason. The Marchegiano family also drew on its Italian ancestry to help dictate much of its lifestyle in America. Rocco's parents, for instance, loved opera. The family also ate Italian food and had wine with dinner. Beyond their home as well, the Marchegianos had no choice but to be conscious of their ethnicity. Brockton was replete with ethnic rivalries, particularly between the Italians and the Irish. On local sandlots and playgrounds young Rocco regularly felt the passions underlying that rivalry.

From the beginning, then, Marciano knew that he was an Italian. And he never forgot, even after he became rich and famous and the heavyweight champion of the world. He very much remained visibly bound to his Italian heritage. He would mutter, for example, certain Italian sayings, and Italian music appealed to him. Then, of course, there was the matter of food. "He was a real Italian," fellow Italian American Lou Duva remembers. "Italian food was his thing. We'd rather go into a little Italian restaurant, him and I, and grab a good Italian meal rather than go to a fancy place where you had to put a tux on or be catered to."[19]

It was more than just language, song, and food, however. Marciano purposely tried to establish a connection with his roots in Italy. After he won the title from Walcott, he sent his parents back to Italy on a dream vacation. He also expressed longing to visit his homeland. "I'd like to spend some time around Naples where mother came from," he told Arch Ward in 1953. "She's always telling me about those Neapolitan opera singers. I naturally want to visit Rome, my dad's boyhood home, and get acquainted with relatives I have never seen. The biggest thrill I can think of would be an audience with the pope."[20]

The most striking example of Marciano's Italian pride involved changing his name. After the first few professional fights, Al Weill wanted to change "Rocco Marchegiano" to something easier to pronounce, perhaps "Rocky March" or "K. O. Clouter." Marciano, however, objected. "Mr. Weill, I'm an Italian boy and I've got to have an Italian name," he reportedly said. He got his way with "Marciano." The episode, claimed one Philadelphia reporter, proved that Marciano was "fiercely proud of his Italian parentage."[21]

To a large extent that was true. Marciano clearly felt a bond with Mario Lanza, Jimmy Durante, and other Italian American celebrities who had parentages similar to his. He also felt a bond with ordinary Italian Americans and tended to grant them access and opportunity. Marciano, observes his brother Sonny, "leaned a little bit more toward the Italians" both during and after his ring career.[22] Indeed, many who surrounded Marciano in the years after his retirement were Italian American.

Beyond the psychological connection was the tangible support that Marciano received from other Italian Americans. It was a time when people tended to root for their own. During the 1930s and 1940s, Italian Americans took great pride in their well-known counterparts in politics (such as New York City mayor Fiorello La Guardia and the mayors of several large cities); entertainment (among them Frank Sinatra); and, especially, sports, which by midcentury had long been at the vanguard of ethnic pride and acceptance. Joe Savoldi, Angelo Bertelli, Charley Trippi, and many other Italian Americans excelled on college gridirons. Several, notably Gene Sarazen, also found success on the links.

It was on major league baseball diamonds, however, that Italian Americans made their biggest mark. There were enough in the game that a young boy in western Massachusetts named A. Bartlett Giamatti (later to become president of Yale University and commissioner of major league baseball) could invent a mythical Italian American all-star team and keep a scorecard on the performances of his heroes. DiMaggio was especially critical. Over the course of a career that stretched from 1936 to 1951 he inspired special pride among fellow Italian Americans. Early in his career, it was common to see Italian flags unfurled in Yankee Stadium whenever DiMaggio got a hit. Many years later Italian Americans who had struggled to find their way into society during the 1930s and 1940s continued to recall the vicarious pride they had taken in DiMaggio's many accomplishments.

Often, the mere participation of DiMaggio and others in the National Pastime was enough to make ordinary Italian Americans burst with pride. That participation was visible proof that they would eventually succeed in other segments of society besides sports. And it struck even those Italian Americans who had already made their mark in other fields, such as Michael A. Musmanno, a judge who had served with distinction in World War II and presided over the Nuremberg trials. When he returned to the United States in 1948 after five years overseas, Musmanno disembarked in New York City and had a celebration dinner (Italian, of course) with his brother and several nephews. "Dessert" was a ball game at Yankee Stadium, with the starting lineup of the Yankees featuring four Italian Americans: DiMaggio, Phil Rizzuto, Vic Raschi, and Yogi Berra. "Here my yearning to see Americans of Italian lineage recognized for demonstrated merit obtained thrilling realization," Musmanno would recall with pride.[23]

That this pride would often dictate rooting interests was no surprise. Consider Providence, Rhode Island, for example. By midcentury, the city had long been a Boston Red Sox stronghold (and remains so today). Around that time, however, there was an upsurge of support for the Yankees among Providence's baseball fans. Earl Lofquist of the *Providence Journal* knew why. "This may be due in small part to the fact that Providence is somewhat in the middle, geographically speaking," he observed. "It is due in larger part to the fact that a very great ball player named Joe DiMaggio plays for the New York Yankees. This introduces a racial note but a highly pleasant one. Providence has a large population of Italian ancestry, and they properly take great pride in their Joe even to a point of seeing no ball club other than the Yankees."[24]

Italian Americans rooted for their own not just in baseball but also in the second-biggest sport of the era, boxing. By midcentury, a number of Italian

Americans had already enjoyed some success in the ring, ranging from "Two Ton" Tony Galento to Rocky Graziano to Jake LaMotta. Then along came Marciano, the most successful Italian American boxer of all, the one who captured the top prize in the sport. The fact that the ethnic walls were beginning to crumble societally did not weaken Italian American support for Marciano. He was, in a sense, their representative. As a result, they rooted for him—passionately.

Others in society may have been inclined to root against Marciano because of his ethnicity. Even though discrimination against Italian Americans was fading, it was still present, and there is no question that many Americans still harbored prejudice against Italian Americans. For instance, one of Marciano's former grade-school teachers, Margaret Sheehan, recalled after he had become famous, "He did have the volatile temperament that is characteristic of his race, but he always was able to control it."[25] Such feelings, however, didn't translate into rooting against Marciano. When he wasn't facing fellow Italian Americans (LaStarza) in his title run, he was fighting blacks (Walcott, Charles, and Moore) or foreigners (Cockell). For those in the early 1950s who viewed matters primarily through such lens, he probably constituted the lesser of two evils.

Among Italian Americans, Marciano was more than just a crowd favorite. He was also a hero, perhaps not of the magnitude of the great DiMaggio but a significant one nonetheless. To show their veneration for the heavyweight champion of the world, Italian American civic and fraternal organizations showered Marciano with awards. And, as Duva puts it, when it came to his fellow Italian Americans, Marciano "attended all the dinners." After he retired his legend and reputation remained intact, and the dinners and the awards kept coming. Right to the end, he remained a hero. Several months before his death in 1969 Marciano was one of four Italian American sports figures (along with DiMaggio, Sarazen, and Vince Lombardi) whom an Italian American group honored at Madison Square Garden with a big ceremony hosted by Ed Sullivan. "He meant a lot to the Italian Americans, naturally," fellow Italian American Angelo Dundee says. "He was loved and was respected."[26]

● ● ●

The media of the early 1950s took notice of Marciano's ethnicity as well. That was particularly true during his rise and early reign, when sportswriters would customarily identify Marciano as an "Italian" or an "Italian American" as part of their descriptions of the boxer. Often they would use his ethnicity in conjunction with a stereotypical but true physical characteristic, such as "the tough Italian," "the sturdy legged Italian," or "the hard-hitting Italiano." They would also occasionally actualize Marciano's ethnicity. One columnist, for example, declared that Marciano knocked out Walcott "with a bolt of Italian lightning."[27]

The persistent references to Marciano's lineage during his rise and early reign were no accident. Although its importance was starting to fade, ethnicity still mattered. And Marciano's was not merely an incidental fact but rather a defining one that governed part of his essence. According to the conventional wisdom of the time, it might even dictate how he would fight. Just a decade earlier, many sportswriters had pointed to Billy Conn's feisty Irish blood as a key factor in compelling him to mix it up with Louis despite being ahead, a decision that led to disaster—a Louis knockout. As Conn's manager Johnny Ray said, "If he hadda Jewish head instead of an Irish one, he'd be the champ."[28] Sportswriters and promoters knew that boxing fulfilled many needs, including ethnic identification. Many themselves saw the world in ethnic terms. They were not afraid to emphasize ethnic rivalries when trying to promote a bout.

Throughout his reign, many sportswriters would treat Marciano's ethnicity with a certain amount of creativity. For instance, in noting that Marciano realized as a boy that he'd have to gain a "better place" for himself through his hands, Tim Cohane of *Look* drew the rather absurd comparison between the fighter and Michaelangelo: "Michaelangelo—what Italian boy has not heard of him?—had done great things with his hands. So would Marciano, even if not in Michaelangelo's way." Nearly three years later, Paul Zimmerman of the *Los Angeles Times* declared, "Like another famous Italian named Caesar, Rocky Marciano looked around today for more worlds to conquer and none worthy of him in sight." Others eschewed historical comparisons and took a stab at humor. Bob Coyne of the *Boston Daily Record,* for example, once drew a cartoon of Marciano's face over the Brockton skyline. The cartoon was entitled "Pizza Pie in the Sky." A more cutting approach came from Hugh Brown of the *Philadelphia Evening Bulletin,* who called Marciano the "crude, short-armed paisan."[29]

Other fell back on stereotypes about Italian Americans in describing Marciano, although sometimes the stereotypes were relatively benign. A. J. Liebling of *The New Yorker* observed, for instance, that Marciano's "outline has a squareness and his skin a terracotta tint that make you think of an Etruscan figurine." And Jack Cuddy of the United Press once called him a "rather handsome Italian with the crisp, curly black hair." Other sportswriters would from time to time describe Marciano as "olive-skinned."[30]

By far, however, the most frequent—and most disparaging—stereotype that sportswriters used to describe Marciano's appearance had to do with the word *swarthy*. They routinely used that adjective in association with Marciano during his rise to the title. It was a word that many had used degradingly in conjunction with the waves of Italian immigrants that arrived in America around the turn of the century. At midcentury the word still lingered. Many, in fact, probably used it to reflect their belief that Italians, under the skewed yet prevailing racial views of the era, were not full-fledged "white people." Calling Marciano "swarthy," then, did not exactly constitute high praise.

Other sportswriters dug deeper and went after Marciano's intelligence. A stereotype about Italians revolved around their mental inferiority. Sportswriters did not evoke the stereotype with another Italian American fighter of the era, Roland LaStarza, because he was, after all, a college man. Marciano, however, had no such background and was therefore fair game. National media outlets that ran profiles of him around the time he won the title leveraged the stereotype in particular. *Time* pointed out that Marciano was "as brilliant in sports as he was dull in books" as a boy and that he had "an unclouded mind in a body sound as brick" as a man. The *Saturday Evening Post* called him "half educated," and *Life* portrayed Marciano as an oaf who was lucky to have Al Weill and Charley Goldman around to think for him.[31]

A few daily columnists picked up the theme and repeated it in subtle ways from time to time. Arthur Daley, for instance, called Marciano "an earnest, stolid young man without much imagination, an excellent temperament for a fighter. He never sees ghosts or goblins." Bill Keefe of the *New Orleans Times-Picayune* was considerably less subtle, declaring, "Rocky never has qualified as an intellectual giant." Later in Marciano's reign, Keefe called him "seemingly dumb" and "[a]lmost as thoughtless as a buzz saw."[32]

All of this was exceedingly unfair, for Marciano was not dumb. Although he had dropped out of high school and lacked much formal education, he nevertheless possessed some native intelligence, which he displayed both in and out of the ring. And, like everything else, Marciano worked at it. He tried to improve his vocabulary, in large part because he was in demand as an after-dinner speaker and wanted to make a good showing. He became well-spoken and articulate, with a soft, modulated voice that had a trace of the famed Boston accent and made him sound, according to A. J. Liebling, like Henry Cabot Lodge, the Brahmin senator from Massachusetts.[33] The heavyweight champion of the world may not have been an intellectual giant but neither was he a dolt as sometimes portrayed.

A stereotype employed in conjunction with Marciano that had more grounding in fact involved the family. Italian Americans have long been associated with supreme loyalty to family, a primarily positive (albeit sometimes limiting) stereotype. With Marciano, the stereotype held true. What did family mean to Marciano? "If I had to use one word, it meant *everything* to him," says his youngest brother Peter.[34] Ironically, though, despite his love of the ideal, Marciano was not a prototypical family man with his own family—wife Barbara, daughter Mary Anne, and, later, son Rocco Kevin, whom Rocky and Barbara adopted in 1968. Marciano had an undeniable love for his children, but he drifted apart from his wife, particularly in the years after his retirement. Nor was an idealistic love of family enough to keep him at home; most of his retirement years were spent on the road.

Marciano's strong feeling for family played itself out more in his relationships with his parents and siblings. He occupied a key role in that family—that of the first son in a traditional Italian household. "The oldest of an Italian family takes over most of the time the father image," explains Peter Marciano. "For example, in my family, my dad—we loved him and he was obviously the guy who led the family. But when you reach a certain age, it's just an automatic thing. If I had a problem, if I needed to go to someone, I would go to Rocky. He was my father. He was the father that took over for my dad because my dad started to get a little bit old."[35] Marciano willingly played the role and took a paternal interest in Peter and his other brothers and sisters.

Even after his marriage to Barbara, Marciano remained extremely close to his parents and siblings and was a frequent presence in the family's Brockton home. W. C. Heinz now says that on the several occasions he interviewed the champion in Brockton he found "a warmth" in that household. He remembers Marciano's father peeling and cutting an apple at the kitchen table. As soon as the father peeled a piece, his youngest son, Peter, would gobble it up. When the father stopped, Peter said, "Pop, how about peeling me another piece of the apple?" After a pause the father replied, "What's the matter with you? You can peel your own piece." After another pause Peter said, "No, Pop, I like the way you do it." It was, remembers Heinz, "a lovely, warm scene."[36]

A few sportswriters cited the continuing "closely-knit family devotion" as one of the secrets of Marciano's success and the reason he had such a "fine character." A few even made an explicit ethnic connection. As one wire service reporter noted, "Some of his well-wishers have criticized Rocky's complete truthfulness in letting members of his family handle his finances; but perhaps those critics do not appreciate what a close-knit unit the usual Italian family is."[37]

Some took this a step further by using an ethnic backdrop to describe individual members of Marciano's family. His father was occasionally a subject, particularly during training camp before the Cockell fight. He was, according to Bill Liston of the *Boston Post,* "having a picnic for himself. It seems that many of the Italian residents of the Napa Valley come from the same town in Italy where Pop Marciano was born and raised and every day is like old home week for Pop." In general, though, Pierino Marchegiano was, according to A. J. Liebling, a man with "a heavy Italian accent and a most un-Italian reserve."[38] He didn't fit the stereotype.

Lena Marchegiano, however, did, and from the beginning she was an integral part of her son's story. Early profiles of Marciano would invariably contain a photograph of his mother, holding a picture of her son or serving him spaghetti and meatballs. Both in those early profiles and thereafter, the press consistently portrayed her as an overweight, happy, emotional Italian who was religious, a bit superstitious, and totally devoted to her son. Much was made in particular of her behavior on fight night. She was too nervous to watch her son fight in person. Instead, she would go to church, take a car ride with a friend, pray some more, and even have friends perform the Italian ceremony of *malocchio,* which was designed to remove the evil eye that might bring harm to loved ones.

All of this was essentially true. Marciano's mother was overweight, happy, emotional, religious, and a bit superstitious, and she did have a fight-night ritual. For all of these reasons and more, many in the press were genuinely fond of her. Heinz, for instance, admits that he "was always charmed by his [Marciano's] mother." Other sportswriters, however, were somewhat condescending in descriptions of Lena Marchegiano. They liked her but would set forth her qualities and rituals with a touch of humor and mockery. Some would even refer to her as "Mamma" or "Mama" or quote her in dialect. For instance, Marciano's mother promised to view the films of her son's fights only after he retired. As *Sports Illustrated* recorded the promise, "When he quits, I looka the pitch." When she kept the promise, a reporter from the magazine was there to record the scene. The resulting article was entitled "Rocky's Mama Sees the Pitch."[39]

One Italian American stereotype that the press did not use with Marciano (or any member of his family) involved the Mob, perhaps the most sensitive and most enduring of all Italian American stereotypes. During the 1920s and 1930s, many of organized crime's most notorious figures (such as Al Capone, Lucky Luciano, and Frank Costello) were Italian American. Aided by Hollywood, the image stuck and eventually encompassed all Italian Americans. That became even truer after World War II, when the nation grew ever more obsessed with the workings of organized crime. Italian Americans did not benefit from the obsession. Much to their chagrin and resentment, they continued to be connected with organized crime and violence.

Marciano, however, avoided the stereotype. Although boxing was rife with gangsters, scandal, and crime, he built what Gerry Hern of the *Boston Post* called a "personal reputation for integrity." Marciano was proud of that reputation. Pierino Marchegiano, a proud man himself, identified his most memorable moment as the day he was discharged from the army during World War I. A colonel had advised the recent emigrant to America, "Pierino, you can be proud to call yourself an American." The sentiment was passed on to the Marchegiano children. "You take pride in your name and being Italian," their father told them. "And don't disgrace our name. Don't you ever do anything to disgrace the name." Pierino's eldest son Rocky never forgot the lesson. "He always wanted to portray himself as being a good guy," Peter Marciano remembers. "He was very conscious of that. He never wanted to bring any kind of embarrassment to the family."[40]

Even the lure of money wasn't enough to make Marciano consider "playing ball." Once, for instance, before the Cockell fight, a leading figure in the Mafia reportedly visited Marciano in his hotel room and offered him a large sum of money if he would agree to take a dive. "You disgust me," Marciano answered angrily. "I'm ashamed that you're Italian. Get outta here and don't come back." Would Marciano ever fix a fight? "He wouldn't know how," points out the IBC's Truman Gibson. "It just wouldn't be in his lexicon."[41]

There is no evidence that any of Marciano's opponents in his big fights were on the take. That includes Archie Moore, Marciano's opponent for his final fight in 1955. In his book on Sonny Liston, Nick Tosches cites Gibson as alleging that Moore had taken a dive. In an interview for this book, however, Gibson indicates that Tosches "misunderstood me completely." According to Gibson, the rumor of the fix originated when Gibson and Jack Kearns, Moore's behind-the-scenes manager, visited Moore in San Diego shortly after his fight with Marciano. Moore introduced Gibson and Kearns to "his partners," a couple of small-time gamblers. Kearns promptly became enraged, asking Moore, "Why the hell didn't you tell me these guys were you partners? They're bums. They probably had you fix a fight and you didn't tell me." Thereafter Kearns helped spread the rumor of a possible Marciano-Moore fix. "I don't think there's anything to it at all," Gibson concludes.[42]

The Mob, then, usually didn't try to involve itself in engineering the outcomes of Marciano's fights. "There was never any inside stuff with Marciano," maintained Billy Brown, Weill's successor as the matchmaker for the IBC in the 1950s. "Everything happened aboveboard. Marciano could fight.

He didn't need anything. The Rock did it all on his own, with no help from anybody." So the Mob stayed on the sidelines and Marciano stayed clean, leading Jimmy Cannon to declare, with considerable justification, "Rocky Marciano stood out like a rose in a garbage dump."[43]

But it was a dump, and Marciano, as much as he tried, couldn't completely escape the garbage. The Mob ran boxing during the 1940s and 1950s, and its influence was inescapable and pervasive. As David Remnick has pointed out, "After the war there was not a single champion who was not, in some way, touched by the Mafia, if not wholly owned and operated by it."[44]

The most important of the mobsters was, of course, "the underworld commissioner of boxing," Frankie Carbo, whose tentacles seemed to touch every major fighter of the era. Rocky Marciano, too, fell within Carbo's reach. At the very least, Carbo acquiesced to Marciano's rise to the title and enjoyed cordial relations with Team Marciano. Most in the press remained silent about the fact at the time. One who did not was Joe Bostic, a black sportswriter for the *New York Amsterdam News*. "He was the beneficiary of as fine a set of circumstances as any heavyweight aspirant ever had," wrote Bostic of Marciano in June 1954. "Not only was his undercover manager the matchmaker for the powerful IBC, but he had perfect diplomatic relations with the man and mob that controls the game today."[45] There is no question that "the man" in question was Carbo.

In addition, Carbo plainly played a role in arranging some of Marciano's bigger fights. After Marciano's bout with Freddie Beshore in August 1951, for example, Carbo was spotted outside Marciano's dressing room, whispering with Marty Weill about the rumored fight between Marciano and Joe Louis. Less than a year later Carbo was probably involved in putting together the fight between Marciano and Harry Matthews in July 1952. In fact, Jim Norris later testified on Capitol Hill that Weill told him that the bout might not have come off had he not listened to a "certain person," whom Norris presumed to be Carbo.[46] Norris also testified that Carbo helped close Marciano's second fight with Walcott, primarily by applying pressure to Walcott's recalcitrant manager Felix Bocchicchio.

The connection between Carbo and Team Marciano—especially Al Weill—may have gone far deeper than mere acquiescence and matchmaking. Especially toward the end of Marciano's reign, Weill was often mentioned as one of the managers whom Carbo regularly used as a front man. Was Weill acting as a front for Carbo in the case of Marciano? Did Carbo own a piece of Marciano? "In my opinion, Frankie Carbo may have had a piece of Rocky through Al Weill," says Peter Marciano. "Did Rocky know about it? Absolutely. And I don't know this for sure. But if in fact Frankie Carbo did have a piece of Rocky, Rocky was aware of it." Jimmy Breslin is more adamant. He contends that mobsters definitely owned a piece of Marciano and that Weill served as the front man. "He managed Marciano," Breslin says of Weill, "but there were quite a few managers behind the scenes . . . Weill didn't have him. Weill got his cut. That's about it." Breslin believes that Marciano likely was owned by Carbo ("It had to be Carbo," he says) and Mob chieftain Little Augie Carfano. Did Marciano know gangsters had a piece of him? "Sure, he knew gangsters inside out," says Breslin.[47]

Marciano was used to having mobsters around. This fact is illustrated by a story that Breslin tells concerning Joe Weber, the head waiter at Gallagher's, a New York restaurant where Marciano would often eat before a big fight and before the restaurant opened its doors for the evening. Weber was in charge of the meal for Marciano. While the champion would eat, two gangsters would stand guard at a nearby booth. According to Breslin, "they were sitting there with a fucking shotgun. So he would eat and get up and Weber would have to go to the fight with them. They'd make him come along. So he'd get up to the stadium. He'd walk around and he'd sit there nervous. . . . And the minute the bell would ring, it was all over for Weber. He looked to go. He didn't give a fuck what happened. All he knew was that Marciano didn't get sick. If he didn't get sick from the food, then they weren't going to kill him. If he did get sick from the food, they were going to shoot him right in the fuckin' stadium."[48]

In any event, it wouldn't have been shocking if Carbo did own a small piece of Marciano. After all, he owned a piece of just about everyone else. Then again, Carbo might have kept his hands off Marciano because he and the rest of the Mob didn't want to taint an Italian hero. In the final analysis, as Bud Collins points out, "Who knows how much Frankie Carbo had of Rocky?"[49] The answer isn't clear. The ownership of Marciano never really was.

● ● ●

In the early-twenty-first century, ethnicity is still relevant, but it is individual, private, voluntary, and symbolic in nature. As Richard Alba has recognized, Italian Americans in particular are "on the verge of the twilight of their ethnicity."[50] To many, it still matters some. To only a few, however, does it matter greatly. Ethnicity meant far more in the early 1950s. Yet as the coverage of Rocky Marciano illustrates, ethnicity was beginning to mean less and less in American society and culture.

Over the span of his career the number of ethnic-based stereotypes used to describe Marciano gradually declined. As the stereotypes faded, so did the references. By the time that he became champion, the "swarthy" descriptions had largely disappeared. And, after Marciano's fight with LaStarza in 1953, sportswriters were no longer regularly identifying him as an Italian. Part of this was due to familiarity. By 1955 everyone knew that Marciano was Italian. Then again, ethnic awareness had declined dramatically in society, and sports mirrored societal change. Because of the trend toward assimilation and the concept of the melting pot, an athlete's ethnic background mattered far less in 1955 than it had just five years earlier. As Robert Lipsyte points out, "In a time of ethnicity, he was part of an ethnic group that we were growing comfortable with."[51] By the end of his career, to the media and the masses, Rocky Marciano was no longer an Italian hero. He was, instead, an American hero.

The most significant and enduring effect of Marciano's ethnicity was on his image. Bud Collins points out that although Marciano may not have been an all-American boy in the Jack Armstrong mold, his was an American success story nonetheless. "He was a blue collar guy from Brockton and his parents were immigrants," Collins says. "And he worked hard at everything. . . . He had the characteristics of an American success story in that he came from a very humble background and just made himself do it. He wanted a place in the pantheon, so to speak. He yearned to be recognized for what he could do. And he earned that."[52] Yet it was more than that. To the image-makers, Marciano didn't just embody the American Way of Life— he was also living the American Dream. He *was* the American Dream.

His immigrant background made all that possible. As the image-makers were always reminding readers, Rocco Marchegiano wasn't born into privilege. He was nothing but the eldest son of a poor Italian American shoemaker from Brockton. He came up from nothing, and he came out of the melting pot. As the image-makers also pointed out, Rocco Marchegiano's Brockton neighborhood included boys of all backgrounds—Italians, Irish, and Jews. "They were mostly the children of decent factory workers who lived slightly above the subsistence level in small frame houses fringing the playground and its immediate environs," wrote Al Hirshberg in the *Saturday Evening Post*. "Nobody starved, but nobody had any money to waste on luxuries."[53]

But this was America. And America gave a young boy like Rocco Marchegiano the chance to gain a better life if he had the talent, was willing to work hard, and caught a few breaks along the way. That is precisely, of course, what happened with Rocco Marchegiano, who, although the eldest son of a poor Italian American shoemaker from Brockton, grew up to be rich, famous, and the heavyweight champion of the world. As Collins wrote in the *Bos-*

ton Globe upon Marciano's death in 1969, "His success made the public feel there was actually something wholesome about boxing: the mill-town boy, clean through and through, wins the title, respect and riches through hard work." Today, Collins agrees that Marciano was, in a sense, living the American Dream. "I think that there are many people who want to live it and aspire to do it and do do it," he says. "And he was one of them in sports."[54]

In the Age of Simplicity, all of this made the public feel good, for Americans believed in the American Dream. In a sense, it was Marciano's ethnicity that made it possible for him to live it with robust fullness. As the *Boston Herald Traveler* editorialized shortly after his death:

> [T]his was a man whose life style was the legendary American Dream come true. He was a kind of Horatio Alger hero in the flesh, the living embodiment of the virtues parents drum into the minds of their offsprings: Work hard, save your money, live a clean life. Do these things and the rewards will be success (even fame, maybe), wealth and all of the good life that is America's so lavishly to give. Rocky learned the precepts from immigrant parents to whom the American Dream was real and true and not something to be ridiculed and denigrated. He worked hard to develop his one great skill; he married the hometown sweetheart, he lived a clean life, he saved his money. . . . In this age of the anti-hero and the non-hero, Rocky Marciano was the hero with whom the mass of Americans could readily identify, the hero who surmounted all difficulties by dint of hard work, dedication and perseverance. He was a near-classic example of the triumph of classic virtues.[55]

12 Archie

When it came to rags-to-riches stories, Archie Moore made Rocky Marciano look like Little Lord Fauntleroy. Unlike Marciano, Moore didn't have a strong family behind him. Unlike Marciano, he didn't have a real place to call home, just a string of adopted hometowns that tracked his travails. And, unlike Marciano, he didn't have the support and influence of a powerful manager as the backbone of his ring career. He was, in very many ways, on his own. Still, he was not bereft of assets. He had talent. He had personality and the ability to invent and reinvent his persona. He had persistence. Most of all, he had gumption. In the fall of 1955, Moore, the reigning light-heavyweight champion of the world, managed to parlay all that into a shot at the heavyweight champion of the world, Rocky Marciano. In many ways it would be Marciano's biggest fight, and the reason was that multifaceted mystic Archie Moore.

There were, indeed, many sides to Moore. First and foremost, he cast himself as a master craftsman. He had, after all, been boxing professionally since 1936. By 1955 he had picked up all the tricks of his trade, and he let everyone know it, portraying himself as a savant of ring strategy and pugilistic science. Few disagreed. Fellow boxers considered him a master at their craft, which is why featherweight champion Sandy Saddler respectfully called him "Mr. Moore." The press, too, regarded him as a supreme stylist and a master defensive boxer. Praised John Lardner of *Newsweek*, "He is a consummate ring craftsman, perhaps unmatched in our time for a union of style, subtlety, wisdom, and power." He was, echoed Herbert Brean of *Life*, "the last of the great ring technicians."[1]

With Archie Moore, though, boxing wasn't just craft—it was art. He certainly looked like an artiste, with a hairline mustache and a small, wispy Vandyke beard (a "wisp of hair the size of a horsefly" that resembled "a three-cornered Cape of Good Hope postage stamp," according to Lardner). Then there were the robes he donned on his stage. He had a Harlem dress designer, Marie Hardy, make one for each big fight. For his outing with Carl ("Bobo") Olson in 1955 he wore a robe of white baby flannel, imported from England, lined with gold satin, and trimmed with braid and epaulets of ten-karat gold. His fight with Harold Johnson in 1954 saw the unveiling of a robe made of black satin, with gold satin lining, a mandarin collar, and ten-karat-gold edging. That robe, according to Lardner, made Moore look "like a bebop maestro about to take a bath. And the truth is that Archie Moore, at this point in his hard, full life, likes to be thought of as an avant-garde genius of jazz music."[2]

He was, in fact, a devotee of modern jazz and of one jazzman in particular, tenor saxophonist Eli ("Lucky") Thompson. Moore would tell anyone who would listen that Thompson was "the greatest tenor sax man in the world." He had twenty-six hours of Thompson's music on tape and would lug it from town to town, training camp to training camp. Moore also served as a patron and "mouthpiece" for Lucky and his band, touring with them, acting as master of ceremonies, and even picking at a string bass onstage. There was a certain kinship between Archie and Lucky. "[H]e never has received the recognition due him because he won't compromise his art by playing the rhythm-and-blues circuit," Moore declared. "From the first, Lucky and I saw the parallel patterns of our careers." Moore and Thompson even co-wrote a song, "Stay in There." Proclaimed Moore, "It's the theme of our lives." He occasionally imported Thompson into his training camp for some live musical inspiration. "Lucky is my rhythm man," Moore explained. "He plays while I skip rope, and this makes a pulsation which keeps me in time. We're artists who appreciate each other's work."[3]

By 1955 Archie Moore had practiced his art all over the world, in thirty-eight U.S. cities and on three continents to be exact. During his nineteen-year career, his boxing base of operations shifted from St. Louis to San Diego to Australia to Baltimore and then to Toledo. For two short stretches in the early 1950s he was even encamped in Argentina, where he became a particular favorite of Juan Perón. Along the way, Moore fought in such out-of-the-way places as Keokuk, Iowa, Ponca City, Oklahoma, and North Adams, Massachusetts. He was, in the words of Gilbert Millstein of the *New York Times,* "a sort of Ulysses of boxing."[4]

Over the course of his travels, Moore had acquired verbal flair. According to Millstein, he spoke in prose that was "florid and elliptical" and possessed an "overpowering mastery of the language." Echoed Herbert Brean, "Archie employs the English language enthusiastically and is the master of a large polysyllabic vocabulary." That vocabulary routinely dazzled reporters accustomed to boxers who spoke in butchered grammar or mere grunts. Once someone asked Moore how he had acquired it. "Just from talking," he replied.[5]

Moore also cast himself as a homespun philosopher. In camp, he would occasionally meditate while reading the New Testament. And he was constantly regaling the press with bits of wisdom, often in the form of proverbs and platitudes. "You're no philosopher," Moore once said to a training camp observer. "You're too young to be a philosopher." The man replied, "I'm forty-one. I'm older than you, yet you claim to be a philosopher." Answered Moore, "You're older perhaps, but you gotta suffer to be a philosopher. I've suffered, so I'm a philosopher."[6] Like any good philosopher, Moore had theories:

Moore's Theory of Combinations. Moore was scientific when it came to the combinations that he would unleash on unwitting foes. He even developed a code system for his combinations, with each punch in the series having a different number. For example, Moore claimed that he knocked out Bobo Olson in 1955 with a 4-6-9 combination. He refused to reveal the code, however. "I won't tell you the numbers to my combinations," he told *Sports Illustrated.* "Those are my secrets."[7]

Moore's Theory of Ballistics. Moore claimed to have studied the science of ballistics and applied his learning to his ring style. Before the Marciano fight, he regaled reporters with a long dissertation on the parallels between ballistics and boxing, citing the velocity of a bullet, its trajectory, and its effect on the target to illustrate his point.

Moore's Theory of "Escapology." Moore developed and practiced the theory of escapology, his method for avoiding grave danger in the ring. "I try to build a bridge," he explained. "With each punch I try to build a bridge so I can escape over it if something goes wrong. That's what you call escapology. That's what *I* call escapology."[8]

Moore's Theory of "Relaxism." Moore also believed that it was important for a fighter to be able to relax, hence his theory of relaxism. Like escapology, no one was quite sure what relaxism entailed. Once, when Moore was attempting to explain the theory of relaxism to a sportswriter, he became so relaxed that he, alas, fell asleep.

Above all, Archie Moore was a mystic. In fact, he shrouded every detail of his life and career in a cloak of mystery. The accounts he gave of past events—even the mundane—were often vague, contradictory, and confusing. No one knew his real name, for example. Some sportswriters identified it as "Archibald Lee Moore." Others said it was "Archibald Louis Moore." Others said it was "Archibald Lee Louis Moore." A few gave up and listed him as "Archibald Lee (or Louis) Moore." Moore never bothered to clarify the matter.

Nor did he provide an accurate accounting of his place of birth. Sometimes he said he was born in Benoit, Mississippi. At other times he pegged the place of his birth as Collinsville, Illinois. To add to the confusion, Moore's mother swore that her son was born in Benoit, although a few sportswriters claimed he was born in St. Louis. Why the confusion over such a trivial detail? As Moore explained, "I just like to confound you writers."[9] He succeeded.

Confusion also reigned over the date of Moore's birth (and thus his age). Again, mother and son differed. Moore's mother claimed that he was born on December 13, 1913, which would have made him forty-one in 1955. Moore, of course, disagreed. He claimed that he was born on December 13, 1916, which would have made him thirty-eight when he fought Marciano. "I guess my mother should know, since she was there," he once admitted. "But I have given it a lot of thought and have decided that I must have been three when I was born."[10] Many believed Moore had noted the publicity that Walcott had gotten over the issue of his age and decided to copy it. Indeed, as with Walcott, Moore's age became the frequent subject of jokes and guessing games. Some even claimed that he was forty-five when he fought Marciano. No one knew for sure, and that's the way Archie Moore wanted it.

There were other points of confusion. How many ex-wives did he have, three or four? Was he a Democrat or Republican? ("Neither," revealed Moore. "I'm a diplomat.") And how did he gain enough weight to fight heavyweights? Here at least Moore offered some cryptic clues. In the days before he fought the gigantic Cuban heavyweight Nino Valdes in May 1955, Moore walked around with a thermos slung over his shoulder. From time to time he would slyly swig from it. Reporters naturally bit. What was in the thermos? "I'd rather not talk about it," Moore protested. "It's a secret strength extract—a kind of goose juice—that I got from the natives while I was boxin' down in Argentina."[11] In fact, the thermos was filled with beef broth.

Yet when Moore fought as a light heavyweight, how did he manage to lose weight to make the 175-pound limit? He cited a secret weight-loss method that he had acquired one day in 1940 in Australia when he came upon an aborigine who was throwing a boomerang. Moore claimed that he had traded his red sweater for the aborigine's secret weight-loss method (and the boomerang, of course). No one believed that Moore really had any such secret method. They knew he made weight the same way every other fighter did—by starving himself and running extra miles in the days before a fight. Moore stuck to his story, however. In defense, he said, "Have you ever seen a fat Australian?" To add to the mystery, he would often eat behind a screen at training camp when reporters were present. Years later he finally revealed his "secrets" for losing weight: drinking sauerkraut juice and chewing but not swallowing meat.[12]

The mystery that surrounded Moore was, of course, quite intentional. "Remember that Archie is a professional guide," New York sportswriter Lester Bromberg once said. "He'll take you exactly where he wants you to go."[13] Few took Moore at face value, recognizing that he was purposely mysterious about anything that might bring him publicity, and few seemed especially bothered by his half-truths and flights of fancy. There was an underlying good-naturedness about it, and besides it made good press.

His penchant for attracting attention was born in large part out of necessity. Indeed, for the longest time no one—the press, the public, and even his own manager—paid much attention to Archie Moore at all. It started when he was a child. Born Archie Lee Wright, he was a product of a broken home. After his parents separated when he was small, he and his sister Rachel eventually landed in St. Louis with his mother's brother, Cleveland Moore, and his wife, Willie P. Moore (whom Archie called "Auntie"). Although the Moores adopted Archie and gave him a new last name, life didn't get any easier, for the Moores lived in "Kerry Patch," a tough slum area of St. Louis.

Things got even tougher when Moore was in his early teens and both his Uncle Cleveland and his sister Rachel died. Several years later, he quit high school and turned to a life of petty crime, stealing from empty houses and streetcars. When he was nabbed taking change from a conductor's box on a streetcar, he was sent away to reform school. He was only fifteen.

When he got out of reform school he decided to take the straight and narrow path—through boxing. He made his amateur debut in April 1935 at the Pine Street YMCA in St. Louis. He kept boxing after entering the Civilian Conservation Corps, fighting in Missouri and Arkansas, sometimes under the name the Fourth of July Kid. After his discharge in the spring of 1936, Moore got a New Deal job with the Works Progress Administration and kept looking for amateur bouts. It was then he decided to turn professional as a middleweight.

It was not an easy road. Moore had several disadvantages. To begin with, he was black, and in the mid-1930s many black fighters still had trouble getting quality fights against quality opponents. To make matters worse, Moore, for all his skill, didn't have a "rock 'em, sock 'em" style that would have had promoters clamoring for his services. Nor did he have the type of managerial backing that would have influenced promoters to notice him. He did have a parade of managers between 1936 and 1944, but none managed to catapult Moore into the big time. Instead, he fought primarily in small clubs, first in the Midwest and then on the West Coast. He wasn't making much money.

Still, Moore was winning far more than he was losing. With a trip to Australia in the summer of 1940 he gained an international reputation. He returned to the United States as the number-four-ranked middleweight in the world. Then his career went into a tailspin when he developed an ulcer, thought to be caused by improper eating, financial woes, and general frustration. In February 1941, after a fight with Eddie Booker, he underwent emergency surgery to fix the ulcer. By the time he left the hospital, his weight had plummeted from 160 pounds to 110. He did not fight again until January 1942.

Moore finally seemed on the verge of a breakthrough in the mid-1940s when he hooked up with a new manager, Jimmy Johnston. Nicknamed the "Boy Bandit" because of his shock of black hair and his wily, scheming ways, Johnston was one of the ring's great characters, full of stories, quips, and grudges. He also knew the ropes of the fight game. Soon, Johnston had Moore (now fighting as a light heavyweight) on track to a title shot. Then, in May 1946, Johnston suddenly died. Moore's immediate title chances died with him. Although he would continue to remain a leading light-heavyweight contender, it would be six long years before he got a shot at the title.

His manager throughout this time was Jimmy Johnston's brother Charley, who was quieter than his older brother but just as influential in his own way. In the early 1950s he would become a key figure in the International Boxing Guild, the boxing managers' association that wielded considerable power. In the end, he would manage Moore for nearly a decade, which was incredible given that the two men had a strange and uneasy relationship. Johnston didn't advise Moore on boxing matters ("What could I tell him?" he asked). For some reason—probably because Johnston didn't want to risk his other, more important interests by ruffling the feathers of the powers-that-be—he was reluctant to wield his influence to help Moore. "Are you ashamed of my ability?" a frustrated Moore once asked him. "Do you think I can't fight?" Johnston answered sarcastically, "I don't want you to get hurt." Moore called him "Milquetoast."[14]

By early 1949 Archie Moore had had enough. In Toledo, he found himself fighting someone named the Alabama Kid for the paltry sum of $300. Moore planned to quit after the fight. Once he sent the Alabama Kid packing, he took the few hundred dollars he had to his name and went to the local Ford dealership to buy a used car that could take him to San Diego. There he met Bob Reese, owner of the dealership. "We had a few things to do to the car, so he kept coming in and we got to talking," Reese recalled. "The more I saw of him—the way he conducted himself—the more I liked him. Before he left I said, 'Why don't you make Toledo your home? Maybe we can find something of interest for you here.'"[15] Reese became Moore's patron. He put him on his payroll for $75 a week and helped sort out his tangled finances. Finally, Archie Moore had some support.

His career instantly caught fire. Between 1949 and 1951 he fought thirty-three times, winning all but three bouts. By 1952, even though he had been fighting for sixteen long years and was in his mid-thirties, he had never looked better. Then, in December 1952 in St. Louis, he finally got his title shot. Pressure from the public and the sanctioning authorities left light-heavyweight champion Joey Maxim with no choice—he had to give Moore a crack at the crown. Of course, Moore had to take a financial bath to get his shot, resulting in a meager purse of less than $2,000. After the fight, he had to borrow $10,000 from the IBC in order to pay his expenses, buy some Christmas gifts, and get out of town. He left St. Louis, however, with the title, having defeated Maxim in a fifteen-round decision. He was world champion.

The next few years brought nothing but fistic success for Archie Moore. He kept fighting and winning, successfully defending his light-heavyweight title against Maxim (a highly regarded fighter) in June 1953 and then again in January 1954. In August 1954, after eighteen years of fighting, he finally headlined a show at Madison Square Garden. Moore's long-awaited Garden debut was a smash, as he knocked out Harold Johnson in the fourteenth round. He was finally and completely in the big time.

● ● ●

Yet he wasn't satisfied. Although he cast himself as a philosopher, he was an activist at heart. "I'm not a dreamer," he once explained. "I'm a practical man. I don't believe in the theory that he who waits gets. You have to go out and get what you want."[16] What Archie Moore most wanted in the fall of 1954 was a fight against the heavyweight champion of the world, Rocky Marciano. When that didn't seem to be in the offing, Moore took matters into his own hands and launched a mass-media campaign that was thoroughly innovative, often hilarious, and ultimately effective.

The campaign wasn't completely unprecedented. Managers had used them before on behalf of their fighters, and Moore himself had successfully employed such a campaign in 1951 and 1952 in order to fight Joey Maxim. In the fall of 1954 he decided to repeat the tactic, only on a grander scale than had ever been attempted. Once again, he would act as the point man, with his manager, the indifferent Charley Johnston, remaining on the sidelines. Moore did have some help, however, from Bob Reese and other Toledo patrons. Reese agreed to front money for Moore's campaign, which in the end totaled more than $50,000. Moore's team also included Michael V. DiSalle (the former mayor of Toledo and the former director of the Office of Price Stabilization under the Truman administration); Dr. Nicholas P. Dallis (creator of the *Rex Morgan, M.D.* and *Judge Parker* comic strips, who had already created a character, "Archer Moran," for the *Morgan* strip in honor of Moore); and other Toledo captains of industry. They all wanted to help Archie Moore.

In October 1954, Moore began meeting with his Toledo backers to map out the campaign. Their strategy was simple—two or three times a week they would bombard sports editors and sportswriters across the nation with communiqués advocating a Marciano-Moore match. "My business is not prize fighting but merchandising and I was out to merchandise Archie," Reese explained later. "I knew I had a good product. He had ability and confidence, and he'd take on any fighter, bar none."[17]

On November 17, 1954, Moore and company launched their campaign by sending 427 night letters to sports editors and sportswriters across the United States. Later they expanded their mailing list to nearly five hundred. They kept at it for the better part of nine months, well into the spring of 1955. Moore remained firmly at the center of it all. "Archie acted as his own messenger boy," Reese would recall. "He and I would meet in my office at 7 or 7:30 every morning and talk over what we would do that day. Then Archie would carry the stuff to the printer, pick it up, help stuff envelopes, and take the telegrams to Western Union." Often, Moore himself wrote the communiqués, signing them "Archie Moore, the old gus who's chasing our Heavyweight Champion" or "the Father Time that Marciano and Weill want no part of."[18]

It wasn't just letters. Moore and his Toledo backers were creative in getting their point across. They conducted a poll of sportswriters on the issue of a potential Marciano-Moore fight and then released the results, claiming that 992 of the 1,134 respondents wanted to see the match (with 787 indicating that they believed that Marciano would win). They distributed drawings caricaturing Marciano, courtesy of Walt Buchanan, the cartoonist for the *Toledo Blade,* who agreed to provide his services free of charge. They placed a classified advertisement—"INFORMATION WANTED on how to make Rocky Marciano defend his heavyweight title"—in forty newspapers, and more than a thousand citizens replied. They sent Christmas cards to sportswriters and enclosed a financial statement to show the small amount Moore would net from the fight. They sent personal letters to Marciano himself, with Moore firing off a year-end greeting wishing him a happy new year and asking him to make a resolution to fight Archie Moore in 1955. And they distributed wanted posters featuring Marciano's picture and signed by "Sheriff" Archie Moore.

Initially, sportswriters paid little attention to Moore's campaign. Soon, though, they began reprinting his appeals on a regular basis. It became apparent that Rocky Marciano was merely a pawn in Archie Moore's elaborate game. As Moore later admitted, "Our target was Rocky's manager, Al Weill. We have always felt that he, as an astute student of styles, knows I can give Marciano a tough time. We felt that he wanted no part of the fight." Moore also felt that the IBC would not pressure Weill "to take the fight unless they had to."[19] The plan, then, was to break the resistance of Weill and the IBC through the public pressure engendered by a bombardment of letters, telegrams, and other communications, all claiming that Moore was being ducked.

To bolster his claim, Moore could draw on some history. He claimed that leading contenders (the top middleweights of the late 1930s and the top light heavyweights of the late 1940s) had avoided him before. "What kept me down all these years?" Moore asked rhetorically. "I can only say it was my ability; they were afraid to fight me." Many agreed. Moore, observed Budd Schulberg of *Sports Illustrated,* "learned the hard way that the better you were the less chance you had to get in there for the big one." Echoed Wendell Smith of the *Pittsburgh Courier,* "No one was interested in him, neither the public nor the opposition. Maybe the public didn't catch on to

Archie because he couldn't catch on to the top fighters who were ducking him."[20] Moore was good enough to win but not colorful enough to draw a big gate. Why, then, would a top contender risk fighting him for a small purse? Moore, the party line concluded, was forced to fight in obscurity against toughs no one else would face.

Not everyone bought the party line, however. Some pointed to his record, which stood at 120-19-5 in the fall of 1955 and was, in some respects, spotty. Red Smith observed that Moore had been knocked down (and out) on several occasions. "Archie's address is Toledo, not Olympus," Smith noted. Smith also disputed the fact that good fighters had ducked Moore, pointing out that top men like Ezzard Charles, Harold Johnson, Jimmy Bivins, and Lloyd Marshall had all given Moore fights. "What barred Archie from the championship class was the indifference of the fight public," Smith maintained. "For years, fans acknowledged Moore's ability with a wide yawn. Championship matches are made not necessarily between the two best men, but rather between those whom the customers are most eager to see." Echoed John Ahern of the *Boston Globe*, "[T]his stuff about Moore getting the brush off for being so tough is pure, simple, unadulterated baloney. It's true he was passed over by promoters, but the reason they did duck him was his style rather than his toughness."[21]

Was Al Weill in particular guilty of ducking Moore? Some pointed to the fact that before the launch of Moore's campaign in late 1954 there had been no public outcry for the fight. That was largely true. In the various discussions of 1953 and 1954 concerning Marciano's potential opponents, Moore's name surfaced only once in a great while. There certainly was no widespread demand for a Marciano-Moore bout. "Weill wasn't ducking Moore, the fighter," Shirley Povich of the *Washington Post* argued, "he was avoiding Archie's lack of importance as an opponent for his man Marciano. . . . [I]t was Archie's lack of gate-appeal that most seriously concerned Weill. A return bout with Ezzard Charles held the promise of more revenue and so did a fight with Don Cockell." Echoed Red Smith, "Joey Maxim didn't duck Archie. Neither did Marciano, of course. As soon as circumstances created a real demand for this match, Al Weill accepted it."[22]

Regardless of the impact of his campaign, the fact that he scored several impressive victories in the first half of 1955 helped Moore's cause considerably. In early May, he outdecisioned Nino Valdes, the number-one heavyweight contender, and thus became the new number-one heavyweight contender himself. Then, in late June, Moore defended his light-heavyweight title against middleweight champion Bobo Olson in front of more than twenty-seven thousand in the Polo Grounds. It was a strange matchup and necessitated huge prefight weight fluctuations. Olson went from a svelte 160 pounds to an overstuffed 170, while Moore went from 196 to 175. Moore had enough strength left, however, to knock out Olson in the third round with his "4-6-9 combination." In his sweltering dressing room after the fight the victor asked IBC head Jim Norris, "Now do I get that crack at Marciano?" Then Moore grabbed Burt Lancaster, the actor, to pose for a few pictures together. Lancaster kept shouting above the din, "Greatest fighter in the world, greatest fighter in the whole world."[23] At long last, Archie Moore had arrived.

By now both the press and the public were clamoring for a Marciano-Moore match. The IBC moved quickly to meet the demand, scheduling the fight for September in Yankee Stadium. "The public forced the IBC and Weill to give me this match," the triumphant Moore proclaimed.[24] Archie Moore had finally gotten his man.

● ● ●

It was Archie Moore's moment. The Olson victory in June had put him in the national spotlight, and by fall he had become a national sensation, "an object of the most intense scrutiny on the part of both sportswriters and the lay public."[25] It was difficult to pick up a sports or general-interest magazine and not see a picture or story on Moore. Everyone, it seemed, was discovering Archie Moore.

He quickly demonstrated that he was not about to relinquish the moment when he began training for the fight in North Adams, Massachusetts. The odd choice of location annoyed both the IBC and the New York press, which regarded the town as an out-of-the-way dump. Moore arrived with his bizarre entourage in tow. The group included James ("Cheerful") Norman, Moore's principal trainer and reportedly the only man to have his ear. Cheerful, a former welterweight, tipped the scales at 280 pounds. Moore evidently had a penchant for big trainers, because Tiny Payne was also a mountain of a man. (The other trainers who occasionally worked with Moore, Hiawatha Gray and Bertie Briscoe, were considerably less mountainous.) Poppa Dee was also on hand. An elderly gentleman pushing eighty, he formerly had operated a barbershop in Detroit and was now a doorman at a Detroit hotel. He was also Moore's "personal advisor." In fact, Poppa was a ballyhoo man and in camp to hawk souvenirs and help the challenger talk it up—not that Moore needed help in that regard.

Moore took North Adams by storm. He would drive through the center of town in a red Ford Thunderbird ("I think a sport should have a sport car," he explained) while wearing a blue yachting cap ("it lends an impression that you own a yacht"). From his car, he would waive to townspeople and yell "How's North Adams' finest?" to the police.[26] He was savoring every minute. Along the way, he also did some training for the fight, often accompanied by the person and saxophone of Lucky Thompson. In the gym, despite the presence of Johnston, Cheerful Norman, and the other trainers on hand, Moore was his own boss. He even bandaged his own hands. Training sessions were self-directed, free-flowing, and loose.

They were also an afterthought. Moore was clearly unwilling to let training stand in the way of his other, more important, hobbies and interests. He ran up mountains, played softball, and practiced archery with local youngsters. He practiced shooting a warden's pistol. He dabbled in developing film. He fooled around on the French horn. He wrote a letter to President Eisenhower, inviting him to the fight (the president couldn't make it). He delivered a lecture on music, "From Bach to Pop to Bop," at a fraternity at nearby Williams College. And he began flying lessons, a pursuit that alarmed Jim Norris, the IBC, and everyone else who had a financial stake in the fight.

Most of all, Archie Moore kept talking. Each day in training camp he would hold court for an appreciative and spellbound audience, offering lengthy, off-the-cuff discourses on a wide variety of subjects. He had never had such a stage before. As Red Smith observed, "He's an actor by preference, a spellbinding spieler. He even makes up like a Shakespearean ham, with his Mephistophelean mustache and chin whiskers. All his life he's been playing summer stock in converted barns. Now, for the first time, he's hit Broadway. He has an audience worthy of his immeasurable art. It must be a great comfort to him." On rare occasions the pressure to perform got the better of Moore. Once, about a week before the fight, he lashed out at "unsociable newspaper men." On another occasion he accused the press of "trying to make me the villain in this fight. I can tell that you fellows have Marciano as the fair-haired golden boy of the fight."[27] In general, though, good feelings reigned between Moore and the press. It was all great fun.

Not for Rocky Marciano, however, who continued to be the subject of Moore's jibes. On one occasion, for example, Moore reportedly said, "I have nothing but the utmost respect for Rocky. He has done a great job getting where he is with limited ability." Then again, it was hard to tell whether Moore actually said such things. Harry Mendel, the IBC's infamous ballyhoo man, was also stationed in the challenger's camp and once again tasked with directing his invective against Rocky Marciano. It was a curious assignment for Mendel. In a sense, his services weren't necessary. Marciano's previous title challengers (Walcott, LaStarza, Charles, and Cockell) were all reserved men who needed some prodding to say something mean about the champion. Moore had no such reserve. As Arthur Daley noted, he acted as "his own minister of propaganda."[28] Mendel therefore found himself in a unique and unsettling position: He needed to justify his job. On the other hand, it was a plum assignment. Moore was a publicity man's dream. He would say anything. Mendel could invent anything and attribute it to Moore, and everybody would believe it.

For one last time, Mendel launched a smear campaign against Marciano. Or was it really a ballyhoo battle against Moore? Indeed, Mendel and Moore engaged in a game of one-upmanship throughout camp. Once, for instance, when asked about his reported accusation that Marciano was a foul fighter, Moore replied, "Harry Mendel writes that stuff. Anybody could tell the difference between what I write and what Mendel writes. That's his job, public relations, but I'm in charge of my public relations." Another time Moore proclaimed, "Actually, I didn't say that Rocky has lost his punch. Harry Mendel said I said it. He misquoted me."[29]

More often than not though, Mendel and Moore were not in competition but in cahoots. After the fight, Mendel admitted that he had spent most of his time helping Moore think up insults about Marciano. He added with a laugh, "I believed a lot of the stuff I wrote, too." It was at a press conference after the fight that Marciano asked Mendel, "Did Archie really say all those bad things about me, Harry?" "Why, Rocky," Mendel replied, "you don't think I'd tell a lie, do you?" Everyone in the room laughed.[30]

That was after the fight, however. Before the fight was Marciano really laughing at Moore's stream of barbs, which had begun all the way back in November 1954? Some maintained that he was, in fact, livid. As Allie Colombo confided to one reporter, "Rocky never says anything when he reads bad stories about himself. He just grunts and doesn't talk for a while. But every time he grunts I know somebody is in real trouble. And the last time Moore's name was mentioned, Rocky grunted. So figure it out for yourself." Others drew a similar conclusion. According to Bill Liston of the *Boston Post,* "the Rock is inwardly sizzling with rage." Jerry Nason of the *Boston Globe* described Marciano as "a seething mass of white-hot lava on the verge of erupting" from a year's worth of ridicule and abuse.[31]

Marciano was, for sure, annoyed at some of Moore's barbs. He was also incredulous at the amount of invective emanating from North Adams: "You know, I don't believe a lot of things I have been reading about Archie Moore lately. . . . He's been around too long to have said some of those foolish things." To the extent that he did believe them, Marciano seemed to recognize the humor underlying Moore's boasts. "They don't bother me," he said of the insults. "That's Moore's character. I mean he's quite a character, isn't he?"[32] The fact that Moore's talk spurred ticket sales also helped lessen the sting of his needling. After the fight Marciano would give him great credit for feeding the gate.

From the beginning, ticket sales boomed, not just at the box office in Yankee Stadium but at all the movie theaters around the country on the closed-circuit network. Everyone was talking about the fight; more excitement and anticipation surrounded it than any other Marciano fight, or any other heavyweight fight in years for that matter. A few even rated it as the biggest boxing match since the Dempsey-Tunney battles in the 1920s.

The reason, of course, was Moore. By the time of the fight he had fully displayed what Gerry Hern of the *Boston Post* called "a genius at whipping up the public's innate resentment of alleged injustice." He had succeeded in casting himself as the ultimate and heroic outsider bucking the system. Conversely (and strangely enough), the champion was almost lost in the shuffle. Perhaps, Shirley Povich mused, Marciano had even "become a bit of a hostile character. That's on account of Moore, who has been playing the underdog role so shrewdly that for the first time in his title career, Marciano may not be the sentimental favorite."[33] Marciano, of course, still had many fans who would root for him on fight night. By this point in his career, however, he was an old story. Moore, the old man, was the new story.

Moreover, Marciano's camp at Grossinger's was deathly quiet compared to the Moore maelstrom in North Adams, although Weill tried his best to whip up some excitement. He didn't have Lucky Thompson, but he did have Yancey Henry, a former fighter of his who had started a bebop trio called, appropriately enough, the Yancey Henry Trio. Yancey and his band showed up at Marciano's camp and serenaded paying customers with "When Irish Eyes Are Smiling," an odd selection to say the least. Stealing another page from Moore's book, Weill pranced around camp in a blue yachting cap, which, as Red Smith noted, made Weill look like the First Lord of the Admiralty.[34] The effort to create a Moore-style splash thus failed.

At least an air of relaxation prevailed at Grossinger's. Many noted that they had never seen Marciano more relaxed, carefree, or impressive in camp. Perhaps that was because he had insisted on a less-demanding training regimen. He got his way, sparring only 116 rounds in preparation, the lightest workload before any of his title fights. "This time I haven't worked so hard or so long, and there is no sign of staleness whatsoever," Marciano explained. "I was trying to do too much in those days. Now I take time off whenever I feel I need it. The new program has worked wonders." Charley Goldman didn't like it, however. "We argued a lot about it, but that's the way he wanted it and that's the way it was," he sighed.[35] In the weeks be-fore the fight, Goldman was plainly worried about his fighter.

He was about the only one. Marciano was a prohibitive 18-5 betting fa-vorite. Although most believed that the confident and experienced Moore would test the champion—particularly if he managed to cut Marciano—no one thought Moore would win. In one prefight poll conducted by the As-sociated Press, a staggering sixty-four of sixty-eight respondents picked Marciano. Confidence in the champion only grew after the jam-packed weigh-in. Moore seemed nervous and rattled as he was forcibly escorted to the scales, almost like a man going to the gallows. Had he finally talked himself over the edge? Fortunately, Vincent Nardiello was on hand to sup-ply answers. "I never saw Moore like this," Doctor Nardiello admitted. "The last time I examined him he was cocky and calm, not a bit nervous. And today, he really surprised me. I expected him to be cool and calm like Rocky. But he wasn't. Of course, he is highly imaginative and that would add to the tension. He's really keyed up."[36] As the fight was postponed a day be-cause of the threat of Hurricane Ione, everyone continued to ponder the psyche of the man of the hour: Archie Moore.

●　●　●

The next night, September 21, 1955, Moore was back to his old, confident, flamboyant self. For the 61,574 fans looking on in Yankee Stadium, the nearly 400,000 watching on the closed-circuit network (133 theaters in 92 cities, the largest ever), and the estimated 250 million listening on radio, he was clearly the center of attention. He did not disappoint. Before the fight he had promised a special robe for the occasion, although he had refused to reveal any details. When reporters tried to pry the information out of Marie Hardy, his robe designer, she, too, said, "It's a secret. I can't tell you. Archie says not to." Now, Moore delivered on his promise with a garment that Hugh Brown of the *Philadelphia Evening Bulletin* called "a dilly," a black and gold silk robe with wide Louis XIV cuffs. "No Othello was ever more lavishly costumed," declared Budd Schulberg.[37] The large crowd roared in amazement at the sight of Moore's robe.

Tension built as ring announcer Johnny Addie introduced a group of past and present champions sitting at ringside. Tension broke, if only for a mo-ment, when a dwarf suddenly and mysteriously appeared in the middle of the ring. Then the drama returned as Addie introduced the combatants, identifying Moore from San Diego and Toledo (or, as Moore called them, the "Twin Cities"). Then Moore went to work on Marciano's psyche. In his corner, arms folded, he shot the champion a hypnotic glare and repeated it when the two fighters met at center ring for instructions. Marciano was unfazed. Then came another reprieve when referee Harry Kessler titillated everyone by beginning his microphoned instructions, "Good evening, Rocky and Archie." Finally, amid the crackling atmosphere, the fight everyone had been talking about for months began.

It did not disappoint. Although it wasn't a back-and-forth classic (like the first Marciano-Walcott) or an epic bloodbath (like the first Marciano-Charles), it had certain elements of each. It also had more than sixty-one thousand fans in Yankee Stadium standing and roaring throughout. It began, though, not with a roar but a yawn. Nothing happened in the first round. Then, in the second, Archie Moore nearly won the fight. A wild Marciano miss left him wide open, and Moore seized the moment, delivering a short, well-timed, and powerful right to Marciano's jaw. Before anyone realized what had happened, the champion was down on the canvas on all fours.

Over his entire career Marciano had been knocked down only once, against Walcott in their first fight. Now he was down again. Fans in Yankee Stadium and around the country were stunned. So was Marciano. Some ringside observers thought he was in real trouble and had never been closer to defeat. Marciano later admitted that he "blacked out just a second." He also said, however, "I was dazed but my head cleared quickly."[38] Indeed, he was quickly up at the count of two. He wore a look of confusion and puzzlement and was halfway turned to the ropes, but he was on his feet.

The knockdown also took referee Harry Kessler by surprise, so much so that he made a significant blunder. At the time, the mandatory eight-count was not in effect for championship bouts in New York. Kessler forgot. After Marciano had gotten up at the count of two, Kessler remained in front of him, continuing the count for two or three more seconds as he wiped the dazed Marciano's gloves and blocked Moore's entry. Then Kessler realized his error, stepped aside, and finally let Moore move in for the kill. Moore, however, had lost a few precious seconds. Some felt that Kessler's mental lapse may have disconcerted Moore and cost him a shot at finishing the dazed Marciano. In later years Moore himself advanced that claim, and with much bitterness. In 1985 he recalled "standing there looking [Kessler] right in the eyes and he's looking in my eyes. And he sees the hate in my eyes, he sees it all right. And he knows I hate him. I hate him to this day."[39]

To a large extent though, Moore had no one to blame but himself. Before the fight he had criticized Walcott for letting Marciano get away in their first fight. Walcott, Moore proclaimed, shouldn't have walked away with pride after the knockdown, but instead he kept his eyes fixed on Marciano.

"He lost his rhythm, lost a half step gettin' back to his man, and that cost him the fight," Moore pointed out. Now, ironically, Moore repeated the mistake. After Marciano got up and Kessler finally stepped away, Moore landed a variety of well-orchestrated blows but never managed to mount an assault that might have put down the champion for good. "I couldn't understand why Archie didn't come at me then," Marciano said. "I wasn't groggy, but I was dazed, and I couldn't see out of my left eye for a while."[40]

Immediately after the fight, Moore, somewhat tellingly, didn't mention Kessler's mental lapse as the reason for his failure to finish. He did, however, offer a number of other explanations. He said he was surprised that he had knocked Marciano down so early in the fight. He said he wasn't warmed up enough. He said he should have stepped in more with his follow-up punches. The bottom line? As Moore said, "When he got up, I let him get away."[41] And Marciano did, indeed, get away. Toward the end of the second round he was starting to land some punches again. At round's end, Moore walked back to his corner, plainly discouraged. He knew that a golden opportunity had come and gone.

That was the end of the surprises. From then on, the fight slowly but surely swung to Marciano. Some felt that the turning point came late in the third round. Until then, it had been Moore's round, with the challenger skillfully evading Marciano's wild lunges, scoring some counters of his own, and making the champion look like an amateur. As the round wound down, however, Marciano chased his man across the ring, raining a torrent of punches over the covered-up Moore. Most missed, and those that did connect seemed to glance off the challenger. The tide, though, had turned. "From then on the fight was mine," Marciano said later. Agreed Budd Schulberg, "[T]his round was a turning point, for it proved that no matter how brilliantly Archie boxed he could not stop the champion's forward progress. He could not prevent the champion from jarring him. The science of self-defense was inadequate to the problem of how to stop a human tank like Marciano from running over him."[42]

Marciano was beginning to take charge of the fight, but not in his preferred manner. By this point in his career he was tired of being called crude. He had hoped to silence critics by dispatching Moore in a more polished, skillful manner. After he hit the canvas in the second round, however, his handlers urged him to return to the style that had always given him great success (albeit lukewarm reviews). "In the third round we sent Rocky out to crowd Moore," Al Weill said after the fight. "Archie never got another chance to free-wheel in the ring."[43]

Marciano began to carry the fight in the expected manner, by staying on top of Moore and uncorking repeated barrages at him. It was an effective style but one that would nevertheless result in the same old criticism of Marciano after the fight—that he was wild, awkward, and crude. Some criticism would be scathing. Proclaimed Ned Cronin of the *Los Angeles Times,* "Rocky did everything but perform an appendectomy on Moore. . . . Without question, Marciano is the most primitive fighter since Luis Angel Firpo. Primitive in this case is a rather elegant term for dirty fighting." Echoed Curley Grieve of the *San Francisco Examiner,* "This was a primitive Marciano exhibition of unscientific fighting, a cross between gladiator tactics in a Roman circus and the life and death battle of a Neanderthal man defending his cave."[44]

Others, however, would point out that Marciano only seemed wild because of Moore's defensive abilities. Indeed, after the fight Moore would earn a host of kudos for his defensive brilliance. They were well deserved. As Marciano accelerated the pace, Moore drew upon all his experience, skill, and tricks to stem the attack. He bobbed. He blocked punches. He covered up like what Red Smith called "a rolling, weaving turtle," exposing only his arms, elbows, and shoulders. All those tactics caused Marciano considerable frustration. In trying to find his target, he had to cut through a moving tangle of arms and hunched shoulders. "I don't think I ever threw any more punches in a fight than I did tonight against Archie," he said later. "I just couldn't seem to get the clean shot at him. He'd hide beneath those arms and bob and weave and roll with punches so that the only thing I could do was to keep pitching them."[45]

Moore was doing more than just covering up, however. He was continuing to punish the champion with well-timed shots of his own. Time after time, he would suddenly emerge from his shell and lash out with a stinging, well-placed blow. Most found their mark. Some even visibly shook Marciano. Then Moore would retreat into his shell. This was part of Moore's strategy, which amounted to an early, modified version of the "rope a dope" later popularized by Muhammad Ali. Moore's plan was to ride the ropes and hope Marciano would eventually punch himself out. Not everyone approved of the tactic. "Did you see that?" manager Charley Johnston asked after the fight. "Did you ever see a smart fighter do that? . . . I told Archie, I yelled at him, to get away from the ropes and maneuver the champ into the middle of the ring. He wouldn't do it." The strategy never produced its desired effect. "I thought he'd wear himself out," Moore admitted after the fight.[46]

Marciano never did wear out. He only got stronger. He really stepped up the pace of his attack in the sixth round and effectively won the fight in the process. Twice he knocked down Moore. Early in the round he put him down for a count of four courtesy of a right-left combination. Then, late in the round, Marciano dropped Moore for a count of eight, courtesy of a chopping right. In between, he gave what Budd Schulberg called "a demonstration of continuous punching that had to be seen to be believed." Moore absorbed more punishment than seemed possible but drew upon his defensive mastery and considerable courage to survive. Almost incredibly, he even fought back for a stretch. The round ended with an after-bell exchange sparked by Marciano. ("That was unintentional," Moore said after the fight, "and I hit him back unintentionally.") Then the battered Moore and the weary Marciano each returned to their corners. It had been, praised Joseph C. Nichols of the *New York Times,* a round destined to be referred to "by this generation as comparable to any single round in heavyweight title history."[47]

Marciano was filled with confidence. "I knew that I had him in the sixth round when I started backing him on his heels," he said. "That's what I should have been doing right at the start but I didn't. I gave him too much punching room in the early rounds and he took too much advantage of it." Now it was merely a matter of time. Moore's right eye was beginning to close and he was banged up, prompting Nardiello, the attending ringside physician, to visit his corner at the end of the sixth. More important, while Marciano was getting stronger, the aging Moore was tiring. Charley Johnston knew that and urged Moore to go for a knockout in the seventh round. He did, but he didn't get one. Marciano kept advancing and hurling bombs, and it was Moore who hit the canvas again, although Kessler (probably erroneously) ruled it a slip rather than a knockdown. Moore, however, did stage a rally of sorts in the seventh. A. J. Liebling of the *New Yorker* called it his "finest stand."[48]

It was also his final stand. In the eighth round, Marciano again stepped up his attack. He pounded the challenger all over—in the middle of the ring, on the ropes, and in the corners—for the entire three-minute round. Moore kept fighting back, emerging from his cocoon once in awhile to fire deadly shots. He was increasingly unable to cope with the champion's constant barrage of firepower, however. Toward the end of the eighth, Marciano punctuated his latest assault with his best punch of the fight, a straight right to the jaw. Moore went down. At the count of six he was still holding the rope and showed no signs of rising when the bell rang to end the round. He had been saved by the bell. After the round Nardiello paid another visit to Moore's corner, this time asking the challenger if he wanted the fight stopped. "No," Moore replied. "It's a championship. I want to be counted out in the ring."[49]

That's precisely what happened. The proud, defiant, and still-dangerous Moore came out of his corner for the ninth round and landed a few stinging blows. But he was unable to sustain his attack because his legs were completely gone. He was unable to resist the Marciano onslaught any longer. It was pure power and strength now as Marciano flailed away with both hands, delivering an avalanche of blows. Some of his punches missed. Some Moore blocked. Others landed, however, and sapped the challenger's last ounces of energy. One last assault punctuated by a pair of left hooks to the head finally put Moore down for good. He tried to rise but was counted out, his left arm hooked over the middle rope.

With the fight over, Marciano's fans—like in the old days—started to rush over press row to hail their hero in the ring. Amid the developing melee, Marciano first went over to pay tribute to his fallen foe. As he explained later, "I said you're better than I thought you were. You were great, the best I ever fought. And Archie told me, 'Man, you're all right.'" Moore had a slightly different recollection of Marciano's postfight greeting: "He said I was the greatest fighter he ever fought and he thanked me for helping him make a lot of money."[50] Indeed, it was Marciano's biggest payday by far. His purses for his other title defenses had ranged from the approximately $250,000 he had received for his June 1954 fight with Charles to the approximately $115,000 he had received for his May 1955 bout with Cockell. For fighting Archie Moore, Marciano received the whopping sum of $470,997. No wonder he held no grudges over the months of ridicule.

Archie Moore exited the stage in style. Before he left the ring, he draped his majestic robe over his shoulders and paused for a second to comb his hair. Moments later he dramatically swept into his dressing room, announcing to the assembled reporters, "Gentlemen, I'll be with you in a minute." A few moments later he declared, "I've got no excuses. Rocky's consistency overpowered me. He's a great fighter. I tried to make the men in my corner proud of me. I enjoyed the fight. Rocky, I'm sure enjoyed it. If the people enjoyed it half as much as I, I'm satisfied." In the end, Moore asked the press, "Any more questions, boys? Me, I'm going fishin'. You are welcome to come visit me." When reporters asked Moore where he would be entertaining visitors, he responded, "Oh, I live all over the USA. Let's all go home."[51] With that, Archie Moore headed for Greenwich Village to listen to his friend Lucky Thompson play at the Café Bohemia.

● ● ●

In the days after the fight Moore received a bucketful of praise for his boxing skill, defensive mastery, dangerous hitting, and, most of all, for his courage. His gallant performance had a lot to do with helping make the fight what Abramson called "one of the all-time memorable battles of Queensbury history." It was, agreed Nichols, "one of the most savagely fought, thrilling duels in modern prize ring history." Schulberg saw it as "a beautiful spectacle of pain and skill and endurance and die-slow courage and a resoluteness that makes champions and wins wars." Few would have disagreed with Red Smith when he observed, "The biggest fight in years was one of the best in years."[52]

Ultimately, the star of the show was Rocky Marciano. The evening may have started out as Moore's but it ended as Marciano's. He received widespread praise of a familiar kind. Hugh Brown proclaimed him "perhaps the finest conditioned athlete in the world." Such conditioning led directly to the stamina, which one reporter described as "almost inhuman," that he displayed once again in the ring. He was also lauded for what Matt Ring of the *Philadelphia Evening Bulletin* called "almost superhuman strength." Confirmed Moore, "Marciano is far and away the strongest man I've encountered. You can avoid him some of the time, but not all of the time." Marciano was, added Moore, "a mauler with determination to keep going, and that determination is what makes him a great champion."[53]

For the first time, though, Marciano received widespread recognition as a great champion, not just from Moore but from people throughout the fight game. Many, of course, had been on the Marciano bandwagon for quite a while. As far back as the LaStarza fight in 1953, some were ready to proclaim his greatness as champion, and Marciano won over more critics with each successive fight. After the first fight with Ezzard Charles in 1954, for instance, New York sportswriter Bill Corum rhapsodized, "I think that he is a great champion, the Rock from the land of Plymouth Rock. . . . He's a helluva man in the ring, this Rocky of ours." Others had jumped on the Marciano bandwagon after his dramatic knockout of Charles in the rematch later in 1954. Some former detractors grudgingly admitted that Marciano was the best of his era. Others began to mention him in the same breath with Dempsey and Louis, as the greatest of all time. As Arthur Daley instructed readers in the wake of the fight, "Rocky Marciano is a great champion, folks. It's about time he began to receive the recognition he so richly deserves."[54]

Before Marciano faced Archie Moore in the fall of 1955, though, many continued to withhold final judgment on the champion—to the extent they considered the matter at all. There had always been a natural tendency to focus on Marciano's opponent rather than Marciano himself in the wake of his victories. In his title fights against Walcott, LaStarza, Charles, and Cockell, the losers had received as much, if not more, praise for gallantry as the winner did for a triumphant performance. As Daley noted, "[T]he plaudits never went to him. They went to the fellows he'd beaten. It was almost as if the drama critics ignored the Barrymores in order to rave about the impressive acting of some supernumerary."[55]

Moreover, some of the reviews on Marciano were decidedly mixed, and for reasons that were stylistic. Throughout his reign Marciano continued to appear crude. As W. J. McGoogan of the St. Louis Post-Dispatch observed on the eve of the Marciano-Moore fight, "It is surprising that a champion like Marciano with such a record does not win more acclaim than he has, but there are still many good boxing men who declare flatly that Rocky is lucky to be champion because he can't do anything more than punch and not too accurately at that."[56]

Even the spotless record itself, which stood at a perfect 48-0 before his match with Moore, remained a source of criticism. Hadn't he fattened it up against a bunch of New England nobodies? Who had he beaten in the big time besides old has-beens (Walcott and Louis) or never-weres (Matthews and LaStarza)? And did he really stack up against the great champions of yesteryear? Jack Dempsey fanned the flames here, alleging before the Marciano-Moore fight that Marciano not only would have lost to the great (Louis, Dempsey, and Johnson) but also to the not-so-great (Max Schmeling, Jack Sharkey, and Max Baer). Marciano, Dempsey declared, was "just average . . . Rocky has too many faults to be a great fighter."[57] Others did not go as far but reached a similar conclusion: Marciano was not a great heavyweight champion.

The Archie Moore fight gave Rocky Marciano a chance to answer his critics once and for all. In a prefight column entitled "This Fight Will Determine Rocky's Worth," Wendell Smith observed, "The critics have had a difficult time trying to decide whether the stocky, solid champion is great or just an ordinary titleholder who has thrived on mediocre opposition. . . . This should be the night Marciano establishes himself one way or the other for all time. This will be the night he'll have to call on all his skills, all his savvy, all that is buried deep within him, for he has never faced a man like Archie before."[58]

If the Moore fight was a final examination, Marciano passed it with flying colors. Red Smith believed that it was Marciano's finest fight because he survived Moore's sniping and battered his seemingly impregnable defenses with a relentless attack unparalleled in heavyweight annals. The victory over Moore, agreed Hugh Brown, "was the most impressive of Marciano's sanguinary, spectacular career." Similarly, Arthur Daley called it "the supreme performance" of Marciano's career, one in which he wore "an aura of superhuman grandeur." Later, the man who knew Marciano's boxing abilities the best—Charley Goldman—would tell his pupil, "Rocky, that was your peak fight."[59]

In the wake of the Moore fight, recognition of Rocky Marciano's greatness as a champion was as complete as it would ever be. True, some continued to harp on his flaws, but Marciano was never going to win over those people, for they were the purest of the purists and would never find his style acceptable. To some, he was and would forever remain an ugly duckling.

But his performance against Moore captured the undecided vote. Perhaps some realized that they had unfairly held him to the standard of the great Joe Louis, or that they had allowed themselves to fixate on minor flaws while ignoring his incredible strengths. As Budd Schulberg declared after the Marciano-Moore bout, "The experts still fault him for his lack of finesse. . . . The old-timers talk of Sullivan and Jeffries and Dempsey. We have another such immortal slugger in our midst. Are we too close to his shortcomings to recognize his incomparable virtues?" The title of Schulberg's article supplied the answer: "A Champion Proves His Greatness."[60]

Part 3: Receding

13 The Wanderer

And then, somewhat suddenly, Rocky Marciano quit. On April 27, 1956, at the relatively young age of thirty-three, he announced that he was retiring from the ring.

The retirement was not a complete shock. The day before his September 1955 fight with Archie Moore, several sportswriters, citing sources close to the champion, reported that the Moore fight would be his last. Al Weill was enraged by the reports and vigorously denied them, but his fighter gave the story fresh legs after the bout. "My mother wants me to retire," Marciano announced to the press in his dressing room. "My wife wants me to retire— my whole family wants me to quit. It's been a tough life for them all. I don't know what I will do. I want time to think it over."[1] The next day, however, Marciano announced that he would indeed return to the ring in June 1956 in the hope of capturing his fiftieth straight victory.

During the winter of 1956, though, Marciano developed second thoughts during a long South American vacation that he and Barbara took. Meanwhile, rumors kept cropping up. Most people continued to believe that Marciano was going to return. Why wouldn't he? Wasn't he at the peak of his powers? How could he pass up another big payday? Conventional wisdom was wrong. On the morning of April 27, he called Barbara from Michigan and told her that he had decided to retire. Several hours later, Marciano was in New York at a hastily arranged press conference at the Hotel Shelton. Flanked by Weill and Charley Goldman on one side and Jim Norris of the IBC on the other, he formally announced that he was quitting.

His stated reason was his family. "I am retiring because of my wife and baby," he announced to the press. Barbara Marciano had been after him to retire for some time, and the Marcianos' daughter, Mary Anne, was three. He felt guilt here, too, proclaiming that he had been a "poor father." The fact that his mother and father wanted him to quit as well made the decision easy, at least on the family front. "I want to start living for my family," a remorseful Marciano declared.[2]

Other factors weighed in favor of retirement as well. Marciano may have been worried about his creaky back, which had first given him problems early in his career and continued to loom as a potential problem. The back hadn't prevented him from capturing and defending the crown, but who knew how long it would hold up? Moreover, he had attained financial security. His fights had grossed him approximately $1.7 million. That was before Weill's cut and taxes, of course, but Marciano's net share was still substantial, estimated at between $250,000 and $450,000. He had also made extra cash from barnstorming. As he said at his retirement press conference, "I am comfortably fixed, and I am not afraid of the future."[3]

He also knew that his considerable postretirement prospects in business and public relations hinged at least in part on his status as "the undefeated heavyweight champion of the world." A fiftieth victory would have certainly been nice, but why risk the perfect 49–0 record that would continue to create revenue? Now that he had been beaten Moore, Marciano had nothing left to prove. His legacy was secure. Why put it in jeopardy?

Even so, Marciano might have fought on. As his brother Peter points out, however, "He felt that there really wasn't anybody out there that could challenge him." By early 1956 Walcott had long been retired, and Charles had faded badly. A rematch with Moore was always a possibility, but would that pack fans in after the conclusive 1955 fight? The other leading contenders—Nino Valdes, Hurricane Jackson, and Bob Baker—excited no one. A young, talented Floyd Patterson was starting his rise through the ranks, but he seemed a year or two away and didn't seem overly eager to fight Marciano. Because of the sour aftertaste of the Cockell fight, Marciano was unwilling to accept any kind of bum-of-the-month program. What he looked for was someone to stir his pride and fill his wallet. No one fit the bill. "There was nobody in sight to fight," Marciano said later. "I kept hoping that they could make a June fight for me and then I could quit. But the time went on and nobody showed up."[4]

All of this surely entered into his decision, but two primary considerations led Rocky Marciano to retire. The first had to do with his relationship with Weill. Publicly, Marciano said all the right things about his manager. "If I had to do it over again, I'd want a man like Al Weill," he said a week after announcing retirement. "In fact, I'd want Al Weill." To some extent Marciano was telling the truth, for he knew he wouldn't have scaled the heights he had as fast, if at all, without the influential Weill behind him. Privately, though, Marciano admitted that he had built up a considerable dislike if not hatred for his manager and that he retired in large part to get away from him. "I'm getting out while I can," he said on the morning that he retired. "I'm dumping this guy before he dumps me."[5]

Marciano could no longer tolerate Weill's ego, which would often assume significant and visible proportions. Jimmy Breslin remembers that ego emerging time and time again during interviews. "He would begin by 'The fighter did this,'" Breslin said. "Then the ego would come in and he'd say, 'We got him in the fourth round.' Then, later on, it would come out to, 'Did you see me hit that bum in the seventh round?'" Weill's ego naturally entered his relationship with Marciano. "Without me you're nothing," the manager would frequently remind his fighter. Weill would often treat Marciano as his serf as well. Once, for instance, in the presence of Jimmy Cannon, Weill sent Marciano out to fetch him a box of cigars. On another occasion Cannon asked Marciano a question, and Marciano stumbled a bit when answering. Weill immediately put his hand over Marciano's mouth and said, "Don't talk until you learn how to speak." Eventually, the abuse and control alienated Marciano. In the words of his brother Sonny, "He grew tired of being manipulated."[6]

There was also the matter of money. Marciano had always been angry that Weill was receiving half of his earnings under their contract. Then came news from the West Coast in mid-April 1956, several weeks before Marciano retired. In government hearings being conducted there, allegations surfaced that San Francisco promoter Jimmy Murray had paid Weill a sum of $10,000 off the top from the receipts of the Marciano-Cockell fight (which, if true, would have meant that Weill deprived Marciano of several thousand dollars). Weill, of course, denied the allegations. "I wish it was so, but it isn't," he said. "I haven't seen any $10,000." Marciano, at least publicly, accepted Weill's explanation. "I believe Al is an honest guy," he said. "We've been together for nine years, and Al wouldn't do that to me. Besides, $10,000 is pennies compared to a million-dollar gate."[7]

Privately, though, Marciano was enraged and hurt. Recalls Peter Marciano, "Rocky had some very, very strong evidence that he [Weill] was beating him out of a lot of money . . . I think he felt hurt and he felt like Al Weill really went behind his back." It may have been the last straw in the deteriorating Marciano-Weill relationship. It may also have led him to step out of the ring. Lou Duva recalls that Marciano and Weill "had their falling outs quite a few times. I think the real reason he quit—it wasn't because of his back, it was because of Al Weill."[8]

Burnout was the other prime reason that caused him to step away. Although Marciano had fought professionally for less than eight years, they were intense years. On the way up, he was fighting all the time. After he became a leading contender and then champion, he fought a lot less—only twice a year as champion. But when he wasn't fighting, Marciano was training. Constantly. By the time of the Cockell fight in the spring of 1955, he was tiring of the grind. The Moore fight in the fall of 1955 should have rejuvenated him, given its huge buildup and the atmosphere that preceded the bout, but it didn't. In training camp before that fight he confided to intimates that he had lost his hunger. Others, including Charley Goldman, noticed the same thing. He was weary of it all—the months away from home, the special diets, the miles of roadwork, and especially the hours in the gym. "He was getting to a point in his life where he started to dislike going into the gym," remembers Peter Marciano. "He kind of got turned off by the certain odor . . . that's in a gym, in a boxing/training facility. It's a very distinct odor—and it was starting to turn him off."[9]

He had enough of an edge, of course, to beat Moore. In the wake of that fight, though, he failed to recapture his hunger. His friends knew. They noticed that he was putting on more between-fight weight than usual. More important, he wasn't taking walks anymore. Goldman saw Marciano a month or so after the Moore fight. "Hey, you look bloaty, Rock," the trainer said. "Yeh, Charley, I am," the fighter replied. "And you know something? I haven't even been taking walks." Goldman later said, "Right then, I knew."[10] Shortly thereafter Marciano made it official and quit the ring.

His retirement brought a shower of praise from the press, much of which had a "we didn't realize what we had" quality to it. Although his greatness as a fighter was still the subject of some debate, most gave him credit for

his perfect 49-0 record. For one last time Marciano the man received glowing praise for his personality and his qualities of spirit, even from those who
doubted his greatness as a fighter. To the end, his image outside the ring
remained as perfect and unassailable as his record in it.

Other sportswriters, however, treated news of his retirement with a healthy
dose of skepticism. Marciano, after all, was still young and at or near his peak.
By his own admission, he had at least two or three good fights left. Given all
of this, many felt that he would be unable to resist the lure of the ring and
another big payday. Some were even conspiratorial about it. Marciano, they
said, had temporarily quit to help IBC head Jim Norris, who was just then
battling the government in a trial taking place in New York with respect to
the antitrust litigation. Marciano's retirement would allow Norris to counter
government claims and point out that the IBC no longer had an exclusive
contract with the heavyweight champion of the world. The theory was
groundless. It was also ironic, considering that Marciano had developed a
few grudges against Norris over time. An alternate theory, only somewhat
more plausible, involved the elimination tourney that the IBC announced
around the time of his retirement. Marciano had abdicated, some thought,
so a new king—perhaps Patterson—could rise to the throne. Then, once the
new king was accepted, the old king (Marciano) could come back to try to
reclaim his throne—in a fight that would have a monster gate, of course.

There were several sportswriters who begged Marciano not to come back.
They felt that he had nothing left to prove. They also genuinely liked Marciano, and memories of the unsuccessful comeback of another fighter they
genuinely liked—Joe Louis—were still fresh and painful. They didn't want
to see Marciano tumble from grace and tarnish his reputation as well.
Marciano, too, wanted to avoid that fate. He was, after all, the man who
had knocked Louis through the ropes that night in the Garden. As he said
at his retirement press conference, "I'm going to profit by other people's
mistakes. If Joe Louis couldn't make a successful comeback, I'm not going
to attempt it."[11] To prove he was serious, Marciano went up to Grossinger's the day after he announced his retirement and symbolically nailed up
the entrance to his old training quarters. The Rocky Marciano era was over.

● ● ●

True to his word, he never came back. For sure, Jim Norris and the IBC tried
their hardest. After Patterson won the heavyweight championship in late
1956, Norris, with his empire starting to crumble around him, desperately
tried to convince Marciano to come out of retirement to fight the new champion. He even offered the old champion a $1 million guarantee. But Mar-

ciano wouldn't bite. He did, however, seem to take particular delight in toying with the affections and aspirations of Norris and Weill. Sonny Marciano remembers attending a meeting in Florida shortly after his brother quit and Norris and Weill making a long, impassioned plea for Marciano to come out of retirement. According to Sonny, his brother enjoyed watching his former bosses squirm and then shut down the discussion by saying, "I was looking forward to this day when I could look you both in the eye and tell you that I don't need it anymore, I don't need boxing, and I don't need you."[12]

In 1959, though, Marciano did briefly contemplate a return to the ring. Lou Duva reveals that Marciano came close to signing a deal to fight Ingemar Johansson, the big Swede who had knocked out Patterson to become the new champion. Negotiations took place at the Victoria Hotel in New York, with Marciano slated to receive $1.4 million ("a tremendous figure at that time," says Duva) and Duva slated to work Marciano's corner. In preparation, Marciano underwent secret training sessions in Ocala, Florida. For a while he was serious, cutting down on meals and doing roadwork with his old zeal. Eventually, though, his various business interests interfered. Besides, Cus D'Amato, Patterson's manager, successfully managed to block the Marciano-Johansson deal from being consummated. After a month, Marciano called off the comeback.[13]

He didn't fade away, though. He had never tired of the limelight and was in no hurry to leave it. His status as an ex-champion ensured that he could stay in it. He was always at big fights in the late 1950s and 1960s, coming down the aisle, hopping into the ring, and taking a bow. Sometimes he was at ringside, providing color commentary for television. He also hosted a syndicated television show, *The Main Event,* in 1961. Marciano would briefly interview a guest (usually a past boxing great such as Jersey Joe Walcott or a celebrity such as George Raft, Jonathan Winters, or Joe DiMaggio) and supply the voice-over analysis for clips from a great fight of the past, often one of his own.

Marciano found other outlets for capitalizing on his boxing fame. He dabbled in celebrity refereeing and also endorsed products and appeared in televised advertisements. The lofty title of "the undefeated heavyweight champion of the world" kept Marciano in demand as a legend of his sport. He was also active in an array of charitable causes throughout his retirement years, often with little attendant fanfare. "It was his personality to not make a big thing of it," recalls Peter Marciano.[14]

Marciano also involved himself in the business end of boxing by owning small pieces of several fighters. He testified on Capitol Hill on several occasions during the 1960s, joining other former champions in endorsing the idea of a federal boxing czar to help clean up the sport and rule it with an iron fist. As he explained, "It would be like a policeman on the corner with a big stick. You just wouldn't find any trouble on that corner."[15] Marciano was so enamored with the idea that he offered to serve as the czar at one point.

By the mid-1960s, some fans were seeing Marciano not as a czar but as a returning champion. The spark was the reigning champion, Muhammad Ali. Many sportswriters and fans—especially older ones—didn't like his style, his brashness, his politics, or his religion. As Robert Lipsyte observes, for sportswriters, "Ali was really the litmus test. And it was generational. . . . Here was Ali, who had everything. And the older generation didn't really know how to deal with it because everything flew in the face of what Mr. Man, the heavyweight champion of the world, was supposed to be about." In the 1970s, of course, most would come to see Ali as a figure of respect, affection, and even love. In the mid-1960s, though, many saw him in terms of fear and hate, so much so that Jack Olsen of *Sports Illustrated* observed that Ali was, at the time, "the most hated figure in sport."[16]

Given the racial overtones of all this, and the complete lack of white contenders within the ranks, it was no surprise that many turned their lonely eyes to a Great White Hope from the past: Rocky Marciano. As Bud Collins of the *Boston Globe* observed upon Marciano's death in 1969, "Rocky was a champion people could understand. They saw him as uncomplicated, a family man who trained hard, punched people thoroughly and well, and was good to his parents."[17] Many white Americans neither understood nor liked Ali. They did understand and like Marciano, and by the mid-1960s they wanted him back.

For a while in the fall of 1966, it appeared that they would get him back. There were rampant rumors that Marciano would come out of retirement to fight Ali. At one point, a rich Texan came forward and offered him $4 million to do so. Marciano thought about it and declined the offer. It was a wise decision. He would have found himself in the middle of a racial passion play. Moreover, the forty-three-year-old Marciano had no chance of defeating Ali, who was then at the peak of his powers. A decade earlier it might have been a good match, but not now. As *Sports Illustrated* observed, "Forty-three is no age for a white hope."[18]

Eventually, Marciano did fight Ali—sort of. In 1969 a Miami advertising executive named Murray Woroner came up with the idea of staging a simulated, computer-generated match between Marciano and Ali on closed-circuit television. Because both men were alive and well (Marciano on the banquet circuit, Ali in exile), Woroner could pay them to act out various scenarios in front of the cameras. Then he could feed data on both fighters into the computer, have the computer spit out how a mythical fight between the two would unfold, match the film to the computerized script, and release it across the country, keeping the outcome very much in suspense. And that's what he proceeded to do. Woroner called his brainchild "Superfight."

So, in the summer of 1969, Marciano went on a diet, lost fifty pounds, and put on what boxing historian Bert Sugar called "the worst-looking toupee I've ever seen." Over the course of a week he and Ali boxed more than seventy-five one-minute rounds in a Miami warehouse as the cameras rolled. "They both had a pot on them," recalls a bemused Angelo Dundee. "They were way out of shape. But thank God for the camera work. They looked like they were throwing punches. Slow motion, and they speeded them up with the cameras." Dundee remembered one especially amusing moment: "Muhammad threw a jab that came from the back that picked up the toupee. And Rocky says, 'Cut the cameras, cut the cameras.' He didn't want anybody to know that he had a rug on."[19]

Before Superfight, Marciano was not a big fan of Ali's. "He never did like Muhammad," recalls Dundee. "He said he talked too much." Lipsyte says that Marciano had "told me that he was ashamed of Muhammad Ali because he felt that, in retrospect, it somehow stained the honor of his own championship—it kind of reflected badly on the heavyweight champion." During Superfight, though, according to Dundee, Marciano became "very friendly with Muhammad." Peter Marciano recalls that Ali "always addressed Rocky as 'Champ.' Never called him 'Rocky.' Never called him 'Mr. Marciano.' It was 'Champ.' It was the highest respect that you could give." Still, a competitive fire existed between the two men, at least from Marciano's standpoint. Indeed, after Superfight, Marciano said to Duva, "Ask him about his ribs." When Duva did so, Ali responded, "Oh, man, that guy's crazy" and lifted his shirt to reveal big red welts.[20]

In the end, Woroner's computer produced and Woroner edited. Although few took Superfight seriously—it was, after all, pure American schlock—it did draw extensive media attention. It also drew a large crowd. On the night of January 20, 1970, fans in more than a thousand theaters across the United States paid a combined total of more than $2.5 million to see Superfight. Marciano won via knockout in the thirteenth round. The fact that Marciano had died by the time Superfight was shown only added to the surreal nature of the spectacle. Ali, though, was alive and well. On "fight night" he watched from a Philadelphia theater, supposedly unaware of the outcome like the rest of the fans. At fight's end he grumbled, "That computer was made in Alabama."[21]

Ali shouldn't have been too surprised, for Superfight—what Lipsyte now calls "that ugly computer fight"—managed to unearth festering racial feelings. To many, Marciano (the white champion of decency) had worn the crown with dignity, whereas Ali (the black champion of militancy) had done nothing but demean it. As boxing historian Jeffrey T. Sammons has pointed out, "The staged morality play was a soothing tonic to many Americans who longed to see Ali dethroned in the ring." One reporter allegedly told Ali before the bout, "You won't submit to White America's old image of black fighters, you won't even submit to White America's Army. . . . They want your ass whipped in public, knocked down, ripped, stomped, clubbed, pulverized and not just by anybody, but by a real Great White Hope, and none's around. That's where the computer comes in."[22] And that's where Rocky Marciano came in as well. He had, in a sense, come full circle. He was the Great White Hope once again.

● ● ●

Between his real and surreal flirtations with his old sport, Marciano led a life that was unorthodox, not just for an ex-champion but for anyone else. As champion, his life had been exhausting but predictable: train, fight, barnstorm, then do it all over again. Now his lifestyle became dizzying. After 1956 it involved a succession of hotels and motels and airplanes and restaurants. Marciano was always on the move. One day he would be in Fort Lauderdale, the next he would be gone to Chicago to try and close a business deal. Then it was on to Las Vegas for a personal appearance. Next he would be off to New York to hang out with friends on Broadway, with perhaps a quick stopover in Brockton to see his parents. Although there was an established pace—frenetic—there was no set pattern. Instead, he lived his life in disorganized, unpredictable fashion. He even coined a term to describe his wanderings—*bouncing*.[23]

In the course of his bouncing, Marciano primarily concentrated on making money. He attacked the business world the way that he attacked opponents in the ring: fast and furious and with more than a little bit of wildness. He founded and invested in countless numbers of businesses—a sausage company in Ohio, a restaurant in Maryland, a bowling alley in Florida, a chain of spaghetti restaurants in California, and many, many more. His business partners in these ventures included Jimmy Tomatoes, a hanger-on from the days as champion, with whom he lost heavily in a failed tomato and potato farm venture due to an unexpected Florida frost. Another business partner was, oddly enough, Charley O. Finley, later the notorious penny-pinching owner of the Oakland A's.

There were other many other business partners, of course, as Marciano constantly traveled the country, looking for the next deal and the next sure thing. Some of his ventures made money. Others flopped. Too often, Marciano's thirst for making a deal was not backed by the diligence needed to make the deal a success. He didn't like lawyers, nor did he like banks. He was also exceedingly private when it came to his deals. As Truman Gibson recalls, "In business, Rocky didn't take too much advice about his affairs . . . Rocky would not listen to anyone. We tried to talk with him and he said, 'Well, I know what I'm doing.' He was not a guy that listened to people or really discussed his affairs."[24]

His inherent innocence made him an easy mark for charlatans and scams. "Early on, I think he was taken by people's sincerity," recalls Sonny Marciano. "He was honest and he thought people are like that." The same naiveté hurt him in another postretirement business enterprise: lending money. In the years after his retirement, Marciano loaned hundreds of thousands of dollars to hundreds of people. It was common for him to have a half-million dollars on the street at any given time. A typical Marciano loan had a small interest rate and was unsecured. It also was not recorded in writing. Instead, the trusting Marciano tried to keep track of outstanding loans in his head. Sometimes he remembered who owed him what, and other times he did not. Sometimes he collected on the loan, and other times he did not. As his accountant and friend Frank Saccone recalled, "Rocky was a very articulate, intelligent man, but when it came to business, he was so, so stupid."[25]

● ● ●

In the end, Marciano amassed a considerable fortune in his postretirement years. Along the way, he cultivated an extensive network of friends and associates who participated in his bouncing. Most in the network were average citizens (usually of Italian American descent) who were drawn to Marciano and his lifestyle. There was Saccone, the Brockton accountant who accompanied him on many business trips. There was Dale Miltimore, a former short-order cook and cab driver who served as Marciano's chauffeur. There was Lindy Ciardelli, a wealthy, self-made businessman from San Jose who shared Marciano's love of the fast life. And there were Ben Danzi in New York, Bernie Castro in Florida, Dominic Santarelli in Chicago, and dozens of others, along with multiple personal managers and scores of pilots who carted Marciano around the country in small airplanes.

Marciano's postretirement network also involved women. He had wealth. He had fame. He was constantly on the road. And the road offered certain temptations. "The girls used to fall over him," recalls Sonny Marciano. "We'd go into Toots Shor, and they'd be with Dean Martin, and everybody wanted to sit with Rocky. And Frank Sinatra—they all wanted to be at Rocky's table. And the young girls who tagged along would be in awe of Rocky."[26] Marciano was willing to take advantage of the opportunities that were presented to him on a regular basis.

The spartan regimen that he had kept as champion might have been a factor. As Peter Marciano speculates, "Here he was, after he retired, and girls would kind of like throwing themselves at him. And he said to himself, 'You know, I gave up so much early on. You know, I missed a lot. I want to find out what it was like.'"[27] An even greater factor might have been his marriage to Barbara, which soured and caused Marciano considerable unhappiness after his retirement. Perhaps Marciano viewed sex as a prerogative of power, fame, and celebrity. Whatever the reason, he became a womanizer.

His network also included mobsters. Because Marciano was an Italian American who had been heavyweight champion of the world, Mob guys tended to have a high degree of respect for the Rock. To a large extent the respect was mutual. After all, Marciano liked Italians, he liked big money, and he liked to move fast. His Mob friends were all that, and they had an extra aura of danger about them. As a result, Marciano developed a fascination and even some admiration for members of the underworld. "From our vantage point, they were sincere and friendly and exciting to be with," explained Marciano's friend Ernie Clivio. "They would do everything they could to make us comfortable and show us a good time. Anything else that went on was not our business. Rocky would no more be involved with the shady stuff than I would."[28]

Marciano became friendly with underworld figures throughout the country. He became a business associate of Cleveland racketeer Pete DiGravio and was on his way to visit him when DiGravio was shot to death on a golf course in 1968. He became close friends with Chicago mobster Frankie Fratto, who possessed a long and inglorious criminal record. He even visited the notorious Mafia don Vito Genovese in prison shortly before the latter's death in early 1969.

And he became friends with Frankie Carbo. At the end of his career, Marciano, in a white lie for public consumption, claimed that he had only met Carbo twice. In fact, after meeting Carbo through Weill, Marciano developed a fairly closely relationship with "the underworld commissioner of boxing." He saw Carbo as having class, someone who knew how to dress, how to live, how to move, how to command respect, and how to treat other Italians. Moreover, Marciano liked the aura of danger and excitement that surrounded Carbo, although he hated Carbo's control, and often abuse, of fighters. The Marciano-Carbo relationship, then, was strictly personal and not business.

Marciano—despite his business ties to DiGravio and his associations with the likes of Fratto, Genovese, and Carbo—was never involved in the Mob's illicit dealings. He had too much personal integrity for that type of business. Besides, the Italian underworld viewed Marciano as an Italian folk hero who needed to retain that status. As Peter Marciano recalls, "The Mob guys protected Rocky. They made it known to everyone, 'Don't mess with this man. This is our guy. This is our knight in armor.'"[29] Rocky Marciano needed to remain pure, and despite his associations with gangsters and mobsters that's the way he stayed.

● ● ●

His activities and behavior in the years after his retirement bring sharper focus to Marciano the man. When he reigned as champion, of course, his pristine image reigned. The image-makers of the day made little effort to discover "the real Rocky Marciano" or provide a glimpse into his psyche. After he retired, some of that finally began to come out. Much of this was due to Marciano himself. Once he gave up his regular grind of training, fighting, and barnstorming, he was free to live life as he chose. That life was, in many ways, revealing, as were the personality traits he exhibited along the way. In many instances, the sportswriters, stuck on Marciano's image, failed to report his postretirement activities and behaviors until after he died in 1969. No matter. Such details nevertheless provide a fuller picture of Marciano the man.

Some of the qualities and personality traits he had displayed as champion (both within and outside his image) became more evident after he retired. In some cases they also became more pronounced, particularly his fixation with money. Marciano's old fear of going broke never dissipated. Peter Marciano recalls that his brother was deeply affected when he read about a boxer who had spent all his money and was totally broke.[30] Marciano vowed that the same fate would not befall him, to the point that he once stated that he would rather die then go broke.

Marciano's fear drove a constant pursuit of money—or, to be more exact, cash. Once, for instance, According to an August 23, 1993, *Sports Illustrated* story, he refused to accept a $5,000 check for a speech in Montreal. When his befuddled hosts managed to scrape together $2,500 in cash, though, Marciano happily accepted. Checks involved banks, which Marciano didn't trust. In contrast, the sight of dollar bills seemed to soothe his fears. Besides, cash made it easier to evade obligations to the IRS—or to Al

Weill pursuant to the Marciano-Weill contract that was still in place for a short time after his retirement.

In his life after boxing, observed Jim Murray of the *Los Angeles Times,* "Rocky chased a buck the way he chased Ezzard Charles." He was not only chasing a buck but keeping it in all sorts of strange places. He stashed money in curtain rods. He stuffed it in light fixtures. He hid it in old-fashioned toilets. He placed it everywhere except banks. "Rocky was from the old school," Peter Marciano once recalled. "He didn't trust accountants, bankers and lawyers. He hid the money, and he spread it out. Trying to find it would be an exercise in futility."[31]

Not that the members of his family didn't try. In the years after his death they spent a lot of time searching for Marciano's hidden fortune, which certainly amounted to hundreds of thousands of dollars and may have even been millions (no one knows for sure). Speculation raged over where the cash might reside. Some felt it was somewhere in Altoona, Pennsylvania, where Marciano would often secretly visit. Others believed that it resided in safe-deposit boxes, Swiss bank accounts, or family beach houses. Still others felt it was buried in a bomb shelter that one of Marciano's friends, Bernie Castro, had built on his Florida estate. In the end, no one was sure where Marciano had hidden his money. No one ever found it, and in all likelihood no one ever will.

One thing is certain—whatever money Marciano did make in the years after his retirement, he did not spend it carelessly. "He was very careful of his money and parsimonious," Gibson recalls. "Everything had a price tag with Rocky." Even those who hold Marciano in high regard recognize that he could be thorny when it came to the subject of money. "He never worked for nothing, to be honest with you," admits Duva. "He never spent too much money." Echoes another Marciano fan, Angelo Dundee, "Rocky was frugal. He had that thing about being a frugal guy."[32] In his quest to keep his money, Marciano's greatest enemy became the telephone company. For some reason he felt it was out to get him, and he would go to great lengths to avoid paying for calls. Reversing charges, using slugs, or employing wire contraptions—Marciano did it all to beat the telephone company out of a dime.

Marciano arranged his life so that he didn't have to spend a dime. His network of friends and associates took care of all his travel and lodging needs. He also knew the restaurants where he wouldn't have to pay for meals. When he ate in places that did expect payment for food, he made sure he surrounded himself with people who would pick up the tab. He even became enraged on those few occasions when plans went awry and he was expected to foot the bill. Confirms Peter Marciano, "He knew that if people wanted to be with him, yeah, they had to pick up the tab. No questions about it. He was out with big people with big money and they were getting a lot of mileage [out of his name]—insurance guys, guys in business, 'Yeah, this is my friend, Rocky Marciano.'"[33]

There was plainly a method to his madness. "Rocky was the world's greatest schemer," Dale Miltimore remembers. "He could leave town with thirty cents in his pocket and tour the country and he'd come back with the same thirty cents. He never had transportation, money, or a system, just the connections to get all of these things. The plane tickets, the hotel rooms, the meals, were always on somebody, but never Rocky." All of this required a certain persistence. Jimmy Breslin remembers how Marciano would patiently wait in airports to hitch a ride with a private pilot so that he wouldn't have to fly commercial. "He'd go to the fucking airport and he'd stand there until somebody recognized him," Breslin recalls. "Then he'd ask the guy where he was going."[34] More often than not Marciano would find his man—and avoid the airfare.

All of this also required some gumption. One story about his stratagem for personal appearances made its rounds among sportswriters. "He would arrive that afternoon and they would pick him up at the airport and he would have a small overnight case and he would be in a shirt and jeans," says Robert Lipsyte of the *New York Times*. "And they would ask where was his luggage. And he said he didn't have any. And they said, 'Well, we were kind of thinking that you'd wear a suit and tie.' And he'd say, 'Gee, I'm sorry.' But there would always be somebody on the committee who owned a local haberdashery. So it would end up that he would get completely outfitted and maybe even a new suitcase to put the stuff in."[35]

The story was essentially true. Jimmy Breslin recalls Marciano using the same ploy when he worked with him early in the 1960s. "You're doing a television show in New York and he'd come down Sunday night—you're doing it Monday—looking like he was homeless," says Breslin. "And he'd show up at the show Monday and they'd have to send out for a jacket, slacks. And he'd kid around and say, 'Geez, can't you make it for a bigger guy.'" When asked about his most striking recollection of Marciano, Breslin, who liked Marciano, laughs and says, "Coming down with no clothes."[36]

During his retirement years, when money was at issue Rocky Marciano occasionally stepped out of character. Usually a man who tried to avoid any sort of negative publicity, he nevertheless went to court (and lost) with gardener Cooper Kirk over $706. Although gentle and easygoing outside the ring, Marciano nevertheless slugged writer Gene Schorr over a dispute about money and received a judgment against him for $5,000 in the resulting lawsuit in addition to a stern lecture from the judge on the subjects of fame and self-restraint. On another occasion, Marciano, usually the most loyal of friends, nevertheless allowed his long relationship with Nicky Sylvester to become strained for a time over the disputed amount of $40. Money plainly mattered greatly to Rocky Marciano.

● ● ●

Many would regard these aspects of Marciano's character—womanizing, association with gangsters, and a strange fixation of money—as flaws. Undeniably, and to a large extent, they were. At the same time, however, they must be put into perspective.

Indeed, several of Marciano's shortcomings were understandable, for example, his fixation on money. As Bud Collins points out, in light of Marciano's background, the way he tried to hoard money was "rather understandable. He really was one of those guys who never felt that he still wasn't poor." Breslin goes a step further and suggests that Marciano, when it came to cheapness, was the rule rather than the exception among boxers. "He came out of a town with no money and a prizefighter starting gets $50," Breslin says. "There's no money. And they're cheap." Breslin even alleges that some of Marciano's stranger habits in this regard, such as his schemes against the telephone company, were par for the course among boxers. "There hasn't been one prizefighter in the history of the business who didn't have a dodge on telephones," Breslin says. "That's because the phones were there."[37] In sum, then, when it came to money Rocky Marciano may have been an extreme example, but he was hardly the only example among boxers.

Similarly, Marciano's associations with gangsters—although plainly not flattering to the man—must be viewed in context. Marciano had such associations, but so did most other fighters of the era. Many, in fact, had associations far more nefarious than Marciano's, whose connections to underworld figures were driven by hero worship and ethnic commonality but for the most part did not cross the line between personal and business. Besides, there was a certain inevitability to all this. As Breslin observes, "In that business, who are you going to be close to? The cardinal?"[38]

In the years since Marciano's death, what has really damaged public perception of him is, ironically, his squeaky-clean image. Because his image was so flawless, any information that has leaked out concerning flaws tends to have a certain shock value. In such a scenario, the fact that his flaws may have been somewhat understandable and common can easily be overlooked. Rather, what can seem to matter more—what seems to stand out and shock—is the fact that the flaws fail to correspond to his larger-than-life image.

At the same time, however, Marciano plainly and genuinely possessed many of the positive personality traits that were at the heart of his image. The remembrances of W. C. Heinz are instructive in this regard. In writing several articles on the champion during the early 1950s, Heinz got to know Marciano quite well. The stories he tells a half-century later suggest that image-makers weren't merely engaging in a flight of fancy when it came to the subject of Rocky Marciano. For instance, Heinz remembers once walking with Marciano on Lexington Avenue in New York when Marciano suddenly stopped in the middle of the sidewalk and asked, "You know what somebody told me about Toots Shor?" Heinz did not. Marciano replied, "He told me that Toots Shor could take you out in one punch." With that, Heinz started to laugh. "What are you laughing at?" Marciano immediately asked. Replied Heinz, "You're the heavyweight champion of the world, and you're romanticizing a fat saloonkeeper." As Heinz remembers today, "But that's the way he was. That simplicity."[39]

On another occasion, toward the close of Marciano's career, Heinz was involved in a bidding war to ghostwrite Marciano's autobiography, which eventually appeared in the *Saturday Evening Post*. Heinz was driving in a car with Marciano and Allie Colombo to pick up another sportswriter who was also vying for the job. Suddenly Colombo said, "Look, Rocky, you don't want this guy. You want Bill to write the story. He's been with you. He understands it. He's a better writer." Replied Marciano, "That's right. But you see, I don't mind knocking a guy out in the ring, but I just don't like to hurt anybody's feelings." The incident, Heinz says, demonstrated that Marciano "was not a strong-willed man in that sense," and that he was man "with great empathy, great sympathy."[40]

Sonny and Peter Marciano tell similar stories of kindness about their older brother. For instance, Peter remembers his older brother gently rebuking him for stepping on a grasshopper. "Peter, that's God's creature," Rocky said. "Why would you step on a grasshopper? They're not hurting you." Similarly, Sonny Marciano remembers his older brother defending homosexuals on several occasions in the face of insults and slurs from people in the company of the heavyweight champion of the world. At one function, for example, someone called an artist a queer, causing Marciano to reply, "Does that change things—the fact that he's a queer? Does that make him less of a human being than you or I?" Concludes Sonny, "I think he had a great deal of compassion for the downtrodden—for people that didn't get the opportunity and that didn't get that chance for fulfillment."[41]

These, then, were Rocky Marciano's qualities of decency and kindness and spirit and character. Moreover, in his retirement years he also lived up to many other aspects of his image. One example concerned his loyalty. Although Marciano didn't pay any cash to members of his network who helped facilitate his life after 1956, he did repay them in kind, often in the form of business contacts. Some of his friends nicknamed him "the Golden Key." Explained Lindy Ciardelli, "Rocky had a knack, a special talent, for being able to make things happen . . . Rocky knew all the key people. He was always with guys who would get things done, and who knew how to move and protect his interests on the money. Rocky had the Golden Key to open all the doors."[42]

Marciano was willing to open those doors for friends. "He always introduced me to people, and set me up with the right connections for big accounts," Frank Saccone has recalled. "Wherever we went, he made certain I was really taken care of, wined and dined, the whole bit." Echoed Dale Miltimore, "Rocky would do things for you because he wanted to. He was the kind of a guy who showed his appreciation in strange ways, and anybody who was ever loyal to him never regretted it."[43] There were numerous people who associated with Marciano in the years after his retirement who saw their bank accounts swell because of his loyalty.

With friends, Marciano was also extremely generous with his time. "He was always there in a position to help you out," Lou Duva says. "Any time he could help you, he would help you out." Once, for instance, Marciano was taking a limousine from New York City back to Brockton. "We had this affair going on and we needed a guest speaker," remembers Duva. "And so I called him on the cell [car] phone. . . . He had the guy turn the car around, came down to our dinner, spoke there. He had never met the guy, and he spoke as if he knew him for ten years. Signed autographs, took pictures, and everything."[44]

Marciano was even generous with money when it came to friends and family. "Rocky was so generous with the ones that he loved," says Peter Marciano. "I could name you twenty-five people—guys that grew up with him, that borrowed money from him, that never paid him back. . . . With his family—with his mother and his father, and his siblings, his brothers and sisters—he would go out of his way. 'What can I do for you? I want to do something for you.'" Marciano also provided friends and family with exposure. For instance, Sonny Marciano remembers the efforts Rocky made to promote Sonny's baseball career. "He would always put me in front of him, would always want me to be in the interview," recalls Sonny. "They didn't want me—they wanted Rocky. And he'd always want to talk about, 'This is my brother Sonny. Signed a pro baseball contract.' And he would want me to feel good. He was a very unselfish man."[45]

Marciano was also good to fellow members of the boxing fraternity. Heinz was always struck by his "affinity for the fighters that he fought." It wasn't just affinity. Marciano possessed genuine concern for other boxers. When old fighters slurred words in front of him, remembers Sonny Marciano, "it would bother him. He was very protective of his fellow fighters." Those strong feelings often translated into favors. "He was always good to fighters like Ezzard Charles, Joe Walcott, Joe Louis, all those kind of guys," Duva recalls. "They were part of his life. He went out of his way to do things for them." Duva specifically cites Marciano's efforts to arrange speeches and personal appearances for fellow fighters: "If he was offered $5,000, which he was many times, to speak at some big affair, he would substitute somebody else, some other fighter who was down and out. . . . He'd tell the guy, 'Look, just give the guy $2,500 and I'll give you a date some other time.'"[46]

Along the way, Marciano developed close friendships with numerous boxers, including many he had fought. Duva remembers appearing on a radio show in Miami with Marciano and Joe Louis in the wake of the famous fight in 1964 when Cassius Clay shocked the world by defeating Sonny Liston. After the interview, Marciano, Louis, and Duva were in the same car, which was going down a driveway, when Marciano suddenly got out and began to run alongside the vehicle. "C'mon, Lou," he said. "Joe, let's do it." A startled Louis asked, "Rocky, you take too many punches? What happened? What are we running for?" Replied Marciano, "Did you hear about what they said about that kid out there, Cassius Clay—that he's going to get a million dollars for his next fight?" Louis immediately got out of the car too and said, "Let me run with ya." "That's how close these guys were," remembers Duva.[47]

Marciano was a good friend to boxers and non-boxers alike. "Rocky would always loan me anything I wanted," recalled Willie Pep, the former featherweight champion and a close friend of Marciano. "He'd hold out the cash and tell me to take as much as I needed. If you were a man of your word, The Rock was always right there anytime you needed him." Echoed Dale Miltimore, "Friend? There was never one like Rocky. Rocky really cared about his friends."[48] Many others felt the same way. It was, therefore, no accident that Marciano was surrounded by scores of people after he retired. For sure, they latched onto Marciano in great part because he was a celebrity. They stuck around, however, and even participated in his crazy, topsyturvy lifestyle, because they thought he was a good man and a good friend.

Perhaps is the most telling fact of all—how many, and how much, people genuinely liked Rocky Marciano. All of the sportswriters interviewed for this book (W. C. Heinz, Furman Bisher, Bud Collins, Jimmy Breslin, and Robert Lipsyte) liked Marciano, and several liked him a lot. Former opponent Roland LaStarza says, "The man was a nice guy, that's all. What can I say?" And other members of the boxing fraternity go even farther. Marciano was, praises Lou Duva, "a great guy, great guy." Adds Angelo Dundee, "Rocky, let me tell you something: the nicest guy you ever wanted to meet. A gentleman."[49]

In the final analysis, then, Rocky Marciano the man stands up fairly well against his pristine, all-American-boy image. For sure, he had undeniable flaws. He may have cheated on his wife. He may have exercised poor judgment in associating with members of the underworld. And his love for the almighty dollar certainly drove some behavior that was strange at best and often destructive. As Furman Bisher observes, though, although Marciano had his shortcomings, "Compared to today's standards, he would be virtually a choir boy." "Was he a perfect man?" Peter Marciano asks. "No. But, again, who is?"[50] Moreover, Marciano had a good side and possessed ample and admirable qualities of spirit and character. He may not have lived up to his image in all respects, but neither did he substantially betray it.

● ● ●

If his postretirement wanderings provide a fuller picture of Marciano the man, that picture nevertheless remains incomplete and somewhat unclear. Not many people, even among his closest friends, fully understood Rocky Marciano. Certainly, his fear of poverty played a large part in shaping his existence, but even that does not fully explain the unique and unpredictable life he led after retirement.

Perhaps it was action that drove Marciano, for what he craved, perhaps even as much as money, was excitement. He spent his years as champion in the fast lane, and he was determined to stay there after he stepped down. As Joan Flynn Dreyspool of *Sports Illustrated* observed with some prescience at the time of his retirement, "There has always been more of the showman in Rocky Marciano than some people may have thought. The limelight has never really lost its appeal—perhaps because his vigorous training schedules have not allowed him much of it." In the succeeding years, Marciano spent much of his time trying to stay in the limelight and find action. "He allowed himself to indulge and to get back some of the things that he said no to before," recalls Peter Marciano. "And he wanted it all." Echoes Sonny Marciano, "He wanted to get the very most out of life. He just wanted to cover it all."[51]

Along the way, Marciano acquired a certain recklessness. Once, for instance, as he drove down a Boston highway with Saccone, he became enraged at missing his exit. To return to it, he banged a U-turn and drove into oncoming traffic, weaving between on-rushing cars and screaming, "Get out of the way, you mothers!" The moment he got back to the exit, he became calm once again. Unsurprisingly, he had several wrecks and near-disasters on the road. As brother Sonny recalls, "He was a terrible driver."[52] Marciano was also fearless when it came to airplanes. He would fly in the worst conditions and in the smallest aircraft and remain placid throughout.

To Marciano, this merely represented the proper way of living. "There's no question he was reckless," Sonny Marciano recalls. "But he didn't know he was reckless. It was a way of life. . . . He was of the opinion not to look for danger, but that in order to live a rich, full life you need to walk the tightrope and you need to live dangerously. . . . That was Rocky—life to the fullest." Some of his family and friends attributed his recklessness to feelings of invincibility and indestructibility carried over from the ring. "Rocky didn't think that he would die," observes Sonny. "He didn't fight that way and he didn't think that way. Never negative thoughts."[53]

Restlessness was also an innate part of his personality. As Sonny Marciano recalls, "He was restless early on. . . . My mother used to get him on that when the family was around together. He couldn't sit down to watch a whole television show. A half-hour or an hour show was just too long for him. He had things to do and things to accomplish." In the years after his retirement, though, Marciano became even more restless. As Jim Murray noted upon his death, "Rocky lived life lately as if it were the fifteenth round and he was behind on points. Everytime I saw him of late, he was on the dead run."[54]

The answers to what Marciano was running to or from may have been in his marriage. The union between Rocky and Barbara had begun on the right foot in the early 1950s. Problems soon developed, however. For one thing, the couple was unsuccessful in attempts to have a big family. After daughter Mary Anne was born in 1952, Rocky and Barbara didn't conceive another child, and along the way Barbara suffered five miscarriages. The Marcianos did adopt a son, Rocco Kevin, in 1968, one year before Marciano's death. Many in the Marciano family believe that the child was a product of one of Marciano's extramarital dalliances.

Marciano's celebrity (both as champion and ex-champion) also took its toll on his relationship with Barbara. Sonny Marciano remembers, "She always said, 'I wish you worked at a nine-to-five job where you'd come home and we'd share.' She truly loved Rocky. . . . It was a tough life for her. She had to wait for him."[55] While she was waiting—or perhaps because she was waiting—Barbara developed a drinking problem. She lost interest in traveling and living life in the fast lane. She put on a lot of weight, and both her health and appearance began to decline.

All of this posed a problem for Marciano, who disliked heavy drinking, wanted to live life on the go, and admired physical beauty in a woman. Although he continued to get along with Barbara, he may have begun to view her much as a sister rather than a wife. His frustration with the marriage plainly grew over time. Even a change in locale in the late 1950s from the ranch house in Brockton to a waterfront home in Fort Lauderdale failed to improve matters. In another era Marciano would probably have sought a divorce, but that wasn't an attractive option in the late 1950s or 1960s, particularly given his strict Catholic upbringing.

Marciano stayed in the marriage but not with full participation. Even his undeniable love for his children wasn't enough to keep him at home for very long. Instead, he sought solace on and from the road. The solution only worked partially, however, and it caused some unhappiness, for Marciano believed in the concept of family. "He was not happy with himself because of his situation with his wife," Peter Marciano now says. "This really bothered him a great deal."[56] It is quite possible then that the state of Marciano's marriage drove his need for action and his increased sense of restlessness in the years after retirement—as well as considerable guilt, loneliness, and unhappiness.

Ultimately, though, no one can really be sure of any of this, for Rocky Marciano revealed little of his inner self, even to his closest friends. As one friend observed, "Nobody ever knew Rocky except Rocky, and that was exactly the way he wanted it." Even Peter Marciano concedes that his brother was "very complex. Extremely complex."[57] The great irony of Rocky Marciano's life is that this purportedly simple man and symbol of the Age of Simplicity was somewhat mysterious and complex. In fact, he wasn't simple at all.

14 Rocky

Rocky Marciano's days of wandering ended suddenly and tragically. August 31, 1969, was the eve of his forty-sixth birthday. Marciano was in Chicago and scheduled to fly home to Fort Lauderdale for a birthday celebration that evening. Then a friend—Frank Farrell, an insurance executive—asked him to deliver a speech at a Des Moines steak house that night. Marciano agreed to postpone the trip home and make the appearance. In the early evening, he and Farrell boarded a small, single-engine airplane piloted by Glenn Belz. The weather that night was poor, with a low cloud ceiling and limited visibility, and Belz was not the most experienced of pilots. Somewhere over a field near Newton, Iowa, the aircraft lost power, struck a lone tree in the middle of the field, and skidded into a small ravine. All three passengers on board were instantly killed. Marciano's body was found pinned beneath the wreckage of the battered airplane.

His death was both sad and shocking and elicited a flood of tributes from former opponents. "This is the saddest news I've ever heard," Joe Louis said. "He was a man all youth looked up to and a personal friend of mine," observed Jersey Joe Walcott. "I'm not only saddened, but also deeply hurt." Ezzard Charles said simply, "I am very sorry to hear about it. I always liked Rocky." Fittingly, Archie Moore, from a ring in San Diego, read a poem that he had composed for Marciano:

> At the end of the trail
> When the master calls
> However we stand
> We must surely fall
> Our memories will be measured
> By our good deeds
> We know you have spread them
> Large and Small wish you Godspeed.[1]

In the wake of Marciano's death, several members of Congress, including one from Michigan named Gerald Ford, spoke on the floor of the U.S. House of Representatives to honor him. Editorials lauding him appeared in several newspapers, and, of course, sportswriters rolled out their tributes as well. For one last time they showered praise on Marciano the man. Jim Murray's reaction was typical: "'Champ' will never have quite the same meaning for me."[2]

There was more than a touch of nostalgia to their tributes, for sportswriters who had covered Marciano in the early 1950s were now dealing with a far different sports world. Television's impact was undeniable and pervasive. Boxing was no longer a preeminent sport. Athletes were more pampered, more politicized, more socially aware, more racially conscious, and more controversial than they had been. The world had changed markedly since the Age of Simplicity and become dizzyingly complex. Older sportswriters such as Red Smith, Arthur Daley, and Jimmy Cannon (as well as their older readers) were trying to make sense of it all. To them, the death of Marciano was one more indication—a tragic one—that their old world order was crumbling.

A year earlier, in 1968, Paul Simon and Art Garfunkel had sung, "Where have you gone, Joe DiMaggio?" They may well have substituted Marciano's name for DiMaggio's. Marciano, like DiMaggio, was one of the last larger-than-life heroes. By the late 1960s it had only been a little more than a decade since he had reigned, but it seemed like an eternity. Changes had swept, and were continuing to sweep, through American society, and many longed for a simpler time and simpler heroes. Those who had come of age before the 1960s were actively trying to make sense of a new generation that only several weeks before Marciano's death had gathered en masse at Woodstock. Like others of his generation, and as a true Fifties Man, Marciano probably didn't understand free love, long hair, draft dodging, lack of patriotism, disrespect for authority, and a sense of rebellion. The times, they had indeed changed.

●   ●   ●

In the years after his death, Rocky Marciano slowly began to fade from public consciousness. In part, that was due to the passage of time. The renaissance of Muhammad Ali during the 1970s also obscured the memory of Marciano, for Ali's personality overshadowed all in boxing who had come before him. Moreover, shockingly few people at the heart of the Rocky Marciano story were around to retell it by the mid-1970s. In a strange twist of fate, the three men who had been closest to Marciano during his career—Allie Colombo, Charley Goldman, and Al Weill—all died within a year of him. Barbara Marciano died young, as did others connected to the story such as Jim Norris and Ezzard Charles. Only a few remain who were professionally connected with Marciano; Roland LaStarza is alive and well and living in Florida, and Truman Gibson continues to practice law in Chicago. And, of course, Marciano left a still-vibrant family that includes brothers, sisters, nieces, nephews, and two children.

With most who were part of the story long gone, however, all that remains for many is Marciano's perfect record. He is still an immortal of the sports world, if for no other reason than his yet-unmatched 49-0 record. He also remains in the public consciousness, albeit at its edge. Proof of this came in 1999, when ESPN, with much fanfare and suspense, engaged in a year-long celebration of its list of the fifty greatest athletes of the century. Each of the top fifty received a half-hour special capturing his or her career and impact. No such special was accorded to Rocky Marciano, who, alas, finished fifty-first.

●   ●   ●

Marciano deserves to be remembered more often and more prominently. As a fighter, it is clear that he was the best heavyweight of his age. He was also one of the best of all time. Angelo Dundee puts Marciano in the top echelon of heavyweight champions. "He belongs there," he says. "Undefeated heavyweight champ of the world. He's top ten. He belongs there." Jimmy Breslin goes even farther: "I don't know who was better than Marciano." Was he the best of all time? "He was very close to it."[3]

Yet Marciano usually gets short shrift. In rating heavyweight champions of the past and present, many regard Joe Louis and Muhammad Ali as first-tier and place Jack Dempsey, Joe Frazier, Larry Holmes, and others in the second. Although a few believe that Marciano belongs in the first tier, most place him in the second, a notch below Louis and Ali.

The most frequently raised objections to Marciano's greatness relate to his brief reign, stylistic weaknesses, and failure to fight quality opposition. Each objection has validity. Marciano's reign was indeed remarkably short—less than four years—and he defended his crown only a half-dozen times. In contrast, Louis reigned continuously for almost twelve years, with a wartime interruption. Ali's multiple reigns in the 1960s and 1970s were interrupted by a long exile from the sport as well as a few losses along the way, although combined, he, too, ruled for a long time (more than seven years). Both Louis and Ali defended their crown more often than Marciano defended his. Marciano's reign didn't have the same shelf life.

Marciano's flaws of style, of course, were harped on throughout his career. Try as he might, he always remained wild, awkward, and crude in the ring, even during his best fights and greatest moments. Neither Louis nor Ali, nor a host of other heavyweights throughout the ages, for that matter, had those distinct—and glaring—weaknesses.

It is also fair to question the quality of Marciano's opposition, as sportswriters did throughout his career. This is particularly valid with respect to the first thirty-five fights or so of his career when he fought his share of club fighters and obscure journeymen. In his last dozen or so bouts, though, Marciano faced the best heavyweights then fighting, some of whom were very good. Charles, for instance, was an underrated heavyweight still in his prime when they met, and Walcott and Moore were great fighters who despite advanced age were still lethal and accomplished ring craftsmen. Louis may have had little left when he met Marciano, but the skill that did remain made him a formidable opponent. It is significant that all four of these men were champions at one time or another. They most assuredly were not stiffs, nor were some of the other men whom Marciano faced, such as Roland LaStarza, Rex Layne, and Harry Matthews. They may not have been of championship caliber, but they were quality fighters nonetheless.

Marciano (or, more accurately, Al Weill) may have ducked Moore and even LaStarza for a stretch, but ultimately he avoided no one. He fought the best heavyweights of his era. The answer to the question of "Who'd he ever beat?" is "Everybody of his era." And, really, what more can you ask? As Angelo Dundee says of Marciano, "He was the best of his times. Period."[4]

As were Louis and Ali. The heavyweight division happened to have been stocked with talent when Ali fought (e.g., Sonny Liston, Joe Frazier, George Foreman, and Ken Norton). But did Joe Louis really meet better opponents than Marciano did? Granted, Louis beat some very good fighters, men such as Max Schmeling, Billy Conn, and Walcott. Yet Marciano, too, beat some very good fighters. And Louis also beat a host of members of his bum-of-the-month club. The quality of opposition, then, should only be a minor asterisk on Marciano's record.

Ultimately, of course, Marciano's perfect and unmatched record attests to his supreme talents as a fighter. Other great fighters had the occasional off-night, and when they did, they lost. Even Louis had an off-night, losing to Max Schmeling in 1937. So did Ali against Ken Norton in 1973, Leon Spinks in 1978, and, to a lesser extent, Joe Frazier in 1971. Marciano, too, had off-nights, but he never lost. No other heavyweight in history can make such a claim. It is stunning that Marciano was only knocked down twice (in the first Walcott fight in 1952 and the Moore fight in 1955) and only came close to losing a few times (the first Lowry fight in 1949, the first LaStarza fight in 1950, the first Walcott fight in 1952, and, perhaps, the second Charles fight in 1954). Even when he was not at his best he usually had enough to win comfortably.

How, then, would Marciano have fared against Louis or Ali? It is always a somewhat foolish exercise to compare the athletes of different eras. As Dundee cautions, "You don't try to say, 'Well, so-and-so could have beat so-and-so.' That's bullshit." Yet such comparisons are also inevitable. Duva makes such a comparison—and a distinction as well. Although he states that Marciano was not as great as Ali or Louis, he also points out, "As far as styling goes, Louis was a stylist. For Fancy Dan and promotion, Muhammad Ali was the guy. But in raw terms of fighting, you had to go with Rocky Marciano."[5]

One could surmise that Louis might have been too polished for Marciano, and Ali too fast. But each of those fighters would have had trouble coping with Marciano's primary strengths—his punching power, his ability to take a punch, his stamina, and his determination—which were supreme and in some cases unmatched. At the very least, Marciano would have held his own against an "in his prime" Louis or Ali. Like them, he was a great fighter. Also like them, he belongs in the first tier of the greatest heavyweight champions of all time.

Comparative boxing abilities aside, Rocky Marciano should be remembered, if for no other reason than as a symbol of his times. He was not the only person to symbolize the early 1950s, of course. Dwight Eisenhower is associated with that era, as are men and women from other disciplines. From the world of sports, however, which always supplies powerful metaphors, images, and representatives to capture the essence of an era, no individual came to symbolize the early 1950s with more accuracy and impact than Rocky Marciano. A few other athletes (football's Otto Graham and basketball's George Mikan) also fit the tenor of the times, but they labored in more obscure sports and did not enjoy the spotlight that was cast upon the heavyweight champion of the world. The other sports heroes of the early 1950s who had equal star power to Marciano's were either holdovers from the 1940s (Ted Williams and Stan Musial) or up-and-comers who would blossom more fully later in the 1950s (Willie Mays and Mickey Mantle). Marciano's prime, on the other hand, coincided perfectly with the Age of Simplicity. It was his time.

As a cultural icon of his age, Rocky Marciano came to personify the cherished American Way of Life that emerged to counter the communist threat, both abroad and at home. He also came to embody the American Dream, a concept in which the nation believed and pursued in the early 1950s with earnest vigor. He was, in short, the ideal. He was the sports hero who represented who Americans were and what they strived for as a society in the early 1950s. Marciano the man, of course, while possessing many of the outstanding qualities at the heart of his image, was considerably more complex than his image indicated. He had flaws and even a bit of mystery. But the fact that Marciano's image had a few holes and was represented with a few inaccuracies did not detract from its power. It was close enough to reality to retain a lasting impact.

In the end, the fact that Marciano did not have the same type of social impact of Louis or Ali was, in a sense, a function of time and circumstance. He was certainly every bit as representative of his times. Joe Louis came to symbolize early–1940s patriotism, and two decades later Muhammad Ali came to symbolize mid–1960s freedom and rebellion. In between, Rocky Marciano came to symbolize early–1950s simplicity. He was, indeed, the rock of his times.

Notes

Interviews

Each of the following interviews was conducted via telephone, except for my interview with Peter Marciano, which took place in Canton, Massachusetts.

Furman Bisher, May 11, 2001
Jimmy Breslin, May 4, 2001
Bud Collins, May 15, 2001
Angelo Dundee, May 1, 2001
Lou Duva, May 1, 2001
Truman Gibson, May 3, 2001
W. C. Heinz, May 4, 2001
Roland LaStarza, May 1, 2001
Robert Lipsyte, May 3, 2001
Louis "Sonny" Marciano, June 13, 2001
Peter Marciano, June 7, 2001

Chapter 1: Holyoke

1. *Boston Post,* May 2, 1956, p. 17.

2. Interview with Sonny Marciano; R. Marciano as told to Gross and Hirshberg, *Saturday Evening Post,* September 22, 1956, pp. 26–27, 71–74.

3. *Philadelphia Evening Bulletin,* September 26, 1952, p. 88.

4. Killory is quoted in *Saturday Evening Post,* September 20, 1952, pp. 32–33, 154–56; Minnehan is quoted in *Boston Globe,* September 29, 1952, pp. 1, 7.

5. Holden is quoted in *Saturday Evening Post,* September 20, 1952, pp. 32–33, 154–56; Marciano is quoted in *New York Times,* June 6, 1954, sec. 5, p. 2.

6. Marciano as told to Gross and Hirshberg, *Saturday Evening Post,* September 15, 1956, pp. 24–25, 54–58; Holden is quoted in *Boston Sunday Globe,* September 28, 1952, pp. 1, 62.

7. *Saturday Evening Post,* September 15, 1956, pp. 24–25, 54–58.

8. *Cosmopolitan,* June 1954, pp. 62–67.

9. *Boston Globe,* September 3, 1969, p. 48.

10. Interview with Sonny Marciano.

11. *Boston Post,* July 15, 1951, pp. 23, 25.

12. *Philadelphia Evening Bulletin,* September 29, 1952, p. 33.

13. Ray Fitzgerald, *Champions Remembered* (Brattleboro: Stephen Greene Press, 1982), p. 152.

14. *Boston Sunday Globe,* October 21, 1951, p. 51.

15. Cannon is in *Boston Record American,* September 4, 1969, p. 58; interview with Sonny Marciano.

16. P. Marciano is quoted in *Chicago Tribune,* September 4, 1969, sec. 3, pp. 1, 2; R. Marciano as told to Gross and Hirshberg, *Saturday Evening Post,* October 20, 1956, pp. 36, 147–50.

17. Interview with Peter Marciano; interview with Sonny Marciano.

18. Weill is quoted in *The New Yorker,* November 17, 1951, pp. 102–18; Marciano is quoted in Everett M. Skehan, *Rocky Marciano* (1977, repr. London: Robson Books, 1998), p. 284.

19. Marciano is quoted in *Boston Record American,* September 3, 1969, p. 42, and *Sports Illustrated,* August 23, 1993, pp. 54–68.

20. *Cosmopolitan,* June 1954, pp. 62–67.

21. M. Piccento is quoted in *Sports Illustrated,* January 23, 1956, pp. 28–32, 47; R. Marciano is quoted in *Look,* October 30, 1956, pp. 95–105; interview with Sonny Marciano.

22. Interview with Sonny Marciano; R. Marciano is quoted in *Good Housekeeping,* May 1954, pp. 26–27, 142–44.

23. *Saturday Evening Post,* September 29, 1956, pp. 44–45, 68–74.

24. *The New Yorker,* October 11, 1952, pp. 73–84.

25. Interview with Jimmy Breslin.

26. *Los Angeles Times,* September 1, 1969, pt. 3, pp. 1, 3.

Chapter 2: Providence

1. *Boston Herald Traveler,* September 3, 1969, p. 35.

2. *Saturday Evening Post,* September 20, 1952, pp. 32–33, 154–56.

3. *Saturday Evening Post,* October 13, 1956, pp. 36, 159–62.

4. Liebling is in *The New Yorker,* November 17, 1951, pp. 102–18; Cannon is in *Boston Record American,* October 24, 1969, p. 69.

5. Weill is quoted in *Newsweek,* September 27, 1954, p. 62; Marciano as told to Gross and Hirshberg, *Saturday Evening Post,* September 15, 1956, pp. 24–25, 54–58.

6. *Life,* September 22, 1952, pp. 107–18; interview with Truman Gibson.

7. Interview with Angelo Dundee; interview with Lou Duva.

8. Interview with Jimmy Breslin; Liebling is in *The New Yorker,* November 17, 1951, pp. 102–18.

9. *New York Times,* October 24, 1969, p. 57.

10. *Boston Record American,* October 24, 1969, p. 69.

11. Daley is in *New York Times,* September 26, 1952, p. 28; Marciano as told to Gross and Hirshberg, *Saturday Evening Post,* October 13, 1956, pp. 36, 159–62.

12. Ronald K. Fried, *Corner Men: Great Boxing Trainers* (New York: Four Walls Eight Windows, 1991), pp. 179.

13. Interview with Angelo Dundee; Arcel is quoted in Fried, *Corner Men,* p. 159.

14. Goldman is quoted in *The New Yorker,* October 11, 1952, pp. 73–84, and Fried, *Corner Men,* p. 161; interview with Jimmy Breslin.

15. Goldman is quoted in *Chicago Tribune,* June 18, 1954, pt. 3, pp. 1, 5; interview with Angelo Dundee; Goldman is quoted in *Boston Herald Traveler,* September 2, 1969, p. 24.

16. *San Francisco Examiner,* September 14, 1955, p. 35.

17. *Life,* February 12, 1951, pp. 110–17.

18. Goldman is quoted in *Life,* February 12, 1951, pp. 110–17, and Fried, *Corner Men,* p. 162.

19. Interview with Angelo Dundee; Cannon is in *Boston Record American,* November 14, 1968, p. 78; interview with W. C. Heinz; interview with Angelo Dundee.

20. Goldman is in *Collier's,* January 17, 1953, pp. 20–25, and is quoted in *Boston Post,* September 27, 1952, p. 11.

21. *Look,* January 15, 1952, pp. 70–72.

22. *Boston Sunday Globe,* April 29, 1956, pp. 44, 48.

23. *Providence Journal,* August 31, 1948, p. 7.

24. Everett M. Skehan, *Rocky Marciano* (1977, repr. London: Robson Books, 1998), p. 94.

25. Goldman is quoted in *Providence Journal,* August 31, 1948, p. 7; the Goldman-Marciano conversation is in Fried, *Corner Men,* pp. 165–66.

26. Interview with W. C. Heinz; interview with Angelo Dundee.

27. Goldman is quoted in *Washington Post and Times Herald,* September 15, 1955, p. 28; interview with Lou Duva.

28. Interview with Sonny Marciano.

29. *Providence Journal,* April 28, 1956, pp. 1, 4.

30. Ray Fitzgerald, *Champions Remembered* (Brattleboro: Stephen Greene Press, 1982), p. 154.

31. *Sports Illustrated,* August 23, 1993, pp. 54–68.

32. Weill is quoted in *Boston Herald-Traveler,* September 2, 1969, pp. 21, 24; *Washington Post,* October 1, 1948, p. 7B.

33. *Washington Post and Times Herald,* September 15, 1955, p. 28.

34. *Boston Record American,* September 3, 1969, p. 42.

35. *Providence Journal,* May 3, 1949, p. 10.

36. Marciano is quoted in Skehan, *Rocky Marciano,* p. 122; Weill is quoted in *Saturday Evening Post,* September 20, 1952, pp. 32–33, 154–56.

37. Weill is quoted in *Saturday Evening Post,* September 20, 1952, pp. 32–33, 154–56; Marciano as told to Gross and Hirshberg, in *Saturday Evening Post,* October 13, 1956, pp. 36, 159–62.

38. *Providence Journal,* October 11, 1949, p. 14.

39. *Providence Journal,* November 8, 1949, p. 14.

40. *Providence Journal,* December 20, 1949, p. 8.

41. Ibid.

Chapter 3: New York

1. *Boston Daily Record,* May 4, 1956, p. 64.

2. Interview with Roland LaStarza.

3. *Providence Sunday Journal,* March 26, 1950, sec. 2, p. 2.

4. *New York Times,* March 25, 1950, p. 17.

5. LaStarza is quoted in *New York Herald Tribune,* March 25, 1950, p. 13; interview with Roland LaStarza.

6. Abramson is in *New York Herald Tribune,* March 25, 1950, p. 13, and March 26, 1950, sec. 4, p. 3; New England reporter is in *Boston Daily Record,* March 27, 1950, p. 57.

7. *New York Herald Tribune,* March 26, 1950, sec. 4, p. 3.

8. Abramson is in *New York Herald Tribune,* March 26, 1950, sec. 4, p. 3; Ring is in *Philadelphia Evening Bulletin,* March 25, 1950, p. 11.

9. *Saturday Evening Post,* October 13, 1956, pp. 36, 159–62.

10. *Providence Sunday Journal,* May 1, 1949, sec. 2, p. 6.

11. Interview with Angelo Dundee.

12. *Providence Evening Bulletin,* December 19, 1950, p. 36.

13. *St. Louis Post-Dispatch,* September 15, 1952, pp. 4B–5B.

14. Goldman is quoted in *Time,* September 22, 1952, p. 50, and in *The New Yorker,* November 17, 1951, pp. 102–18; interview with W. C. Heinz.

15. Goldman is quoted in *The New Yorker,* November 17, 1951, pp. 102–18; interview with Jimmy Breslin.

16. Interview with Lou Duva; interview with Angelo Dundee.

17. Goldman is quoted in *Washington Post and Times Herald,* September 15, 1955, p. 28, and *Saturday Evening Post,* September 20, 1952, pp. 32–33, 154–56.

18. *Providence Evening Bulletin,* March 25, 1950, p. 4.

19. Interview with Truman Gibson.

20. Ibid.

21. Ibid.

22. Ibid.

23. Ibid.; interview with Jimmy Breslin.

24. *Sports Illustrated,* January 17, 1955, pp. 11–13, 47–50.

25. Remnick is in, and Pacheco is quoted in, David Remnick, *King of the World: Muhammad Ali and the Rise of an American Hero* (New York: Random House, 1998), pp. 61–62, 188.

26. *New York Times,* December 9, 1960, p. 40.

27. *New York Times,* December 10, 1960, p. 17.

28. *Sports Illustrated,* January 17, 1955, pp. 11–13, 47–50.

29. Interview with W. C. Heinz.

30. Interview with Truman Gibson.

31. Ibid.; interview with Jimmy Breslin.

32. *New York Times,* December 10, 1960, p. 17.

33. *Providence Sunday Journal,* March 25, 1951, sec. 2, p. 6.

34. Daley is in *New York Times,* September 22, 1952, p. 28; Lofquist is in *Providence Sunday Journal,* September 17, 1950, sec. 2, p. 2.

35. *Providence Journal,* June 6, 1950, p. 13.

36. Marciano is quoted in *Boston Sunday Globe,* July 27, 1952, p. 53; Siegel is in *Boston Traveler,* July 11, 1950, p. 34.

37. *Providence Evening Bulletin,* November 14, 1950, p. 34.

38. Lofquist is in *Providence Journal,* March 29, 1951, p. 11, and *Providence Journal,* May 2, 1951, p. 11.

39. *Sports Illustrated,* January 23, 1956, pp. 28–32, 47.

40. Interview with Robert Lipsyte; interview with Angelo Dundee; interview with Lou Duva.

41. Everett M. Skehan, *Rocky Marciano* (1977, repr. London: Robson Books, 1998), p. 197.

42. *Providence Journal,* May 23, 1950, p. 10.

43. *Saturday Evening Post,* October 13, 1956, pp. 36, 159–62.

44. Marciano is quoted in *Boston Daily Record,* July 14, 1951, p. 26; Goldman is quoted in *Life,* September 22, 1952, pp. 107–18.

45. Marciano is quoted in *Boston Post,* July 13, 1951, pp. 1, 13; Jensen is quoted in *Boston Evening American,* July 13, 1951, p. 28.

46. Goldman is quoted in *Boston Post,* May 12, 1955, pp. 1, 15; Marciano is quoted in *Boston Post,* July 13, 1951, pp. 1, 13.

47. Ibid.; the descriptions of the knockout are in *Boston Daily Record,* July 13, 1951, p. 42, and *Boston Post,* July 13, 1951, pp. 1, 13.

48. *New York Times,* July 13, 1951, p. 15.

49. *Boston Evening American,* July 13, 1951, p. 28.

50. Thomas is in *Providence Evening Bulletin,* July 11, 1951, p. 36; Siegel is in *Boston Traveler,* July 12, 1951, p. 16.

51. *Washington Post,* July 14, 1951, p. 8; Marciano is quoted in *Boston Post,* September 28, 1952, p. 35.

Chapter 4: The Great White Hope

1. Randy Roberts, *Papa Jack: Jack Johnson and the Era of White Hopes* (New York: Free Press, 1983), p. 19.

2. Sullivan is quoted in David Remnick, *King of the World* (New York: Random House, 1998), p. 222; Jeffries is quoted in Roberts, *Papa Jack,* p. 31.

3. Roberts, *Papa Jack,* pp. 73–74.

4. Ibid., p. 68.

5. London is quoted in Roberts, *Papa Jack,* p. 68; Jeffries is quoted in Remnick, *King of the World,* p. 222.

6. Jeffrey T. Sammons, *Beyond the Ring: The Role of Boxing in American Society* (Urbana: University of Illinois Press, 1988), p. 51.

7. Chris Mead, *Champion: Joe Louis, Black Hero in White America* (New York: Charles Scribner's Sons, 1985), p. 183.

8. Mead, *Champion,* p. xii.

9. For the quoted descriptions of Layne, see *Boston Post,* September 28, 1952, p. 35; *Louisville Courier-Journal,* October 26, 1951, sec. 2, p. 17; and *Boston Post,* July 12, 1951, p. 15.

10. *Los Angeles Times,* September 21, 1952, pt. 2, p. 9.

11. *Boston Globe,* September 24, 1952, pp. 1, 8.

12. Wray is in *St. Louis Post-Dispatch,* October 23, 1951, p. 2B; Bisher is in *Atlanta Constitution,* October 30, 1951, p. 10; Garrison is in *Charlotte Observer,* July 31, 1952, p. 4B.

13. Bisher is in *Atlanta Constitution,* September 25, 1952, p. 19; Baird is in *New Orleans Times-Picayune,* September 28, 1952, sec. 6, p. 3.

14. Anderson is in *Pittsburgh Courier,* July 21, 1951, p. 14; Bostic is in *New York Amsterdam News,* September 27, 1952, pp. 1, 29; *New York Amsterdam News,* September 27, 1952, p. 29.

15. *Pittsburgh Courier,* July 3, 1954, p. 16.

16. Lacy is in *Baltimore Afro-American,* October 4, 1952, p. 13, and September 19, 1953, p. 16; Bostic is in *New York Amsterdam News,* June 26, 1954, p. 26.

17. *Pittsburgh Courier,* June 5, 1954, p. 14.

18. John Morton Blum, *V Was for Victory: Politics and American Culture during World War II* (San Diego: Harcourt Brace Jovanovich, 1976), p. 220.

19. Harvard Sitkoff, *The Struggle for Black Equality, 1954–1980* (New York: Hill and Wang, 1981), p. 17.

20. Sitkoff, *The Struggle for Black Equality,* p. 14.

21. Gallico is cited in Remnick, *King of the World,* p. 225; Corum is cited in Mead, *Champion,* p. 119.

22. Mead, *Champion,* p. 50.

23. Susan E. Tifft and Alex S. Jones, *The Trust* (Boston: Back Bay Books, 2000), pp. 275–76.

24. Liebling is in *The New Yorker,* October 11, 1952, pp. 73–84, October 2, 1954, pp. 75–87, and October 8, 1955, pp. 104–20; the quoted description of Walcott is in *Atlanta Constitution,* May 16, 1953, pp. 1, 5; the quoted description of Charles is in *Baltimore Sun,* June 19, 1954, p. 15; the quoted description of Moore is in *Newsweek,* August 23, 1954, p. 73.

25. Lewis is in *Cleveland Press,* July 14, 1951, p. 7; Gibbs is in *Baltimore Sun,* September 23, 1952, p. 15.

26. *New York Times,* June 15, 1954, p. 39.

27. *New Orleans Times-Picayune,* September 19, 1954, sec. 6, p. 2.

28. Stone is in *Birmingham Post-Herald,* June 18, 1954, p. 10, and September 23, 1955, p. 13.

29. *Saturday Evening Post,* September 20, 1952, pp. 32–33, 154–56; *Boston Evening Globe,* February 13, 1952, pp. 1, 29; the United Press reporter is in *St. Louis Post-Dispatch,* February 10, 1952, pp. 6E.

30. Interview with Jimmy Breslin.

31. Daley is in *New York Times,* June 6, 1954, sec. 5, p. 2, June 7, 1954, p. 28, and June 8, 1954, p. 31.

32. Interview with Truman Gibson.

33. *New York Amsterdam News,* September 20, 1952, p. 27.

34. *New York Times,* July 25, 1985, pp. B7, B10.

35. Abramson is in *New York Herald Tribune,* September 21, 1952, sec. 3, p. 5; Ring is in *Philadelphia Evening Bulletin,* February 13, 1952, pp. 1, 29.

36. Ring is in *Philadelphia Evening Bulletin,* August 18, 1952, pp. 1, 24; Lewis is in *Cleveland Press,* September 22, 1952, p. 24.

37. *Boston Globe,* September 24, 1952, pp. 1, 8.

38. *San Francisco Examiner,* June 18, 1954, pp. 36, 39.

39. *Baltimore Afro-American,* June 26, 1954, p. 16.

40. *Philadelphia Evening Bulletin,* September 22, 1955, pp. 1, 2.

41. *New Orleans Times-Picayune,* September 23, 1955, p. 31.

42. Interview with Robert Lipsyte; interview with Jimmy Breslin.

43. Greene is in *Detroit News,* September 20, 1955, pp. 29–30; Bisher is in *Atlanta Constitution,* September 20, 1955, p. 7.

44. Interview with Bud Collins.

45. Breit is in *The New York Times Magazine,* September 20, 1953, pp. 24–25, 59, 62; *New York Herald Tribune,* April 28, 1956, sec. 3, pp. 1, 2.

46. The quoted descriptions of Marciano's connections with the IBC are in *Cleveland Press,* July 25, 1952, p. 24, *New York Herald Tribune,* July 28, 1952, p. 17,

and *Boston Globe,* July 29, 1952, pp. 1, 8; Bostic is in *New York Amsterdam News,* July 21, 1951, p. 15, and *New York Amsterdam News,* February 16, 1952, p. 24.

47. *Boston Evening Globe,* July 28, 1952, p. 8.

48. Interview with Jimmy Breslin; interview with Robert Lipsyte; interview with Lou Duva.

49. Interview with Furman Bisher.

Chapter 5: The Uncrowned Champion

1. Louis is quoted in *Time,* October 9, 1950, p. 55.

2. *New York Amsterdam News,* October 27, 1951, p. 27.

3. *Look,* October 2, 1956, pp. 56–60.

4. *Pittsburgh Courier,* October 27, 1951, p. 8.

5. Louis is quoted in *Chicago Daily Tribune,* October 16, 1951, pt. 3, p. 2, and *Providence Evening Bulletin,* October 24, 1951, p. 50; Marciano is quoted in *Boston Evening Globe,* October 24, 1951, p. 28.

6. Marciano is quoted in *Boston Evening Globe,* October 25, 1951, p. 20, *San Francisco Examiner,* October 23, 1951, p. 27, and *New York Times,* September 13, 1953, sec. 5, p. 2.

7. *New York Herald Tribune,* October 26, 1951, p. 21.

8. *The New Yorker,* November 17, 1951, pp. 102–18.

9. Ring is in *Philadelphia Evening Bulletin,* October 26, 1951, p. 37; Lacy is in *Baltimore Afro-American,* October 20, 1951, p. 15.

10. Abramson is quoted in *New York Herald Tribune,* October 26, 1951, p. 21; the veteran fight man is quoted in *Chicago Tribune,* October 26, 1951, pt. 4, p. 1.

11. *Washington Post and Times Herald,* September 14, 1954, p. 41.

12. Marciano as told to Gross and Hirshberg, *Saturday Evening Post,* September 29, 1956, pp. 44–45, 68–74; Goldman is quoted in *Sports Illustrated,* December 5, 1955, pp. 15–16.

13. Marciano is quoted in *Boston Post,* October 27, 1951, p. 8; Seamon is quoted in *Louisville Courier-Journal,* October 27, 1951, sec. 2, pp. 3, 6.

14. Marciano as told to Gross and Hirshberg, *Saturday Evening Post,* September 29, 1956, pp. 44–45, 68–74; Liebling is in *The New Yorker,* November 17, 1951, pp. 102–18.

15. *St. Louis Post-Dispatch,* September 11, 1955, p. 2E.

16. Liebling is in *The New Yorker,* November 17, 1951, pp. 102–18; Marciano is quoted in *Boston Evening Globe,* October 27, 1951, p. 5; Louis is quoted in *New York Times,* October 27, 1951, p. 12.

17. *The New Yorker,* November 17, 1951, pp. 102–18.

18. Marciano is quoted in *Boston Globe,* October 27, 1951, p. 4; Goldman is quoted in *St. Louis Post-Dispatch,* October 27, 1951, p. 6A.

19. Marciano is quoted in *Boston Globe,* October 27, 1951, p. 4; Louis is quot-

ed in *Detroit News,* October 27, 1951, p. 11, and *Boston Globe,* October 27, 1951, p. 4.

20. *The New Yorker,* November 17, 1951, pp. 102–18.

21. *New York Times,* October 27, 1951, p. 12.

22. *Boston Globe,* October 27, 1951, p. 4.

23. Marciano is quoted in *Time,* November 5, 1951, p. 97, and *Los Angeles Times,* October 27, 1951, pt. 3, pp. 1–2.

24. Interview with Peter Marciano; interview with Lou Duva; Falloni is quoted in *Boston Herald Traveler,* September 2, 1969, pp. 1, 24.

25. Smith is in *New York Herald Tribune,* October 28, 1951, sec. 3, p. 3; Daley is in *New York Times,* October 28, 1951, sec. 5, p. 2.

26. Goldman is quoted in *Saturday Evening Post,* September 20, 1952, pp. 32–33, 154–56; Lofquist is in *Providence Journal,* April 18, 1952, p. 10.

27. LeDuc is in *Detroit News,* October 28, 1951, pt. 2, p. 2; Louis is quoted in *Pittsburgh Courier,* November 3, 1951, p. 14.

28. *Boston Post,* October 23, 1951, p. 16.

29. Marciano is quoted in *Boston Sunday Globe,* October 21, 1951, p. 51, and Don Dunphy, *Don Dunphy at Ringside* (New York: Henry Holt, 1988), p. 81.

30. Goldman is quoted in *Washington Post and Times Herald,* September 15, 1955, p. 28; Weill is quoted in *Saturday Evening Post,* September 20, 1952, pp. 32–33, 154–56; Hern is in *Boston Post,* October 30, 1951, p. 18.

31. Ring is in *Philadelphia Evening Bulletin,* February 13, 1952, pp. 1, 29; Thomas is in *Providence Evening Bulletin,* February 14, 1952, p. 43.

32. Interview with Sonny Marciano; Marciano as told to Gross and Hirshberg, *Saturday Evening Post,* October 13, 1956, pp. 36, 159–62.

33. *Providence Journal,* April 18, 1952, p. 10.

34. *Philadelphia Evening Bulletin,* February 7, 1952, p. 37.

35. *Philadelphia Evening Bulletin,* February 14, 1952, p. 41.

36. Marciano is quoted in *New York Herald Tribune,* February 14, 1952, p. 22; Pollock is in *Philadelphia Evening Bulletin,* February 15, 1952, p. 32.

37. *Boston Post,* February 15, 1952, p. 21.

38. Gibbs is in *Baltimore Sun,* February 15, 1952, p. 20; Pollock is in *Philadelphia Evening Bulletin,* February 15, 1952, p. 32; Keane is in *Boston Globe,* February 14, 1952, pp. 1, 12.

39. Dawson is in *New York Times,* February 14, 1952, p. 33; Ring is in *Philadelphia Evening Bulletin,* February 14, 1952, pp. 1, 41.

40. Goldman is in *Collier's,* January 17, 1953, pp. 20–25; Thomas is in *Providence Evening Bulletin,* May 13, 1952, p. 26.

41. *Denver Post,* July 28, 1952, p. 19.

42. *Sports Illustrated,* May 22, 1961, pp. 90–104.

43. Ibid.

44. *New York Herald Tribune,* July 26, 1952, p. 13.

45. Nason is in *Boston Globe,* July 28, 1952, p. 5; Hurley is quoted in *Boston Evening Globe,* July 26, 1952, p. 6.

46. The Matthews-Hurley exchange is quoted in *New Orleans Times-Picayune,* July 28, 1952, p. 24; Matthews is quoted in *Washington Post,* July 28, 1952, p. 8.

47. Norris is quoted in *Sports Illustrated,* May 22, 1961, pp. 90–104; Goldman is quoted in *Washington Post,* July 27, 1952, p. 2C.

48. *New York Herald Tribune,* July 29, 1952, pp. 21, 23.

49. *San Francisco Examiner,* July 29, 1952, pp. 19, 20.

50. Goldman is quoted in Ronald K. Fried, *Corner Men: Great Boxing Trainers* (New York: Four Walls Eight Windows), p. 171, and *Boston Post,* July 29, 1952, p. 15.

51. *Sports Illustrated,* May 22, 1961, pp. 90–104.

52. The "limp rag doll" description is in *Los Angeles Times,* July 29, 1952, pt. 4, pp. 1, 3; Goldman is quoted in *New York Herald Tribune,* July 29, 1952, p. 21; Weill is quoted in *The New Yorker,* October 11, 1952, pp. 73–84.

53. Hurley is quoted in *Providence Evening Bulletin,* July 29, 1952, p. 20, and *Los Angeles Times,* July 29, 1952, pt. 4, p. 3; Matthews and Hurley are quoted in *Providence Evening Bulletin,* July 29, 1952, p. 20.

54. Marciano is quoted in *New York Times,* July 29, 1952, p. 24; Ring is in *Philadelphia Evening Bulletin,* July 29, 1952, pp. 1, 39, 41.

Chapter 6: Jersey Joe

1. The quoted description of Walcott is in *New York Times,* May 15, 1953, p. 29; Walcott is quoted in *Saturday Evening Post,* June 12, 1948, pp. 20–21, 136–41; the Walcott-Mendel exchange is quoted in *Chicago Tribune,* May 4, 1953, pt. 4, p. 2.

2. Finch is in *Los Angeles Times,* September 23, 1952, pt. 4, p. 1; Considine is in *San Francisco Examiner,* May 14, 1953, p. 34.

3. *Saturday Evening Post,* June 12, 1948, pp. 20–21, 136–41.

4. *Saturday Evening Post,* June 19, 1948, pp. 28, 118–22.

5. Considine is in *San Francisco Examiner,* May 14, 1953, p. 34; Bisher is in *Atlanta Constitution,* May 19, 1953, p. 7; Bocchicchio is quoted in *Chicago Daily Tribune,* May 8, 1953, pt. 4, pp. 1–2.

6. *Time,* December 15, 1947, pp. 47–48.

7. *Life,* July 30, 1951, pp. 66–67.

8. Corum is in *San Francisco Examiner,* May 17, 1953, p. 48; the Blondell anecdote is in *Life,* July 5, 1948, pp. 57–58.

9. *New York Herald Tribune,* September 21, 1952, sec. 3, p. 5.

10. Smith is in *New York Herald Tribune,* September 21, 1952, sec. 3, p. 5, and September 25, 1952, p. 30; Abramson is in *New York Herald Tribune,* September 14, 1952, sec. 3, p. 5.

11. *New York Times,* September 23, 1952, p. 27.

12. Walcott is quoted in *Baltimore Afro-American,* September 20, 1952, p. 16,

and *New York Herald Tribune,* September 14, 1952, sec. 3, p. 5; Ring is in, and Walcott is quoted in, *Philadelphia Evening Bulletin,* September 4, 1952, p. 36.

13. *Saturday Evening Post,* September 29, 1956, pp. 44–45, 68–74.

14. *Baltimore Afro-American,* September 6, 1952, p. 16.

15. Marciano is quoted in *Baltimore Afro-American,* September 6, 1952, p. 16; Colombo is quoted in *Boston Globe,* November 13, 1968, p. 38.

16. Goldman is quoted in *New York Herald Tribune,* September 23, 1952, p. 28; Donaghey is in *Philadelphia Evening Bulletin,* September 23, 1952, pp. 57–58; Reinauer is quoted in *Boston Post,* September 23, 1952, pp. 1, 26.

17. *Philadelphia Evening Bulletin,* September 2, 1969, pp. 59, 63.

18. Martin is in *Baltimore Sun,* September 23, 1952, p. 15; Smith is in *Pittsburgh Courier,* September 13, 1952, p. 14; Baird is in *New Orleans Times-Picayune,* September 23, 1952, p. 18.

19. *Pittsburgh Courier,* September 20, 1952, p. 14.

20. Daley is in *New York Times,* September 25, 1952, p. 40; Fleisher is cited in *Denver Post,* May 14, 1953, p. 33.

21. The quotation is taken from the video of the fight.

22. *New York Herald Tribune,* June 16, 1954, p. 23.

23. *New York Times,* June 7, 1954, p. 28.

24. *New York Times,* September 25, 1952, p. 40.

25. Daley is in *New York Times,* September 24, 1952, p. 41; Walcott is quoted in *San Francisco Examiner,* September 24, 1952, pp. 35, 37.

26. *The New Yorker,* October 11, 1952, pp. 73–84.

27. *Boston Post,* September 25, 1952, p. 22.

28. Interview with Jimmy Breslin.

29. Daley is in *New York Times,* September 24, 1952, p. 41; Liebling is in *The New Yorker,* October 11, 1952, pp. 73–84.

30. *New York Herald Tribune,* September 25, 1952, p. 30.

31. Abramson is in *New York Herald Tribune,* September 24, 1952, pp. 1, 30; Liebling is in *The New Yorker,* October 11, 1952, pp. 73–84; Daley is in *New York Times,* September 2, 1969, p. 54; Pollock is in *Philadelphia Evening Bulletin,* September 25, 1952, p. 37; Liebling is in *The New Yorker,* October 11, 1952, pp. 73–84.

32. Abramson is in *New York Herald Tribune,* September 24, 1952, pp. 1, 30; Smith is in *New York Herald Tribune,* September 24, 1952, p. 30.

33. Marciano is quoted in *Newsweek,* October 6, 1952, pp. 102–6; Daley is in *New York Times,* September 25, 1952, p. 40; Lacy is in *Baltimore Afro-American,* October 4, 1952, p. 15.

34. Ring is in *Philadelphia Evening Bulletin,* September 24, 1952, pp. 1, 29, 32; Walcott is quoted in *San Francisco Examiner,* September 24, 1952, pp. 35, 37.

35. Smith is in *New York Herald Tribune,* May 15, 1953, p. 27; Liebling is in *The New Yorker,* October 11, 1952, pp. 73–84.

36. *Boston Post,* September 25, 1952, p. 22.

37. Salsinger is in *Detroit News,* September 25, 1952, pp. 59–60; Smith is in *New York Herald Tribune,* September 24, 1952, p. 30; Marciano is quoted in *New York Herald Tribune,* September 25, 1952, p. 30.

38. *New York Herald Tribune,* May 15, 1953, p. 27.

39. *Chicago Tribune,* May 6, 1953, pt. 4, p. 3.

40. Kaese is quoted in *Boston Globe,* May 15, 1953, p. 16; Marciano is quoted in *Detroit News,* May 15, 1953, p. 67, and *New York Herald Tribune,* May 12, 1953, p. 28.

41. Smith is in *New York Herald Tribune,* May 16, 1953, p. 15; Abramson is in *New York Herald Tribune,* May 17, 1953, sec. 3, pp. 1, 3; Marciano as told to Gross and Hirshberg, *Saturday Evening Post,* October 6, 1956, pp. 42–43, 126–28.

42. Bocchicchio is quoted in *Atlanta Constitution,* May 16, 1953, pp. 1, 5; the Walcott-Sikora exchange is in *Pittsburgh Courier,* May 23, 1953, p. 14.

43. Bocchicchio is quoted in *Chicago Tribune,* May 16, 1953, pt. 2, p. 1, and *Los Angeles Times,* May 16, 1953, pt. 3, p. 2; Florio is quoted in *Pittsburgh Courier,* May 23, 1953, p. 14.

44. *New York Herald Tribune,* May 19, 1953, p. 30.

45. *Boston Daily Record,* May 2, 1956, p. 83.

46. *New York Herald Tribune,* May 16, 1953, p. 15.

47. *Washington Post,* May 16, 1953, pp. 1, 14.

48. Sikora is quoted in *New York Herald Tribune,* May 17, 1953, sec. 3, p. 3; Ring is in *Philadelphia Evening Bulletin,* May 18, 1953, pp. 1, 37; Marciano is quoted in *New York Herald Tribune,* May 17, 1953, sec. 3, pp. 1, 3.

49. Florio is quoted in *Baltimore Afro-American,* September 26, 1953, p. 15; Braddock is quoted in *Washington Post,* May 17, 1953, p. 3C.

50. *Denver Post,* May 17, 1953, p. 2B.

51. Ring is in *Philadelphia Evening Bulletin,* May 16, 1953, pp. 1, 15, 16; Bostic is in *New York Amsterdam News,* May 23, 1953, pp. 31, 38; Smith is in *New York Herald Tribune,* May 16, 1953, p. 15; Ward is in *Chicago Tribune,* May 20, 1953, pt. 3, p. 1.

52. Linthicum is in *Baltimore Sun,* May 17, 1953, p. 2D; McCurley is cited in *Philadelphia Evening Bulletin,* May 17, 1953, sec. 2, p. 5; Corum is in *San Francisco Examiner,* May 17, 1953, p. 48.

53. *New York Herald Tribune,* May 17, 1953, sec. 3, pp. 1, 3.

54. *Cleveland Press,* May 16, 1953, pp. 1, 10.

Chapter 7: The Ideal

1. Chris Mead, *Champion: Joe Louis, Black Hero in White America* (New York: Charles Scribner's Sons, 1985), pp. 52–54.

2. Interview with Robert Lipsyte.

3. Jeffrey T. Sammons, *Beyond the Ring: The Role of Boxing in American Society* (Urbana: University of Illinois Press, 1988), p. 184.

4. Stephen J. Whitfield, *The Culture of the Cold War* (Baltimore: Johns Hopkins University Press, 1991), p. 17.

5. Whitfield, *The Culture of the Cold War,* p. 53.

6. David Halberstam, *The Fifties* (New York: Villard Books, 1993), pp. 508–14.

7. Mead, *Champion,* p. 9.

8. *Boston Sunday Globe,* October 28, 1951, pp. 1, 12; *Chicago Tribune,* May 16, 1953, pt. 2, pp. 1, 2.

9. *New Orleans Times-Picayune,* October 24, 1953, p. 14.

10. B. Marciano is quoted in *Boston Evening Globe,* September 15, 1953, p. 14, and *Chicago Tribune,* May 16, 1953, pt. 2, pp. 1, 2.

11. The quoted description of Marciano as "a devoted family man" is in *Detroit News,* September 23, 1953, pp. 71–72; Cohane is in *Look,* February 10, 1953, pp. 87–91; Goldman is in *Collier's,* January 17, 1953, pp. 20–25.

12. For Marciano's interviews with Ward and Daley, see *Chicago Tribune,* September 21, 1953, pt. 4, p. 1, and *New York Times,* September 11, 1953, p. 28.

13. Bentley is quoted in *Chicago Tribune,* September 4, 1969, sec. 3, pp. 1, 2; P. Marciano is quoted in *Boston Globe,* May 13, 1955, p. 41.

14. Hirshberg is in *Saturday Evening Post,* September 20, 1952, pp. 32–33, 154–56; Garrison is in *Charlotte Observer,* June 15, 1954, p. 6–B.

15. Nichols is in *New York Times,* June 18, 1954, p. 27; the Brockton resident is quoted in *Cosmopolitan,* June 1954, pp. 62–67.

16. *Cosmopolitan,* June 1954, pp. 62–67.

17. Daley is in *New York Times,* September 22, 1952, p. 28; Cohane is in *Look,* February 10, 1953, pp. 87–91.

18. Jennings is in *Philadelphia Sunday Bulletin,* September 28, 1952, p. 9; Smith is in *Life,* September 22, 1952, pp. 107–18.

19. Cohane is in *Look,* January 27, 1953, pp. 67–71; Daley is in *New York Times,* September 23, 1953, p. 40; Marciano is quoted in *Time,* September 22, 1952, p. 50.

20. Abramson is in *New York Herald Tribune,* March 24, 1950, p. 27; Zimmerman is in *Los Angeles Times,* September 25, 1952, pt. 4, p. 1.

21. *Chicago Daily Tribune,* April 24, 1953, pt. 3, p. 3.

22. The quoted descriptions of Marciano's religiousness are in *Detroit News,* September 23, 1953, pp. 71–72, and *Chicago Tribune,* September 25, 1953, pt. 4, pp. 1, 2; Liston is in *Boston Post,* September 26, 1952, p. 27; Cohane is in *Look,* February 10, 1953, pp. 87–91.

23. Breit is in *The New York Times Magazine,* September 20, 1953, pp. 24–25, 59, 62; Marciano is quoted in *Boston Globe,* September 3, 1969, pp. 45, 48.

24. The Marciano–party host exchange is in *New York Times,* June 6, 1954, sec. 5, p. 2; Smith is in *New York Herald Tribune,* September 14, 1954, p. 28; Cohane is in *Look,* February 10, 1953, pp. 87–91; *Life,* September 22, 1952, pp. 107–18.

25. Smith is in *Life,* September 22, 1952, pp. 107–18; Cohane is in *Look,* February 10, 1953, pp. 87–91; the ice cream picture is in *Saturday Evening Post,* September 22, 1956, pp. 26–27, 71–74.

26. Cohane is in *Look,* October 30, 1956, pp. 95–105; Daley is in *New York Times,* June 6, 1954, sec. 5, p. 2; Cannon is in *Boston Record American,* September 7, 1969, p. 59; Goldman is quoted in *New York Times,* June 6, 1954, sec. 5, p. 2.

27. Breit is in *The New York Times Magazine,* September 20, 1953, pp. 24–25, 59, 62; Pett is in *St. Louis Post-Dispatch,* September 11, 1955, p. 2G.

28. Marciano is quoted in *New York Times,* September 11, 1953, p. 28; Goldman is quoted in *Boston Evening Globe,* September 17, 1952, p. 30; Breit is in *The New York Times Magazine,* September 20, 1953, pp. 24–25, 59, 62.

29. Cannon is in *Boston Sunday Advertiser,* September 7, 1969, p. 59; Daley is in *New York Times,* September 24, 1953, p. 47, and May 18, 1955, p. 39; Woodward is in *Boston Evening Globe,* September 22, 1953, p. 39; Martin is in *San Francisco Examiner,* September 14, 1955, p. 35; Sullivan is in *San Francisco Examiner,* May 19, 1955, pp. 34, 39.

30. Daley is in *New York Times,* September 25, 1952, p. 40; Cooke is in *New York Herald Tribune,* April 28, 1956, sec. 3, p. 1; Liebling is in *The New Yorker,* October 11, 1952, pp. 73–84.

31. Murray is in *Boston Evening Globe,* September 2, 1969, p. 25; the golf anecdote and the Franklin Field anecdote are in *Washington Post and Times Herald,* April 28, 1956, p. 8; Gillooly is in *Boston Sunday Advertiser,* April 29, 1956, p. 30; Breit is in *The New York Times Magazine,* September 20, 1953, pp. 24–25, 59, 62.

32. Marciano is quoted in *St. Louis Post-Dispatch,* September 11, 1955, p. 2G; Brown is in *Philadelphia Sunday Bulletin,* June 20, 1954, sec. 2, p. 3; Daley is in *New York Times,* September 20, 1955, p. 36.

33. *Time,* September 22, 1952, p. 50; Smith is in *Life,* September 22, 1952, pp. 107–18.

34. Daley is in *New York Times,* September 25, 1952, p. 40, September 11, 1953, p. 28, June 6, 1954, sec. 5, p. 2, and September 11, 1955, sec. 5, p. 2.

35. Keefe is in *New Orleans Times-Picayune,* October 22, 1953, p. 39, and October 23, 1953, p. 26; Kaese is in *Boston Globe,* September 20, 1952, p. 7; Smith is in *Boston Globe,* September 3, 1969, pp. 45, 48.

36. *New York Times,* September 13, 1953, sec. 5, p. 2.

37. *St. Louis Post-Dispatch,* April 29, 1956, p. 3E.

38. Halberstam, *The Fifties,* pp. ix–xi.

39. Marciano is quoted in *New York Times,* September 11, 1953, p. 28, and June 6, 1954, sec. 5, p. 2; Marciano as told to Gross and Hirshberg, *Saturday Evening Post,* September 15, 1956, pp. 24–25, 54–58.

40. Ward is in *Chicago Tribune,* September 26, 1953, pt. 2, p. 1; Daley is in *New York Times,* September 13, 1953, sec. 5, p. 2.

41. The quoted descriptions of Marciano are in *Saturday Evening Post,* September 20, 1952, pp. 32–33, 154–56, and *Life,* September 22, 1952, pp. 107–18; Goldman is quoted in *Life,* September 22, 1952, pp. 107–18; quoted descriptions of Marciano are in *Life,* September 22, 1952, pp. 107–18, and *Detroit News,* September 25, 1952, p. 62.

42. Interview with Bud Collins; Marciano is quoted in *Philadelphia Evening Bulletin*, September 27, 1952, p. 12.

43. *San Francisco Examiner*, April 28, 1955, p. 30.

44. Interview with Bud Collins; interview with Robert Lipsyte; interview with Jimmy Breslin.

45. Lewis is in *Cleveland Press*, June 19, 1954, p. 10; the Marciano-Liston exchange is in *Boston Post*, May 8, 1955, pp. 33, 35.

46. The "Havana-curtain" description is in *Boston Post*, September 27, 1952, p. 9; Daley is in *New York Times*, September 2, 1969, p. 54.

47. Interview with Jimmy Breslin; Ward is in *Chicago Tribune*, May 16, 1953, pt. 2, pp. 1, 2.

48. Lewis is in *Cleveland Press*, September 19, 1952, p. 20, May 12, 1953, p. 34, June 15, 1954, p. 28, and June 19, 1954, p. 10; interview with Jimmy Breslin.

49. Jerome Holtzman, *No Cheering in the Press Box* (New York: Henry Holt, 1995), p. 259.

50. *Time*, September 22, 1952, p. 50.

51. Interview with Furman Bisher; interview with Bud Collins.

52. Interview with Robert Lipsyte.

53. Interview with W. C. Heinz; interview with Robert Lipsyte; interview with Jimmy Breslin.

54. Interview with Bud Collins; interview with Furman Bisher.

55. *Boston Post*, September 26, 1952, p. 27.

56. *Washington Post and Times Herald*, September 20, 1955, p. 20.

57. Holtzman, *No Cheering in the Press Box*, p. 146.

Chapter 8: The Ugly Duckling

1. *Pittsburgh Courier*, June 6, 1953, p. 14.

2. Ibid.

3. Heinz is in *Saturday Evening Post*, September 19, 1953, pp. 36, 152–56; Brown is in *Philadelphia Evening Bulletin*, September 24, 1953, p. 45; the description of LaStarza as a Notre Dame halfback is in *New York Times*, September 22, 1953, p. 41.

4. For quoted descriptions of LaStarza, see *Detroit News*, September 23, 1953, pp. 71–72 ("college man") and *Louisville Courier-Journal*, September 24, 1953, sec. 2, p. 7 ("college-educated boxer").

5. *Saturday Evening Post*, September 19, 1953, pp. 36, 152–56.

6. Ibid.

7. Interview with Roland LaStarza.

8. LaStarza is quoted in *Saturday Evening Post*, September 19, 1953, pp. 36, 152–56; interview with W. C. Heinz.

9. LaStarza is quoted in *New York Times*, September 22, 1953, p. 41, *San Francisco Examiner*, September 21, 1953, p. 47, and *Saturday Evening Post*, September 19, 1953, pp. 36, 152–56.

10. Interview with Peter Marciano; interview with Roland LaStarza.

11. Marciano is quoted in *Boston Post,* September 28, 1952, p. 35; the quoted "skeleton in Rocky Marciano's fistic closet" description is in *New York Herald Tribune,* September 25, 1953, pp. 1, 16; Marciano is quoted in *Boston Post,* September 24, 1953, pp. 1, 21.

12. *New York Herald Tribune,* September 25, 1953, p. 16.

13. *New York Herald Tribune,* September 26, 1953, p. 14.

14. Marciano is quoted in *Boston Post,* September 25, 1953, p. 34; LaStarza is quoted in *Chicago Tribune,* June 8, 1954, pt. 6, p. 6; Marciano is quoted in *New York Times,* September 25, 1953, p. 24.

15. Interview with Roland LaStarza.

16. Ibid.; interview with Peter Marciano.

17. Marciano is quoted in *New York Times,* September 25, 1953, p. 24; the anecdote involving Marciano and LaStarza's father is in *Philadelphia Evening Bulletin,* September 25, 1953, pp. 1, 37.

18. *San Francisco Examiner,* September 25, 1953, pp. 38, 43.

19. *Los Angeles Times,* September 25, 1953, pt. 4, p. 2.

20. *Cleveland Press,* September 23, 1953, p. 22.

21. *New York Times,* June 7, 1954, p. 28.

22. *Newsweek,* October 5, 1953, p. 76; Brown is in *Philadelphia Evening Bulletin,* September 25, 1953, p. 37; Considine is in *Atlanta Constitution,* September 25, 1953, pp. 12, 14.

23. Martin is in *Louisville Courier-Journal,* June 19, 1954, sec. 2, p. 3; Goldman is quoted in Ronald K. Fried, *Corner Men: Great Boxing Trainers* (New York: Four Walls Eight Windows, 1991), p. 172.

24. Cannon is cited in *Newsweek,* October 5, 1953, p. 76; Abramson is in *New York Herald Tribune,* September 26, 1953, p. 14; Salsinger is in *Detroit News,* September 26, 1953, pp. 13–14.

25. *Louisville Courier-Journal,* June 19, 1954, sec. 2, p. 3.

26. Goldman and Marciano are quoted in *Washington Post and Times Herald,* June 14, 1954, p. 19.

27. The "inverted tree trunks" description is in *The New York Times Magazine,* September 20, 1953, pp. 24–25, 59, 62; Liebling is in *The New Yorker,* October 11, 1952, pp. 73–84.

28. Interview with Jimmy Breslin; Charles is in *Pittsburgh Courier,* September 25, 1954, p. 14; the Marciano-Smith exchange is in *New York Herald Tribune,* September 12, 1952, p. 21.

29. Reynolds is quoted in *New York Times,* November 15, 1992, sec. CN, p. 21; interview with Roland LaStarza; interview with Angelo Dundee.

30. Wolf is in *Los Angeles Times,* June 13, 1954, pt. 2, p. 8; Goldman is quoted in *New York Herald Tribune,* May 13, 1953, p. 29.

31. *Detroit News,* September 12, 1955, p. 25.

32. Smith is in *New York Herald Tribune*, September 26, 1953, p. 15; Schulberg is in *Sports Illustrated*, October 3, 1955, pp. 36–39.

33. *Boston Post*, May 20, 1955, p. 23.

34. Brown is quoted in *Boston Evening Globe*, May 16, 1953, p. 7; Charles is quoted in *Washington Post and Times Herald*, September 21, 1955, p. 29; Baird is in *New Orleans Times-Picayune*, September 19, 1955, p. 28.

35. Interview with Peter Marciano; interview with Lou Duva.

36. Salsinger is in *Detroit News*, May 12, 1953, p. 37; Goldman is quoted in *Boston Post*, September 19, 1953, p. 7.

37. McGoogan is in *St. Louis Post-Dispatch*, June 18, 1954, p. 6C; Abramson is in *New York Herald Tribune*, September 18, 1955, sec. 3, p. 7.

38. LaStarza is quoted in *New York Times*, September 25, 1953, p. 24; Daley is in *New York Times*, September 20, 1955, p. 36; Moore is quoted in *Life*, October 3, 1955, pp. 34–35.

39. Interview with W. C. Heinz; Marciano is quoted in *Boston Post*, September 21, 1952, p. 31; Goldman is quoted in *St. Louis Post-Dispatch*, September 11, 1955, p. 2G.

40. Interview with Lou Duva; interview with Angelo Dundee.

41. Povich is in *Washington Post*, September 2, 1969, p. D1; Goldman is quoted in *St. Louis Post-Dispatch*, September 11, 1955, p. 2G.

42. Interview with W. C. Heinz.

43. Goldman is quoted in *Sports Illustrated*, December 3, 1956, p. 32; Breit is in *The New York Times Magazine*, September 20, 1953, pp. 24–25, 59, 62.

44. R. Marciano is quoted in *St. Louis Post-Dispatch*, September 11, 1955, p. 2G; interview with Sonny Marciano; interview with Peter Marciano.

45. Marciano is quoted in *Chicago Tribune*, June 18, 1954, pt. 3, pp. 1, 5, and *Sports Illustrated*, January 23, 1956, pp. 28–32, 47.

46. Interview with Peter Marciano; Grayson and Attell are quoted in *Look*, October 16, 1956, pp. 61–68; Abramson is in *New York Herald Tribune*, June 18, 1954, pp. 1, 20.

47. Goldman is quoted in *New York Herald Tribune*, September 23, 1952, p. 28, and September 7, 1955, sec. 3, p. 1.

48. Interview with Roland LaStarza; interview with Angelo Dundee; interview with Jimmy Breslin.

49. Martin is in *Louisville Courier-Journal*, June 19, 1954, sec. 2, p. 3; Simmons is quoted in *Detroit News*, September 12, 1955, p. 25; LaStarza is quoted in *Chicago Tribune*, June 8, 1954, pt. 6, p. 6.

50. Liebling is in *The New Yorker*, October 8, 1955, pp. 104–20; Zimmerman is in *Los Angeles Times*, September 20, 1955, pt. 4, pp. 1, 3; Moore is quoted in *Los Angeles Times*, September 23, 1955, pt. 4, pp. 1, 2; Brown is quoted in *The New Yorker*, October 2, 1954, pp. 75–87.

51. Charles is quoted in *New York Times*, September 18, 1954, p. 20; Moore is quoted in *Life*, October 3, 1955, pp. 34–35.

52. Marciano is quoted in *New York Times,* September 2, 1955, p. 21; Colombo is quoted in *San Francisco Examiner,* May 12, 1955, pp. 31, 34; Goldman is quoted in *New York Times,* May 12, 1953, p. 36.

53. Povich is in *Washington Post and Times Herald,* September 22, 1955, p. 53; Goldman is quoted in *Life,* February 12, 1951, pp. 110–17; interview with Peter Marciano.

54. Liebling is in *The New Yorker,* October 8, 1955, pp. 104–20; Marciano is quoted in *Sports Illustrated,* January 23, 1956, pp. 28–32, 47; Charles is quoted in *Washington Post and Times Herald,* June 16, 1954, p. 27.

55. Cannon is in *Boston Record American,* September 3, 1969, p. 42; the Marciano-Smith exchange is in *New York Herald Tribune,* June 16, 1954, p. 23; interview with Peter Marciano.

56. Marciano is quoted in *The New York Times Magazine,* September 20, 1953, pp. 24–25, 59, 62; Colombo is quoted in *Boston Globe,* September 4, 1969, p. 49.

57. Abramson is in *New York Herald Tribune,* September 18, 1955, sec. 3, p. 7; Moore is quoted in *New York Times,* September 8, 1955, p. 39; Patterson is quoted in Fried, *Corner Men,* p. 170.

58. Interview with Bud Collins; interview with Jimmy Breslin.

59. *Charlotte Observer,* September 18, 1955, p. 3D.

60. *Newsweek,* June 14, 1954, p. 64.

61. Smith is in *New York Herald Tribune,* June 16, 1954, p. 23, and *New York Herald Tribune,* September 13, 1955, sec. 3, p. 1.

62. *Washington Post and Times Herald,* September 15, 1955, p. 28.

Chapter 9: The King and His Kingdom

1. Interview with Jimmy Breslin.

2. *Charlotte Observer,* September 19, 1955, p. 14A.

3. Carberry is in *Denver Post,* May 14, 1953, p. 33; Povich is in *Washington Post and Times Herald,* September 22, 1955, p. 53.

4. Kaese is in *Boston Globe,* June 16, 1954, p. 25; Nason is in *Boston Evening Globe,* September 19, 1955, pp. 1, 10.

5. *The New Yorker,* October 11, 1952, pp. 73–84.

6. *Chicago Tribune,* May 9, 1953, pt. 2, p. 1.

7. The "almost like a scientist" description and the Nardiello quote are in *New York Times,* September 21, 1953, p. 31; Nardiello is also quoted in *Chicago Tribune,* September 21, 1953, pt. 4, p. 1.

8. Nardiello is quoted in *New York Times,* September 22, 1953, p. 41, *New York Herald Tribune,* September 24, 1953, p. 29, and June 2, 1954, p. 29, and *New York Times,* September 15, 1955.

9. Cooke is in *New York Herald Tribune,* September 17, 1955, sec. 3, p. 1; Ward is in *Chicago Tribune,* May 12, 1953, pt. 3, p. 1.

10. Mendel is quoted in *Chicago Tribune,* April 25, 1953, pt. 2, p. 3; Weill is quoted in *Chicago Tribune,* May 5, 1953, pt. 3, p. 3.

11. Stapler is in *Detroit News,* May 3, 1953, pt. 2, p. 4; Charles is quoted in, and Kaese is in, *Boston Globe,* June 16, 1954, p. 25.

12. LaStarza is quoted in *Detroit News,* September 24, 1953, pp. 67, 68, and September 23, 1953, pp. 71, 72.

13. *Boston Evening Globe,* May 14, 1953, pp. 1, 26.

14. Smith is in *New York Herald Tribune,* May 14, 1953, p. 27, and September 18, 1952, p. 31.

15. Ward is in *Chicago Tribune,* September 23, 1953, pt. 4, p. 1; Sullivan is in *San Francisco Examiner,* June 12, 1954, p. 21.

16. Smith is in *New York Herald Tribune,* September 18, 1955, sec. 3, p. 1; Nason is in *Boston Evening Globe,* June 16, 1954, p. 32.

17. Smith is in *New York Herald Tribune,* May 15, 1953, p. 27, and September 23, 1952, p. 28.

18. *Cleveland Press,* September 23, 1952, p. 29.

19. *The New Yorker,* October 2, 1954, pp. 75–87.

20. *New York Herald Tribune,* September 18, 1954, p. 13.

21. *Philadelphia Evening Bulletin,* September 24, 1952, p. 32

22. *Sports Illustrated,* October 3, 1955, pp. 36–39.

23. Ibid.; Povich is in *Washington Post and Times Herald,* September 22, 1955, p. 53.

24. *Sports Illustrated,* April 18, 1966, pp. 95–103.

25. Jack Cannon and Tom Cannon, eds., *Nobody Asked Me, but . . . the World of Jimmy Cannon* (New York: Holt, Rinehart and Winston, 1978), pp. 116–18.

26. Heinz is in *Cosmopolitan,* June 1954, pp. 62–67; Smith is in *New York Herald Tribune,* May 12, 1955, p. 27.

27. Interview with Robert Lipsyte.

28. Marciano is quoted in *Washington Post and Times Herald,* September 22, 1955, p. 53, and *Boston Post,* September 16, 1955, pp. 1, 23.

29. Reinauer is quoted in *Philadelphia Evening Bulletin,* September 23, 1952, pp. 57–58; the quoted descriptions of Wergeles's duties are in *Newsweek,* January 10, 1955, p. 53, and *Boston Evening Globe,* September 19, 1955, p. 10.

30. *Boston Evening Globe,* September 23, 1952, p. 42.

31. Breit is in *New York Times,* September 14, 1954, p. 33; Marciano is quoted in *Chicago Tribune,* September 4, 1969, sec. 3, pp. 1, 2.

32. *Chicago Tribune,* September 4, 1969, sec. 3, pp. 1, 2.

33. *Saturday Evening Post,* October 20, 1956, pp. 36, 147–50.

34. *Chicago Tribune,* September 2, 1969, sec. 3, pp. 1, 2.

35. *Boston Daily Record,* May 1, 1956, p. 30.

36. Cohane is in *Look,* April 5, 1955, pp. 97–99; the Marciano-Weill exchange is quoted in *Boston Daily Record,* May 1, 1956, p. 30.

37. *San Francisco Examiner,* April 2, 1955, p. 21.

38. *Sports Illustrated,* December 3, 1956, p. 32.

39. *Boston Evening Globe,* September 25, 1952, p. 18.

40. Salsinger is in *Detroit News,* September 23, 1953, pp. 71–72; interview with Bud Collins; Marciano is quoted in *New Orleans Times-Picayune,* October 24, 1953, p. 14.

41. Cannon is in *Sports Illustrated,* September 6, 1954, p. 67; Schulberg is in *Sports Illustrated,* September 27, 1954, pp. 58–60; Nason is in *Boston Evening Globe,* September 19, 1955, pp. 1, 10.

42. *Washington Post and Times Herald,* April 28, 1956, p. 8.

43. Marciano is quoted in *New York Times,* September 11, 1953, p. 28, *St. Louis Post-Dispatch,* September 11, 1955, p. 2G, *Sports Illustrated,* January 23, 1956, pp. 28–32, 47, and *Boston Record American,* September 2, 1969, p. 69.

44. *San Francisco Examiner,* May 7, 1955, p. 20.

45. *New York Times,* February 26, 1966, p. 25.

46. Interview with Truman Gibson.

47. Ibid.

48. *Sports Illustrated,* December 5, 1960, p. 12, and June 12, 1961, p. 11.

49. Interview with Jimmy Breslin; interview with Robert Lipsyte.

50. Interview with Robert Lipsyte.

Chapter 10: Ezzard

1. *Boston Post,* June 15, 1954, p. 16.

2. Heinz is in *Saturday Evening Post,* June 7, 1952, pp. 34, 127–29; Smith is in *New York Times,* May 30, 1975, p. 23.

3. *Saturday Evening Post,* June 7, 1952, pp. 34, 127–29.

4. Ibid.

5. The nightclub anecdote is in *Saturday Evening Post,* June 7, 1952, pp. 34, 127–29; Charles is quoted in *Sports of the* Times: *The Arthur Daley Years,* ed. James Tuite (New York: Quadrangle, 1975), pp. 201–3.

6. Arcel is quoted in *The New Yorker,* July 10, 1954, pp. 44–54; Abramson is in *New York Herald Tribune,* June 13, 1954, sec. 3, p. 4; Daley is in *New York Times,* June 20, 1954, sec. 5, p. 2; Salsinger is in *Detroit News,* June 16, 1954, pp. 67, 73.

7. Charles is quoted in *New York Times,* June 8, 1954, p. 31 and *Newsweek,* June 16, 1952, pp. 101–2; the quoted descriptions of Charles's performance are in *Chicago Tribune,* June 17, 1954, pt. 6, pp. 1, 4 and *Philadelphia Sunday Bulletin,* June 13, 1954, sec. 2, p. 5; *Time,* June 16, 1952, p. 59.

8. *Boston Globe,* June 17, 1954, p. 12.

9. The description of Charles is in *Boston Evening Globe,* June 17, 1954, pp. 1, 14; Ring is in *Philadelphia Evening Bulletin,* June 18, 1954, pp. 1, 28.

10. Smith is in *Pittsburgh Courier,* June 12, 1954, p. 14; Daley is in *New York*

Times, June 17, 1954, p. 39; Brown is in *Philadelphia Evening Bulletin,* June 16, 1954, p. 40; Lardner is in *Newsweek,* June 14, 1954, p. 64.

11. Salsinger is in *Detroit News,* June 16, 1954, pp. 67, 73; Martin is in *Louisville Courier-Journal,* June 19, 1954, sec. 2, p. 3.

12. *Saturday Evening Post,* June 7, 1952, pp. 34, 127–29.

13. *Charlotte Observer,* June 15, 1954, p. 6–B.

14. *Saturday Evening Post,* June 7, 1952, pp. 34, 127–29.

15. *Saturday Evening Post,* June 7, 1952, pp. 34, 127–29.

16. *Pittsburgh Courier,* May 22, 1954, p. 15.

17. *Newsweek,* July 4, 1949, p. 66.

18. The "stinkeroo" description is in *Time,* July 4, 1949, p. 34; *Life,* July 4, 1949, p. 32.

19. Lofquist is in *Providence Journal,* July 14, 1951, p. 7; the quoted descriptions of Charles are in *Cleveland Press,* June 12, 1954, p. 10 (Snooks) and *Atlanta Constitution,* June 16, 1954, p. 14 (Ezzard the Gizzard).

20. Smith is in *New York Times,* May 30, 1975, p. 23 and *New York Herald Tribune,* September 15, 1954, p. 28; Daley is in *New York Times,* June 20, 1954, sec. 5, p. 2; Salsinger is in *Detroit News,* September 15, 1954, pp. 65, 67.

21. Charles is quoted in *Newsweek,* January 22, 1951, p. 78 and *Detroit News,* June 16, 1954, pp. 67, 73; interview with W. C. Heinz.

22. *New York Times,* May 29, 1975, p. 38.

23. Weill is quoted in *Philadelphia Evening Bulletin,* September 25, 1953, pp. 1, 37; Charles is quoted in *New York Times,* April 6, 1954, p. 39.

24. *New York Herald Tribune,* June 10, 1954, p. 28.

25. *Cleveland Press,* June 12, 1954, p. 10.

26. Marciano is quoted in *Boston Post,* June 16, 1954, p. 21; Weill is quoted in *Boston Post,* June 16, 1954, pp. 1, 21.

27. Povich is in *Washington Post and Times Herald,* June 16, 1954, p. 27; Charles is quoted in *Boston Evening Globe,* June 16, 1954, p. 32; Sullivan is in *San Francisco Examiner,* June 12, 1954, p. 21.

28. Louis is quoted in *New York Herald Tribune,* June 14, 1954, p. 21; Charles is quoted in *New York Herald Tribune,* June 15, 1954, p. 29; Weill is quoted in *San Francisco Examiner,* June 9, 1954, p. 31.

29. *New York Herald Tribune,* June 17, 1954, p. 29.

30. Smith is in *Pittsburgh Courier,* June 12, 1954, p. 14; Abramson is in *New York Herald Tribune,* June 17, 1954, p. 29.

31. Zimmerman is in *Los Angeles Times,* June 18, 1954, pt. 4, pp. 1, 2; Smith is in *Chicago Tribune,* June 18, 1954, pt. 1, p. 1, pt. 3, p. 5.

32. Abramson is in *New York Herald Tribune,* June 18, 1954, pp. 1, 20; Charles is quoted in *Pittsburgh Courier,* June 26, 1954, p. 15.

33. *Los Angeles Times,* June 19, 1954, pt. 3, pp. 1, 2.

34. Brown is quoted in *The New Yorker,* July 10, 1954, pp. 44–54; Marciano is quoted in *New York Herald Tribune,* June 18, 1954, p. 21.

35. *Washington Post and Times Herald,* September 13, 1954, p. 13.

36. Interview with Jimmy Breslin; Goldman is quoted in *New Orleans Times-Picayune,* June 19, 1954, p. 16.

37. *San Francisco Examiner,* June 18, 1954, p. 36.

38. *Philadelphia Sunday Bulletin,* June 20, 1954, sec. 2, p. 3.

39. The crowd is quoted in *New York Herald Tribune,* June 18, 1954, p. 20 and *Los Angeles Times,* June 18, 1954, pt. 4, pp. 1, 2.

40. Smith is in *New York Herald Tribune,* June 18, 1954, p. 20; Whorton is in *Los Angeles Times,* June 18, 1954, pt. 4, p. 2; Brown is in *Philadelphia Evening Bulletin,* June 18, 1954, p. 30; Liebling is in *The New Yorker,* July 10, 1954, pp. 44–54.

41. Charles is quoted in *Pittsburgh Courier,* June 26, 1954, p. 15; Brown is quoted in *Pittsburgh Courier,* June 26, 1954, p. 14; Smith is in *New York Herald Tribune,* June 19, 1954, p. 10.

42. Marciano's handlers are quoted in *Washington Post and Times Herald,* June 20, 1954, p. 1C; Marciano is quoted in *Washington Post and Times Herald,* June 18, 1954, p. 37; Zimmerman is in *Los Angeles Times,* June 18, 1954, pt. 4, pp. 1, 2.

43. *The New Yorker,* July 10, 1954, pp. 44–54.

44. *Time,* June 28, 1954, p. 68; Whorton is in *Los Angeles Times,* June 18, 1954, pt. 4, p. 2; Marciano is quoted in *Washington Post and Times Herald,* September 14, 1954, p. 41.

45. Smith is in *New York Herald Tribune,* June 19, 1954, p. 10; Martin is in *Louisville Courier-Journal,* June 19, 1954, sec. 2, p. 3; Ring is in *Philadelphia Evening Bulletin,* June 18, 1954, pp. 1, 28; Weill is quoted in *Boston Evening Globe,* June 18, 1954, p. 10.

46. Wilfrid Smith is in *Chicago Tribune,* June 18, 1954, pt. 1, p. 1, pt. 3, p. 5; Wendell Smith is in *Pittsburgh Courier,* June 26, 1954, p. 14.

47. Martin is in *Louisville Courier-Journal,* June 19, 1954, sec. 2, p. 3; Lewis is in *Cleveland Press,* June 18, 1954, p. 34.

48. Charles is quoted in *San Francisco Examiner,* June 18, 1954, pp. 36, 39; Marciano is quoted in *Washington Post and Times Herald,* June 20, 1954, p. 1C; Charles is quoted in *New York Herald Tribune,* June 18, 1954, pp. 21, 24.

49. *Washington Post and Times Herald,* June 19, 1954, p. 15.

50. *Philadelphia Evening Bulletin,* June 19, 1954, p. 11.

51. Charles is quoted in *Boston Evening Globe,* September 14, 1954, p. 34 and *Boston Globe,* September 11, 1954, p. 7.

52. *St. Louis Post-Dispatch,* June 20, 1954, p. 3F.

53. Louis is quoted in *New York Times,* September 13, 1954, p. 29; Charles is quoted in *Detroit News,* September 15, 1954, pp. 65, 67.

54. Wolf is in *Los Angeles Times,* September 13, 1954, pt. 4, p. 2; Sullivan is in *San Francisco Examiner,* September 14, 1954, pp. 27, 30.

55. *New York Herald Tribune,* September 18, 1954, p. 13.

56. *New York Herald Tribune,* September 19, 1954, sec. 3, pp. 1, 5.

57. Marciano is quoted in *St. Louis Post-Dispatch,* September 18, 1954, p. 6A and *Los Angeles Times,* September 18, 1954, pt. 3, p. 2.

58. Daley is in *New York Times,* September 18, 1954, p. 20; Schulberg is in *Sports Illustrated,* September 27, 1954, pp. 58–60.

59. *Washington Post and Times Herald,* September 20, 1954, p. 15.

60. Charles and Marciano are quoted in *Los Angeles Times,* September 18, 1954, pt. 3, p. 2.

61. Marciano is quoted in *New York Herald Tribune,* September 19, 1954, sec. 3, pp. 1, 5; Ring is in *Philadelphia Evening Bulletin,* September 18, 1954, pp. 1, 17; Smith is in *New York Herald Tribune,* September 18, 1954, p. 13; Marciano is quoted in *Los Angeles Times,* September 19, 1954, pt. 2, p. 12.

62. Charles's handlers are quoted in *San Francisco Examiner,* September 18, 1954, p. 22; Brown is quoted in *Sports Illustrated,* May 16, 1955, pp. 40–43; Weill is quoted in *San Francisco Examiner,* April 24, 1955, p. 55.

63. Marciano is quoted in *Washington Post and Times Herald,* September 20, 1954, p. 15; Charles is quoted in *Los Angeles Times,* September 18, 1954, pt. 3, p. 2; Berl is quoted in *Boston Evening Globe,* September 3, 1969, p. 51.

64. *Boston Post,* September 19, 1954, p. 34.

65. Marciano is quoted in *Detroit News,* September 18, 1954, pp. 17, 18 and *New York Times,* September 18, 1954, p. 20.

66. Charles is quoted in *New York Times,* September 18, 1954, p. 20; Marciano is quoted in *Los Angeles Times,* September 18, 1954, pt. 3, p. 2; the description of Charles grinning and the Charles-Marciano exchange are in *San Francisco Examiner,* September 18, 1954, p. 22.

67. Charles is quoted in *Los Angeles Times,* September 18, 1954, pt. 3, p. 2; Smith is in *Chicago Tribune,* September 18, 1954, pt. 1, p. 1, pt. 2, p. 4; Abramson is in *New York Herald Tribune,* September 19, 1954, sec. 3, pp. 1, 5.

68. Smith is in *New York Herald Tribune,* September 19, 1954, sec. 3, p. 1; Marciano is quoted in *Charlotte Observer,* September 19, 1954, p. 2–D; the quoted "finest performance" description is in *New York Times,* September 19, 1954, sec. 5, p. 2; Nason is in *Boston Evening Globe,* September 3, 1969, p. 51.

69. *Chicago Tribune,* September 18, 1954, pt. 2, pp. 1, 4.

70. *Time,* September 27, 1954, p. 46.

Chapter 11: The Italian Hero

1. Marciano is quoted in *Boston Post,* May 16, 1955, pp. 1, 19; Weill is quoted in *San Francisco Examiner,* February 28, 1955, p. 38.

2. *Life,* March 7, 1955, pp. 118–20; Marciano is quoted in *San Francisco Examiner,* May 7, 1955, p. 20.

3. *Sports Illustrated,* May 16, 1955, pp. 44–45.

4. *New York Times,* May 16, 1955, p. 30.

5. *San Francisco Examiner,* March 27, 1955, p. 52.

6. *San Francisco Examiner,* May 14, 1955, p. 19.

7. *New York Herald Tribune,* May 16, 1955, p. 21.

8. *Chicago Tribune,* May 18, 1955, pt. 4, p. 3.

9. Wilson is cited in *Time,* May 30, 1955, p. 51; Nichols is in *New York Times,* May 17, 1955, p. 34; Marciano is quoted in *New York Herald Tribune,* May 17, 1955, p. 23.

10. *Time,* May 30, 1955, p. 51; Daley is in *New York Times,* May 18, 1955, p. 39; Marciano is quoted in *Washington Post and Times Herald,* September 13, 1955, p. 16.

11. *Newsweek,* May 30, 1955, p. 77.

12. Andrews is cited in *New York Times,* May 18, 1955, p. 38; the *Evening News* is cited in *Boston Evening Globe,* May 17, 1955, p. 34; Wilson is cited in *Time,* May 30, 1955, p. 51; *London Times,* May 18, 1955, p. 4.

13. *Sports Illustrated,* May 30, 1955, pp. 42–43.

14. Richard Polenberg, *One Nation Divisible: Class, Race, and Ethnicity in the United States since 1938* (New York: Viking Press, 1980), p. 35.

15. *Life,* May 1, 1939, pp. 62–69.

16. Richard D. Alba, "The Twilight of Ethnicity among Americans of European Ancestry," in *Ethnicity and Race in the U.S.A.: Toward the Twenty-first Century,* ed. Richard D. Alba (London: Routledge and Kegan Paul, 1985), p. 143; Polenberg, *One Nation Divisible,* p. 55.

17. John Morton Blum, *V Was for Victory: Politics and American Culture during World War II* (San Diego: Harcourt Brace Jovanovich, 1976), p. 63.

18. Polenberg, *One Nation Divisible,* p. 145.

19. Interview with Lou Duva.

20. *Chicago Tribune,* September 25, 1953, pt. 4, pp. 1, 2.

21. Marciano as told to Gross and Hirshberg, *Saturday Evening Post,* September 20, 1952, pp. 32–33, 154–56; the Philadelphia reporter is in *Philadelphia Evening Bulletin,* September 26, 1952, p. 88.

22. Interview with Sonny Marciano.

23. Michael A. Musmanno, *The Story of the Italians in America* (Garden City: Doubleday, 1965), p. 216.

24. *Providence Sunday Journal,* September 11, 1949, sec. 2, p. 2.

25. *Boston Globe,* September 26, 1952, pp. 1, 19.

26. Interview with Lou Duva; interview with Angelo Dundee.

27. For the ethnic descriptions of Marciano, see *St. Louis Post-Dispatch,* October 28, 1951, p. 2D, and *Cleveland Press,* May 15, 1953, p. 44 ("Italian"); *San Francisco Examiner,* June 17, 1954, pp. 39, 43 ("Italian American"); *Chicago Tribune,* July 29, 1952, pt. 3, p. 1 ("the tough Italian"); *New York Times,* May 10, 1953, p. 55 ("the sturdy legged Italian"); *New Orleans Times-Picayune,* May 15, 1953, pp. 29, 31 ("the hard-hitting Italiano"); and *Atlanta Constitution,* May 14, 1953, p. 9 ("with a bolt of Italian lightning").

28. Chris Mead, *Champion: Joe Louis, Black Hero in White America* (New York: Charles Scribner's Sons, 1985), p. 181.

29. Cohane is in *Look,* January 27, 1953, pp. 67–71; Zimmerman is in *Los Angeles Times,* September 23, 1955, pt. 4, pp. 1, 2; Coyne is in *Boston Daily Record,* May 3, 1956, p. 64; Brown is in *Philadelphia Evening Bulletin,* September 22, 1955, p. 48.

30. Liebling is in *The New Yorker,* October 11, 1952, pp. 73–84; Cuddy is in *Providence Evening Bulletin,* July 9, 1951, p. 31; the "olive-skinned" description is in *Providence Journal,* July 13, 1951, p. 8, and *San Francisco Examiner,* September 24, 1953, p. 28.

31. *Time,* September 22, 1952, p. 50; *Saturday Evening Post,* September 20, 1952, pp. 32–33, 154–56; *Life,* September 22, 1952, pp. 107–18.

32. Daley is in *New York Times,* September 23, 1952, p. 27; Keefe is in *New Orleans Times-Picayune,* May 11, 1953, p. 24, September 15, 1955, p. 39, and September 22, 1955, pp. 38, 40.

33. *The New Yorker,* October 11, 1952, pp. 73–84.

34. Interview with Peter Marciano.

35. Ibid.

36. Interview with W. C. Heinz.

37. The quoted description of Marciano's family devotion and character is in *Philadelphia Sunday Bulletin,* September 28, 1952, sec. 2, p. 9; the wire service reporter is in *Detroit News,* September 25, 1952, p. 62.

38. Liston is in *Boston Post,* May 16, 1955, pp. 1, 19; Liebling is in *The New Yorker,* October 11, 1952, pp. 73–84.

39. Interview with W. C. Heinz; the "Mamma" and "Mama" descriptions are in *Life,* September 22, 1952, pp. 107–18, and *Sports Illustrated,* May 14, 1956, pp. 25–26; Marciano's mother is quoted in *Sports Illustrated,* June 11, 1956, pp. 26–27.

40. Hern is in *Boston Post,* July 24, 1952, p. 16; interview with Sonny Marciano; interview with Peter Marciano.

41. The Marciano-gangster exchange is in *Sports Illustrated,* August 23, 1993, pp. 54–68; interview with Truman Gibson.

42. Interview with Truman Gibson.

43. Brown is quoted in Everett M. Skehan, *Rocky Marciano* (1977, repr. London: Robson Books, 1998), p. 165; Cannon is cited in Ray Fitzgerald, *Champions Remembered* (Brattleboro: Stephen Greene Press, 1982), p. 164.

44. David Remnick, *King of the World* (New York: Random House, 1998), p. 46.

45. *New York Amsterdam News,* June 12, 1954, p. 24.

46. The reference to Carbo and M. Weill whispering is in *Boston Evening American,* August 28, 1951, p. 32; Norris is quoted in *Washington Post,* December 9, 1960, pp. D1, D3.

47. Interview with Peter Marciano; interview with Jimmy Breslin.

48. Interview with Jimmy Breslin.

49. Interview with Bud Collins.

50. Alba, *Ethnicity and Race in the U.S.A.,* p. 152.

51. Interview with Robert Lipsyte.

52. Interview with Bud Collins.

53. *Saturday Evening Post*, September 20, 1952, pp. 32–33, 154–56.

54. Collins is in *Boston Globe*, September 2, 1969, p. 25; interview with Bud Collins.

55. *Boston Herald Traveler*, September 2, 1969, p. 26.

Chapter 12: Archie

1. Lardner is in *Newsweek*, August 23, 1954, p. 73; Brean is in *Life*, July 18, 1955, pp. 48–50.

2. Lardner is in *Newsweek*, August 23, 1954, p. 73 and *Newsweek*, January 10, 1955, p. 53.

3. Moore as told to Cohane, *Look*, September 20, 1955, pp. 80–88; Moore is quoted in *Time*, September 12, 1955, pp. 52, 55.

4. *The New York Times Magazine*, September 11, 1955, pp. 26, 58–64.

5. Millstein is in *The New York Times Magazine*, September 11, 1955, sec. 6, pp. 26, 58–64; Brean is in, and Moore is quoted in, *Life*, July 18, 1955, pp. 48–50.

6. *Baltimore Afro-American*, September 17, 1955, p. 15.

7. *Sports Illustrated*, September 19, 1955, pp. 18–21, 40–43.

8. Ibid.

9. *Washington Post and Times Herald*, September 4, 1955, p. C4.

10. *New York Times*, December 10, 1998, p. B16.

11. *Saturday Evening Post*, September 17, 1955, pp. 26–27, 86–90.

12. *New York Times*, December 10, 1998, p. B16.

13. *Saturday Evening Post*, September 17, 1955, pp. 26–27, 86–90.

14. Johnston is quoted in *Life*, July 18, 1955, pp. 48–50; the Moore-Johnston exchange is in *Look*, April 5, 1955, pp. 97–99.

15. *Saturday Evening Post*, September 17, 1955, pp. 26–27, 86–90.

16. *Baltimore Afro-American*, September 17, 1955, p. 15.

17. *Saturday Evening Post*, September 17, 1955, pp. 26–27, 86–90.

18. Reese is quoted in *Business Week*, July 30, 1955, pp. 28–29; see also *Life*, July 18, 1955, pp. 48–50.

19. *Look*, September 20, 1955, pp. 80–88.

20. Moore is quoted in *Washington Post and Times Herald*, September 4, 1955, p. C4; Schulberg is in *Sports Illustrated*, September 5, 1955, pp. 47–48; Smith is in *Pittsburgh Courier*, September 10, 1955, p. 12.

21. Smith is in *New York Herald Tribune*, September 19, 1955, sec. 3, p. 1; Ahern is in *Boston Globe*, September 16, 1955, p. 21.

22. Povich is in *Washington Post and Times Herald*, September 8, 1955, p. 31; Smith is in *New York Herald Tribune*, September 19, 1955, sec. 3, p. 1.

23. *Pittsburgh Courier*, July 2, 1955, p. 12.

24. *New York Herald Tribune*, September 13, 1955, sec. 3, p. 1, 3.

25. *The New York Times Magazine*, September 11, 1955, sec. 6, pp. 26, 58–64.

26. Moore is quoted in *Time,* September 12, 1955, pp. 52, 55, and *The New York Times Magazine,* September 11, 1955, sec. 6, pp. 26, 58–64.

27. Smith is in *New York Herald Tribune,* September 18, 1955, sec. 3, p. 1; Moore is quoted in *New York Herald Tribune,* September 14, 1955, sec. 3, pp. 1, 2, and *Washington Post and Times Herald,* September 14, 1955, p. 49.

28. Moore is quoted in *Charlotte Observer,* September 19, 1955, p. 14-A; Daley is in *New York Times,* September 20, 1955, p. 36.

29. Moore is quoted in *Washington Post and Times Herald,* September 14, 1955, p. 49, and *Baltimore Afro-American,* September 10, 1955, p. 16.

30. Mendel is quoted in *Boston Post,* September 22, 1955, p. 15; the Marciano-Mendel exchange is in *Boston Post,* September 23, 1955, pp. 1, 26.

31. Colombo is quoted in *Boston Post,* September 13, 1955, p. 17; Liston is in *Boston Post,* September 20, 1955, pp. 1, 20; Nason is in *Boston Evening Globe,* September 19, 1955, pp. 1, 10.

32. Marciano is quoted in *Boston Post,* September 16, 1955, pp. 1, 23 and *New York Herald Tribune,* September 11, 1955, sec. 3, p. 4.

33. Hern is in *Boston Post,* September 20, 1955, p. 20; Povich is in *Washington Post and Times Herald,* September 20, 1955, p. 20.

34. *New York Herald Tribune,* September 15, 1955, sec. 3, p. 1.

35. Marciano is quoted in *Los Angeles Times,* September 19, 1955, pt. 4, p. 1; Goldman is quoted in *Boston Globe,* September 19, 1955, p. 7.

36. *Boston Post,* September 21, 1955, p. 23.

37. Hardy is quoted in *Boston Globe,* September 20, 1955, p. 8; Brown is in *Philadelphia Evening Bulletin,* September 22, 1955, p. 48; Schulberg is in *Sports Illustrated,* October 3, 1955, pp. 36–39.

38. Marciano is quoted in *Los Angeles Times,* September 22, 1955, pt. 4, p. 3, and *Boston Post,* September 22, 1955, pp. 1, 14.

39. *Washington Post,* September 20, 1985, pp. D1–D3.

40. Moore is quoted in *Sports Illustrated,* September 19, 1955, pp. 18–21, 40–43; Marciano is quoted in *New York Times,* September 23, 1955, p. 28.

41. *Pittsburgh Courier,* October 1, 1955, p. 12.

42. Marciano is quoted in *New York Times,* September 22, 1955, p. 37; Schulberg is in *Sports Illustrated,* October 3, 1955, pp. 36–39.

43. *San Francisco Examiner,* September 23, 1955, pp. 34, 40.

44. Cronin is in *Los Angeles Times,* September 23, 1955, pt. 4, p. 3; Grieve is in *San Francisco Examiner,* September 22, 1955, pp. 36, 39.

45. Smith is in *New York Herald Tribune,* September 22, 1955, sec. 3, p. 1; Marciano is quoted in *Boston Post,* September 22, 1955, pp. 1, 14.

46. *San Francisco Examiner,* September 23, 1955, pp. 34, 40.

47. Schulberg is in *Sports Illustrated,* October 3, 1955, pp. 36–39; Moore is quoted in *Los Angeles Times,* September 23, 1955, pt. 4, pp. 1, 2; Nichols is in *New York Times,* September 22, 1955, p. 37.

48. Marciano is quoted in *Boston Post,* September 22, 1955, pp. 1, 14; Liebling is in *The New Yorker,* October 8, 1955, pp. 104–20.

49. *New York Herald Tribune,* September 23, 1955, sec. 3, pp. 1, 2.

50. Marciano is quoted in *Chicago Tribune,* September 23, 1955, pt. 4, pp. 1, 2; Moore is quoted in *Pittsburgh Courier,* October 1, 1955, p. 12.

51. Moore is quoted in *Sports Illustrated,* October 3, 1955, pp. 36–39, and *New York Herald Tribune,* September 22, 1955, sec. 3, p. 2.

52. Abramson is in *New York Herald Tribune,* September 22, 1955, sec. 3, pp. 1, 2; Nichols is in *New York Times,* September 22, 1955, p. 37; Schulberg is in *Sports Illustrated,* October 3, 1955, pp. 36–39; Smith is in *New York Herald Tribune,* September 22, 1955, sec. 3, p. 1.

53. Brown is in *Philadelphia Evening Bulletin,* September 22, 1955, p. 48; the "almost inhuman" description is in *New York Herald Tribune,* September 22, 1955, sec. 3, p. 1; Ring is in *Philadelphia Evening Bulletin,* September 22, 1955, pp. 1, 49; Moore is quoted in *Time,* October 3, 1955, p. 62, and *Chicago Tribune,* September 22, 1955, pt. 6, p. 1.

54. Corum is in *Denver Post,* June 20, 1954, p. 3B; Daley is in *New York Times,* September 19, 1954, sec. 5, p. 2.

55. *New York Times,* September 19, 1954, sec. 5, p. 2.

56. *St. Louis Post-Dispatch,* September 18, 1955, p. 3D.

57. *San Francisco Examiner,* September 5, 1955, p. 24.

58. *Pittsburgh Courier,* September 17, 1955, p. 13.

59. Smith is in *New York Herald Tribune,* September 23, 1955, sec. 3, p. 1; Brown is in *Philadelphia Evening Bulletin,* September 22, 1955, p. 48; Daley is in *New York Times,* September 23, 1955, p. 28; Goldman is quoted in *Look,* October 30, 1956, pp. 95–105.

60. *Sports Illustrated,* October 3, 1955, pp. 36–39.

Chapter 13: The Wanderer

1. *Los Angeles Times,* September 22, 1955, pt. 4, p. 3.

2. Marciano is quoted in *New York Herald Tribune,* April 28, 1956, sec. 3, pp. 1, 2, *Boston Traveler,* April 27, 1956, pp. 1, 36, and *Boston Evening Globe,* April 27, 1956, pp. 1, 29.

3. *New York Times,* April 28, 1956, pp. 1, 13.

4. Interview with Peter Marciano; R. Marciano is quoted in *Boston Post,* April 30, 1956, pp. 1, 13.

5. Marciano is quoted in *Boston Daily Record,* May 4, 1956, p. 65, and *Boston Evening Globe,* September 2, 1969, p. 28.

6. Interview with Jimmy Breslin; Weill is quoted in *Saturday Evening Post,* October 13, 1956, pp. 36, 159–62; Cannon's anecdote is in *Boston Sunday Advertiser,* September 7, 1969, p. 59; interview with Sonny Marciano.

7. Weill is quoted in *Sports Illustrated,* April 30, 1956, p. 36; Marciano is quoted in *Sports Illustrated,* May 7, 1956, pp. 24–25, 28.

8. Interview with Peter Marciano; interview with Lou Duva.

9. Interview with Peter Marciano.

10. *Sports Illustrated,* December 3, 1956, p. 32.

11. *New York Herald Tribune,* April 28, 1956, sec. 3, pp. 1, 2.

12. Interview with Sonny Marciano.

13. Interview with Lou Duva.

14. Interview with Peter Marciano.

15. *New York Times,* June 1, 1961, p. 40.

16. Interview with Robert Lipsyte; Olsen is in *Sports Illustrated,* April 11, 1966, pp. 89–104.

17. *Boston Globe*, September 2, 1969, p. 25.

18. *Sports Illustrated,* September 26, 1966, p. 61.

19. Sugar is quoted in Thomas Hauser, *Muhammad Ali: His Life and Times* (New York: Simon and Schuster, 1991), pp. 196–97; interview with Angelo Dundee.

20. Interview with Angelo Dundee; interview with Robert Lipsyte; interview with Angelo Dundee; interview with Peter Marciano; interview with Lou Duva.

21. *Boston Evening Globe,* January 21, 1970, p. 30.

22. Interview with Robert Lipsyte; Jeffrey T. Sammons, *Beyond the Ring: The Role of Boxing in American Society* (Urbana: University of Illinois Press, 1988), p. 209.

23. Everett M. Skehan, *Rocky Marciano* (1977, repr. London: Robson Books, 1998), pp. 271, 287.

24. Interview with Truman Gibson.

25. Interview with Sonny Marciano; Saccone is quoted in *Sports Illustrated,* August 23, 1993, pp. 54–68.

26. Interview with Sonny Marciano.

27. Interview with Peter Marciano.

28. Skehan, *Rocky Marciano,* p. 324.

29. Interview with Peter Marciano.

30. Ibid.

31. Murray is in *Boston Evening Globe,* September 2, 1969, p. 25; P. Marciano is quoted in *Boston Globe,* August 27, 1989, sec. SW, pp. 1, 6.

32. Interview with Truman Gibson; interview with Lou Duva; interview with Angelo Dundee.

33. Interview with Peter Marciano.

34. Miltimore is quoted in Skehan, *Rocky Marciano,* p. 272; interview with Jimmy Breslin.

35. Interview with Robert Lipsyte.

36. Interview with Jimmy Breslin.

37. Interview with Bud Collins; interview with Jimmy Breslin.

38. Interview with Jimmy Breslin.

39. Interview with W. C. Heinz.

40. Ibid.

41. Interview with Peter Marciano; interview with Sonny Marciano.

42. Skehan, *Rocky Marciano,* p. 282.

43. Saccone is quoted in Skehan, *Rocky Marciano,* p. 309, and Miltimore on p. 281.

44. Interview with Lou Duva.

45. Interview with Peter Marciano; interview with Sonny Marciano.

46. Interview with W. C. Heinz; interview with Sonny Marciano; interview with Lou Duva.

47. Interview with Lou Duva.

48. Pep is quoted in Skehan, *Rocky Marciano,* p. 283, and Miltimore on p. 335.

49. Interview with Roland LaStarza; interview with Lou Duva; interview with Angelo Dundee.

50. Interview with Furman Bisher; interview with Peter Marciano.

51. Dreyspool is in *Sports Illustrated,* May 7, 1956, pp. 24–25, 28; interview with Peter Marciano; interview with Sonny Marciano.

52. Skehan, *Rocky Marciano,* p. 337; interview with Sonny Marciano.

53. Interview with Sonny Marciano.

54. Ibid.; Murray is in *Boston Evening Globe,* September 2, 1969, p. 25.

55. Interview with Sonny Marciano.

56. Interview with Peter Marciano.

57. Marciano's friend is quoted in Skehan, *Rocky Marciano,* p. 218; interview with Peter Marciano.

Chapter 14: Rocky

1. Louis is quoted in *New York Times,* September 2, 1969, p. 44; Walcott is quoted in *Boston Evening Globe,* September 2, 1969, p. 28; Charles is quoted in *Boston Herald Traveler,* September 2, 1969, p. 24; Moore is quoted in *Boston Globe,* September 3, 1969, p. 48.

2. *Boston Evening Globe,* September 2, 1969, p. 25.

3. Interview with Angelo Dundee; interview with Jimmy Breslin.

4. Interview with Angelo Dundee.

5. Ibid.; interview with Lou Duva.

Bibliographic Essay

At the heart of the research underlying this book are contemporaneous newspaper articles from Rocky Marciano's era. In particular, I researched and reviewed articles about Marciano at the key junctures in his life (his most important pre-title fights, all of his title fights, his retirement, and his death) in twenty-three newspapers: the *Atlanta Constitution, Baltimore Afro American, Baltimore Sun, Birmingham Post-Herald, Boston Globe, Boston Post, Charlotte Observer, Chicago Defender, Chicago Tribune, Cleveland Press, Denver Post, Detroit News, Los Angeles Times, Louisville Courier-Journal, New Orleans Times-Picayune, New York Amsterdam News, New York Herald Tribune, New York Times, Philadelphia Evening Bulletin, Pittsburgh Courier, San Francisco Examiner, St. Louis Post-Dispatch,* and *Washington Post.*

In addition to those publications, I consulted the following newspapers for coverage of various points in Marciano's early career: the *Boston Daily Record, Boston Evening American, Boston Herald, Boston Traveler, Brockton Daily Enterprise, Providence Evening Bulletin,* and *Providence Journal.*

I also relied not only on oral history but also on numerous books and magazine articles concerning Marciano and the primary subjects contained in this book. In what follows, I identify the key sources underlying each chapter (beyond the endnotes, which provide citations for the direct quotations within chapters).

Chapter 1: Holyoke

A firsthand account of Marciano's boyhood in Brockton as well as his early pre-career adulthood (involving his succession of manual labor jobs, stint in the army, struggles as a frustrated athlete, and first fight with Epperson in Holyoke) can be found in Rocky Marciano as told to Milton Gross and Al Hirshberg, "They Said I'd Get Murdered!" *Saturday Evening Post,* September 22, 1956, pp. 26–27, 71–74. This article is the second installment in a six-part autobiographical serial that Marciano wrote for the *Saturday Evening Post* several months after his retirement in the fall of 1956 (from the September 15, 1956, issue to the October 20, 1956, issue, inclusive). The serial is particularly valuable as a whole because it provides Marciano's personal views (albeit somewhat sanitized) on numerous aspects of his career. Another invaluable and comprehensive source for Marciano's early years is Everett M. Skehan, *Rocky Marciano: The Biography of a First Son* (Boston: Houghton Mifflin, 1977), reprinted as Everett M. Skehan, *Rocky Marciano* (1983, repr. London: Robson Books, 1998), pp. 3–74.

Other accounts of Marciano's early life can be found among the numerous profiles written about him during his rise and early reign, including Tim Cohane, "Rocky Marciano . . . Poor Man's Dempsey," *Look,* January 15, 1952, pp. 70–72; Marshall Smith, ". . . and New Champion?" *Life,* September 22, 1952, pp. 107–18; Al Hirshberg, "Can Any Man Living Beat Him?" *Saturday Evening Post,* September 20, 1952, pp. 32–33, 154–56; Tim Cohane, "The Rocky Marciano Story . . . with Heart and Hands," *Look,* January 27, 1953, pp. 67–71; and W. C. Heinz, "Brockton's Boy," *Cosmopolitan,* June 1954, pp. 62–67..

Chapter 2: Providence

Many magazine articles written about Marciano during his rise and early reign contain portraits of his mentors Al Weill and Charley Goldman (including Smith, ". . . and New Champion?"; Hirshberg, "Can Any Man Living"; and Cohane, "The Rocky Marciano Story"). Most of these articles also feature an account of Marciano's initial meeting with Weill and Goldman in June 1948, as do Tim Cohane, "How Marciano Licked Al Weill," *Look,* October 2, 1956, pp. 56–60; Rocky Marciano as told to Milton Gross and Al Hirshberg, "The Worst Experience of My Life," *Saturday Evening Post,* September 29, 1956, pp. 44–45, 68–74; and Skehan, *Rocky Marciano,* pp. 69–85. For a slight variation of that story, see Charley Goldman with Tom Meany, "How Marciano Can Be Beaten," *Collier's,* January 17, 1953, pp. 20–25.

For additional profiles of Al Weill that emphasize his shrewdness and like personality traits, see Cohane, "How Marciano Licked Al Weill," and "Kingmaker," *Newsweek,* September 27, 1954, p. 62. For a kinder, gentler view of Weill's personality, see A. J. Liebling, "A Reporter at Large: Broken Fighter Arrives," *The New Yorker,* November 17, 1951, pp. 102–18; and A. J. Liebling, "A Reporter at Large: Equalizer," *The New Yorker,* October 11, 1952, pp. 73–84. For a retrospective, affectionate portrait of Goldman, see Ronald K. Fried, *Corner Men: Great Boxing Trainers* (New York: Four Walls Eight Windows, 1991), pp. 159–87. For a profile of Goldman written in the early 1950s, see "Fight Trainer," *Life,* February 12, 1951, pp. 110–17. Other articles from the era containing glimpses into Goldman's character include Liebling, "Broken Fighter Arrives," and Liebling, "Equalizer."

For Marciano's firsthand account of his early professional career, see Marciano as told to Gross and Hirshberg, "The Worst Experience."

Chapter 3: New York

For a firsthand account of the Carmine Vingo near-tragedy, see Marciano as told to Gross and Hirshberg, "The Worst Experience."

Numerous sources detail the founding, operations, and practices of the International Boxing Club. Among the best are Jeffrey T. Sammons, *Beyond the Ring: The Role of Boxing in American Society* (Urbana: University of Illinois Press, 1988), pp. 130–83, which contains an excellent, blow-by-blow account of the saga, and David Remnick, *King of the World* (New York: Random House, 1998), pp. 43–68, which, among other things, contains a fine portrait of Frankie Carbo. The weekly issues of *Sports Illustrated* throughout the 1950s are also invaluable in this regard. Perhaps the best source on the IBC and the synergistic empires of Jim Norris and Frankie Carbo, however, remains Barney Nagler, *James Norris and the Decline of Boxing* (Indianapolis: Bobbs-Merrill, 1964), which was written only a few years after the IBC reigned supreme over the sport of boxing.

For information on the Marcianos' marriage, see Harold Graham, "My Husband Can Lick Your Husband," *Good Housekeeping,* May 1954, pp. 26–27, 142–44. A more recent (and less-sanitized) account can be found in William Nack, "The Rock," *Sports Illustrated,* August 23, 1993, pp. 54–68.

For the published judicial opinion resolving Marciano's legal dispute with his amateur manager Gene Caggiano, see *Caggiano v. Marchegiano,* 99 N.E.2d 861–865 (Mass. 1951).

Chapter 4: The Great White Hope

Much of this chapter concerns the emergence and development of the Great White Hope, which took place in the first part of the twentieth century, particularly during the careers of heavyweight champions Jack Johnson and Joe Louis. To this end, I relied primarily upon three sources: Randy Roberts, *Papa Jack: Jack Johnson and the Era of White Hopes* (New York: Free Press, 1983), the definitive account of Johnson's life and career; Chris Mead, *Champion: Joe Louis, Black Hero in White America* (New York: Charles Scribner's Sons, 1985), the best source on Louis and the pioneering role that he played; and Sammons, *Beyond the Ring,* pp. 30–129, which provides a superb contextual history of boxing. All three of these works provide excellent information and analysis on the history of the Great White Hope, as well as the racial symbolism and passion involved in the first part of the twentieth century when a white man met a black man in the ring.

For more on the struggles of black heavyweights who fought between Johnson and Louis (topics also covered in the works by Mead and Sammons), see Randy Roberts, *Jack Dempsey: The Manassa Mauler* (Baton Rouge: Louisiana State University Press, 1979). In addition, for a brief but valuable account of the history of race and the heavyweight title (involving Johnson, Louis, and Muhammad Ali, among others), see Remnick, *King of the World,* pp. 221–32.

For an excellent examination of civil rights and the status of race relations from the 1930s into the mid-1950s, see Harvard Sitkoff, *The Struggle for Black Equality, 1954–1980* (New York: Hill and Wang, 1981), pp. 11–39. Other sources that are useful along these lines include Robert Weisbrot, *Freedom Bound: A History of America's Civil Rights Movement* (New York: W. W. Norton, 1990), and August Meier and Elliott Rudwick, *From Plantation to Ghetto,* 3d ed. (New York: Hill and Wang, 1976). For an examination of civil rights and race relations during World War II, see John Morton Blum, *V Was for Victory: Politics and American Culture during World War II* (San Diego: Harcourt Brace Jovanovich, 1976), pp. 182–220. For an examination of civil rights during the years after World War II, see David McCullough, *Truman* (New York: Simon and Schuster, 1992), pp. 569–70, 586–89, 638–40, and 644–46.

This chapter contends that the ordeals of Joe Louis and Jackie Robinson took the edge off racism in sports in the early 1950s. Along those lines, the best source for Louis's role in integrating the big-time world of professional sports is Mead, *Champion.* Also useful in this regard is Sammons, *Beyond the Ring,* pp. 96–129. The best account of Robinson's ordeal in breaking the color line in 1947 remains Jules Tygiel, *Baseball's Great Experiment: Jackie Robinson and His Legacy* (New York: Oxford University Press, 1983). Another source useful in this regard, especially for Robinson's testimony against Paul Robeson as well as for Robinson's postcareer civil rights activities, is David Falkner, *Great Time Coming: The Life of Jackie Robinson, from Baseball to Birmingham* (New York: Simon and Schuster, 1995).

Chapter 5: The Uncrowned Champion

For a superb account of Marciano's October 1951 fight with Joe Louis, see Liebling, "Broken Fighter Arrives."

For a two-part profile of Jack Hurley, Harry Matthews's colorful manager, see Jack Olsen, "Don't Call Me Honest," *Sports Illustrated,* May 15, 1961, pp. 76–96, and Jack Olsen, "Fifty Percent of Harry," *Sports Illustrated,* May 22, 1961, pp. 90–104.

Chapter 6: Jersey Joe

An excellent source for the life and career of Jersey Joe Walcott is the two-part article that he wrote for the *Saturday Evening Post* in the summer of 1948 before his rematch with Joe Louis. See Jersey Joe Walcott with Lewis Burton, "I'll Lick Joe Louis Again," *Saturday Evening Post,* June 12, 1948, pp. 20–21, 136–41, and June 19, 1948, pp. 118–22.

For Marciano's firsthand account of the two Marciano-Walcott fights detailing, among other things, Marciano's theory on how he was blinded during the first fight, see Rocky Marciano as told to Milton Gross and Al Hirshberg, "Dirty Work at Ringside," *Saturday Evening Post,* October 6, 1956, pp. 42–43, 126–28.

Chapter 7: The Ideal

Three profiles published around the time of the first Marciano-Walcott fight crystalized and cemented Marciano's image, both in words and pictures: Smith, ". . . and New Champion?"; Hirshberg, "Can Any Man Living?"; and Cohane, "The Rocky Marciano Story" (in addition to Tim Cohane, "The Rocky Marciano Story . . . Profile of a Puncher," *Look,* February 10, 1953, pp. 87–91). A fourth article that appeared around the same time, although considerably shorter, also manages to capture the official Marciano persona: "Personality," *Time,* September 22, 1952, p. 50.

For an earlier profile during Marciano's rise that details key components of his developing image, see Cohane, "Rocky Marciano." For articles toward the end of his reign that reiterate and reinforce his official image, see the autobiographical serial in the *Saturday Evening Post* (September 15, 1956–October 20, 1956), as well as Tim Cohane, "Why Marciano Will Never Fight Again," *Look,* October 30, 1956, pp. 95–105.

For two excellent profiles during Marciano's reign that probe beneath his official persona (and therefore depart greatly from the stock profiles churned out by the image-makers throughout his reign), see Harvey Breit, "A Lamb in Lion's Clothing," *New York Times Magazine,* September 20, 1953, pp. 24–25, 59, 62, and Joan Flynn Dreyspool, "Conversation Piece: Subject: Rocky Marciano," *Sports Illustrated,* January 23, 1956, pp. 28–32, 47. For a superb article exploring Marciano's relationship with his hometown of Brockton, Massachusetts, see Heinz, "Brockton's Boy."

This chapter begins with images that sportswriters constructed for two great heavyweight champions who preceded Marciano, Jack Dempsey and Joe Louis. For more on Dempsey's image, see Roberts, *Jack Dempsey.* For more on Louis's image, see Mead, *Champion,* as well as Remnick, *King of the World,* pp. 221–32.

The chapter also contains a parallel between Marciano's image and the ideal man of the 1950s ("Fifties Man"). For an excellent book concerning the societal and cultural mores of the early 1950s, see Stephen J. Whitfield, *The Culture of the Cold War* (Baltimore: Johns Hopkins University Press, 1991). Other sources that are also useful in this regard include David Halberstam, *The Fifties* (New York: Villard Books,

1993), and Ellen Schrecker, *The Age of McCarthyism: A Brief History with Documents* (Boston: St. Martin's Press, 1994).

Moreover, this chapter analyzes the canons of sportswriting that prevailed during Marciano's era and governed his image accordingly. For an analysis of the gee-whiz school of sportswriting, see Murray Sperber, *Shake Down the Thunder: The Creation of Notre Dame Football* (New York: Henry Holt, 1993), pp. 175–77, 424, a superb and scholarly account of the early days of Notre Dame football. For a biography on a member of the gee-whiz school still writing in the early 1950s, see Thomas B. Littlewood, *Arch: A Promoter, not a Poet: The Story of Arch Ward* (Ames: Iowa State University Press, 1990).

For an analysis of sportswriting in the early 1950s (primarily through character sketches of three dominant sportswriters of the era, Red Smith, Arthur Daley, and Jimmy Cannon), see Robert Lipsyte, *Sportsworld: An American Dreamland* (New York: Quadrangle, 1975), pp. 170–83. For a biography of Smith, see Ira Berkow, *Red: A Biography of Red Smith* (New York: Times Books, 1986). For the collected work of Daley, see James Tuite, ed., *Sports of the Times: The Arthur Daley Years* (New York: Quadrangle, 1975). For the collected work of Cannon, see Jack Cannon and Tom Cannon, eds., *Nobody Asked Me, but . . . the World of Jimmy Cannon* (New York: Holt, Rinehart and Winston, 1978). For profiles of Cannon as well as analyses of the transformation in the style of sportswriting that took place from the mid-1950s to the early 1960s, see David Halberstam, *October 1964* (New York: Villard Books, 1994), pp. 172–81, and Remnick, *King of the World*, pp. 145–59. For a superb analysis of sportswriting from the 1920s to the 1950s in the words of the sportswriters themselves, see Jerome Holtzman, *No Cheering in the Press Box* (New York: Henry Holt, 1995).

For an analysis of the interplay between television and sports in the 1950s and 1960s, see Robert W. McChesney, "Media Made Sport: A History of Sports Coverage in the United States," in *Media, Sports, and Society,* ed. Lawrence Wenner (Newbury Park, Calif.: Sage Publications, 1989), pp. 49–67.

Finally, for several scholarly works concerning the subject of hero-making and athletes, see Peter Williams, *The Sports Immortals: Deifying the American Athlete* (Bowling Green: Bowling Green State University Popular Press, 1994); Janet C. Harris, *Athletes and the American Hero Dilemma* (Champaign: Human Kinetics Publishers, 1994); and David L. Porter, "America's Greatest Sports Figures" in *The Hero in Transition,* ed. Ray B. Browne and Marshall W. Fishwick (Bowling Green: Bowling Green State University Popular Press, 1983).

Chapter 8: The Ugly Duckling

For a profile of Roland LaStarza written around the time that he met Marciano for the heavyweight title, see W. C. Heinz, "He's Mad at the Champ," *Saturday Evening Post,* September 19, 1953, pp. 36, 152–56.

Much of this chapter concerns Marciano's strengths and weaknesses as a boxer—

especially Charley Goldman's work in accentuating those strengths and minimizing those weaknesses. For a thorough analysis of Goldman's work with Marciano, see Fried, *Corner Men,* pp. 159–87. For an article in the same vein but with a twist, see Goldman with Meany, "How Marciano Can Be Beaten."

Chapter 9: The King and His Kingdom

No one captured the romance and glamour associated with "the kingdom" of heavyweight championship boxing in the early 1950s better than A. J. Liebling of *The New Yorker.* All told, Liebling wrote essays on five of Marciano's seven title fights: his two fights with Jersey Joe Walcott ("Equalizer" and "A Reporter at Large: Long Toddle, Short Fight," *The New Yorker,* May 30, 1953, pp. 33–45); his two fights with Ezzard Charles ("A Reporter at Large: Public and Private Mills," *The New Yorker,* pp. 44–54, and "A Reporter at Large: Doc Picks Rock," *The New Yorker,* October 2, 1954, pp. 75–87); and his fight with Archie Moore ("A Reporter at Large: Ahab and Nemesis," *The New Yorker,* October 8, 1955, pp. 104–20). Although all of these essays are superb, the ones concerning the two Marciano-Walcott fights probably best capture the excitement surrounding a heavyweight championship fight in the early 1950s.

For more on Stillman's Gym, the nerve center of boxing and the headquarters for the fight mob in the early 1950s, see Fried, *Corner Men,* pp. 31–53.

For a glimpse into how Marciano felt about being "the heavyweight champion of the world," see Rocky Marciano as told to Milton Gross and Al Hirshberg, "It Was Worth It," *Saturday Evening Post,* October 20, 1956, pp. 36, 147–50, and Dreyspool, "Conversation Piece." For an examination and criticism of the stock historical image of the "heavyweight champion of the world," see Lipsyte, *Sports World,* pp. 74–76.

There are numerous sources detailing the repeated scandals and widespread corruption that the sport of boxing endured, starting in the mid-1950s and extending into the early 1960s (one of the chief factors that eroded the sport's popularity and the kingdom of heavyweight championship boxing). Among the most valuable are Sammons, *Beyond the Ring,* pp. 130–83; Remnick, *King of the World,* pp. 43–68; and, especially, Nagler, *James Norris.* For an excellent analysis of the Cheasty trial that Truman Gibson alleges was the impetus of the legal problems that contributed to the downfall of the IBC, see Evan Thomas, *The Man to See: Edward Bennett Williams: Ultimate Insider: Legendary Trial Lawyer* (New York: Simon and Schuster, 1991), pp. 104–18.

Perhaps the best information relating to this general subject, however, can be found in the weekly issues of *Sports Illustrated* throughout this era. The magazine's ongoing exposé of corruption in boxing is a journalistic tour de force. Some of the many noteworthy articles that the magazine published during this time period include Budd Schulberg, "Boxing's Dirty Business Must Be Cleaned Up Now," *Sports Illustrated,* November 1, 1954, pp. 11, 58–60; Harry Thomas, "Jim Norris Is Part of Boxing's

Dirty Business," *Sports Illustrated,* December 13, 1954, pp. 10–16; Robert Coughlan, "How the IBC Runs Boxing," *Sports Illustrated,* January 17, 1955, pp. 11–13, 47–50; Martin Kane and James Shepley, "The Case against the IBC," *Sports Illustrated,* April 23, 1956, pp. 26–29, 59; Martin Kane, "IBC: Guilty as Charged," *Sports Illustrated,* May 18, 1957, pp. 16–17; Martin Kane, "Things Will Not Be the Same," *Sports Illustrated,* February 9, 1959, pp. 34–37; and Gilbert Rogin, "Norris' Last Stand," *Sports Illustrated,* December 19, 1960, pp. 12–16.

For information on some of boxing's other internal problems in the early 1950s (e.g., overexposure on television and the decline of the amateur ranks), see Sammons, *Beyond the Ring,* pp. 130–83; McChesney, "Media Made Sport," pp. 49–67; and Arthur Daley, "Is Boxing on the Ropes?" *New York Times Magazine,* January 31, 1954, pp. 19, 22, 23, 25.

Chapter 10: Ezzard

For a penetrating and contemporaneous profile of Ezzard Charles, see W. C. Heinz, "The Strange Case of Ezzard Charles," *Saturday Evening Post,* June 7, 1952, pp. 34, 127–29. Also helpful in this regard is a six-part series published by a weekly black newspaper, the *Pittsburgh Courier,* in the spring of 1954. See Bill Nunn, Jr., "Ez Charles— as I Know Him," *Pittsburgh Courier,* May 15, 1954, p. 15, May 22, 1954, p. 15, May 29, 1954, p. 15, June 5, 1954, p. 16, June 12, 1954, p. 16, and June 19, 1954, p. 11.

Chapter 11: The Italian Hero

The source on which I relied the most concerning ethnicity is Richard Polenberg, *One Nation Divisible: Class, Race, and Ethnicity in America in the United States since 1938* (New York: Viking Press, 1980). In addition, I found the multiple works of historian Richard D. Alba relating to the subject of ethnicity (with respect to Italian Americans in particular) to be extremely valuable. See Richard D. Alba, *Italian Americans: Into the Twilight of Ethnicity* (Englewood Cliffs: Prentice-Hall, 1985); Richard D. Alba, ed., *Ethnicity and Race in the U.S.A.: Toward the Twenty-first Century* (Boston: Routledge and Kegan Paul, 1985), pp. 134–58; and Richard D. Alba, *Ethnic Identity: The Transformation of White America* (New Haven: Yale University Press, 1990).

For more on the effect of World War II on ethnicity, see Blum, *V Was for Victory,* pp. 63–64. For an article that demonstrates the impact of ethnicity on the popular perceptions of athletes in the age preceding the early 1950s, see Noel F. Busch, "Joe DiMaggio," *Life,* May 1, 1939, pp. 62–69.

For more on the Italian American experience in America, see Humbert S. Nelli, *From Immigrants to Ethnics: The Italian Americans* (New York: Oxford University Press, 1983); Jerre Mangione and Ben Morreale, *La Storia: Five Centuries of the Italian American Experience* (New York: HarperCollins, 1992); Erik Amfitheatrof,

The Children of Columbus: An Informal History of the Italians in the New World (Boston: Little, Brown, 1973); Michael A. Musmanno, *The Story of the Italians in America* (Garden City: Doubleday, 1965); and Patrick J. Gallo, *Old Breed, New Wine: A Portrait of the Italian-Americans* (Chicago: Nelson-Hall, 1981).

Chapter 12: Archie

Many profiles of Archie Moore during the months preceding his September 1955 fight with Rocky Marciano contain details of his life, career, and colorful personality. See, for example, Tim Cohane, "Archie Moore: At Thirty-eight He Wants to Fight Marciano," *Look,* April 5, 1955, pp. 97–99; Herbert Brean, "A Fighting Man Who Is a Writing Man Too," *Life,* July 18, 1955, pp. 48–50; Archie Moore with Tim Cohane, "My Rocky Road to Rocky," *Look,* September 6, 1955, pp. 94–99; Archie Moore with Tim Cohane, "I'll Make Him Fight My Way," *Look,* September 20, 1955, pp. 80–88; Gilbert Millstein, "In This Corner, at Long Last, Archie Moore!" *New York Times Magazine,* September 11, 1955, pp. 26, 58–64; and W. C. Heinz, "The Mystery of Archie Moore," *Saturday Evening Post,* September 17, 1955, pp. 26–27, 86–90. Most of these articles contain information concerning Moore's public relations campaign to get his fight with Marciano, as does "Promoting a Boxer into a Title Chance," *BusinessWeek,* July 30, 1955, pp. 28–29.

Chapter 13: The Wanderer

For Marciano's firsthand account of some of the factors that led to his decision to retire, see Rocky Marciano as told to Milton Gross and Al Hirshberg, "I Fought All the Way," *Saturday Evening Post,* September 15, 1956, pp. 24–25, 54–58. In another installment in his autobiographical serial, Marciano provides his side of the story concerning one primary retirement consideration, his stormy relationship with manager Al Weill. See Rocky Marciano as told to Milton Gross and Al Hirshberg, "He Ran My Life," *Saturday Evening Post,* October 13, 1956, pp. 36, 159–62; see also Cohane, "How Marciano Licked Al Weill," and Skehan, *Rocky Marciano.*

An excellent contemporaneous account of the controversy swirling around Muhammad Ali during the mid-1960s (a factor that renewed and further solidified Marciano's status as the "great white hope") is by Jack Olsen: "A Case of Conscience," *Sports Illustrated,* April 11, 1966, pp. 89–104, April 18, 1966, pp. 95–103, April 25, 1966, pp. 49–67, May 2, 1966, pp. 37–53, and May 9, 1966, pp. 35–53. Retrospective analyses of this stormy period of Ali's career can be found in Remnick, *King of the World,* and Thomas Hauser, *Muhammad Ali: His Life and Times* (New York: Simon and Schuster, 1991), pp. 113–70.

The most comprehensive source for Marciano's postretirement life (and a critical source for this chapter) is Skehan, *Rocky Marciano,* pp. 263–363. A shorter and more controversial account can be found in Nack, "The Rock."

Chapter 14: Rocky

For a brief yet contained account of Marciano's entire career, see Ray Fitzgerald, *Champions Remembered* (Brattleboro: Stephen Greene Press, 1982), pp. 149–64.

Few full-length books exist on Rocky Marciano. Perhaps the most noteworthy is Skehan's *Rocky Marciano*, which was invaluable in supplying biographical and personal details. Although Skehan's book is difficult to find, it is worth making that effort, especially for readers interested in Marciano the man. Two other full-length books exist concerning Marciano, one long out of print and one more recent: Bill Libby, *Rocky: The Story of a Champion* (New York: Messner Books, 1971), and Michael N. Varveris, *Rocky Marciano: The Thirteenth Candle: The True Story of an American Legend* (Youngstown, Ohio: Ariana Publications, 2000). Although neither was instrumental in the research that I conducted for this book, they are nevertheless available for readers interested in additional information and alternative insights concerning Rocky Marciano.

Index

Russell Sullivan received a B.A. from Yale University and a J.D. from Harvard Law School. As the vice president and general counsel for Linkage, Inc., in Lexington, Mass., he has written and edited several books and publications on various business topics. He lives in the Boston area with his wife, Laura, and their two sons, Ramsey and Owen.

Sport and Society

The University of Illinois Press
is a founding member of the
Association of American University Presses.

Composed in 10/13 Sabon
with Helvetica Neue display
by Jim Proefrock
at the University of Illinois Press
Designed by Dennis Roberts
Manufactured by Thomson-Shore, Inc.

University of Illinois Press
1325 South Oak Street
Champaign, IL 61820-6903
www.press.uillinois.edu